Periodization: Theory and Methodology of Training

4th edition

Tudor O. Bompa, PhD
York University

Human Kinetics

Library of Congress Cataloging-in-Publication Data

Bompa, Tudor O.
    Periodization : theory and methodology of training / by Tudor O.
Bompa. -- 4th ed.
      p. cm.
    Rev. ed. of: Theory and methodology of training. 3rd ed. c1994.
    Includes bibliographical references (p.   ) and index.
    ISBN 0-88011-851-2
    1. Physical education and training.   I. Bompa, Tudor O. Theory
and methodology of training.   II. Title.
GV711.5.B65   1999
613.7'11—DC21   98-54460
                                      CIP

ISBN: 0-88011-851-2

Acquisitions Editor: Martin Barnard; **Developmental Editor:** Sydney Slobodnik; **Managing Editor:** Cynthia McEntire; **Assistant Editors:** John Wentworth, Katy Patterson, Amy Flaig, Leigh LaHood; **Copyeditor:** Denelle Eknes; **Proofreader:** Kathy Bennett; **Indexer:** Marie Rizzo; **Graphic Designer:** Robert Reuther; **Graphic Artist:** Tom Roberts; **Cover Designer:** Jack Davis; **Photo Editor:** Amy Outland; **Photographers (interior):** Tom Roberts, Terry Wild Studios, Beth Schneider; **Illustrators:** Tom Roberts, Kim Maxey, Sharon Smith; **Printer:** Versa Press

Human Kinetics books are available at special discounts for bulk purchase. Special editions or book excerpts can also be created to specification. For details, contact the Special Sales Manager at Human Kinetics.

Printed in the United States of America   10 9 8 7 6 5 4 3 2

Human Kinetics
Web site: www.humankinetics.com

United States: Human Kinetics, P.O. Box 5076, Champaign, IL 61825-5076
800-747-4457
e-mail: humank@hkusa.com

Canada: Human Kinetics, 475 Devonshire Road, Unit 100, Windsor, ON N8Y 2L5
800-465-7301 (in Canada only)
e-mail: hkcan@mnsi.net

Europe: Human Kinetics, P.O. Box IW14, Leeds LS16 6TR, United Kingdom
+44 (0)113 278 1708
e-mail: humank@hkeurope.com

Australia: Human Kinetics, 57A Price Avenue, Lower Mitcham, South Australia 5062
08 8277 1555
e-mail: liahka@senet.com.au

New Zealand: Human Kinetics, P.O. Box 105-231, Auckland Central
09-309-1890
e-mail: hkp@ihug.co.nz

To Romana

Contents

Part III   Training Methods   313

Chapter 13 **Speed, Flexibility, and Coordination Training . .367**

Acknowledgments

This is the fourth edition of one of my most cherished books.

Many individuals have positively influenced me in setting my own professional standards. I will never forget the example set by Professor Constantin I. Bucur, former chairperson of the Politechnical University of Timisoara, Romania. Professor Bucur, Dr. Octavian Popescu, and Professor Ion Bulugioiu, my lifelong friend, introduced me to the magical world of researching, writing, and presenting my work.

With great pleasure, I express my gratitude to Professor Marcel Hebbelinck, of Vrije Universiteit, Brussels, my academic mentor and guide through my doctoral work. Through his lifelong achievements, Professor Hebbelinck set the high professional standards I am trying to reach.

I acknowledge the contribution of Yusuf Omar, who co-authored chapter 5. He spent hundreds of hours researching the sources used in this chapter.

Sincere thanks to my editor, Patricia Galacher, for the incredible work she did making the text flow and easier to read.

I would also like to sincerely thank the professionals at Human Kinetics for their contributions. I am indebted to Martin Barnard, whose logical suggestions helped me create a more rational text and to Syd Slobodnik and Cynthia McEntire, who closely guided me through the intricate maze of publishing a book. Human Kinetics, many thanks for your high standards of professionalism!

Finally, I would like to thank Tamara, my wife; Romana and James, my daughter and son-in-law; and last but not least, Karina, my three-year-old granddaughter, who often wanted to play with Bicu (her grandfather) when he had to sit in his office and add a few more words to this text.

Many thanks to all of you.

PART I

Training Theory

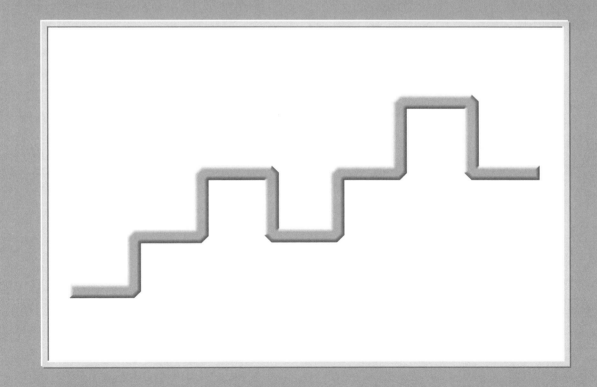

The Basis for Training

Athletic performance has dramatically progressed over the past few years. Performance levels unimaginable before are now commonplace, and the number of athletes capable of outstanding results is increasing. Why such dramatic improvements? There is no simple answer. One factor is that athletics is a challenging field, and intense motivation has encouraged long, hard hours of work. Also, coaching has become more sophisticated, partially from the assistance of sport specialists and scientists. A broader base of knowledge about athletes now exists, which is reflected in training methodology. Sport sciences have progressed from descriptive to scientific.

Most scientific knowledge, whether from experience or research, aims to understand and improve the effects of exercise on the body. Exercise is now the focus of sport science. Research from several sciences enriches the theory and methodology of training, which has become a science of its own (figure 1.1). The athlete is the subject of the science of training. The athlete represents a vast source of information for the coach and sport scientist.

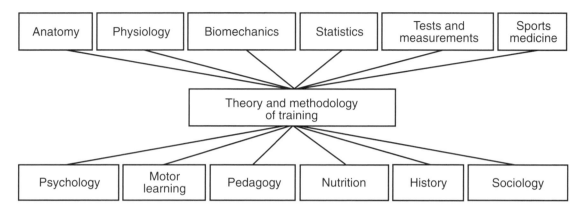

Figure 1.1 Auxiliary sciences

During training, the athlete reacts to various stimuli, some of which may be predicted more certainly than others. Physiological, biochemical, psychological, social, and methodological information is collected from the training process. All this diverse information comes from the athlete and is produced by the training process. The coach, who builds the training process, may not always be in a position to evaluate it. However, we must evaluate all the feedback from the training process to understand the athlete's reactivity to the quality of training and properly plan future programs. In light of this, it becomes clear that coaches require scientific assistance to ensure that they base their programs on objective evaluations.

Theory and methodology of training is a vast area. Closely observing the information available from each science will make coaches more proficient in their training endeavors. The principles of training are the foundation of this complex process. Knowing the training factors will clarify the role each factor plays in training, according to the characteristics of a sport or event.

Chapters 11-13, which cover the methodology of developing biomotor abilities (strength, speed, endurance, flexibility, and coordination), will help the coach select the optimal training method. The planning section shows how to train athletes to achieve maximum performance at the desired time. A training program must include regeneration and recovery between training lessons to ensure continuous improvement in the athlete's performance.

Scope of Training

Training is not a recent discovery. In ancient times, people systematically trained for military and Olympic endeavors. Today athletes prepare themselves for a goal through training. The physiological goal is to improve body function and optimize athletic performance. The main scope of this training is to increase athletes' work and skill capabilities and to develop strong psychological traits. A coach leads, organizes, and plans training, and educates the athlete. Many physiological, psychological, and sociological variables are involved. Training is primarily a systematic athletic activity of long duration, which is progressively and individually graded. Human physiological and psychological functions are modeled to meet demanding tasks.

The aspiration toward high results in competitions should be closely linked with physical excellence. Individuals should strive toward harmoniously combining spiritual refinement, moral purity, and physical perfection. Physical perfection signifies multilateral, harmonious development. The athlete acquires fine and varied skills, cultivates high psychological qualities, and maintains extremely good health. The athelte learns to cope with highly stressful stimuli in training and competitions. Physical excellence should evolve through an organized and well-planned training program based on a high volume of practical experience.

Paramount to training endeavors for novices and professionals is an achievable goal, planned according to individual abilities, psychological traits, and social environment. Some athletes seek to win a competition or improve previous performance; others consider gaining a technical skill or further developing a biomotor ability as a goal. Whatever the objective, each goal needs to be as precise and measurable as possible. In any plan, short or long term, the athlete needs to set goals and determine procedures for achieving them before beginning training. The deadline for achieving the final goal is the date of a major competition.

Objectives of Training

To improve skill and performance, athletes, led by the coach, must meet the training objectives. The general objectives presented in this chapter will be useful for comprehending the concepts in this book.

Multilateral Physical Development

Athletes need multilateral physical development as a training base as well as overall physical fitness. The purpose is to increase endurance and strength, develop speed, improve flexibility, and refine coordination, thus achieving a harmoniously developed body. We expect athletes with a strong base and a good overall development to improve athletic performance faster and better than those without this foundation. In addition, such athletes will have a superior body form, which increases their self-esteem and reflects a strong personality.

Sport-Specific Physical Development

Sport-specific development improves absolute and relative strength, muscle mass and elasticity, specific strength (power or muscular endurance) according to the sport's requirements, movement and reaction time, and coordination and suppleness. This training creates the ability to perform all movements, especially those required by the sport, with ease and smoothness.

Technical Factors

Technical training involves developing the capacity to perform all technical actions correctly; perfecting the required technique based on a rational and economical performance, with the highest possible velocity, high amplitude, and a demonstration of force; performing specific techniques under normal and unusual circumstances (e.g., weather); improving the technique of related sports; and ensuring the ability to perform all movements correctly.

Tactical Factors

Tactical factors include improving strategy by studying the tactics of future opponents, expanding the optimal tactics within athletes' capabilities, perfecting and varying strategies, and developing a strategy into a model considering future opponents.

Psychological Aspects

Psychological preparation is also necessary to ensure enhanced physical performance. Psychological training improves discipline, perseverance, willpower, confidence, and courage.

Team Capability

In some sports (team sports, relays, rowing, cycling, etc.), team preparation is one of the coach's main objectives. The coach can accomplish this by establishing harmony in the team's physical, technical, and strategic preparation. The coach must establish such a concord for psychological preparation, meaning sound relationships, friendships, and common goals among teammates. Training competitions and social gatherings consolidate the team and enhance the feeling of belonging. The coach must encourage the team to act as a unit and should establish specific plans and roles for each athlete according to the needs of the team.

Health Factors

Strengthening each athlete's health is important. Proper health is maintained by periodic medical examinations, a proper correlation of training intensity with individual effort capacity, and alternating hard work with an appropriate regeneration phase. Following illness or injury, the athlete must begin training only when completely recovered, ensuring adequate progression.

Injury Prevention

Prevent injuries by following all safety precautions; increasing flexibility beyond the level required; strengthening muscles, tendons, and ligaments, especially during the initiation phase of a beginner; and developing muscle strength and elasticity to such a degree that when athletes perform unaccustomed movements accidents will be unlikely.

Theoretical Knowledge

Training increases athletes' knowledge of the physiological and psychological basis of training, planning, nutrition, and regeneration. Coaches should discuss athlete-coach, athlete-opponent, and teammate relationships to help athletes work together to reach the set goals.

This summarizes some general training objectives that a coach may consider in developing a training program. Specific characteristics of most sports and of individuals performing them may require the coach to be selective or to establish additional training objectives. Pursue training objectives in a successive manner. The early program should develop the functional basis of train-

Your goal is to develop the capacity to perform all technical actions correctly

ing, then move toward achieving sport-specific goals. For instance, Ozolin (1971) suggests first developing general endurance followed by specific or anaerobic endurance. Another example is the Romanian gymnasts who commence each annual training program with a phase (approximately one month) of strength development before starting technique work. The sequential approach is also extensively used in long-term training programs.

Classification of Skills

Several attempts have been made to classify physical exercises. One criterion was based on the idea that if a person looked good, then he or she was healthy and strong. The founder of German gymnastics, Friederich Jahn, employed as a criterion the equipment the athletes used (Eiselen 1845). Leshaft (1910) divided all exercises into three groups. The first group included simple exercises (calisthenics); the second group incorporated more complex exercises and exercises with progressive loading (jumping, wrestling); and the third group was complex exercises (games, skating, fencing).

Aside from classifying athletes into individual sports (track and field, gymnastics, boxing) and team sports (basketball, volleyball, rugby), a widely accepted classification uses biomotor abilities as a criterion. Biomotor abilities include strength, speed, endurance, and coordination (Grantin 1940). This classification is highly practical for coaches (Farfel 1960). Sport skills can be classified into three groups of exercises: cyclic, acyclic, and acyclic combined.

Cyclic skills are used in sports such as walking, running, cross-country skiing, speed skating, swimming, rowing, cycling, kayaking, and canoeing. The main characteristic of these sports is that the motor act involves repetitive movements. Once athletes learn one cycle of the motor act, they can duplicate it continually for long periods. Each cycle consists of distinct, identical phases

The coach helps the team work together as a unit to reach the set goals

that are repeated in the same succession. For example, the four phases of a rowing stroke, the catch, drive through the water, finish, and recovery, are part of a whole. The athlete performs them in the same succession during the cyclic motion of rowing. All cycles the athlete performs are linked; the present one is preceded and will be followed by another one.

Acyclic skills show up in sports such as shot putting, discus throw, most gymnastics, team sports, wrestling, boxing, and fencing. These skills consist of integral functions performed in one action. For instance, the skill of discus throwing incorporates the preliminary swing, transition, turn, delivery, and reverse step, but the athlete performs them all in one action.

Acyclic combined skills consist of a cyclic movement followed by an acyclic movement. Sports such as all jumping events in track and field, figure skating, tumbling lines and vaulting in gymnastics, and diving use acyclic combined skills. Although all actions are linked, we can easily distinguish between the acyclic and cyclic movements. For instance, we can distinguish the acyclic movement of a high jumper or vaulter from the preceding cyclic approach of running.

The coach's comprehension of these skill classifications plays an important role in the selection of the appropriate teaching method. The whole (entire skill) method of teaching seems to be the most efficient for cyclic sports, because it is difficult to break down the respective skills of running, speed skating, or cross-country skiing. For acyclic skills, breaking down a skill and teaching the components separately (the parts method) results in quicker retention. For example, you can divide the hitch kick technique in the long jump into components (steps) until the athletes accomplish each part properly; then they can learn it as a whole.

Classification of Sports

Voluntary motor acts result from a complex ensemble of muscle contractions performed under dynamic or static conditions, and involve force, speed, endurance, coordination, and amplitude. Categorizing sports is based on training objectives and on physiological and skill similarities necessary to attain and ensure an adequate performance. With this in mind, Gandelsman and Smirnov (1970) divided all sports into seven groups:

- Perfect the coordination and form of a skill.
- Attain a superior speed in cyclic sports.
- Perfect the strength and speed of a skill.
- Perfect the skill performed in a contest with opponents.
- Perfect the conduct of different means of travel.
- Perfect the activity of the central nervous system (CNS) under stress and low physical involvement.
- Develop the ability to perform in various events in combined sports.

The first group includes gymnastics, modern rhythmic gymnastics, figure skating, and diving. Performance often depends on the perfection of coordination, technical complexity of a skill, and artistic presentation, because points are based on subjective judgment. Most skills are acyclic, although some are cyclic (the approach in tumbling and vaulting in gymnastics, jumps in figure skating). The acyclic structures of most skills are diverse, defining a variety of types and intensities of training work, which leads to many adjustments in body functions.

The second group includes sports such as running, walking, speed skating, rowing, cycling, canoeing, cross-country skiing, and swimming, in which superior velocity is the main objective. Another attribute is the cyclic manner in which the athletes perform the skill. The speed they develop for the competition distance of these sports depends on their perfection of the cyclic movements and their ability to overcome fatigue. Fatigue becomes more difficult for long-distance athletes, mainly because of the stress on the cardiorespiratory system.

Sports in the third classification relate to developing maximum force to improve performance. Athletes can develop force either through increasing the mass they use during an exercise and maintaining the rate of constant acceleration (weightlifting) or increasing the acceleration rate while maintaining constant mass (throwing and jumping events). The first case refers to developing strength and the second to developing power.

The fourth group includes all team sports and individual sports performed against opponents (boxing, wrestling, judo, fencing). Excellent sensory organ functioning and the capacity to perceive and act quickly under continually changing contest circumstances are required qualities. Decisions made in a complex game situation depend on the athlete's capacity to perceive external stimuli. The quickness and precision of interpretation can prevent opponents from performing a successful tactical maneuver or lead to a team's success.

The fifth group of sports incorporates activities such as horseback riding, sailing, motor sports, and waterskiing. This group is not researched as much, although some skills are beneficial for daily life. In some sports (sailing, motorcycling, etc.), the equipment quality influences the outcome of the competition; however, athletes must perfect the skills of handling the equipment. The development of these complex skills requires many hours of training. Processing information received by the central nervous system (CNS) through proprioceptors must be extremely fast, because athletes have to make quick decisions during a race. Good physical preparation with specific strength development according to the needs of the sport is important to athletes' success. Aside from strength and reaction time, balance and endurance are among the dominant biomotor abilities athletes need when competing in this group of sports.

Although the activities in the sixth group (shooting, archery, chess) are well-recognized sports, they are not physical exercises because the motor component is low. As Gandelsman and Smirnov (1970) have suggested, however, these sports reflect the main tendency of modern training, the CNS's increased role of guiding the activity. During training and competition, the CNS is under a great deal of stress. Though a competitor does not experience high physical involvement, chess players and shooters participate in well-planned physical exertion. Both sports require excellent endurance, allowing the competitors to focus their concentration, patience, and psychological self-control during a prolonged competition. Upper-body strength is beneficial for shooting so the athlete can hold the weapon still, without deviating from the target.

Finally, combined sports incorporate many events (e.g., decathlon) or different sports such as the modern pentathlon (horseback riding, fencing, swimming, and cross-country running). Women's heptathlon, triathalon, and biathlon are also in this group. Physiological and psychological interpretations must be made according to the specifics of each event in the combined sport, because most include activities from various sports and zones of intensities. The variety of events or sports that dictate the type of training to use is complex, resulting in all-around athletes.

The classification of sports Gandelsman and Smirnov (1970) proposed is schematic. It is, however, beneficial for the coach to have a good understanding of the attributes of all sports activities, because a sport included in one group may have some features characteristic of another group. Understanding the features and related characteristics of a sport may improve the coach's training endeavors, making possible a more effective outcome and a more varied training program. Table 1.1 summarizes sport classifications.

System of Training

A system is an organized or methodically arranged set of ideas, theories, or speculations. A system should encompass accumulated experience as well as pure and applied research findings in an organized whole. A system should not be imported, although it may be beneficial to first study other systems when developing one. Furthermore, in creating or developing a better system, you must consider a country's social and cultural background.

A sport system should include the physical education and sport organization of a nation, considering school programs, recreation and sport clubs, the organizational structure of sport governing bodies, and the systems of athletic training.

The organization of a nation's system should first define its goals, and, based on that, structure itself so that all echelons and units are linked in a solid and sequential setup (figure 1.2). The suggested system has a pyramid structure:

TABLE 1.1   Characteristics of the Classification of Sports Groups

Group #	Training goals	Example of sports	Skill structure	Dominant intensity	Dominant biomotor ability	Functional demand
1	Perfect the coordination and form of a skill.	Gymnastics, figure skating	Acyclic	Alternative	Complex blending of coordination, strength, and speed	CNS, neuromuscular
2	Attain a superior speed in cyclic sports.	Running, rowing, swimming, Nordic skiing	Cyclic	All intensities from maximum to low. Alternative	Speed, endurance	CNS, neuro-muscular, and cardio-respiratory
3	Perfect the strength and speed of a skill.	Weightlifting, throwing, jumping	Acyclic and cyclic combined	Alternative	Strength, speed	Neuro-muscular, CNS
4	Perfect the skill performed in a contest with opponents.	Team sports, some individual sports	Acyclic	Alternative	Coordination, speed, strength, endurance	CNS, locomotor, cardio-respiratory
5	Perfect the conduct of different means of travel.	Sailing, horseback riding, motorcycling	Acyclic and cyclic combined	Alternative	Coordination, speed	CNS
6	Perfect the activity of the CNS under stress and low physical involvement.	Shooting, chess, archery	Acyclic	Low	Coordination, endurance	CNS
7	Combine sports.	Decathalon, biathlon, heptathlon, triathlon	All	Specific to each event	Complex blending of most abilities	CNS, locomotor, cardio-respiratory

at the base are the youngsters in physical education; the peak encompasses the high-performance unit, the nation's athletic ambassadors

A national sport system should consider the nation's values, traditions, climate, and sports emphasis, especially for young participants. Young people must develop the basic skills and abilities to benefit from physical instruction, as well as to perform appropriately in most sports. The latter refers to track and field, swimming, and gymnastics. The emphasis on track and field is to develop the basic skill required in most sports (running, jumping, and

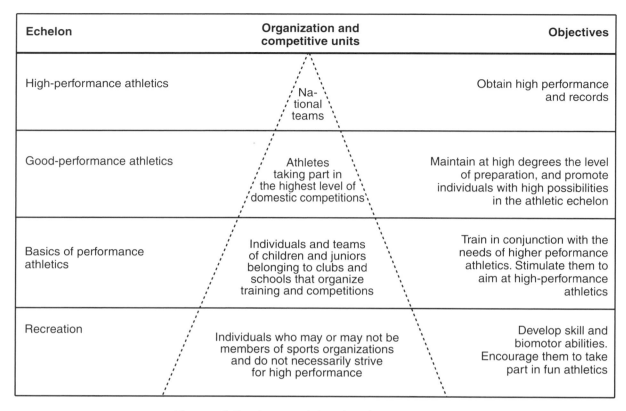

Echelon	Organization and competitive units	Objectives
High-performance athletics	National teams	Obtain high performance and records
Good-performance athletics	Athletes taking part in the highest level of domestic competitions	Maintain at high degrees the level of preparation, and promote individuals with high possibilities in the athletic echelon
Basics of performance athletics	Individuals and teams of children and juniors belonging to clubs and schools that organize training and competitions	Train in conjunction with the needs of higher peformance athletics. Stimulate them to aim at high-performance athletics
Recreation	Individuals who may or may not be members of sports organizations and do not necessarily strive for high performance	Develop skill and biomotor abilities. Encourage them to take part in fun athletics

Figure 1.2   A potential national sports system

throwing). Swimming encourages appropriate development of the cardiorespiratory function and lifeguard abilities. Gymnastics improves balance and coordination. These three sports are part of children's general instruction in most European countries, especially Russia, Germany, and Romania.

Creating a training system for a sport may stem from the general knowledge in the theory and methodology of training, scientific findings, the experience of the nation's best coaches, and the approach used in other countries. The highlight of developing a training system should be creating a model for both short- and long-term training. All coaches should then apply the model. This approach does not exclude the possibility of individual expression. Each individual has a place within the system, and a coach may attempt to enrich the system through his or her talents. Furthermore, by using their abilities and skills, coaches should apply the system according to the club's specifics, the social and natural environments, and athletes' individual characteristics.

Sport specialists and scientists occupy an important place in creating and evolving a training system. Their research, especially applied research, could enrich training know-how; improve methods of athlete evaluation, selection, peaking, and recovery and regeneration following training; and increase knowledge of how to cope with stress.

The quality of a training system depends on direct and supportive factors (figure 1.3). Although each link in the system has a role, the utmost importance lies with the direct factors, training and evaluation of training.

The direct result of a quality training system should be a high level of performance. Training quality does not depend on one factor, the coach. Instead, it depends on many factors, some not commanded by the coach, which could affect the athlete's performance (figure 1.4). Hence, all factors that affect the quality of training should be effectively used and constantly improved.

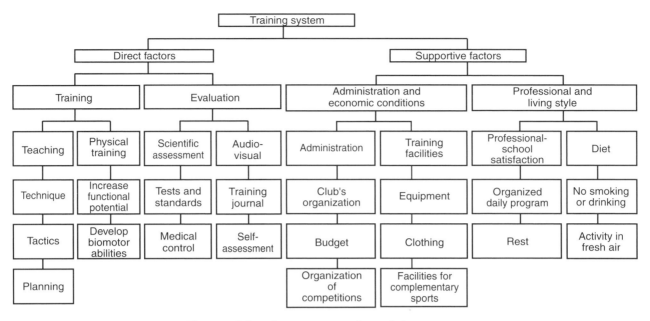

Figure 1.3 Components of a training system

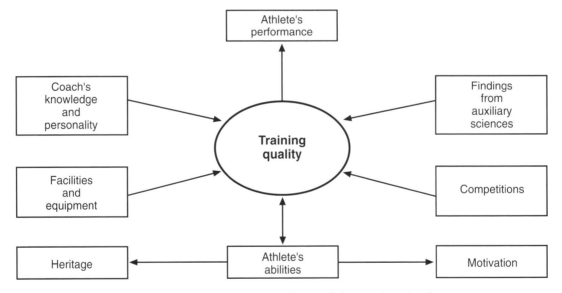

Figure 1.4 Training quality and factors involved

Training Adaptation

A high level of performance is the result of many years of well-planned, methodical, and hard training. During this time, the athlete tries to adapt his or her organs and functions to the specific requirements of the chosen sport. The adaptation level is reflected by performance capabilities. The greater the degree of adaptation, the better the performance.

Training adaptation is the sum of transformations brought about by systematically repeating exercise. These structural and physiological changes result from a specific demand that athletes place on their bodies by the activity they pursue, depending on the volume, intensity, and frequency of training. Physical training is beneficial only as long as it forces the body to adapt to the stress of the effort. If the stress is not a sufficient challenge, then no adaptation occurs. On the other hand, if a stress is intolerable, then injury or overtraining may result.

The time required for a high degree of adaptation depends on the skill complexity and the physiological and psychological difficulty of the event or sport. The more complex and difficult the sport, the longer the training time required for neuromuscular and functional adaptation.

A systematic and organized training program induces several alterations. Although researchers observed the most organic and functional changes in endurance athletes (Astrand and Rodahl 1970; Mathews and Fox 1976), most athletes experience neuromuscular, cardiorespiratory, and biochemical modifications. Psychological improvements also result from physical exercise.

Research in anatomical adaptation has shown that material (bone composition) strength decreases with high-intensity exercise. Also, mechanical properties of bones do not strictly depend on chronological age but on the mechanical demands of the athlete. Low-intensity training at an early age may, therefore, stimulate long bone length and circumference increases. High intensity, on the other hand, may inhibit bone growth (Matsuda et al. 1986).

Researchers also believe that bone adaptation to exercise is a function of age. Immature bones are more sensitive to cycle load changes than mature bones. Strength training at a young age accelerates the maturation process, causing permanent suppression of bone growth (Matsuda et al. 1986). The purpose of training, therefore, is to stress the body so that it responds in adaptation and not aggravation.

Athletes performing strength and power training at near or maximal voluntary contraction increase the cross-sectional area of muscle fibers (hypertrophy). The growth of a muscle and its weight are due largely to hypertrophy, occasionally muscle fiber splitting (hyperplasia), and the increase of protein content.

Researchers often link high performance in power or speed events with genetics and the dominant muscle fiber type. Simoneau et al. (1985) suggests, however, that fiber type composition is not determined solely by genetics. Researchers have observed conflicting results within transfer from fast-twitch to slow-twitch muscle fiber type. Some results verify that when the stimulus is appropriate, the potential to convert one fiber type to another does exist. Therefore, adaptation to fiber type areas could depend on the nature and duration of the training program as well as the pretraining status of the athlete. Thus, it is not solely a genetic factor.

We do not fully understand enhancements of explosive power performance and the corresponding biological adaptation of a specific training stimulus. Gravity normally provides most of the mechanical stimulus responsible for developing muscle structure during everyday life and training. It is reasonable to assume, therefore, that high-gravity conditions could influence the muscle mechanics of even well-trained athletes. Researchers report improvements as a result of fast adaptation to the simulated high-gravity field. They suggest that adaptation has occurred both in neuromuscular functions and in metabolic processes (Bosco et al. 1984).

Performance improvements are also due to changes in the neuromuscular system. During sustained maximal or submaximal activities, the average firing rate of a motor unit increases over time. This neuromuscular strategy can increase the length of time the athlete holds the contraction. During submaximal prolonged activity, as contractile failure develops in active motor units, new units maintain force output. During sustained, maximal voluntary contraction, however, units with the highest initial frequencies showed the most rapid rate of decrease.

High-speed and short-duration activity are responsible for small adaptive changes in enzymes (protein products that induce chemical reactions) and increases in creatine phosphate (CP). The more intensive an activity, the higher its enzyme action, as with oxidative glycolytic metabolism. The greater the hypertrophy, the higher the oxidative enzyme activities. Aerobic exercise is ineffective in changing the glycolytic processes; therefore, the longer an athlete participates in training, the more hypertrophied are his or her slow-twitch muscle fibers (Sale 1989).

Endurance training at a prolonged and moderate intensity improves aerobic capacity, mainly through levels of myoglobin (an oxygen binding pigment that stores and diffuses oxygen), mitochondrial enzymes (both in size and number), glycogen stores, and a greater oxidative capacity. Prominent adaptations to prolonged activity are enhanced respiratory capacity and respiratory rates, increased oxygen transport, augmented cardiac output, and structural changes in the volume density of muscle mitochondria. Thus, the increase in maximum oxygen consumption demonstrates enhanced aerobic capacity for prolonged exercises and increases enzyme activity in working muscles. A major benefit of increased enzyme levels is the oxidation of fatty acids, which improves the organism's ability to use fat as an energy source. Researchers believe that increases in muscle mitochondria and myoglobin account for approximately 50% of the increase in maximal oxygen consumption. The other 50% is probably accounted for by better oxygen transport through the cardiovascular system (de Vries 1980). The dominant aerobic training also increases the anaerobic capacity by a considerable margin (Gollnick et al. 1973b).

Supercompensation Cycle

Supercompensation refers mostly to the relationship between work and regeneration as biological bases for physical and psychological arousal before a main competition. All individuals have a specific level of biological functioning that predominates during normal daily activities. When an individual trains, a series of stimuli disturb the normal biological state by burning supplementary foodstuff. The outcome of this burning is fatigue and high lactic acid concentration in the blood and the cells. At the end of a training lesson, the level of fatigue temporarily reduces the body's functional capacity. The abrupt drop of the homeostasis curve (figure 1.5) illustrates the rapid acquisition of fatigue, which assumes a simultaneous reduction of functional capacity. Following training, and between training sessions, the body replenishes the biochemical sources of energy during a phase of compensation. For an athlete's normal biological behavior, there must always be a balance between energy expenditure and replenishment. During compensation, you must replenish and balance what you consume during training. If not, the depletion of energy deposits will result in performance deterioration.

The return of the curve toward a normal biological state is slow and progressive, suggesting that the body's energy regeneration and replenishment is a slow process, requiring several hours. If the time between high-intensity training sessions is longer, the body fully replaces the energy sources (especially

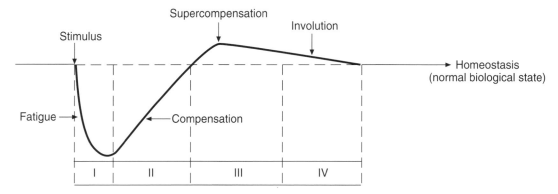

Figure 1.5 Supercompensation cycle of a training lesson (modified from Yakovlev 1967)

glycogen). The athlete achieves this by acquiring some reserves, allowing the body to rebound into a state of supercompensation. Every time supercompensation occurs, the athlete establishes a new, increased homeostatic level with positive benefit for training and performance. Consider supercompensation the foundation of a functional increase of athletic efficiency, resulting from the body's adaptation to the training stimulus and the replenishment of glycogen stores in the muscle. If the resulting phase or the time between two stimuli is too long, supercompensation will fade, leading to involution or a phase of little performance improvement.

The *supercompensation cycle* (figure 1.5) is as follows. After applying exercises in training, the body experiences fatigue (phase I). During the rest period (phase II), biochemical stores are not only replenished but also exceed normal levels. The body compensates fully, followed by a rebounding or supercompensation phase (phase III), when a higher adaptation occurs duplicated by a functional increase of athletic efficiency. If the athlete does not apply another stimulus at the optimal time (during the supercompensation phase), then involution occurs (phase IV), which is a decrease with loss of the benefits obtained during the supercompensation phase.

Following the optimal stimuli of a training lesson, the recovery period, including the supercompensation phase, is approximately 24 hours (Herberger 1977). Variations in supercompensation depend on the type and intensity of training. For instance, following an aerobic endurance training lesson, supercompensation may occur after approximately 6 to 8 hours. On the other hand, intense activity that places a high demand on the CNS may need more than 24 hours, and sometimes as much as 36 to 48 hours, for supercompensation to occur.

However, elite athletes who follow training programs that do not allow 24 hours between training lessons experience a second workout before supercompensation can occur. As suggested in figure 1.6, the improvement rate is higher when athletes participate in more frequent training sessions if the sessions are not so frequent that they prevent the supercompensation phase. Long intervals between training stimuli (figure 1.6a) result in smaller overall improvement than short intervals (figure 1.6b). In the latter case, however, the athlete must alternate the energy systems tapped, as suggested in the planning of microcycles.

The strength of various stimuli has a direct effect on the body's reaction to training. As illustrated in figure 1.7, a phase in which you overemphasize

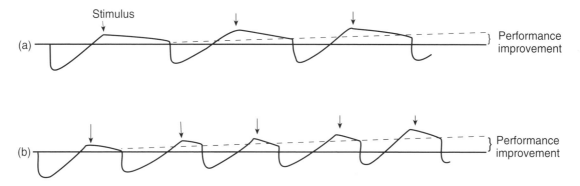

Figure 1.6 The sum of training effect (adapted from Harre 1982)

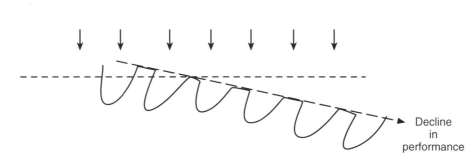

Figure 1.7 Decline in performance from prolonged maximal intensity stimuli

maximal intensity stimuli may lead to exhaustion and a decrease in performance. This is the typical approach of some overzealous coaches who intend
to project an image of being tough and hard working, and who believe that
athletes must reach exhaustion in each workout. Under such circumstances,
athletes never have time to compensate because the depth of the fatigue curve
sinks deeper, a reality that requires longer to regenerate, not another hard
workout. Regeneration will allow compensation and ultimately
supercompensation to occur.

To constantly increase performance the coach must regularly challenge the
athlete to elevate the ceiling of adaptation. In practical terms this means that
the coach must plan high-intensity stimuli alternately, so that days of high-
intensity training alternate with low-intensity days. This will enhance compensation and lead to the desired state of supercompensation (figure 1.8).

It is a biological necessity to reach supercompensation following some training sessions, because the adaptation processes of the body are superior to the
previous session. This means that the athlete has now reached a new homeostasis level, which demonstrates higher levels of training adaptation. As a result, the new supercompensation cycle will start from that point (figure 1.9).

If, on the other hand, the compensation curve does not reach or surpass the previous
homeostasis level, the athlete does not benefit from the supercompensation. High
levels of fatigue, provoked by continuous high-intensity training, hampers
supercompensation and its biological benefits for improving training and
achieving peak performance (figure 1.10).

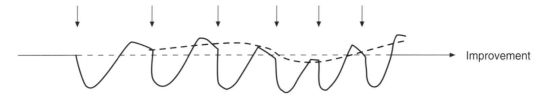

Figure 1.8 Alternating maximal and low-intensity stimuli produces a wavelike improvement curve

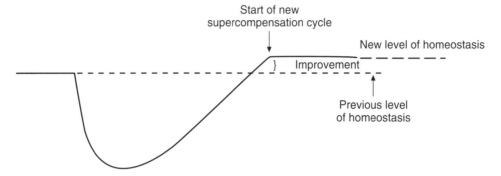

Figure 1.9 A new and higher homeostasis level means that the next supercompensation cycle starts from that point

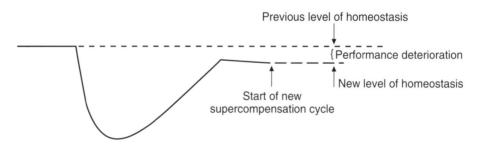

Figure 1.10 A decreased homeostasis level means that the next supercompensation cycle starts at a point lower than the previous level

Detraining

Provided that all expected physiological and psychological alterations occur from prolonged training, maintaining the achieved level or making further improvement requires intensive training stimuli. When such a stimuli ceases, an athlete risks functional and even psychic disturbances, which Israel (1972) calls the syndrome of decreasing the training status or *detraining*. There are two main reasons for ceasing training: one is illness, accident, or training interruption during the transition (off-season) phase and the other is retirement.

In the first case, the athlete loses training benefits within a short time. The speed of detraining varies from several weeks to several months. Researchers have noted a sizable decrease (6-7%) in maximum volume of oxygen, physical working capacity, and total hemoglobin and blood volume following just one week of complete rest (Friman 1979). Athletes completely lose fitness benefits after 4 to 8 weeks of detraining (Fox, Bowes, and Foss 1989); therefore, coaches should carefully monitor and reevaluate the duration of the transition phase (off-season), especially in professional team sports.

In the case of retirement, functional disturbances occur within a few days following the interruption of training. Israel (1972) indicated that headache, insomnia, exhaustion, lack of appetite, and psychological depression are among the usual symptoms. Although such symptoms are not pathological, if the cessation of training persists athletes may display them for a long time, even years, indicating the inability of the human body to adjust quickly to inactivity. Obviously, in such circumstances the best therapy is physical activity.

For injured or sick athletes, the coach should cooperate with the physician in prescribing adequate, if any, physical training. Although physical activity is not advisable during most illnesses, injured athletes may be able to endure limited exertion, lessening detraining and maintaining some physical preparation. During recuperation, especially following illness, training must be progressive with the body's readaptation to previous stimuli. The athlete may increase the training duration from 10 or 15 minutes to 60 minutes and later to 90 minutes, with a load up to 50% of that used before the illness. Under such circumstances, according to Israel (1972), the heart rate may reach between 140 and 170 beats per minute.

Of special concern to each coach should be athletes who retire from training. During their careers, athletes ought to learn that after retirement training has to lessen progressively. The coach should organize detraining over many months, even years, so the athlete's body can progressively slow to low activity. Many Olympic athletes have had organized detraining programs. Some German athletic stars, such as swimmers Cornelia Ender and Roland Mathes, and the rowing team from Dresden, Germany, had detraining programs organized over 4 years.

The coach can plan the content, volume, and intensity of training according to each individual's free time and sporting facilities. Among the first training parameters to reduce progressively are the number of lessons and their intensity. You can reduce the number of lessons to three to five per week, with a progressively lower intensity. You should also reduce the volume of training, especially the duration, over time. The content of physical activity should be diverse. In most cases, you can consider exercises from other sports, because athletes become saturated with those from their specialty. Running, swimming, and cycling are suitable for most athletes, because they maintain an adequate level of fitness and athletes can perform them individually. Detraining is a concern to all athletes. Following retirement, all athletes should remain physically active for their general, physical, and mental well-being.

Sources of Energy

Energy is an athlete's capacity to perform work. Work is the application of force, contracting muscles to apply force against a resistance. Energy is a necessary prerequisite for performing physical work during training and competitions. Ultimately, we derive energy from converting foodstuff at the muscle cell level into a high-energy compound known as adenosine triphosphate (ATP), which is then stored in the muscle cell. ATP, as its name suggests, consists of one molecule of adenosine and three molecules of phosphate.

Perfecting cyclic movements and overcoming fatigue are critical in obtaining superior velocity

Energy required for muscular contraction is released by converting high-energy ATP into ADP + P (adenosine diphosphate + phosphate). As one phosphate bond is broken into ADP + P energy is released. There is a limited amount of ATP stored in the muscle cells, thus we must continually replenish ATP supplies to facilitate ongoing physical activity.

The body can replenish ATP supplies by any of three energy systems, depending on the type of physical activity: the ATP-CP system, the lactic acid system, and the oxygen (O_2) system (figure 1.11).

Anaerobic Systems

The anaerobic system refers to the ATP-CP system, also called anaerobic alactic since lactic acid is not produced during it; the phosphagen system; and the lactic acid system.

ATP-CP System

Because muscles can store only a small amount of ATP, energy depletion occurs rapidly when strenuous activity begins. In response, creatine phosphate (CP) or phosphocreatine, which is also stored in the muscle cell, breaks down into creatine (C) and phosphate (P). The energy released is used to resynthesize ADP + P into ATP. We can then transform this once more to ADP + P, causing the release of energy required for muscular contraction. The transformation of CP into C + P does not release energy that is usable directly for muscular contraction. Rather, the body must use this energy to resynthesize ADP + P into ATP.

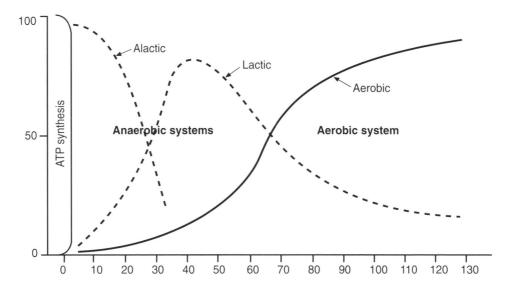

Figure 1.11 Main sources of energy in sport activity (modified from Dal Monte, Sardella, Faccini, and Lupo 1985)

Because CP is stored in limited amounts in the muscle cell, this system can supply energy for only 8 to 10 seconds. It is the chief source of energy for extremely quick and explosive activities, such as 100-meter dash, diving, weightlifting, jumping and throwing events in track and field, vaulting in gymnastics, and ski jumping.

Restoration of Phosphagen

Through restoration, the body recovers and replenishes energy stores to preexercise conditions. Through its biochemical means, the body attempts to return to physiological balance (homeostasis), which is when it has the highest efficiency. Phosphagen restoration occurs rapidly (Fox, Bowes, and Foss 1989). In the first 30 seconds, it reaches 70% and in 3 to 5 minutes, it is fully restored (100%).

Lactic Acid System

For intensive events up to approximately 40 seconds (200 meters, 400-meter sprinting, 500-meter speed skating, some gymnastics events), the ATP-CP system first provides energy, followed after 8 to 10 seconds by the lactic acid system. The lactic acid system breaks down glycogen stored in the muscle cells and the liver, releasing energy to resynthesize ATP from ADP + P. Due to the absence of O_2 during the breakdown of glycogen, a by-product called lactic acid (LA) forms. When high-intensity work continues for a prolonged period, large quantities of lactic acid accumulate in the muscle causing fatigue, eventually stopping physical activity.

Restoration of Glycogen

Full restoration of glycogen requires a long time, even days, depending on the type of training and diet. For intermittent activity, typical of strength or interval training (say 40 seconds work, 3 minutes rest), restoration takes 2 hours to restore 40%, 5 hours to restore 55%, and 24 hours for full restoration (100%). If the activity is continuous, typical of high-intensity endurance activities, restoration of glycogen takes much longer: 10 hours to restore 60% and 48 hours to achieve full restoration (100%).

From this information (Fox et al. 1989), we can see that the time an athlete needs for restoring glycogen after continuous activity is twice as long as after intermittent activity. We can explain the difference between the two by the fact that intermittent work consumes less glycogen; therefore, the body requires a shorter time for resynthesizing glycogen.

Liver glycogen decreases considerably following a demanding training session. For a normal, or carbohydrate-rich diet, it takes 12 to 24 hours to replenish the liver glycogen. During training there could be a LA accumulation in the blood, which has a fatiguing effect on the athlete. Before returning to a balanced resting state, the body has to remove LA from the systems; however, it takes some time to achieve this (Fox et al. 1989): 10 minutes to remove 25%, 25 minutes to eliminate 50%, and 1 hour and 15 minutes to remove 95%. An athlete can facilitate the normal biological process of LA removal by 15 to 20 minutes of light aerobic exertion such as jogging or using a rowing machine. The benefit of this activity is that sweating continues, which maintains the elimination of LA and other metabolic residues.

Fitness level is another element that facilitates restoration of energy stores. A good aerobic base can reduce the time necessary to replenish glycogen stores.

Aerobic System

The aerobic system requires 60 to 80 seconds to produce energy for resynthesizing ATP from ADP + P. The heart rate and respiratory rate must increase sufficiently to transport the required amount of O_2 to the muscle cells, allowing glycogen to break down in the presence of oxygen. Glycogen is the source of energy used to resynthesize ATP in both the lactic acid and aerobic systems. The aerobic system, however, breaks down glycogen in the presence of O_2, producing little or no lactic acid, which enables the athlete to continue to exercise.

The aerobic system is the primary energy source for events lasting between 2 minutes and 2 to 3 hours (all track events from 800 meters up, cross-country skiing, long-distance speed skating, etc.). Prolonged work beyond 2 to 3 hours may result in the breakdown of fats and proteins to replenish ATP stores as the body's glycogen supply depletes. In any of these cases, the breakdown of glycogen, fats, or protein produces the by-products carbon dioxide (CO_2) and water (H_2O), both of which are eliminated from the body through respiratory and perspiration.

The rate at which athletes can replenish ATP is limited by their aerobic capacity, or the maximum rate at which they can consume oxygen (Mathews and Fox 1971).

Figure 1.12 illustrates the energy source used for specific sports and events. Familiarization with the classification of sports based on the duration of activity and the fuel used will help training specialists create better training programs and calculate proper rest intervals between training bouts.

Overlap of the Two Energy Systems

The body uses or depletes energy sources during exercise according to the intensity and duration of the activity. Except for very short activities, most sports employ both energy systems to varying degrees. Therefore, in most sports the anaerobic and aerobic systems overlap.

A good indicator of which energy system contributes the most in an exercise is the level of lactic acid in the blood. Blood samples may be taken and

Energy pathways	Anaerobic pathways			Aerobic pathway	
	Alactic	Lactic			
Primary energy source	ATP produced without the presence of O_2			ATP produced in the presence of O_2	
Fuel	Phosphate system ATP/CP stored in muscle	Lactic acid (LA) system glycogen $\rightarrow$ LA by-products		Glycogen completely burned in the presence of O_2	Fats / Protein
Duration	0 s 10 s	40 s	70 s	2 min 6 min	25 min 1hr 2hr 3hr
Sports events	Sprinting 100 dash Throws Jumps Weight lifting Ski jumping Diving Vaulting in gymnastics	200-400m 500 speed skating Most gym events Cycling, track 50m swimming	100m swimming 800m track 500m canoeing 1,000m speed skating Floor exercise gymnastics Alpine skiing Cycling, track: 1,000m and pursuit	Middle-distance track, swimming, speed-skating 1,000m canoeing Boxing Wrestling Martial arts Figure skating Synchronized swimming Cycling—pursuit	Long distance track, swimming, speed skating, canoeing Cross-country skiing Rowing Cycling, road racing Triathlon
	Most team sports/racquet sports/sailing				
Skills	Mostly acyclic	Acyclic and cyclic			Cyclic

Figure 1.12   Energy sources for competitive sport

lactic acid levels measured. The threshold of 4 millimoles of lactic acid indicates that the anaerobic and aerobic systems contributed equally to the resynthesis of ATP. Higher levels of lactic acid indicate that the anaerobic or lactic acid system dominates, and lower levels indicate that the aerobic system dominates. The equivalent threshold heart rate is 168 to 170 beats per minute, although individual variation exists. Higher heart rates indicate that the anaerobic system predominates, and lower rates indicate that the aerobic system predominates (Howald 1977). Such tests are paramount if you intend to monitor and especially to design training programs according to the predominant energy systems in a sport (i.e., aerobic and anaerobic).

The fact that O_2 requires 2 minutes to reach the muscle cell led many authors and coaches to believe that around that time energy was derived equally from the anaerobic and aerobic systems. Consequently, sports with a duration of 2 minutes were considered to gain energy equally from both systems, which was incredibly emphasized in many sports (including hockey). Interval training employing short repetitions was and still is dominating many training programs. Such training concepts lead to a good performance at the beginning of the race or game only.

Other research (Keul, Doll, and Keppler 1969) suggests that the splitting, or the 50%-50% contribution of the two energy systems, occurs at 60 to 70 seconds after the start of exercise. Mader and Hollmann (1977) discovered that, even by the end of the first minute of an intensive event, the contribution of the aerobic system is 47%. The dominant role in training, which is the aerobic system for most sports, has been emphasized for a long time (Bompa 1968a). MacDougall (1974) suggested that a well-trained aerobic system "increases the total energy available even though the event is largely anaerobic." High aerobic capacity results in less lactic acid production. Consequently, an athlete with a good aerobic base can work with higher intensity before experiencing lactic acid buildup, as compared with others. Similarly, a high aerobic capacity is beneficial to a performer doing anaerobic work. During the recovery phase following anaerobic training, an athlete with a well-trained aerobic system recovers faster than one who lacks it. To improve training methodology as well as the physiological working capacity, it is vital to increase the total volume of work, emphasizing the aerobic system.

Table 1.2 provides information regarding the performance delivery systems of many sports. This information represents the state of the art, with some elements based on thorough scientific investigation and others employing the guidelines proposed by Mathews and Fox (1976), Dal Monte (1983), and other authors. The latter information seems to be slightly biased on the contribution of the anaerobic systems. Often such analyses consider a rally in racquet sports or a tactical segment of a game in basketball or ice hockey, thus emphasizing the contribution of the alactic and lactic systems. Before taking the information from table 1.2 for granted, try to answer some things yourself. For example, determine if the rest interval between two rallies in volleyball (average 9 seconds) is long enough to remove the lactic acid from the system, resynthesize ATP from ADP + P, and thus resupply the body with the fuel produced under the anaerobic system.

For other team sports, such as football, soccer, and rugby, the energy requirements and thus the training should consider the position the athlete plays in the team. In soccer, for instance, discriminate between a sweeper, whose energy is provided mostly by the anaerobic systems, and a midfielder, who often covers 12 to 16 kilometers per game. The aerobic requirements for the latter are more than obvious. Take into account that an elite ice hockey player skates at a high velocity for more than 5 kilometers per game, and a wide receiver in football often runs at maximum velocity for 25 to 40 segments of 25 to 50 meters during the 2 or 3 hours of a game. Reevaluating the contribution of and especially the need for aerobic training is long overdue.

Summary of Major Concepts

The scope of training is to increase athletes' working capacity, skill effectiveness, and psychological qualities to improve their performance in competitions. Training represents a long-term endeavor. Athletes are not developed overnight, and a coach cannot create miracles by cutting corners through overlooking scientific and methical theories.

As athletes train, they adapt or adjust to it. The better the anatomical, physiological, and psychological adaptation is, the higher the probability of improving athletic performance.

Supercompensation is the leading concept of training. The dynamics of a supercompensation cycle depend on planned training intensities. Good plan-

TABLE 1.2 Energy Delivery Systems (Ergogenesis in Percentage) for Sports

Sports/event		ATP-CP	LA	O₂	Source
Archery		0	0	100.00	Mathews and Fox 1976
Athletics	100m	49.50	49.50	1.00	Mader 1985
	200m	38.27	56.68	5.05	Mader 1985
	400m	26.70	55.30	18.00	Mader 1985
	800m	18.00	31.40	50.60	Mader 1985
	1,500m	20	55	25	Mathews and Fox 1976
	3,000m.s.c.	20	40	40	Mathews and Fox 1976
	5,000m	10	20	70	Mathews and Fox 1976
	10,000m	5	15	80	Mathews and Fox 1976
	Marathon	0	5	95	Mathews and Fox 1976
	Jumps	100	0	0	Mathews and Fox 1976
	Throws	100	0	0	Mathews and Fox 1976
Baseball		95	5	0	Mathews and Fox 1976
Basketball		80	20	0	Dal Monte 1983
Biathlon		0	5	95	Dal Monte 1983
Canoeing	c1 1,000m	25	35	40	Dal Monte 1983
	c2 1,000m	20	55	25	Dal Monte 1983
	c1,2 10,000m	5	10	85	Dal Monte 1983
Cycling	200m track	98	2	0	Dal Monte 1983
	4,000m pursuit	20	50	30	Dal Monte 1983
	Road racing	0	5	95	Dal Monte 1983
Diving		100	0	0	Dal Monte 1983
Driving (motor sports, luge, etc.)		0	0-15	85-100	Dal Monte 1983
Equestrian		20-30	20-50	20-50	Dal Monte 1983
Fencing		90	10	0	Dal Monte 1983
Figure skating		60-80	10-30	20	Dal Monte 1983
Gymnastics (except floor)		90	10	0	Dal Monte 1983
Handball		80	10	10	Dal Monte 1983
Ice hockey		80-90	10-20	0	Dal Monte 1983
Judo		90	10	0	Dal Monte 1983
Kayaking	K1 500m	25	60	15	Dal Monte 1983
	K2, 4 500m	30	60	10	Dal Monte 1983
	K1 1,000m	20	50	30	Dal Monte 1983
	K2, 4 1,000m	20	55	25	Dal Monte 1983
	K1, 2, 4 10,000m	5	10	85	Dal Monte 1983
Rowing		2	15	83	Howald, 1977
Rugby		30-40	10-20	30-50	Dal Monte 1983

(continued)

TABLE 1.2   *(continued)*

Sports/event			ATP-CP	LA	O$_2$	Source
Sailing			0	15	85-100	Dal Monte 1983
Shooting			0	0	100	Dal Monte 1983
Skiing Alpine	Slalom					
		45-50s	40	50	10	Alpine Canada 1990
	Giant slalom					
		70-90s	30	50	20	Alpine Canada 1990
	Super giant					
		80-120s	15	45	40	Alpine Canada 1990
	Downhill					
		90-150s	10	45	45	Alpine Canada 1990
	Nordic		0	5	95	Dal Monte 1983
Soccer			60-80	20	0-10	Dal Monte 1983
Speed skating	500m		95	5	0	Dal Monte 1983
	1,500m		30	60	10	Dal Monte 1983
	5,000m		10	40	50	Dal Monte 1983
	10,000m		5	15	80	Dal Monte 1983
Swimming	100m		23.95	51.10	24.95	Mader 1985
	200m		10.70	19.30	70.00	Mader 1985
	400m		20	40	40	Mathews and Fox 1976
	800m		10	32	60	Mathews and Fox 1976
	1,500m		10	20	70	Mathews and Fox 1976
Tennis			70	20	10	Dal Monte 1983
Volleyball			40	10	50	Gionet 1986
Water polo			30	40	30	Dal Monte 1983
Wrestling			90	10	0	Dal Monte 1983

ning must consider supercompensation, because its application in training ensures the restoration of energy and, most importantly, helps athletes avoid critical levels of fatigue that can result in the undesirable state of overtraining.

To conduct an effective training program, you must understand energy systems, the energy fuel used by each system, and how much time athletes need to restore energy fuels used in training and competition. A good understanding of restoration time for an energy system is the foundation for calculating rest intervals between training activities during a workout, between workouts, and after a competition.

The more comfortable you are with these concepts, the more effective you are in organizing and leading a training program.

Chapter 2

Principles of Training

The theory and methodology of training, a distinct unit of physical education and sports, has specific principles based on the biological, psychological, and pedagogical sciences. These guidelines and regulations, which systematically direct training, are known as the principles of training. These specific principles reflect the particularities of fulfilling important training goals, namely increasing skill and performance levels. Training principles are part of a whole concept, and though we should not view them as isolated units, we describe them separately for a more understandable presentation. Correctly using these training principles will create superior organization and more functional content, means, methods, factors, and training components.

Active Participation

It is vital to understand three factors of this principle: the scope and objectives of training, the athlete's independent and creative role, and the athlete's duties during long preparation phases. The coach should promote independent and conscientious development through leadership and expertise. Athletes must perceive the coach's conduct as improving their skills, biomotor abilities, and psychological traits, so they can overcome the difficulties of training.

Maximize conscientious and active participation in training by periodically and consistently discussing with each athlete his or her progress. Athletes then relate the objective feedback from the coach with the subjective assessment of their performances. By comparing performance abilities with subjective feelings of speed, smoothness, and ease, athletes perceive themselves as strong and relaxed. They will be able to understand the positive and negative aspects of performance, what they need to improve, and how to do it. Training involves active listening and participation from both the coach and the athletes. Athletes should take care of their well-being. Because personal problems may impact performance, athletes should share them with the coach, so they can deal with the problem through a common effort.

Do not limit active participation to the training session. Athletes are responsibile for their actions when not supervised by the coach. Alcohol consumption and smoking affect performance; consequently, athletes should

Active listening and participation from both the coach and athletes enhances success

vigorously resist such temptations. During free time, social activities provide satisfaction and relaxation but athletes must be sure to get adequate rest. This will ensure that physical and psychological regeneration occurs before the next training lesson. Athletes who do not faithfully observe all the requirements of nonsupervised training should not expect maximum performances. Ritter (1982) suggests the following rules from this principle.

First, the coach should elaborate training objectives with the athlete and should actively establish objectives according to the athlete's ability. Second, the athlete should actively participate in planning and analyzing long- and short-term training. The athlete should be capable of self-assessment, so he or she will have a positive role in these matters. Experienced athletes are expected to be more involved than beginners. You can sometimes encourage elite athletes to develop their own programs. Modify those programs according to their quality and the athletes' objectives. The notes and comments athletes make in their training journals are important in designing a program. A critical evaluation of the previous plan may also be useful.

Third, the athlete should periodically pass tests and standards so there will be a clear picture of the performance level and improvement in a given period. The appropriate conclusions may then be drawn based on objective information. Base future programs on this important analysis.

Finally, the athlete must undertake individual assignments (homework) or individual training sessions without supervision. Often athletes and coaches cannot afford more than one organized training lesson per day. Still athletes may have high objectives for themselves, knowing that they will not be easy to achieve. Such athletes may have to compete against individuals who have more training time. One efficient way to overcome this problem is for individuals to supplement their training with additional activity at home before school or work. Supplementary training lessons reflect positively on performance. The athlete's rate of endurance development and abilities such as flexibility and strength increase due to self-motivated training. Such an approach is an effective way to make the athletes aware of their roles. They will participate more conscientiously in achieving their objectives.

The coach should also demonstrate a conscientious attitude toward training by setting precise and achievable objectives for the athletes. This will elevate their interest in training and their desire and enthusiasm to participate successfully in competitions. It will enhance the development of psychological traits, such as willpower and perseverance, to overcome training difficulties. Set objectives so they are difficult enough to be challenging yet realistic enough to be achievable (McClements and Botterill 1979). The coach should plan long- and short-term goals for each athlete, in which the latter effectively stimulates athletes' training interests.

Multilateral Development

Necessary multilateral or overall development is accepted in most fields of education and human endeavors. Regardless of how specialized the instruction may become, initially there should be exposure to a multilateral development to acquire necessary fundamentals.

You can often observe extremely rapid development in some young athletes. In such cases, it is paramount that the instructor resist the temptation to develop a specialized training program. A broad, multilateral base of physical development, especially general physical preparation, is a basic requirement to reach a highly specialized level of physical preparation and technical mastery.

Setting precise and achievable objectives for the athlete reflects a good attitude toward training

Such an approach to training is a prerequisite for specializing in a sport or event. Figure 2.1 illustrates the sequential approach to training that is common in East European countries.

The base of the pyramid, which we may consider the foundation of any training program, shows multilateral development. When this development reaches an acceptable level, especially in physical development, the athlete enters the second phase of development. This leads to the highlights of an athletic career, namely training for high performance.

The approach suggested in figure 2.1 is completely different from the North American model, where training specificity is evangelized from childhood to international-level competition. North American sport specialists urge young athletes to perform only sport-specific skills and physical development. A tennis player does drills and exercises specific to tennis no matter what! This narrow approach to training produces robots who can hardly do any other sport. Such a limited approach also may lead to overuse injuries.

The long-term approach does not exclude specificity in training. On the contrary, it is present in any of the three stages of development, but in different proportions (figure 2.2). The followers of multilateral, overall training in the early years of athletic development will build a solid base and avoid overuse injuries, monotony, and staleness in training.

Three longitudinal studies performed in three different countries demonstrate the validity of this principle. In a 14-year East German study (Harre 1982), a large group of 9- to 12-year olds were divided into two groups. The first group trained similar to the approach taken in North America: early specialization in a given sport, using exercises and training methods specific to the sport. The second group followed a generalized program, in which children participated in a variety of other sports, skills, and overall physical training in addition to specific skills and physical training. The results (table 2.1) prove that a strong foundation leads to athletic success.

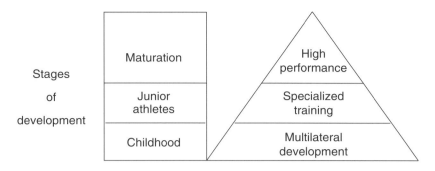

Figure 2.1 Phases of long-term athletic training

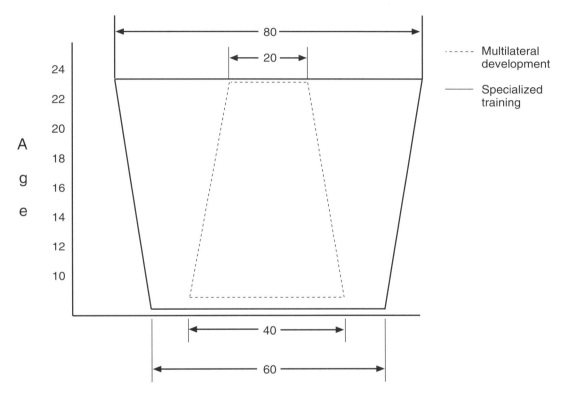

Figure 2.2 Ratio between multilateral development and specialized training for different ages

Nagorni's (1978) Soviet survey presented similar findings. This longitudinal study concluded in most sports, specialization should not start before the age of 15 to 16. Some findings:

- Most of the best Soviet athletes have had a strong multilateral foundation.

- Most athletes started at 7 or 8 years. During the first few years, all participated in various sports, such as soccer, cross-country skiing, running, skating, swimming, and cycling. From 10 to 13, the children also participated in team sports, gymnastics, rowing, and track and field.

- Specialized programs started at 15 to 17, without neglecting earlier sports and activities. Best performances were achieved after 5 to 8 years in the specialized sports.

TABLE 2.1 Comparison Between Early Specialization and Multilateral Development

TRAINING PHILOSOPHY	
Early specialization	**Multilateral program**
Quick performance improvement	Slower performance improvement
Best performance achieved at 15-16 years because of quick adaptation	Best performance at 18 or older, at the age of physiological and psychological maturation
Inconsistent performance in competitions	Consistent performance in competitions
By 18 many athletes burn out, quitting the sport	Longer athletic life
Prone to injuries because of forced adaptation	Few injuries

- Athletes who specialized at a much earlier age achieved their best performances at a junior age level. These performances were never duplicated when they became seniors (more than 18 years). Many retired before reaching senior levels. Only a minority of the early specialized athletes were able to improve performance at the senior age.

- Many top-class Soviet athletes started to train in an organized environment at the junior age level (14-18). They had never been junior champions or held national records, but at the senior age many of them achieved national- and international-class performances.

- Most athletes considered their success possible and facilitated by the multilateral foundation built during childhood and junior age.

Rolf Carlson (1988) analyzed the background and development pattern of elite Swedish tennis players who were very successful in international competition. Carlson divided the subjects into a study group and a control group. The most relevant findings are shown in table 2.2. Both groups of players were equal in skills up to the age of 12 to 14; the difference between them occurred after this age. Additional findings in the control group were that skill development was fast during early adolescence and players participated in an atmosphere of high demand for success. Carlson's study supports the importance of emphasizing an all-around sport engagement and less professional-like training during early childhood and adolescence.

Athletes should participate in multilateral training throughout their careers, from the early stages of development to advanced levels of competition. The principle of multilateral development evolves from the interdependence among all human organs and systems, and between physiological and psychological processes. Numerous interdependent changes follow training. Exercise, regardless of its nature and motor requirements, requires the harmony of several systems and various biomotor abilities and psychological traits. Consequently, at the early stages of an athlete's training, direct training toward proper functional development of the body.

Muscle groups, joint flexibility, stability, and the activation of all the limbs corresponding to the future requirements of the selected sport should be the focus of attention. In other words, it is necessary to develop to a superior level all anatomical and physiological abilities required to perform efficiently at high levels of technical and tactical skill.

TABLE 2.2   Comparison of Control Group and Study Group

Control group	Study group
• All subjects were from urban areas with many training facilities.	• Eight of the 10 best tennis players grew up in rural areas, where the lack of training facilities limited the number of workouts per week to only three! These players therefore engaged in other sports and physical activities
• Specialization started at the age of 11.	• Specialization for most elite players started after the age of 13 to 15.
• From an early age, players participated in a tennis-intensive program.	• One of the best Swedish players revealed that he seldom practiced tennis more than three times a week, 45 minutes a session, until he turned professional!
• After the age of 10, none of the players participated in multilateral development.	• Another elite player stated that he did not train too hard during early adolescence. "You should engage in other sports as well. Today specialization starts too early in age."

Specialization and athletic mastery are functionally based on multilateral development. In any sport, the chance to obtain high performance lies with the individual who participates in plural anatomical and physiological development during the early stages of athletic training. Systematic training includes the skills of a chosen sport along with other skills and motor actions. Such an athlete should be fast like a sprinter, strong like a weightlifter, resistant like a distance runner, and coordinated like a juggler. Many international-class athletes match this ideal.

Employ the multilateral principle mostly when training children and juniors. This does not imply that an athlete will spend all of his or her training time on such a program. On the contrary, as illustrated by figure 2.2, training should be more specialized as an athlete matures and elevates his or her level of mastery. Coaches in all sports may contemplate the merits of this principle. The advantage of multilateral development in a training program brings a variety of exercises and fun through playing games, and this decreases the likelihood of boredom.

Specialization

Whether training on a field, in a pool, or in a gymnasium, from the beginning of an athlete's career the intent and motives are to specialize in a sport or event. Specialization represents the main element required to obtain success in a sport.

Specialization and exercises specific to a sport or event lead to anatomical and physiological changes related to the necessities of the sport. Researchers captivated by the uniqueness of athletes' physiological traits demonstrated that the human body adapts to the activity an individual participates in (Astrand and Rodahl 1970; Mathews and Fox 1976). Such adaptation is not only physiological; specialization applies to technical, tactical, and psychological features as well. Specialization is a complex, not a unilateral, process based on multi-lateral development. From a beginner's first training lesson to a mature athlete's mastery, the total volume of training and the portion of special exercises are constantly progressively increased.

Ozolin (1971) suggests that the means of training, or the specialized motor acts athletes use to obtain a training effect, should be of two natures: exercises from the specialized sport and exercises to develop biomotor abilities. The former refers to exercises that parallel or mimic the movements of the specific sport. The latter refers to exercises that develop strength, speed, and endurance. The ratio between these two exercise groups varies for each sport, depending on its characteristics. In long-distance running, for example, almost 100% of the volume of training consists of sport-specific exercises. In other sports, like high jumping, these exercises represent only 40%; exercises that develop leg strength and jumping power make up the rest. Similarly, contrary to most Western coaches, East European coaches dedicate only 60 to 80% of the total training time to sport-specific exercise. The remaining percentage is dedicated to developing specific biomotor abilities. Coaches use an almost identical approach in boxing, wrestling, fencing, and gymnastics. For seasonal sports like rowing and canoeing, the ratio between the two exercise groups is almost equal.

Coaches should properly understand and apply the principle of specialization in training children and juniors. Multilateral development ought to be the basis from which to develop specialization. Carefully plan the ratio between multilateral and specialized training, considering the modern tendency to lower the age of athletic maturation. The age at which athletes could achieve high performance is significantly lower in sports such as gymnastics, swimming, and figure skating. No one is surprised anymore to see children 2 or 3 years old in the swimming pool or on the ice rink, or 6-year olds in the gym. The same trend appears in other sports: ski jumpers and basketball players start training at age 8. Table 2.3 presents the age a person begins to train, the time when specialization may start, and the age when he or she reaches high performance.

Early age initiation to a sport is not a novelty; the age of introduction to a sport and the age of achieving high performance has dropped dramatically (e.g., woman's gymnastics and swimming) since the early 1960s. Youngsters' high efficiency in athletics, however, seems to be based on the fact that what really counts is biological age and not chronological age. Functional potential, the ability to adapt to a certain stimulus, is more important than age. The rate of developing skills and athletic abilities seems to be higher for young athletes than for mature ones.

Practicing the same sport regularly for several years, with intensity suited to the athlete, leads to specific adjustments in a youngster's body according to the sport. This creates the physiological premises for specialized training later. In sports requiring skill mastery, coordination, or speed (e.g., gymnastics), high results may be achieved at an early age. In sports dominated by cardio-respiratory and muscular endurance (e.g., cross-country skiing, running, rowing, speed skating, cycling), attempts to lower the age of athletic maturation will result in quick burnout. This burnout shortens the time to produce top athletes, according to a Russian study (Ozolin 1971). Endurance demands require an athlete to reach his or her limits in training and especially in competition; therefore, a well-developed and adjusted body is essential. Sometimes, in a coach's desire to reach high levels of performance prematurely, he or she disregards such realities. Athletes must perform difficult training tasks and, even worse, high-intensity training that exceeds their adaptability potential. Under these circumstances, athletes experience an

TABLE 2.3 Age of Starting, Specializing, and Reaching High Performance
in Different Sports

Sport	Age to begin practicing sport	Age to start specialization	Age when high performance is reached
Archery	12-14	16-18	23-30
Athletics			
Sprinting	10-12	14-16	22-26
Mid-distance running	13-14	16-17	22-26
Long-distance running	14-16	17-20	25-28
Jumps	12-14	16-18	22-25
Triple jumps	12-14	17-19	23-26
Long jumps	12-14	17-19	23-26
Throws	14-15	17-19	23-27
Badminton	10-12	14-16	20-25
Baseball	10-12	15-16	22-28
Basketball	10-12	14-16	22-28
Biathlon	10-13	16-17	23-26
Bobsled	12-14	17-18	22-26
Boxing	13-15	16-17	22-26
Canoeing	12-14	15-17	22-26
Chess	7-8	12-15	23-35
Continental handball	10-12	14-16	22-26
Cycling	12-15	16-18	22-28
Diving			
Women	6-8	9-11	14-18
Men	8-10	11-13	18-22
Equestrian	10-12	14-16	22-28
Fencing	10-12	14-16	20-25
Field hockey	11-13	14-16	20-25
Figure skating	7-9	11-13	18-25
Football	12-14	16-18	23-27
Gymnastics			
Women	6-8	9-10	14-18
Men	8-9	14-15	22-25
Ice hockey	6-8	13-14	22-28
Judo	8-10	15-16	22-26

(continued)

TABLE 2.3 *(continued)*

Sport	Age to begin practicing sport	Age to start specialization	Age when high performance is reached
Modern pentathlon	11-13	14-16	21-25
Rowing	11-14	16-18	22-25
Rugby	13-14	16-17	22-26
Sailing	10-12	14-16	22-30
Shooting	12-15	17-18	24-30

Skiing
  Alpine
  Nordic
  Over 30K
  Jumping
	
	7-8
	12-14
	—
	10-12
		
		12-14
		16-18
		17-19
		14-15
			
			18-25
			23-28
			24-28
			22-26

Speed skating	10-12	15-16	22-26
Soccer	10-12	14-16	22-26
Squash & handball	10-12	15-17	23-27

Swimming
  Women
  Men
	
	7-9
	7-8
		
		11-13
		13-15
			
			18-22
			20-24

Synchronized swimming	6-8	12-14	19-23
Table tennis	8-9	13-14	22-25

Tennis
  Women
  Men
	
	7-8
	7-8
		
		11-13
		12-14
			
			20-25
			22-27

Volleyball	10-12	15-16	22-26
Water polo	10-12	16-17	23-26
Weightlifting	14-15	17-18	23-27
Wrestling	11-13	17-19	24-27

inadequate physiological recovery process, leading to exhaustion. This type of program may also affect a person's natural growth and sometimes even personal health.

Individualization

Individualization in training is one of the main requirements of contemporary training. It refers to the idea that coaches must treat each athlete individually according to his or her abilities, potential, learning characteristics, and specifics of the sport, regardless of performance level. Model the whole training concept according to the athlete's physiological and psychological characteristics to naturally enhance training objectives.

Do not perceive individualization as a method to use only in individual technical corrections or specializing an individual for an event or team position. Rather, look upon it as a means through which you can objectively assess and subjectively observe an athlete. In this way, the coach can realize the athlete's training needs and maximize his or her abilities.

Often, coaches apply an unscientific approach in training by literally following training programs of successful athletes, completely disregarding his or her athlete's personality, experience, and abilities. What is even worse is that coaches sometimes implement such programs into the training schedules of juniors. These athletes are both physiologically and psychologically unfit to follow such advanced programs, especially the intensity component. In Ritter's (1982) opinion, coaches' can maximize their effectiveness in training by paying attention to certain rules.

Plan According to Tolerance Level

A comprehensive analysis of the athlete's work capacity and personality development is necessary to determine his or her highest limits of effort tolerance. The coach should plan the training loads accordingly. Each individual's effort capacity depends on the following factors:

• Biological and chronological age, especially for children and juniors whose bodies have not yet reached maturity. Their training, compared with adult athletes, should be more broad, multilateral, and moderate. Juniors more readily tolerate a high volume of training than high intensity or heavy loads. Both high intensity and heavy loads overtax their anatomical structures, especially the bones (which are not ossified yet), ligaments, tendons, and muscles.

• Experience or the starting age of sport participation. The work the coach demands of the athlete should be proportional to his or her experience. Although the improvement rate of athletes differs, the coach still must be cautious about the loads they undertake. Similarly, when athletes of different backgrounds and experiences train in the same group, the coach should not underestimate their individual characteristics and potential.

• Individual capacity for work and performance. Not all athletes who are capable of the same performance have the same work capacity. There are several biological and psychological factors that determine work abilities. Counsilman (1971) provided interesting behind-the-scenes examples regarding the work capacity and pain tolerance of swimmers Mark Spitz and John Kinsella. As opposed to Spitz, Kinsella liked to push himself, yet no other athlete matched Spitz's performances.

• Training and health status. Training status dictates the content, load, and rating in training. Athletes with the same performance level have different levels of strength, speed, endurance, and skill. Such dissimilarities justify individualizing training. Further, we strongly recommend individualization for athletes who experience illness or accidents. Thus, health status also determines the limits of the training capacity. The coach should know these limitations, and only close cooperation between the coach and a physiologist or physician may resolve the problem.

• Training load and the athlete's recovery rate. When planning and rating the work in training, consider factors outside of training that may place a high

Individualization is one of the main requirements of contemporary training, even in a team situation

demand on the athlete. Heavy involvement in school, work, or family and distances to travel to school or training can affect the recovery rate between training lessons. By the same token, the coach should know lifestyle and emotional involvement and should properly regard all these factors when planning the content and stress in training.

• Athlete's body build and nervous system type. This could play an important role in training load and performance capacity. Establish individual characteristics through adequate testing, for which the coach may solicit the assistance of appropriate specialists. Similarly, the coach may study the athlete's behavior in training, competition, and even during social events. Behavior in school, workplace, or with family and friends may also provide important information for the coach. However, in this regard a coach should ask for scientific assistance from both a physiologist and a psychologist.

Individualize Training

Work adaptation is a function of individual capacity. We rarely find precise standards regarding training demands. Children and juniors adapt more easily to a high volume with moderate intensity than to a low volume and demanding stimuli. Ritter (1982) also suggests that adolescents adjust to daily training provided that they do not burn all their energetic reserves and they receive sufficient time to play.

Children, compared to adult athletes, have unstable nervous systems, so their emotional states sometimes alter quickly. This phenomenon requires a harmony between their training and other involvements, especially their school-work. Furthermore, prospective athletes' training must have much variety to keep up their interest and concentration. Also, to enhance a good recovery rate from injuries, maintain a correct alternation between training stimuli and rest. This is especially so for intense exercise, in which the coach should be cautious about the method of doing work in training.

Account for Gender Differences

Sexual differences play an important role in performance and individual capacity in training, especially during puberty. A coach should be aware that individual motor performance relates to chronological and biological age.

Coaches should regard anatomical structure and biological differences appropriately in training. Women tend to withstand strength training that has a rigorous continuity without long interruptions. However, they must properly strengthen abdominal muscles, because of the specifics of hip shape and size, and the lumbar (lower back) region. With endurance training, the main difference between men and women is the degree of intensity they can tolerate. The quantity of training is equivalent between men and women. In determining the variations in women's training and performance, consider the menstrual cycle and the accompanying hormonal activity. The hormonal changes relate to physical and psychological efficiency and capacity. Young female athletes need more consideration than mature females. As with most young athletes, training should start with adaptation to moderate exercises before moving to more intense or heavier training. Determine the amount of work on an individual basis. In many cases, during the postmenstrual phase, training efficiency was found to be higher (Ritter 1982).

Following delivery of a baby, female athletes may start training only after the genital organs resume normal activity. Regular but careful training may start in the 4th postnatal month, but training for competition may commence only after the 10th postdelivery month (Ritter 1982).

Individualization in training also requires that a coach should make individual training plans for each athlete based on and reflecting their personal abilities. Such plans are necessary for each training lesson. The preparation for and conclusion of a training lesson may be organized and performed in a group. For the main part of the lesson, however, the coach must direct attention to individual or small-group needs, provided that the small groups have similar physical and technical abilities.

Variety

Contemporary training is a demanding activity, requiring many hours of work from the athlete. The volume and intensity of training are continuously increasing, and athletes repeat exercises numerous times. To reach high performance, the volume of training must surpass the threshold of 1,000 hours per year. To give an idea of the amount of work an athlete must do, some examples follow. A world-class weightlifter should commit him- or herself to 1,200 to 1,600 hours of heavy work per year. A rower covers 40 to 60 kilometers in two or three training lessons per day. It is a fact of life that a world-class gymnast must train at least 4 to 6 hours per day, during which time he or she may repeat 30 to 40 full routines. Such a high volume of training demonstrates that athletes must repeat certain exercises or technical elements many times. This, unfortunately, may lead to monotony and boredom. This repetitiveness is prominent in sports in which endurance is a dominant factor and the technical repertoire is minimal (running, swimming, rowing, canoeing, cross-country skiing).

To overcome monotony and boredom in training, a coach needs to be creative, with knowledge of a large resource of exercises that allow periodic alteration. Coaches can enrich skills and exercises by adopting movements of similar technical pattern or those that develop biomotor abilities the sport requires. Athletes who intend to improve leg power for volleyball or high jumping, or for that matter any sport requiring a powerful takeoff, do not necessarily have to spike or jump every day. A variety of exercises are available, such as half squats, leg presses, jumping squats, step-ups, jumping or stair-bounding exercises, exercises with benches, and depth jumps. These exercises allow the coach to alternate periodically from one to the other, thus eliminating boredom while maintaining the same training effect.

The coach's capacity to create, to be inventive, and to work with imagination is an important advantage for successful variety in training. Furthermore, a coach should plan the program so athletes will use a high variety of exercises in both the training lesson and microcycle (weekly program). When making a training program, the coach should consider all the skills and movements necessary to fulfill the goals, then plan them alternately for each day. For the training lesson, the coach will maintain interest and avoid monotony by concluding with elements that the athletes enjoy. For example, following a heavy workout, weightlifters may conclude their training by playing 20 minutes of basketball or volleyball, which can bring fun into their training and may develop endurance and coordination. Similarly, during the preparatory phase of training, athletes can develop certain biomotor abilities by using other means of training or by performing sports of great benefit for the athlete. Boxers, wrestlers, rowers, canoers, and other athletes could develop their endurance through cycling, swimming, and cross-country skiing. These suggestions can easily enrich the content of a training program by bringing greater variety, which in the end will reflect positively on the athletes' mental and psychological well-being. Athletes always need variety in training, and it is up to the coach to ensure it.

Modeling

Model training, although not always well organized and often employed randomly, has existed since the 1960s. Although East European sport specialists have acquired knowledge and experience in this area of training for some time, a strong desire to link athletes' training process through modeling has only existed since the 1970s.

I have a strong conviction that modeling will progressively become one of the most important principles in training. As we learn more about the physiological, mechanical, and psychological intimacy of the selected sport, there will be a desire and a logical need to imitate and model the specifics of a sport in training. By doing so, training will become very precise, resulting in a specific adaptation. Only this adaptation will lead to better performances.

In general terms, a model is an imitation, a simulation of a reality, made from specific elements of the phenomenon that we observe or investigate. It is also an isomorphous (similar form as the competition) image, which we obtain through abstraction, a mental process of making generalizations from concrete examples. When creating a model, it is important to set a hypothesis for its evolution and results' analysis.

A model is required to be sole and unique, so it eliminates variables of secondary importance, and reliable, meaning that it is similar and consistent with one existing previously. To meet these two requirements, a model should incorporate only those means of training that are identical to the nature of competition. The goal of a model is to achieve an ideal. Although the abstract notion of the ideal is higher than the concrete reality, it also represents something we strive to reach, an event that should be achievable. Thus, an established model is an abstract representation of the actions that someone is interested in at a given time.

Through model training, the coach directs and organizes training lessons so that the objectives, methods, and content are similar to a competition. Under these circumstances, the competition represents a strong component for training, not just a reference point. The coach's acquaintance with the specifics of competition is a prerequisite for successfully modeling the training process. The coach must fully understand the specifics of the work structure, such as volume, intensity, complexity, and number of games or periods. Similarly, it is extremely important that the coach knows the ergogenesis (generation of work, from the Greek word *ergon,* meaning to work, and *genesis,* meaning generation, production) of his or her sports or events. Familiarity with the contribution ratio of the aerobic and anaerobic systems for a sport or event is important in understanding the aspects to emphasize in training.

Developing a model is not a short process. On the contrary, a future model should rely on previous examples while eliminating errors, a process that may require a few years. The more effort and time you contribute to improving the model, the better it will be. When introducing new elements, they should reflect the coach's gains in knowledge, technique, tactics, and methods of developing biomotor abilities. Figure 2.3 suggests an approach to developing a model.

Creating a model commences with the contemplation phase, during which the coach observes and analyzes the state of training. Following this is the inference stage, when the coach decides which elements of the training concept to retain and which to improve, based on the conclusions of his or her observations. In the next step, the coach introduces new qualitative elements and quantitative components. The qualitative elements refer to the intensity of training, technical, strategic, and psychological aspects, and the quantitative components refer to the volume of training, duration, and number of repetitions required to automatize the new qualitative elements. Based on the additions, the coach elaborates and improves the qualitative and quantitative models. The new model is then tested in training and later in a competition of secondary importance or an exhibition game. Following this, the coach draws conclusions regarding the validity of the new model and eventually makes slight alterations. This phase leads to the ultimate model, which we assume is complete and ready to apply to training for an important competition.

A model has to be specific for an individual or team and specific to the sport or event. A coach or athlete should resist the common temptation to copy the training model of a successful athlete or team. A training model should consider, among many other factors, the athlete's psychological and physiological potential, facilities, and social environment. Each sport or event should have an accepted technical model to apply to all athletes, but with slight alterations to accommodate each athlete's anatomical, physiological, and psychological characteristics. Audiovisual aids would greatly assist the athletes' study and acquisition of the accepted technical model.

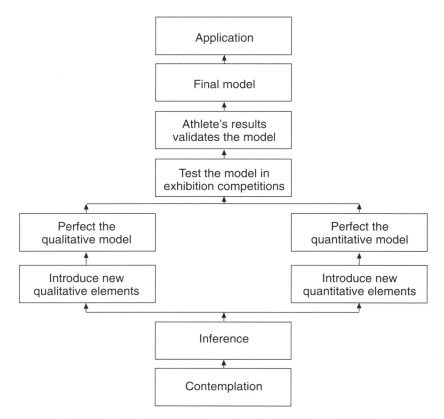

Figure 2.3   Sequence of developing a training model

As mentioned, a training model should simulate the specifics of competitions. It should incorporate training parameters of high magnitude, such as volume and intensity, and use exercises of high efficiency. Each training lesson should be similar to the specifics of a game or race, especially during the competitive phase. For instance, based on the rowing races fatigue coefficient (Bielz 1976; Bompa 1964; Popescu 1957) illustrated in figure 2.4 and the specifics of the sport, a training lesson model for the competitive phase was developed (Bompa 1975). You may derive individualized training plans for each athlete from this model.

The velocity of the boat reaches the highest values in the first part of the race, right after the start, and at the end when the finish takes place. During

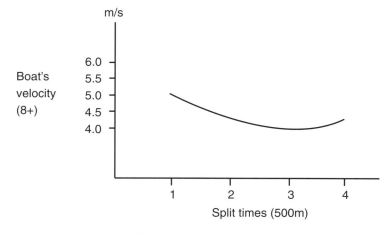

Figure 2.4   Curve of the fatigue coefficient in rowing races (8+ signifies the number of rowers)

the beginning of the race, energy is provided anaerobically, creating an oxygen debt in the athlete. In the main part of the race, the aerobic energy system dominates. As a result of these observations, a training lesson model was developed to reflect these conditions of the race. Hence, the beginning of the lesson always uses high-intensity exercises performed under anaerobic conditions. The main part stresses a high volume of work involving the aerobic system. This is followed by other types of training characterized by high velocity and paralleling the final portion of a race. Such an approach, besides duplicating the model of a race, also develops the psychological traits of will and fighting power, because toward the end of training, the athletes have to perform intense repetitions when already experiencing a high level of fatigue. You may use a similar model in other individual sports with these characteristics (e.g., swimming, running events, canoeing, and speed skating).

With team sports, there are models for training lessons and others to apply in games (Teodorescu 1975). These two models relate strongly to one another, because athletes should perform most training lessons under circumstances similar to the game. In preparation for the game, the coach elaborates an entire model, which is a system containing simple models for each subsystem: technical and tactical, physical, and environmental.

The technical and tactical model consists of each individual player's game plan and actions, which you should integrate with the teammates' model. Similarly, the physical preparation model refers to players' reactions and adaptation to the game's intensity. The environmental model refers to (a) the circumstances under which the athletes play the game, such as equipment, time of the game, quality of officiating, and whether the athletes would perform a workout on the court before the official game; and (b) the sociopsychological climate predicting how hostile spectators may affect team performance. Often, an unfavorable environment could develop high tension that disturbs psychological processes, such as concentration, self-control, combativity, perception, lucidity, quick reaction, and decision making. A friendly audience could stimulate these traits, resulting in a better performance.

The methodology of developing an integral model calls for a sequential approach involving four phases (Teodorescu 1975):

1. Devise the technical and tactical model for each player for both offense and defense.
2. Elaborate the model of tactical combinations for both offense and defense, having in mind future opponents.
3. Establish exercises and drills to learn and perfect the individual's and team's models.
4. Relate individual's and team's models to the physical preparation model. Select complex drills that refer to technical and tactical as well as physical factors. Incorporate all these in the general training plan.

Introduce the environmental model to the players progressively a few weeks after beginning training. You could reproduce elements such as a hostile or noisy audience, if necessary, in certain parts of training so the athletes can develop resistance to the negative effects on performance.

Acquiring the integral model requires a long time. You must divide it into subsystems to allow progressive assimilation, especially during the preparation phase. During the end of this phase, before the exhibition games, incorporate simple models into the integral model and test them against opponents of various abilities. During the precompetitive phase, the coach may plan which competitions to enter, with special regard to tournaments. Do not expect high results in a tournament unless the coach has trained his or her team for it.

During such a rehearsal, the coach should consider the time of the games, their frequency, the time difference between them, and the means the athletes will use to recover before each game.

The concept of modeling also applies in planning long-term training programs, including the annual plan (see the planning chapter). Modeling usually occurs during the transition phase so the coach can make a comprehensive and critical retrospective analysis of the previous year's model. This includes reevaluating whether the objectives, tests and standards, training content, peaking, and other training parameters were set and accomplished adequately. Similarly, the coach should analyze how the athletes coped with training and competition stress and find ways to improve this in the future. The coach should then objectively select the methods and means of training that will materialize in the new model, eliminating those that were ineffective.

Load Progression

Improvement in performance is a direct result of the amount and quality of work the athlete achieves in training. From the initiation stage up to the elite-class athlete, workload in training must increase gradually according to each individual's physiological and psychological abilities.

The physiological basis of this principle is that, as a result of training, the body's functional efficiency and thus capacity to do work gradually increase over a long period. Any drastic increase in performance requires a long time of training and adaptation. The athlete reacts anatomically, physiologically, and psychologically to the increased demand in training load. To improve the nervous system's function and reactions, neuromuscular coordination, and the psychological capacity to cope with the stress of heavy training loads, the athlete needs time and competent training leadership.

The principle of gradual load increase forms a basis for planning athletic training, from a microcycle to an Olympic cycle, and all athletes should follow it regardless of their level of performance. The improvement rate in performance depends directly on the rate and manner in which the athlete increases the training load; however, this pattern varies among sports and geographical regions of the world. A brief examination of the four main theories will help you understand them and evaluate your philosophy.

Standard Loading

In several sports, athletes maintain the same load in training throughout the year. For instance, in most team sports the number of hours of training stays the same throughout the year at approximately 6 to 12 hours per week. A similar situation exists in many clubs in track and field. If power is the dominant ability in events, then athletes use power training with similar exercises and loads throughout the preparatory phase and decrease them during the competitive phase. In both cases coaches use standard loading.

We should clearly state that the repetition of standard loading results in improvements in the early part of the annual plan, followed by a plateau and stagnation of performance during the competitive phase (figure 2.5). As a result, performance may deteriorate during the latter part of the competitive phase because the physiological basis of performance has decreased, and expected improvements from year to year will not occur. Only constantly increasing the training load from year to year will create superior adaptation and thus superior performance.

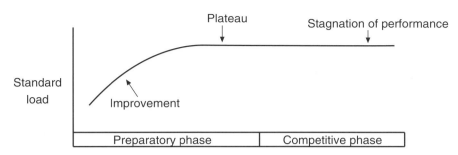

Figure 2.5 A standard load results in improvements only in the early part of the plan

Overloading

The overloading principle represents another traditional loading pattern used in training. According to the original proponents of this principle, performance will increase only if athletes work at their maximum capacity against workloads that are higher than those normally encountered (Hellebrant and Houtz 1956; Lange 1919). Researchers also suggest that the load in training should increase throughout the course of the program (Fox et al. 1989). So, the curve of load increments is constantly going up, as illustrated by figure 2.6.

The overloading principle has evolved from laboratory research, which in most cases is short term, and bodybuilding. Typical of no pain, no gain, overloading is far too taxing and too stressful physiologically and psychologically. On a short-term basis, an athlete may be able to cope with the stress of overloading. On a long-term basis, however, it will lead to critical levels of fatigue, burnout, and even overtraining, because when rigidly applied it does not allow phases of regeneration and psychological relaxation. As is visible in many sports, improper loading often results in overuse injuries and burnout. Many young athletes leave the sport before maximizing their physical capacity because they are constantly, year in and year out, exposed to continuous high-intensity training.

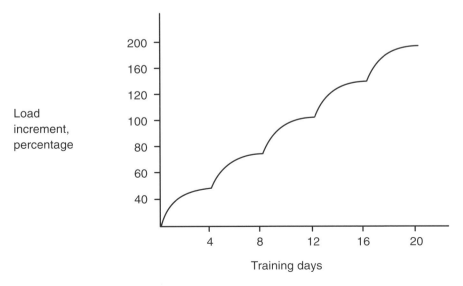

Figure 2.6 Load increments according to the overloading principle (based on data from Hellebrant and Houtz 1956; Fox et al. 1989)

Step Loading

In the past, several studies have investigated methods of increasing the work in training. Researchers found the overloading or the linear and continuous methods were less efficient than the step approach (Harre 1982; Ozolin 1971). As opposed to the overload approach, the step method fulfills the physiological and psychological requirements of following a training load increase with a phase of unloading, during which the athlete adapts and regenerates.

Do not interpret the step approach (figure 2.7) of increasing the training load as a steady increase of equal quantities of work in each training lesson, through an arithmetical addition. One training lesson is insufficient to provoke visible physical or mental changes in the athlete that lead to an adequate adaptation. To accomplish an adaptation, it is necessary to repeat the same type of training lessons or training stimulus several times. Often, you may plan training lessons of the same characteristics for an entire microcycle, following this by another increase in the training load. Figure 2.7 illustrates how the training load increases in a macrocycle, which is a phase of training lasting 2 to 6 (usually 4) weeks. Each vertical line represents a change in training load, and the horizontal line represents the phase of adaptation the new demand requires. The load increases gradually in the first three microcycles, followed by a preparatory decrease or unloading phase, allowing the athlete to regenerate. The purpose of regeneration is to allow the athlete to accumulate physiological and psychological reserves in anticipation of further load increases. Improvement in the degree of training usually occurs following a regeneration phase. The unloading regeneration phase, or the fourth cycle in this example, represents the new, lowest step for another macrocycle. This step is not the same magnitude as the previous low, but it is equal to the medium one, because the athlete has already adjusted to the previous loads. An increase in training load produces a slight physiological and psychological imbalance, followed by an adaptation phase during which the athlete adjusts to the training demand, and concluding with an improvement in training and performance.

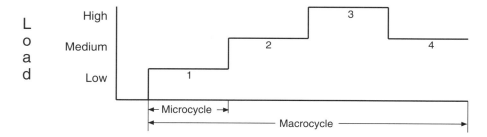

Figure 2.7 Increase of training load in steps (step loading)

There is a direct relationship between the length and height of the step. The longer the length or adaptation, the higher the increase in either or both the volume and intensity of training. An athlete needs to accumulate a large amount of work before performance improves.

As mentioned before, the athlete must perform the training load increase from one step to another carefully and gradually. For endurance sports, in which the main training objective is to increase physiological potential, the increase in training load should not be high. Ozolin (1971) suggests that an increase in load should be around 3 to 6% of an athlete's maximum speed, otherwise he or she must decrease the training volume, resulting in fewer repetitions. In such a case, the individual's working capacity does not increase according to the needs of the racing distance but the needs of a much shorter race.

For sports with high technical complexity, such as team sports, gymnastics, and wrestling, in which technical and tactical mastery are major training objectives, you may base the increase in load on placing higher demands on motor coordination. Consider changing the rhythm of technical movements; combining different technical and tactical elements; introducing new skills; and altering external conditions, such as performing against increased resistance (heavier ball, wrist or ankle weights, waist belt) or reproducing noisy audiences.

When the training load increases, the following elements of progression are available to the coach:

- The number of training sessions per week (i.e., week 1 = 4, week 2 = 5, week 3 = 6)
- The sum of hours of training per week (i.e., week 1 = 8, week 2 = 12, week 3 = 14-16)
- The sum of drills, routines, or miles per week
- The number of high-intensity training sessions per week

Figure 2.8 illustrates how to increase the training load when the progression element is the number of high-intensity training sessions per week (black bars). The level of intensity is high (H), medium (M), low (L), and rest (R). The high-intensity day of the fourth week has vertical lines to symbolize a shorter session and longer rest intervals between repetitions or drills. Similarly, most training sessions are low intensity to facilitate regeneration before the load increases again.

When the training load increases in a given training week (a higher step), athletes experience fatigue in the early part of the week, followed by the body's adaptation to the new load, resulting in improvement toward the end of the week. When adaptation occurs, athletes experience supercompensation with all its benefits, including performance improvement (figure 2.9).

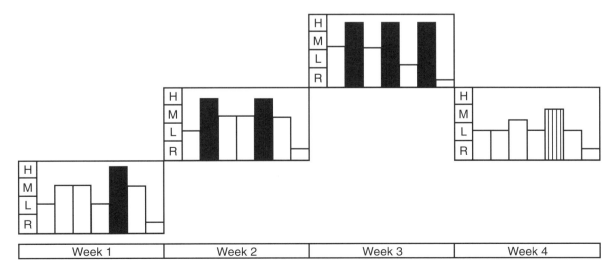

Figure 2.8 How to increase the training load (i.e., number of high-intensity training sessions per microcycle)

Although the increase of training load progresses in steps, in a training plan of longer duration the curve of rating the load has an undulatory shape, which is enhanced by the continuous increase and decrease of the training components (figure 2.10).

During the training process, various exercises, biomotor abilities, and bodily functions develop at a different rate or tempo. Athletes could achieve improvements in flexibility in a short time, 2 or 3 months, although improvement in cardiorespiratory endurance requires much longer, probably up to 12 months. For biomotor development, Ozolin (1971) suggests the following ratio: flexibility improves from day to day, strength from week to week, speed from month to month, and endurance from year to year. The time athletes require from step to step for these abilities also differs drastically. For flexibility an athlete requires perhaps 2 or 3 days; for strength development, a microcycle; and for developing the functional basis of endurance, a macrocycle.

Microcycle	M	T	W	Th	F	Sa	Su
How the body reacts to the new load			F a t i g u e		A d a p t a t i o n		I m p r o v e m e n t
New load							
How the athlete feels			☹		😐		😊

Figure 2.9 A higher step in training results first in fatigue, then adaptation, then improvement

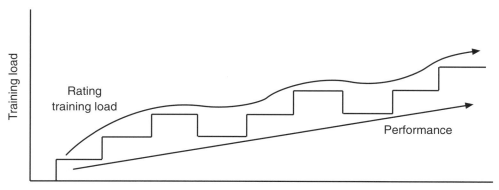

Figure 2.10 The curve of rating load undulates while the performance improves linearly (the arrow)

The ratio of the increase in training load (height of the step) to the adaptation phase (length of the step) is much lower for strength development than for flexibility. The ratio will be lowest for endurance (see figure 2.11). Although the step may be higher for strength or endurance training than for training complex sports, the adaptation phase is much longer, resulting in a lower overall improvement rate. As a guideline, the more complex and difficult the training task, the lower the increase in training load (height of the step) should be. Govern the increase in training load by the rate of performance improvement in a sport. The quicker the rate of performance improvement, the heavier the required training loads, otherwise the athlete will be unable to catch up with contemporary performance.

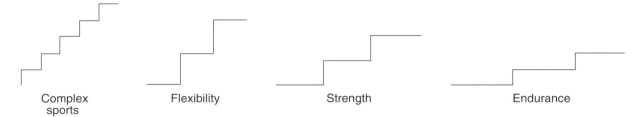

Complex sports   Flexibility   Strength   Endurance

Figure 2.11 Ratios between increase in training load and adaptation

Elevate the magnitude of the training load for smaller training cycles as well as from year to year. Increase both the volume and intensity of training every year, otherwise a stagnation in performance occurs. On the basis of a systematic investigation involving top Soviet athletes, Matveyev (1965) suggests that each year the athlete must increase the volume of training by 20 to 40%, depending on the characteristics of the sport. In most cases, however, the coach determines the elevation of the training volume by the lack of time rather than the athlete's ability to cope with it, implying that time is often a limiting factor in training. Because of the high correlation between the rhythm of increasing an athlete's performance and the index of increasing his or her yearly training load, careful organization and allocation of adequate training time is necessary. Whatever method they use, coaches and athletes must increase the yearly training volume to achieve results, as illustrated by table 2.4.

The dramatic increase during the short period reflected in table 2.4 is a direct result of the increase in number of training lessons per day. If four to six training lessons per week were considered adequate for an elite athlete in the 1960s, it is insufficient nowadays. The increase of the volume of training per year is the outcome of the necessary rise in number of training lessons per day. Athletes training for a top international competition ought to plan two, and in some cases three, training lessons per day. Increasing the number of lessons a week and obviously a year will elevate physical and psychological potential, which will certainly affect performance. The increase in the number of training lessons has to allow for individual capacity, adaptability, training time, performance level, and the need to continuously alternate different training intensities.

Variations of Step Loading

The step-loading method was presented as a basic concept of increasing the training load. I suggest variations of this method here to illustrate the difference between athletes' categories from junior to international class.

TABLE 2.4   Volume of Training 1965-1980

Sport	Elements/Distance	1965	1975	1980
Women's gymnastics	Elements/week Routines/week	2,300 52	3,450 86	6,000 180
Rowing (women)	Kilometers/year	2,300	4,500	6,800
Fencing	Training hours/year	600	980	1,150
Canoeing	Kilometers/year Training hours/year	3,200 960	4,000 1,210	5,175 1,552
Swimming (100m backstroke)	Training hours/year	600	980	1,070
Boxing	Training hours/year	946	1,100	1,280

Note: During the 1990s the volume of training has leveled off.

Although the step method in figure 2.7 (page 46) is valid for most athletes, I suggest a different model (figure 2.12) for junior athletes, in which the first step is a low (L) intensity, the second is either medium (M) or high (H), and the third step is low again. The advantage of using this loading pattern, especially for young athletes in the early stages of development, is that the stressful higher training occurs every second week. This model offers a regeneration cycle every second week immediately after a medium- or high-intensity training. This means that the undesirable physical and psychological stresses are not present too often and, as a result, athletes may avert burnout and eventual injuries.

Figure 2.12   Loading pattern model for young athletes

Flat Loading

For advanced, experienced, international-class athletes, I propose the flat-loading model illustrated in figure 2.13. As seen in this model, the first three steps are of high demand, volume, and intensity, intended to challenge that level of adaptation. The level of work is the highest the athlete can tolerate, followed by a week of regeneration and relaxation (week 4).

I suggest this loading model for the middle part of the preparatory (preseason) phase only. Use the step method for the early part of this phase to allow a progressive increase in training load. This facilitates a progressive adaptation, which is important when you start a new yearly plan.

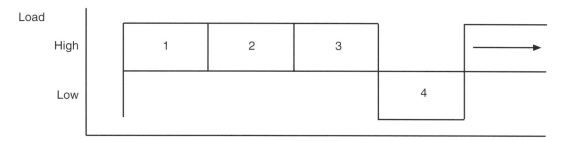

Figure 2.13 Flat-loading pattern for advanced, international-class athletes

Before the beginning of competitions, including exhibitions, planned during the precompetitive phase, loading patterns change again to reflect the needs of peaking and tapering when regeneration cycles are more frequent.

Figure 2.14 illustrates a hypothetical preparatory phase in which the dynamics of the loading pattern change according to the scope of training. In addition to training phases and subphases at the top of the chart, there is another row that specifies the scope of training.

During the general preparatory phase, the scope of training is adaptation, to progressively adapt the body and mind for the next subphase, which challenges athletes to their highest level of tolerance. Now the scope of training is to accumulate as much fitness and technical and tactical skill as possible. During this subphase, training must be demanding. Now is the time to build the physiological foundation for the rest of the annual plan. If you fail to organize an effective and demanding training at this time, then you may compromise the performance you have planned for the year.

From the precompetitive subphase on, including the competitive phase, the training scope is to ready the athletes for the important meets and games to come and to stabilize performance, progressively reaching high and consistent athletic results. During the pre- and competitive phases, the dynamics of the loading pattern depend on the importance and frequency of competitions. Compared with the preparatory phase, therefore, both volume and intensity of training are lower and less frequent. The more competitions, the fewer weeks of high training demand. Similarly, the more important the competition, the lower the training load during the preceding week (a regeneration cycle that should result in the supercompensation so essential for a good performance during competition).

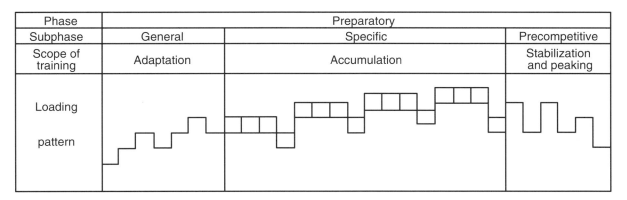

Figure 2.14 How the loading pattern can change for different training subphases for an international-class athlete

Summary of Major Concepts

You must guide the structure and compilation of a training program by specific regulations. Irrespective of the sport a child selects, he or she should not experience only the specifics of that sport. Lay the foundation of a sound training during childhood, through exposure to a holistic, multilateral, multisport program, rather than a narrow, sport-specific training. Such a foundation will result in consistent performance and will be a prescription for injury prevention.

As the athlete matures in age and experience, training becomes more specialized and individualized. It is dominated by specific drills and activities that lead to a faster rate of performance improvement.

Key to performance improvements and planning is the load progression, or how the coach or instructor increases the training load. You will have noticed the suggested difference in step loading between novice and mature athletes. For high-level athletics, from national level up, and professional sports, I propose a more difficult loading pattern, the flat-loading method.

Irrespective of the loading pattern you use, never underestimate the essential role of the regeneration and recovery week. This cycle is critical for removing fatigue, replenishing the energy stores, and providing psychological relaxation for a new increase.

Although step-loading patterns apply mostly to the preparatory phase, during the competitive phase the schedule of competitions dictates the dynamics of loading. This is especially true for team sport athletes who play at least one game per week.

Chapter 3

Preparation for Training

All athletic programs should incorporate the fundamental factors of training, namely physical, technical, tactical, psychological, and theoretical training. They are an essential part of any training program regardless of the athlete's age, individual potential, training level, or training phase. The relative emphasis placed on each factor varies, however, according to these features and the characteristics of the sport or event.

Although training factors are strongly interrelated, there is a manner in which to develop each. As suggested by figure 3.1, physical training is the foundation of the pyramid, the base on which you build performance. The stronger the physical foundation, the higher the technical, tactical, and psychological heights. The winning athlete or team is often the one with better psychological or mental qualities even when the athletes or teams share similar physical, technical, and tactical backgrounds.

Coaches, especially coaches of team sports, often neglect the strong interrelationship between physical and technical training. A shallow base of physical training, often the consequence of a short preparatory (preseason) phase, will result in high levels of fatigue. Fatigue affects athletes' technical skills such as accuracy of passing and shooting. Fatigue also negatively affects tactical judgment, increasing the probability of a team losing the game. It is safe to say that technique is a function of physical training and that tactics are a function of technique. When technical skills are poor or affected by fatigue, a player's tactical ability suffers.

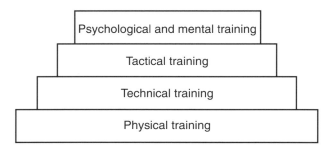

Figure 3.1 The training factors pyramid

The relationships between training factors fall sequentially from physical to technical, to tactical, and finally to psychological. Some overenthusiastic psychologists neglect these relationships, implying that psychology is the winning edge! This may be true, but only if all other factors are equal.

In my opinion, physical training is the cornerstone of all the training factors! Perfect fitness results in the best psychology! Why? Because you have more self-confidence and psychological energy if psychological factors rely on physical improvements. When testing standards show improvements in physical potential, athletes believe in themselves. The coach or psychologist can motivate athletes more easily when arguments are based on real training achievements. It is easier for athletes to gain a positive mental attitude. Any other approach seems phony, and athletes will be less willing to participate in any mental training sessions.

Physical Training

Physical training is one of the most, and in some cases the most, important ingredient in training to achieve high performance. This has been the best kept secret of the East European training system. The main objectives of physical training are to increase the athlete's physiological potential and to develop biomotor abilities to the highest standards. In an organized training program, physical training is developed in the following sequence:

1. A general physical training (G.P.T.)
2. A phase of specific physical training (S.P.T.)
3. A high level of biomotor abilities

Athletes develop the first two phases during the preparatory phase, when they build a solid foundation. The third phase is specific to the competitive period, when the objective is to maintain what was previously gained and perfect their abilities required (figure 3.2).

Training phases	Preparatory phase		Competitive phase
Phase of development	1	2	3
Objective	General physical training	Specific physical training	Perfect specific biomotor abilities

Figure 3.2 Sequential approach to developing physical preparation in an annual plan

The longer the first phase, the better the performance is in the next one. In the first phase, a high volume of moderate-intensity training should prevail. As the program progresses, increase intensity according to the needs of the sport. In some cases, the dynamic characteristics of the sport require that you emphasize intensity from the start. The duration of these phases depends on the needs of the sport and the competition schedule.

Also consider the three-phase approach (figure 3.2) for long-term planning, especially for young athletes. Development focuses on the foundations of training, that is a solid G.P.T., through the first few years of training (2-4). You may follow this phase by a shorter one (1 year), when you build a special foundation for training (S.P.T.). The whole program concludes with the third phase (6-8 months), when you perfect the specific biomotor abilities.

General Physical Training

The main objective of G.P.T., regardless of the specifics of the sport, is to improve working capacity. The higher the working potential, the more easily the body adapts to the continuous increase in physical and psychological training demands. Similarly, the broader and stronger the G.P.T., the higher the level of biomotor abilities the athlete can reach. It is important to emphasize physical potential through G.P.T. For young, prospective athletes, G.P.T. is approximately the same regardless of the sport. For advanced athletes, link it with the specific needs of the sport as well as individual characteristics of the athletes.

Specific Physical Training

Build S.P.T. on the foundation created by G.P.T. The main objective of S.P.T. is to further the athlete's physical development in the physiological and methodical characteristics of the sport. Physiological specialization predominates in successful competitions. Such adjustments in the athlete's potential facilitate a greater amount of work in training and ultimately in competitions. In addition, a high physiological capacity enhances rapid recovery. Yakovlev (1967) claims that an organism that was previously fortified and strengthened would develop to high physiological levels more readily. You can improve specific endurance if you precede such training programs by developing general endurance.

The general endurance developed in cross-country running is inaccurately considered to improve specific endurance for all sports. Such an assumption is valid for middle- and long-distance running; for other sports, regard cross-country running as training for G.P.T. For specific physiological development, stress athletes through training that is directly linked to the sport's technical, tactical, and psychological sophistications. Such a goal is simple to accomplish for cyclic sports, but it is not easy to achieve for sports with complex actions (team sports, gymnastics, throwing and jumping events). In any case, a multiple repetition of parts or full routines, or phases of the game, may achieve the same objective. Selecting appropriate means of training is paramount to final success. Conversely, nonspecific elements may lead to erroneous specialization of the athlete's body development and consequently to inadequate performance.

S.P.T. requires a high volume of training, which is possible only by lowering the intensity. To emphasize the intensity without previously strengthening the athlete's organs and systems could overstress the CNS and the entire body, resulting in exhaustion, fatigue, and injuries.

In such circumstances, the nerve cells, and even the whole body, might reach a state of exhaustion, decreasing the athlete's work capacity. Ozolin (1971) claims that athletes in a medium-intensity program were successful in activities of long duration, displaying high physiological potential. Athletes may not elevate working potential unless they increase both the volume and intensity of training. Because most athletes participate in daily training lessons, the athlete's recovery rate between lessons should influence the increase in training load.

Performing in conditions similar to those of competition also increases S.P.T. Athletes may participate in unofficial competitions without special preparation, especially in the late preparatory phase.

The duration of S.P.T may be 2 to 4 months, depending on the characteristics of the sport and the competition schedule. Long-term planning could be organized for 6 months or up to 1 or 2 years.

Perfecting Specific Biomotor Abilities

Although this phase prevails during the competitive period, developing specific biomotor abilities may commence at the end of the preparatory phase. The objective is to perfect specific biomotor abilities and the athlete's potential to meet the specific needs of the sport. Derive the main training methods from the sport and execute them under increased or decreased load conditions. Increasing the load will develop strength or power, and decreasing it enhances speed. The intensity of an exercise could be equal to the competition's requirement, slightly lower for the decreased load conditions or slightly higher for exercises with increased load conditions.

Duration varies according to the competition schedule. Sports with a long competitive period (soccer, hockey, basketball) have a shorter phase than sports with a short competitive period (cross-country skiing, figure skating). In sports with a long competitive period, perfect biomotor abilities with basic training (at the end of the training lesson). Use the end of the preparatory and beginning of the competitive phases in sports with a short competitive period.

Exercise for Physical Training

In the framework of training, exercise is a motor act repeated systematically. Exercise represents the main training method to increase performance. Exercises vary in effect from narrow to complex. For example, an athlete may perform a simple two-foot takeoff vertical jump with 180-degree rotation, with the goal of developing leg power, but the exercise also enhances balance and space orientation. From the high number of exercises available, a coach should carefully choose those that will best fit the goals and maximize the improvement rate.

Performing an exercise develops an athlete physically, aesthetically, and psychologically (Bucher 1972). Based on forms and structure, we can classify exercises into three categories: exercises for general physical development, specific exercises to develop biomotor abilities, and exercises from the selected sport.

Exercises for General Physical Development

These exercises have indirect action. They contribute to physical preparation, and can be further divided into two groups based on their orientation and effects: (a) exercises performed without implements (calisthenics) or with objects other than those used during competitions (stall bars, benches, skipping ropes, medicine balls), and (b) exercises derived from related sports. All athletes should perform exercises from the first category, especially those lacking general physical development. Perform these exercises during the preparatory phase, and include them during the competitive phase.

Individuals lacking the solid foundation of training based on general physical development exercises seem prone to accidents (overuse injuries). When they reach athletic maturity they infrequently continue to improve. General physical development exercises also improve coordination and enhance learning abilities. Multilateral technical instruction is relevant in sports that require complex motor coordination (gymnastics, diving, team sports, figure skating), in which acquired skills may positively transfer to new skills.

In young athletes, many exercises may lead to injuries because bones and ligaments have not yet matured. Therefore, exercises for general development are desirable. They are less demanding on the body, and when followed in a normal progression, will strengthen muscle and bone, making injuries less likely when the athlete matures. Exercises for general development benefit athletes in sports that cannot be performed year-round because of climate (skiing, football, speed skating, rowing, and rugby). Such exercises assist the athletes in developing a high level of physical preparation for the coming competitive season.

Choose exercises from the category of related sports according to the characteristics and needs of the specific sport. Frequently, wrestlers play minisoccer and basketball to develop general endurance and speed, and for fun. Throwers in volleyball and basketball participate in intensive weight training and perform various bounding exercises. Their training varies yet meets the needs of their events. Some athletes cross-country ski and run. Most athletes should run, because all athletes may benefit from endurance. Some team sports (e.g., basketball) and certain gymnastic elements develop coordination, needed by each athlete. Exercises performed against resistance enhance strength. Encourage other activities, such as swimming and diving, and sports and games, such as basketball and volleyball, for fun, relaxation, and active rest.

Exercises to Develop Biomotor Abilities

These exercises have direct action that improve specific physical training. They enhance technical skills because they are similar to the technical pattern of a skill. During most training phases, specific exercises ought to dominate, because an exercise has a training effect proportional to the time and frequency of its use.

Direct specific exercises to involve the prime movers, which are "muscles that act directly to bring about a desired movement" (*Dorland's Illustrated Medical Dictionary* 1974). However, a training program that incorporates only specific exercises fails to properly develop synergistic muscles or those that cooperate with prime movers. Certain training programs neglect the back and abdominal muscles, although they have an important role in many movements. A training program should introduce compensatory exercises for general development.

Use exercises with a technical pattern and kinematic (motion) structure similar to movements essential to performing the selected sport. Both specific and imitative exercises greatly benefit the athlete's technical and, to a lesser extent, physical improvement. This demonstrates that the strict repetition of a skill, for example spiking in volleyball, does not develop physical abilities (i.e., leg power) to the extent that you may expect. The number of repetitions per training lesson cannot reach the load required to develop higher degrees of power. Similarly, some of the best high jumpers in the world do not high jump more than 500 to 800 times per year. This number of jumps is insufficient to adequately develop leg power. To overcome a slow improvement rate, high jumpers perform tens of thousands of specific exercises aimed at developing leg power (e.g., leg press; bounding exercises; jumping over, on, and off benches; and depth jumping). The number of specific exercises per set that elite athletes perform might be extremely reduced (10-20), but they would repeat each many times per year (50-60 thousand repetitions or more).

Specific exercises are valuable training tools and play an important role in sports with high physical demands (speed, strength, power). Specific exercises should be included during the preparatory, but also are very important during the competitive phase. Often, athletes include them during the preparatory phase, then exclude them during the competitive phase. Research performed in Germany (Harre 1982) concluded that this is the reason some athletes reach a good level of performance early in the competitive season but cannot maintain that level.

Special exercises vary in complexity. Concerning coordination and the biomotor abilities involved, the simpler an exercise is the more efficient and localized is its training effect. For instance, knee flexion exercises develop joint flexibility, strength, speed, and movement time.

The ideomotor (from Greek *idea* and Latin *motor*), or mental imagery method (Cratty 1967) is an effective way to acquire a motor act or improve a biomotor ability. Faraday (1971) observed that a mental representation of a movement is followed by an involuntary, difficult to observe muscle contraction. Krestovnikov (1938) confirmed that a mental representation of a known motor act or movement is paralleled by delicate physiological changes, such as elevating nervous excitability, increasing cardiorespiratory systems, and intensifying metabolic processes.

Ozolin (1971) suggests that mental representation of an exercise, or portion of it, could be used to improve an athlete's degree of training. In fact, during learning, performing an exercise does not occur without a mental representation of it; however, repeating a skill before competition is of much importance. This enables the athlete to repeat a dynamic stereotype (a well-acquired movement),

Knee flexion develops joint flexibility, speed, and strength

such as the technique of performing the event, tactical maneuver, routine, or racing strategy, facilitating a better performance. Ozolin also claims that the ideomotor method may enhance the development of a biomotor ability. Mental representation of a movement performed with high speed may help develop maximum speed. The ideomotor method may also help athletes overcome certain mental barriers, risk certain action, and have courage, confidence, and willpower. Ideomotor exertion, although still underused, may have strong merits in training.

Exercises From the Selected Sport

This category includes all the elements specific to that sport, performed at various speeds, amplitudes, and loads. Athletes may also perform these exercises under unofficial competitive conditions, especially during the preparatory and precompetitive phases. This could be the main means of improving the degree of training and adapting the athlete to the specifics of a competition. An environment similar to the competition (e.g., refereed games or routines in gymnastics and figure skating) could link the components of training. It could also accelerate the athlete's physical, technical, tactical, and psychological adjustment to a competitive atmosphere. Apply this method toward the end of the preparatory phase when the rhythm of increasing training stimuli results in performance improvements. Competition rehearsal may also be valuable for testing the efficiency of technical and tactical skills. Because such competitions are unofficial, increase or decrease the difficulty of the skills. For example, play on a smaller court to emphasize the speed of performing a skill or to increase reaction time; run on inclined fields; jump with a heavy belt; or swim or row against an artificial resistance.

Technical Training

One element that discriminates among various kinds of sports is their specific motor structure. In fact, technique encompasses all the technical structures and elements in a precise and efficient movement through which the athlete performs an athletic task.

Consider technique the specific manner of performing a physical exercise. It is the ensemble of procedures that, through their form and content, ensures and facilitates movement. To succeed in sports, athletes need perfect technique, the most efficient and rational performance of an exercise. The nearer to perfection the technique, the less energy the athlete requires to achieve a given result; therefore, the following equation seems to express an athletic reality:

Good technique = high efficiency

Often, technique is regarded as only the form of a physical movement, but form is always innately linked with its content. Thus, we must view every exercise from two angles—its form and its content. The content of an exercise is characterized through its scope, the activity of the CNS, volitional effort, muscle contraction or relaxation, its force, and inertia.

Technique and Style

Every sport has an accepted standard of perfect technique which every coach and athlete should follow. A model must be biomechanically sound and physiologically efficient to be widely accepted. We would rarely regard the technique of a champion as a model, because it does not always meet these two conditions. Therefore, copying the technique of a winner is not advisable. The model is not a rigid structure, but rather a flexible one, because you should consistently incorporate recent findings. No matter how perfect a model may be, athletes will not always perform it identically. Almost every individual imparts his or her personal characteristics (styles) to the basic technique. The model to follow is a technique, and the individual pattern of performing a skill represents the style. Thus, style distinguishes an individual's pattern of performing a technical model. The main structure of the model is not changed, although the athlete and coach add their personality, character, and anatomical and physiological traits.

Style results from an individual's imagination in solving a technical problem, or manner of performing a motor act. For instance, Perry O'Brien revolutionized the technique of shot putting in the early 1950s with his backward-facing position and original action across the circle. Initially, this was considered O'Brien's style, but later when it was acclaimed and followed by all the athletes, his style became a technique.

In team sports, we consider a certain style of approaching and playing the game the attributes of a specific team. The term style, therefore, has tactical implications as well as application to technical and tactical preparations.

The term technique also incorporates technical elements and technical procedures. Technical elements are the fundamental parts that constitute the

Technique training should be based on individual physical and psychological distinctions

whole technique of a sport. Technical procedures are the various ways to perform a technical element. For instance, shooting in basketball is a technical element. One hand, two hands, or hook shots are technical procedures of that technical element.

Technique and Individualization

The model of a contemporary technique is not always accessible to every beginning athlete. The coach should sometimes introduce a novice to a simplified technique. Even when simplified, however, it must always incorporate the basic elements of the most logical technique. Such plain techniques must ultimately lead to acquiring the whole, correct technique. For instance, in a hammer throw a beginner initially turns once only; then progressively, as ability improves, the coach introduces an additional turn, until the athlete learns the whole technique. The technique of youngsters may differ from that of elite athletes, at least in some sports.

Variations in performing a technique depend strictly on its complexity. The simpler the technique, the fewer individual differences. Cyclic sports offer fewer individual differences than acyclic or acyclic combined sports. Always adapt a technique according to each athlete's characteristics and abilities. The technique of a particular sport or event does not have to be automatically adopted as the only available variant.

When teaching a technical element or the whole technique, always consider the athlete's level of physical training. Inadequate physical training limits acquisition of a skill. Base variations in teaching a technique on individual physical and psychological distinctions. For the role of physical training, Ozolin (1971) claims that if athletes do not improve physical training, they limit their learning and perfecting of a skill. This is especially true in gymnastics. Gymnastics coaches often attempt to teach difficult elements without first developing the necessary strength. The reality that physical training is the foundation of all training factors is shown in figure 3.1.

Athletes are sometimes forced to interrupt their training for whatever reason (illness, accidents). Training interruptions affect mostly the level of physical training. When the athlete returns, he or she may observe that a technique is slightly altered or that a certain technical element cannot be performed (e.g., sit spin in figure skating). Technical deterioration usually accompanies a decline in physical training. When physical training reaches previous levels, the athlete can reestablish the technique: thus, technique is a function of physical training. Technical deterioration is also the result of fatigue, especially for athletes with a low physical training level.

Learning and Skill Formation

Learning means behavior changes accomplished through practice or skill level changes from repeated trials. Learning ability depends on many factors. Motor experience or initial learning level affect learning (Cratty 1967), as does the complexity of a skill (Lachman 1965).

During learning, be aware of these aspects of technique: (a) the external, kinematic structure, or form of the skill; and (b) the internal, dynamic structure, or physiological basis of performing a skill. Ozolin (1971) suggests that technique acquisition occurs in two phases. The first is the learning phase, in which the task is to feature the technique or correct structure of movements, and to perform a skill without useless movement and effort. This phase lasts about 2 years, depending on the athlete's ability and talent and the complexity of the skill (i.e., an athlete can acquire the technique of distance running in 2-6 months). The second is the perfection phase, in which the goal is to improve and master the technique. The duration of this phase is unlimited, because perfecting technique is a major objective for as long as the athlete trains.

Acquiring a skill occurs in three phases (Krestovnikov 1951). During the first phase, useless movements occur because of poor neuromuscular coordination. A nervous irradiation, or dispersing nervous impulses beyond the normal path of conduction, stimulates supplementary muscles. Judge the lack of neuromuscular coordination not as insufficient talent potential, but as a physiological reality. The second phase is that of tensed movements. The third phase establishes a motor skill through adequate coordination of the nervous processes. Thus, the athlete forms the skill or the dynamic stereotype.

In addition to these three phases, we may consider a fourth one: the phase of mastery, characterized by performing fine movements with high efficiency and the ability to adapt the skill performance to eventual environmental changes.

Skill acquisition is based on repetition, which Thorndike (1935) calls the law of exercise. Repetition helps the athlete automate the skill and reach a high level of technical stability.

Evolutional Character of Technique

As a result of coach and athlete innovation, technique continuously evolves. What seems advanced today may be outdated tomorrow. Content and technique of technical training never remain the same. Whether from the coach's imagination, a prominent source of technical novelties, or research in biomechanics of sports, all technical novelties ought to meet the requirements of athletic competition. Any technique has to become a competitional technique; it must be modeled permanently to the specifics of competition. Because competitive rhythm, characteristics, and intensity vary with the opponent's level of preparedness and the environment, the athlete must adjust the technical model, the competitional technique. Do not gear technique only to normal or ideal conditions. Develop the nature of the technique to allow athletes to adjust performance to cope with complex competitive situations. Improving and perfecting technique also must be dynamically linked to physical and psychological traits, because improvement in speed or perseverance may lead to slight technical modifications.

Tactical Training

Tactics and *strategy* are important words in coach and athlete vocabularies. Though they refer to the same thing, the art of performing a skill in a competition with direct or indirect opponents, they signify slightly different concepts. Both terms are borrowed from the military and have a Greek origin. *Strategos* in Greek means general or the art of the general, and *taktika* refers to the matters of arrangement. Strategy and tactics are separately categorized in the theory of warfare, because both terms have unique dimensions. Strategy focuses on wide spaces, long periods, and large movements of forces. Tactics address a smaller scale of space, time, and force. Strategy basically precedes war planning; tactics are the action of the battlefield itself.

In training, strategy refers to organizing the play or competition of a team or athlete. It is a characteristic, a specific philosophy or way of approaching athletic competitions. Strategy is used for a long time, often longer than a competitive phase. Tactics refer to game plans and are an essential part of the strategic framework. Both terms are widely used in everyday language, although geographical preferences exist. In North America, strategy is preferred to tactics; in Eastern Europe the reverse is true. In any case, strategy is the art of projecting and directing the plans for a team or athlete for a whole season or longer. Tactics refer to the attribute of organizing the plans of a team or athlete for a game or competition only.

Tactical training is the means through which athletes absorb methods and possible ways of preparing and organizing offensive and defensive actions to fulfill an objective (i.e., to score, achieve a certain performance, or obtain a victory). Tactical training may follow generally accepted theories, but is specific for each sport. Athletes or teams perform offensive and defensive actions in a competition according to tactical plans established beforehand. Such tactical actions ought to be part of the athlete's strategic framework. During competition, an athlete applies all his or her biomotor abilities and skills according to the real, practical conditions in a confrontation with an opponent. The basis of a successful tactical plan for any sport is a high level of technique. Thus, we may be correct in saying that technique is a limiting factor for tactical maneuvers, or that tactics are a function of an athlete's technique.

The value and importance of tactical training is not the same for every sport. Mastering tactics is one determining success factor in team sports, wrestling, boxing, and fencing, but not for sports such as gymnastics, figure skating, shooting, weightlifting, and ski jumping, in which the athlete's psychological profile assumes greater importance than tactical training.

Tasks and Specificity of Tactical Training

In several sports, elite athletes have achieved almost equal technical and physical training. Often, when all other variables are equal, the victors employ more mature and rational tactics. Although tactical training relies heavily on physical training and is a function of technique, there is an important link between psychological and tactical training.

Tactical mastery is founded on deep theoretical knowledge and the capacity to apply tactics depending on the specifics of the competition. Tactical training may include these tasks:

- Study the principles of the sport's strategy.
- Study competition rules and regulations in the sport or event.
- Investigate and be aware of the tactical abilities of the best athletes in the sport.
- Research the strategy of future opponents as well as their physical and psychological potential.
- Study the specifics of the facilities and environment of the future competition.
- Develop individual tactics for the upcoming competition based on personal strengths and weaknesses, in light of the last two points.
- Analyze past performances in view of future opponents.
- Develop an individual tactical model with variations.
- Learn and repeat this model in training until it becomes a dynamic stereotype.

Tactical acquisition follows the same principles as learning a skill. It depends on multiple repetitions based on a theoretical plan. Because tactical training is a function of good technique and physical training, precede a new tactical maneuver by adequate physical and technical improvement. The possibility exists, however, that these three training factors may develop simultaneously when supplemented with physiological training.

Tactical training, in principle, follows concepts and rules sometimes generalized to several sports. Sports can be classified into five groups based on their tactical similarities.

Group 1 consists of sports in which athletes compete separately, with no direct contact. They follow a certain order drawn before competition, as for alpine skiing, figure skating, gymnastics, diving, in-line skating, and weightlifting.

Group 2 athletes start the competition at the same time, either all together or in small groups. Some cooperation with teammates is possible. The following sports are included: running events in track and field (including relays), cross-country skiing, cycling, and swimming.

Group 3 is characterized by direct competition with the opponent. The result of this bilateral contest is the determinant means of classifying the athletes. Sports in this group are tennis, boxing, wrestling, and fencing.

Group 4 consists of sports in which the opponents are in teams and the athletes have direct contact during the games. Basketball, soccer, hockey, football, and rugby are in this group.

Group 5 is characterized through athletic participation in combined sports. The tactics in combined events include those of each sport and the general plan of participation in competition. The following sports are members of this

Group 1 sports consist of athletes competing separately without direct contact

group: heptathlon and decathlon in track and field, biathlon (shooting and cross-country skiing), triathalon, and modern pentathlon.

Classification facilitates a more comprehensive examination of sport tactics. It also simplifies the subject matter by capitalizing on the similarities certain sports have in their tactical approach. In many cases, a strategy is designed to achieve one or a combination of the following objectives.

Uniform Distribution of Energy

Set specific training tasks leading to a uniform distribution of the athlete's potential. During such tasks the athlete should defeat restricting or opposing factors, such as fatigue. The capacity to maintain a steady velocity or rhythm is essential for success in some sports (especially those in group 2); therefore, it must be part of tactical preparation for competition. In training, an athlete may develop the sense of speed, or the ability to feel the velocity that covers a certain distance, by first using a stopwatch, then by the coach calling the time.

Practice the finish or the final part of a game or competition. In close races, games, or competitions especially, success often depends on the capacity to give everything, to mobilize all forces for the final moment. An athlete may accomplish this either by stressing the end of each repetition or by having the coach announce the time left for performance. The coach's call may stimulate the athlete to intensify the rhythm or speed for the duration of the performance.

Prolong performance, either by informing the athletes before the training lesson begins or by making a sudden decision during training.

Employ several rested sparring partners during training, which would force the athlete or team to constantly perform at a high level.

Group 2 sports have small groups of athletes in competition

The first method is more suitable for sports from groups 2 and 4; the second for groups 1 through 4; the third for groups 2 and 3; and the fourth for groups 2 through 5.

Technical Solutions to Tactical Tasks

Often athletes have to perform under adverse or unusual environmental conditions, such as a wet field, strong wind, cold water, or noisy spectators. The following guidelines may help athletes adapt to such unusual conditions.

1. Perform skills and tactical maneuvers correctly and effectively under unusual circumstances.
2. Organize exhibition games or competitions with partners who follow the same tactics as the future opponents.
3. Create unique situations demanding tactical resolution for each athlete to solve independently using his or her creative potential.

Tactical discipline is an important requirement of training. Often, however, an athlete is exposed to tactical problems that the coach did not foresee. The athlete must solve the problem instantly, based on his or her background, imagination, and creativity. Expose athletes to various situations so that creativity is enhanced during training and exhibition competition.

Methods 1 and 3 are for all five groups, but method 2 is appropriate for groups 3 and 4 only.

Maximize Teammate Cooperation

Limit external conditions (i.e., decrease the available time and playing space). When fatigue is added, athletes experience awkward circumstances that represent challenge and stimulation.

Group 3 sports have athletes in direct competition with the opponent

Perform various tactical maneuvers against a conventional opponent attempting to counteract the play. Create this situation by using the opposing team or spare players during training. Opponents should behave as if they were not familiar with the applied tactics.

Periodically involve spare players in game tactics. Often first-string players coordinate their tactics successfully because they are used to playing together. When the coach replaces some athletes because of illness or fatigue, game harmony suffers; therefore, the coach should frequently involve and familiarize spare players with the team's tactical concepts.

Develop new tactical combinations that improve and upgrade the team's competitive capabilities.

These methods are appropriate for sports from groups 2 and 4.

Perfect the Team's Flexibility

Either change the play from defense to offense or vice versa, or switch among various offensive and defensive tactical maneuvers. Such tactical variations will surprise the opponents; therefore, the switch must occur quickly and smoothly. Consider the following variations:

Group 4 sports have teams in direct contact with opponents

1. Substitute different tactics at a signal from the coach or a designated player (game coordinator or captain).
2. Substitute players who bring new and unexpected game changes to the team.
3. Expose the team to exhibition games against teams that use various styles of play. This would prepare the athletes for similar tactical changes future opponents might implement.

The first method is suitable for groups 2 through 5, and the last two methods are suitable for all five groups.

The Game Plan and Tactical Thinking

Tactical thinking is a fundamental component in tactical training, limited by tactical knowledge and multiple skill repertoire. Tactical thinking encompasses the following abilities:

- To realistically and correctly evaluate the opponent as well as him- or herself
- To instantly recall tactical skills and combinations to use under specific game situations
- To anticipate the opponent's tactics and counteract them
- To disguise or conceal tactics that should prevent the opponents from sensing and counteracting the plan of attack
- To perfectly coordinate individual actions with team tactics

Group 5 sports have athletes competing in combined sports

Based on future competitions, the coach and the athletes create the game plan. Athletes may perform this plan, part of general tactical training, progressively over the last two or three microcycles. A good, detailed plan promotes optimism and good psychological preparation for competition. The plan is the result of anticipation and mental preparation based on previous information and predictions. The game or competition plan may serve the following purposes:

- Inform the athlete of the place, specific facilities, and conditions under which the contest will be organized.
- Introduce and analyze future opponents. The analysis should consider the strong and weak points for each training factor.
- Use the athlete's past performance as a reference to build confidence. Without disregarding the athlete's weaknesses, emphasize the strong points on which to build a realistic optimism.
- Set realistic objectives for the competitions using all these as references.

The game plan and tactical thoughts occur in the following three phases: preliminary planning of the game plan, applying the game plan and its tactical objectives in the game situation, and analyzing the game plan application.

Creating the Preliminary Game Plan

This moment precedes the game and assumes a critical and reasonable analysis of the tactical difficulties the team is likely to encounter. Selecting appropriate solutions to all imagined problems depends on the team's tactical knowledge and skills. The coach should suggest the tactical plan and appropriate tactical objectives based on a comprehensive analysis of the opponent's and his or her team's abilities. According to the team's general plan, the coach designates objectives for each player according to his or her abilities. Next, select the proper system of play and advise athletes how to assess their energy effectively.

However accurate the plan may be during the game, many unperceived technical and tactical occurrences can take place. The plan must, therefore, be flexible to allow the athletes to act with their abilities and imagination as the phase of the game requires.

If possible, avoid changing the athlete's habits during the last few days before the competition to prevent adverse feelings. Reinforce the game plan 2 or 3 days before competition. Organize attractive training lessons. Acknowledge good performance of a skill or tactical maneuver to build the athlete's confidence, create motivation, and increase the desire to start the competition under optimal conditions. It is also important to use relaxation training following each training session to enhance complete physical and mental regeneration before starting the competition. If possible, every single training lesson should follow the model of competition.

In the hours before the competition, remind athletes only of the major point of the plan to reinforce the details. Too many instructions may block the athletes' input (Vanek 1972). Before starting, athletes are quiet in a state of "operational silence". Do not offer any additional advice because athletes are too excited to listen or pay attention. Even if they seem to listen, their attention is oriented toward the competition and they are not receptive to additional advice.

Applying the Game Plan

The second phase refers to implementing the general plan in a game situation. The beginning of a competition is often a short phase in which to test the main elements of the tactical plan. Successfully unveiling the opponent's plan and hiding your own certainly requires experience. In addition, initiative, shrewdness, and the ability to anticipate tactical thinking are important. During the game or match, athletes must solve a link from the chain of tactical elements that a team or individual employs. Puni (1974) inferred that an athlete's tactical objectives refer mostly to knowing how to act every moment of the athletic dispute. The athlete has to comprehend the game's concrete circumstances and decide which tactical action to apply. Comprehending the game's specific circumstances, the athlete, based on tactical knowledge, anticipates the opponent's and teammates' tactical thoughts and intentions. The athlete estimates favorable and unfavorable positions in a given phase of the game, foresees how a phase may evolve, and predicts its eventual repercussions. Correct game comprehension results in the athlete selecting the most favorable tactical skill and avoiding attempting to solve a tactical circumstance instinctively. Tactical thoughts demonstrate analysis, synthesis (combining separate parts into a whole), comparison, and generalization. During the game, tactical thoughts are manifested through quick, simple, and significant gestures or meaningful words.

The application and decision-making process for the game plan results from collaboration between an individual athlete and the rest of the team. Such coordination should lead to a rational, original, rapid, economical, and efficient solution to a difficult tactical problem.

Analyzing the Game Plan Application

The third phase of the game plan is analyzing its application, done with the athletes' constructive contribution. The most appropriate time for this depends on the game outcome. If the result was favorable, plan the discussion for the beginning of the first training lesson. Analyze an unsuccessful effort 2 or 3 days later, allowing more realistic and critical reflection on the past performance, and time to heal psychological wounds.

The analysis should dissect how the plan was made, how correctly the opponent's strengths and weaknesses were evaluated, individual roles in the whole tactical plan, and causes of lack of success. The deeper the analysis, the more valuable the conclusions. At the end of the meeting, however, the coach must be clear and reasonable, with a note of optimism, proposing a few tactical elements to emphasize in training to prepare for future opponents.

Perfecting Technique and Tactical Training

Mastering both technique and strategy is a sport phenomenon in continual evolution. Methods discovered through experience and research contribute substantially to advancing technical and tactical knowledge. The outcome of such explorations leads to an obvious elevation of athletic effectiveness in training and especially in competitions.

For sports in which complex motor skills are important in performance (first and fourth groups), consider the following factors:

- Create and establish an adequate model to match the efficient technique and strategy.
- Disclose the direction and most effective ways of mastering the technique and strategy.
- Employ the most rational approach for perfecting the technique and strategy to produce the best model of achieving mastery in the field.

According to Teodorescu and Florescu (1971), achieving technical and strategic mastery comes from establishing and employing the optimal relationship between three conflicting couples: integration-differentiation, stability-variability, and standardization-visualization.

Integration-Differentiation

The process of learning or perfecting a skill, as well as training an ability, is a multistructural system. Through this system, fulfilling technical and strategic mastery is possible. Within this system unfolds an integration and differentiation process. Integration refers to combining in a whole the components of a skill or tactical maneuver, and differentiation is analytically processing each component.

The classical approach in learning emphasizes progression, from simple to complex technical or tactical elements. For mastery of a skill or tactical maneuver, however, the process is reversed, from studying the complex components and their functions to tracing the components that prevent the function of the whole system. In other words, if the multistructural process (the whole skill or tactical maneuver) does not work properly, the athlete must dissect the skill or maneuver into substructures (parts or functional subsystems). Examine and analyze each substructure separately to discover the fault. If each subsystem works adequately, you may find the fault in the connections of the subsystems (i.e., connective parts or two elements in a gymnastic routine or other sport skill). If after analyzing the connections the fault remains unresolved, it may be necessary to further divide the subsystems until you reach the underlying elements and the imperfection. Improvement methods should aim at the fault or weakest link.

Apply the integration-differentiation processes to either perfecting a technical or tactical model or to changing the model. Figure 3.3 illustrates perfecting a skill by automating the component parts (differentiation process) and resynthesizing the parts into a functional whole (integration process). The outcome of these two procedures will materialize through changes in the accuracy and fineness of the components, which leads to virtuosity and an art of skill performance.

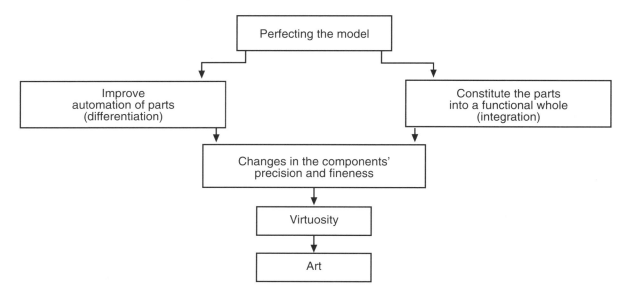

Figure 3.3 The perfecting model (modified from Teodorescu and Florescu 1971)

When you find a technical skill or tactical maneuver insufficient, alter the previous model. Attempt to trace why the mistake occurred (e.g., spiking outside of the court) and change useless components (figure 3.4). As explained, the process of detecting a mistake works backward. The coach figures out that the ball was spiked outside the court, then looks at how the player hit and covered the ball. If the athlete correctly performed this technical element, then the coach observes the airborne body position and the takeoff place in respect to the net to find out whether the athlete is under the ball. The coach decides that the player has a takeoff fault. The player customarily takes off from a place too close to the net, therefore, is always under the ball, restricting a proper cover, which results in sending it outside of the court.

When changing the model, the coach must inhibit the technical element that now appears useless to ensure that acquiring the new technical element is not restricted. The coach can inhibit an incorrect distance for a takeoff by placing tape on the floor to indicate an improved takeoff position. Consequently, as illustrated by figure 3.4, to change a model, inhibit the useless technical element so the athlete can learn and adapt to the newly created condition. Then through training, the parts of the skill will become automated (differentiation) and reintegrated into a whole. This will result in a precise and fine skill, next virtuosity, then art.

Stability-Variability

Sports have many types of movements, technical elements, and tactical schemes. Use these movements and skills in training to enhance variety, elimi-

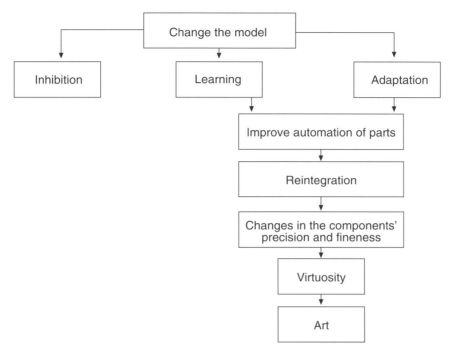

Figure 3.4 Changing an inefficient model
(modified from Teodorescu and Florescu 1971)

nate boredom, and keep the athlete's interest. A variety of exercises, selected according to the needs of the sport, gives a solid background for creating new elements or tactical maneuvers. Variability, for adapting the athlete to an exercise or skill or compensating for an athlete's needs, stabilizes skill and performance level. Furthermore, variability plays the role of blocking the factors that disturb this stability.

Standardization-Individualization

In training, the coach must solve the conflict between standardizing a skill and the athlete's individual traits and characteristics. Thus, the coach has to properly correlate the structure of a technical skill with each individual's psychological and biological particularities.

Phases of Perfecting Technical and Tactical Training

Perfecting technique and tactics rests not only on the coach's knowledge and teaching abilities, but also on the athlete's abilities to acquire new elements. Learning potential depends on the capacity to process new information based on previous models and on individual biomotor abilities. The coach's explanation and the use of preparatory and progressive drills and audiovisual facilities are effective tools for perfecting the athlete's skills. Athletes improve technical and tactical skills in three phases (Teodorescu and Florescu 1971) (figure 3.5).

During the first phase, the main objective is to perfect the components and technical elements of a skill (differentiation). As each component becomes more refined, progressively integrate it into a whole system. Parallel with the perfection process, the athlete must also perfect the dominant or supporting biomotor

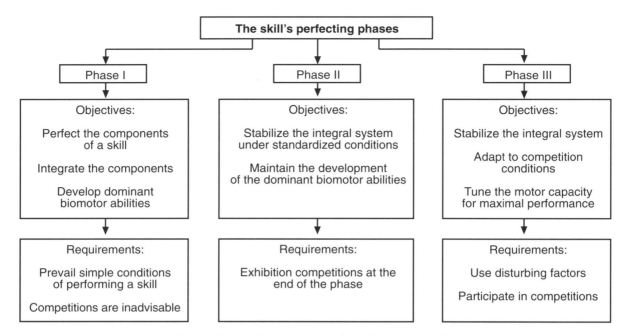

Figure 3.5 Three phases of perfecting the skills (adapted from Teodorescu and Florescu 1971)

abilities, because technique is a function of physical preparation. Because the main objective of the first phase is to perfect the skills, participation in competitions is inadvisable. This phase is suitable for the preparatory phase of the annual plan.

The main objective of the second phase is to perfect the integral system (whole skill) under standardized conditions similar to a competition. Exhibition competitions may be used by the end of this phase. At least, the athlete must maintain the dominant biomotor abilities. You may plan the second phase of perfecting a skill for the end of the preparatory phase.

During the last phase, aim at stabilizing the system and adapting it to the specifics of competition. Consequently, among other methods, the coach may expose the athletes or team to disturbing factors such as noise and fatigue to adjust them to competition circumstances.

Correcting Technical and Tactical Errors

Often technical improvement or skill mastery is delayed because of improper or incorrect learning. Eliminating a technical or tactical fault is every coach's goal. The quicker the athlete can correct a mistake, the faster the improvement. A fault that interferes with improvement could have several causes. Causes for technical or tactical faults fall into three areas.

The athlete may be misperforming a skill. Several factors may limit an athlete's learning. *Psychological limitation* occurs if the athlete sets low achievement goals and is satisfied with the level of skill acquisition. *Insufficient physical training* or lack of correlation among the biomotor abilities, the skill complexity, and the difficulty level would limit an athlete. Because technique is a function of physical training, acquiring a skill may be slowed down, delayed, or limited by insufficiently developing an ability. Coordination is a limiting factor in acquiring a skill, as is strength in certain sports. For instance, an athlete may not learn a technical element in gymnastics without an appropriate level of strength; therefore, technique may be restored as a result of physical improvement. The same is true for some throwing events in athletics. A *misunderstanding or misrepresentation of the technical pattern* of a skill and its correlation with movement, form, and muscular sensation would be a limiting factor. A *new skill* could interfere with skills already acquired. *Fatigue,* which can be caused by poor physical training or inadequate rest, may also limit learning abilities. The athlete may *incorrectly handle or grasp* an implement, object, or apparatus. Finally, there may be *morale or mental causes*, such as lack of self-confidence, desire, and fear of accidents or injuries.

The coach's methodical approach may cause technical faults. The coach may use inappropriate teaching methods or may demonstrate or explain a skill inadequately, incompletely, or incorrectly. There could be a lack of appropriate individualization in teaching a skill, by misunderstanding an athlete's level of biomotor abilities and individual learning capacities or by applying unsuitable teaching methods. Using a random approach in developing a team's strategy or including technical elements in a tactical maneuver could limit the athletes' learning. Personality, behavior, coaching style, and character could be limiting factors, for instance, if the coach lacks patience with athletes or pushes for quick skill acquisition.

There could be organization, equipment, or environmental causes. Using poor quality equipment and apparatus or an imperfect field or court surface affects the quality and rate of improvement. Improper organization or planning does not offer an adequate learning environment. A lack of individual training for slow learners or athletes with incorrect technical or tactical skills will have a detrimental effect. Adverse environment or climate may impair skill acquisition.

We have discussed various means of perfecting technique and strategy. The coach should always be concerned with preventing a mistake, eliminating the need for correction. Through teaching, present additional methodical recommendations intended specifically for correcting a mistake. If this fails, then start correcting a mistake as soon as possible. From the planning point of view, the ideal time to be concerned with an athlete's technical or tactical corrections is during the preparatory phase of the annual plan. Because the stress of competitions is absent, both the coach and athlete can dedicate some quiet time to correct certain faults.

Among the first measures to use for technical remedy is to isolate the fault from other technical elements of a skill. As soon as the athlete no longer has an inhibitory element, such as a technical fault, the coach should begin to teach the element that will replace it. When the athlete acquires the new part of the skill, integrate it with the system or the whole skill. Concurrent with this, develop the biomotor ability the athlete needs as a physical support for the new element.

Always correct a mistake immediately after the warm-up, when the athlete is still fresh and can concentrate on technical accumulation. Because fatigue may affect learning, avoid corrections toward the end of a lesson. If learning takes place in the body of the lesson, then allow a longer time for rest and regeneration between skill repetitions.

An extremely important aspect in correcting technical faults is at what intensity or velocity to do it. In most cases, coaches concentrate on correcting the technique at low intensity and low velocity. In swimming, running, rowing, canoeing, and kayaking, athletes perform technical work at low velocity. What coaches fail to understand is that most athletes can perform a decent skill at low velocity because it generates little fatigue. Technical breakdown occurs at high velocity or under conditions similar to competitions, not at low intensity. The skill's mechanics, the form of performing a skill, breaks down when the athlete experiences fatigue. This is when old faults interfere with an athlete's ability to maintain good form.

The same faulty approach is used to correct skills in jumping and throwing events in track and field, martial arts, and most team sports. In basketball, for instance, players work on shooting accuracy when rested, when fatigue and heart rate are low. Skill deterioration for passing and shooting accuracy occurs when players are fatigued and their concentration low.

The conclusion: fatigue affects the mechanics of a skill. The recommendation: make technical corrections under fatiguing conditions similar to those the athlete experiences in competitions.

Mental practice, or rehearsing the new element, may help the athlete correct a mistake. Also, audiovisual aids are beneficial in making technical corrections. Finally, repeating a new element with a highly skilled athlete (i.e., in team sports) is another method for technical progress.

Theoretical Training

The concept that an athlete has to train practically and theoretically is not yet widely accepted, let alone used. Though rare today, some coaches still believe that they should think for their athletes. Athletes are there to train and compete; the coach does the rest of it. Obviously, this ancient idea may affect the athlete's rate of skill and performance improvement.

Acquiring and applying current theoretical knowledge are important to accelerating the development of athletes' skills and abilities, as well as motivating their training. Concurrent with developing their skills and abilities, coaches must introduce young athletes progressively to the theory of training. They need to experience everything the coach knows about the selected sport. Certainly, the coach must be a knowledgeable individual concerned with his or her own education in the science of sports, thus remaining one step ahead of the athletes.

All the scientific gains the coach makes should not be taboo for the athletes. On the contrary, they should have access to the coach's expertise. The coach's responsibility is not restricted to training; it extends to the athletes' general and sport-specific education. Sharing knowledge from the following areas with athletes may be an adequate guideline for a coach:

- Rules and regulations governing the selected sport.
- The scientific basis for understanding and analyzing the technique of the sport. Biomechanics has the highest implication in technically comprehending and analyzing a skill. Gymnastics, throwing and jumping events in track, diving, and skiing have the most to gain. Correctly understanding the biomechanical bases of skill performance may aid in eliminating injuries.
- The scientific and methodical basis of the biomotor abilities development.
- The planning concept in training. Coaches should refer to periodization of training, preparation for competition, and peaking.
- Anatomical and physiological adaptation following training.
- Causes, prevention, and cure of injuries.
- Sociology of sport (intergroup conflicts).

- Sport psychology, emphasizing communication skills, behavior modification, stressors and how to cope with them, and relaxation techniques.
- Nutrition and athletics, including how it affects performance; the diet to follow according to the phase and type of training; and pre-, during, and postcompetition diets.

Consider the following means for athletes' theoretical training: discussion between the coach and athletes; film analysis; discussions with other athletes and coaches; clinics; relevant periodicals; and other pertinent publications. The coach's explanation and knowledge-sharing processes during training sessions, pre- and posttraining discussions, and conversations while traveling or during camps are important to athletes' theoretical preparation. In his or her activities and involvements, the coach should develop correct moral behavior; cultivate respect for other athletes, referees, and fans; and build a strong patriotic sentiment in the athletes.

Summary of Major Concepts

Irrespective of the sport, training entails physical, technical, tactical, psychological, and theoretical components. There are important relationships among these five factors, especially physical, technical, and tactical training.

Most training programs, especially for team sports, emphasize technical and tactical training, neglecting physical training. However, physical training should be the foundation of every training program because fatigue directly relates to physical conditioning. The weaker an athlete's physical training, the faster he or she will fatigue. When the athlete fatigues, technical and tactical skills deteriorate. A high level of fatigue also affects tactical judgment during the game. This means more mistakes, and as a result, poorer performance. This is why physical training must be the foundation of every training program.

Technique must be trained to perfection. The higher an athlete's level of technique, the less energy he or she requires to perform it. For all sports, especially those in which endurance is an important component, technical proficiency increases the athlete's physical efficiency. For equal performance, a good technician experiences a lower level of fatigue.

Design tactical training and create a game plan well before competitions and games so the athlete has time to practice. If you want to be successful, plan for success!

Variables of Training

Any physical activity leads to anatomical, physiological, biochemical, and psychological changes. The efficiency of a physical activity results from its duration, distance, and repetitions (volume); load and velocity (intensity); and the frequency of performance (density). When planning the dynamics of training, consider these aspects, referred to as the variables of training. Model all these variables according to the functional and psychological characteristics of a competition. Throughout the training phases preceding a competition, define which component to emphasize to achieve the planned performance objective. As a rule, emphasize intensity for sports of speed and power, and volume for endurance sports. Finally, for sports requiring intricate skills, training complexity is primary.

Increase all components of training in proportion to the athlete's overall improvement. Carefully monitor the dynamics of such a balanced increase during all phases of the annual plan and throughout a player's athletic career.

Volume

As a prime component of training, volume is the quantitative prerequisite for high technical, tactical, and physical achievements. The volume of training, sometimes inaccurately called the duration of training, incorporates the following integral parts:

- The time or duration of training
- Distance covered or weight lifted per unit of time
- The repetitions of an exercise or technical element an athlete performs in a given time

Volume implies the total quantity of activity performed in training. Volume also refers to the sum of work performed during a training lesson or phase. When you refer to the volume of a training phase, specify the number of training lessons and the number of hours and days of work.

As an athlete becomes capable of high levels of performance, the overall volume of training becomes more important. For elite athletes, there are no shortcuts for the high quantity of work they must perform. A continual increase in training volume is probably one of the highest priorities of contemporary training. High training volume has a clear physiological justification: athletes cannot physiologically adapt without it. An increasing volume of work is paramount in training for any aerobic sport or event. A similar increase is also necessary for sports requiring the perfection of technical or tactical skills. Only a high number of repetitions can ensure the quantitative accumulation of skills necessary for qualitative improvements in performance.

Performance improves by increasing the number of training lessons and the amount of work accomplished during each lesson for all categories of sports. Recovery also accelerates as the athlete adapts to an elevated quantity of work. The amount of volume increase is a function of individual characteristics and specifics of the sport. For an elite athlete to perform adequately, at least 8 to 12 lessons per microcycle are necessary. Also a high correlation exists between the volume of hours of training per year and desired performance. An athlete expecting to place in the top 20 in the world must perform more than 1,000 hours of training per year. Athletes in international competition ought to consider 800 hours, and national-caliber athletes require at least 600 hours of training. Finally, plan 400 hours of work for an adequate performance in regional or state championships. However, too great an increase in the work volume per training lesson can be harmful. Harre (1982) suggests that such an increase leads to fatigue, low training efficiency, uneconomical muscle work, and increased risk of injury. Consequently, if the volume per training lesson is already sufficient, it is wiser to increase the number of training lessons per microcycle than the volume of work per lesson.

To accurately evaluate the volume of training, select a unit of measurement. For some sports (running, canoeing, cross-country skiing, and rowing), the appropriate unit seems to be space or distance covered during training. The load in kilograms seems to be appropriate for weightlifting or weight training for strength improvement. Time, which regulates other sports (boxing, wrestling, judo, gymnastics, team sports), seems to be a common denominator for most sports, although a coach often must use two measuring units, time and distance, to express the volume correctly (i.e., to run 12 kilometers in 60 minutes).

In training we can calculate two types of volume. *Relative volume* refers to the total amount of time a group of athletes or team dedicates to training during a specific training lesson or phase of training. Relative volume seldom has value for an individual athlete. This means that, although the coach knows the total duration of training, he or she has no information regarding each athlete's volume of work per unit of time. *Absolute volume* measures the amount of work an individual athlete performs per unit of time, usually expressed in minutes. This is a far better assessment of the volume of training athletes perform.

The dynamics of the volume throughout the training phases vary according to the sport and its ergogenesis, the training objectives, the athlete's needs, and the competition calendar.

Intensity

Intensity, the qualitative component of work an athlete performs in a given time, is also an important component of training. The more work the athlete performs per unit of time, the higher the intensity. Intensity is a function of the strength of the nerve impulses the athlete employs in training. The strength of a stimulus depends on the load, speed of performance, and the variation of intervals or rest between repetitions. The last, but not the least, important element of intensity is the psychological strain of an exercise. Muscular work and CNS involvement through maximum concentration determine intensity during training or competition. It is important to acknowledge the psychological element of an exercise and admit that even sports requiring a low level of physical exertion, such as shooting, archery, and chess, have a certain level of intensity.

You can measure intensity according to the type of exercise. Exercises involving speed are measured in meters/second (m/s) or the rate/minute of performing a movement. The intensity of activities performed against resistance can be measured in kilograms or kgm (a kilogram lifted 1 meter against the force of gravity). For team sports the game rhythm determines the intensity.

Intensity varies according to the specifics of the sport. Because the level of intensity varies in most sports and events, establish and use varying degrees of intensity in training. Several methods are available to measure the strength of the stimuli and thus the intensity. For example, with exercises performed against resistance or exercises developing high velocity, use a percentage of the maximum intensity, in which 100% represents best performance. In a 100-meter dash, however, best performance signifies the mean velocity developed over that distance (i.e., 10 meter/second). The same athlete may generate a higher velocity (i.e., 10.2 meter/second) over a shorter distance. I regard this velocity as 105% of maximum and include it in the table of intensities (table 4.1). For exercises performed against resistance, 105% represents a load that the athlete cannot move through the whole range of movement, but may attain isometrically. According to this classification of intensities, a distance runner (i.e., 5,000 or 10,000 meters) may train at 125% or more of the maximum, because the maximum is his or her race pace.

An alternative method of evaluating intensity is based on the energy system used to fuel the activity. This classification (Astrand and Saltin 1961; Farfel

TABLE 4.1 Scale of Intensities for Speed and Strength Exercises

Intensity number	Percentage of maximum performance	Intensity
1	30-50	Low
2	50-70	Intermediate
3	70-80	Medium
4	80-90	Submaximum
5	90-100	Maximum
6	100-105	Supermaximum

With additions from Harre 1982.

1960; Margaria, Ceretelli, Aghemo, and Sassi 1963; Mathews and Fox 1971) is most appropriate for cyclic sports (table 4.2).

Intensity zone one places a strong demand on the athlete to reach higher limits in activities of short duration, up to 15 seconds. These activities are extremely intense, as demonstrated by rapid movement and a high mobility of the information reaching the CNS. The short duration does not allow the autonomic nervous system (ANS) to adapt, so the cardiovascular system does not have time to adjust to the physical challenge. The physical demand of sports specific to this zone (i.e., 100-meter dash) requires a high flow of O_2, which the human body cannot provide. According to Gandelsman and Smirnov (1970), during a 100-meter dash, O_2 demand is 66 to 80 liters per minute. Because the O_2 stored in the tissue does not meet the athlete's needs, he or she may encounter an O_2 debt up to 80 or 90% of that necessary for a fast race. This O_2 debt is repaid by using extra O_2 after the activity, allowing replenishment of ATP-CP stores used during the race. Continuing such activity may be limited by the O_2 supply within the athlete, the amount of ATP-CP stored within the muscle cells, and the athlete's ability to withstand a high O_2 debt.

Zone two, the maximum-intensity zone, includes activities of 15 to 60 seconds (i.e., 200- and 400-meter run, 100-meter swim). Velocity and intensity

TABLE 4.2 Five Zones of Intensity for Cylic Sports

Zone no.	Duration of work	Level of intensity	System producing the energy	ERGOGENESIS%	
				Anaerobic	Aerobic
1	1-15 s	Up to maximum limits	ATP-CP	100-95	0-5
2	15-60 s	Maximum	ATP-CP and LA	90-80	10-20
3	1-6 min	Submaximum	LA and aerobic	70-(40-30)	30-(60-70)
4	6-30 min	Medium	Aerobic	(40-30)-10	(60-70)-90
5	Over 30 min	Low	Aerobic	5	95

Zone 1 activities are extremely intense and of short duration, up to 15 s

are maximum, straining the CNS and locomotor systems and diminishing the ability to maintain a high velocity longer than 60 seconds. The energetic exchanges within the muscle cells reach extremely high levels, yet the cardiorespiratory system has insufficient time to react to the stimulus and is, therefore, still at a low level. The athlete encounters an O_2 debt up to 60 to 70% of the energy requirements of the race. The athlete derives energy predominantly from the ATP-CP system with a low lactic acid (LA) component. The O_2 system does not contribute significantly to the energy requirement, because it participates primarily during exercises of 60 seconds or more. It is also significant that energy demand for one event in this zone, the 400-meter run, is among the highest.

Zone three, also called the submaximum zone, includes activities of 1 to 6 minutes in which both speed and endurance play dominant roles (i.e., 400-meter swim, canoeing, rowing, 1,500-meter run, and 1,000- to 3,000-meter speed skating). The complex nature of these sports and drastic physiological changes (i.e., a heart rate up to 200 beats per minute and a maximum blood pressure of 100 millimeter Hg), hardly may be prolonged more than 6 minutes. Following a race, the athlete may have an O_2 debt of 20 liters per minute and the LA may be up to 250 milligrams (Gandelsman and Smirnov 1970). Under such circumstances the body reaches a state of acidosis, in which it accumulates much more LA than the normal balance (pH7).

The athlete adjusts to the rhythm of the race quickly, especially a well-trained athlete. Following the first minute of the race, the O_2 system helps produce energy and dominates the second part of the race. At the finish, the athlete accelerates the pace. This extra strain pushes the circulatory and respiratory

Zone 2 activities occur in the maximum zone of intensity

Zone 3 activities last 1 to 6 minutes during which speed and endurance play dominant roles

compensating mechanisms to physiological limits and also demands maximum energy production from anaerobic glycolysis as well as the aerobic system, resulting in a high O_2 debt. The body calls on both the LA and aerobic systems to produce the energy required. The percentages of each depend on the event or sport.

Zone four, the medium intensity zone, challenges the athlete's body with activity for up to 30 minutes. Events such as 800- and 1,500-meter swim, 5,000- and 10,000-meter run, cross-country skiing, walking, and long-distance events in speed skating are included. The circulatory system accelerates considerably and the cardiac muscle is stressed over a prolonged time. During the race, the blood O_2 saturation is in deficit (hypoxia), or 10 to 16% below the resting level (Gandelsman and Smirnov 1970). Aerobic energy is dominant (up to 90%), although at the beginning and finish of the race athletes use the anaerobic system as well. Pacing and energy distribution throughout the race are important for athletes involved for a long duration.

Zone five includes activities in which the intensity is low but the volume of energy expenditures is great, as in marathon running, 50-kilometer cross-country skiing, 20- and 50-kilometer walking, and road racing in cycling. This zone is a difficult test for athletes. The extension of work leads to depleting glucides (hypoglycemia) in the bloodstream, a burden on the CNS. The circulatory system is in high demand and heart hypertrophy (a functional enlargement of the heart) is a common characteristic and a functional necessity for athletes competing in these sports and events. These athletes have a high ability to adapt to hypoxia, and following a race often experience a blood O_2 saturation between 10 and 14% below resting level (Gandelsman and Smirnov 1970). The high and prolonged demand makes recovery slow, sometimes up to

Zone 4 activities are in the medium-intensity zone and take up to 30 minutes

2 or 3 weeks, which is one reason why these athletes do not take part in many races (3-5) per year.

For the second and third zones of intensity, perfecting aerobic endurance, uniformly distributing energy, and self-assessing abilities throughout the race are among the determining factors of success. The physiological nature of self-assessment depends on perfecting the function of sensory organs. This is the specialized part of the nervous system that controls the body's reaction to the external environment and, therefore, the development of so-called time, water, track, ball, or implement sense. Time sense comes from rhythmical impulses from the proprioceptors of the muscles and tendons, which repeat at different time intervals. Experienced boxers, runners, and swimmers develop a sense of the time remaining in a round, split times, or the time performed in a race, based on the muscles' sensors. All these senses, with the sense of fatigue, supply information to athletes regarding the state of their bodies and assist in adapting to the training or race session and external environment.

During training, athletes experience various levels of intensity. The body adapts by increasing physiological functions to meet the training demand. Based on these changes, especially heart rate (HR), the coach may detect and monitor the intensity of a training program. A final classification of intensities, on the basis of HR, is suggested in table 4.3 (Nikiforov 1974).

To develop certain biomotor abilities, the intensity of a stimulus must reach or exceed a threshold level beyond which significant training gains take place. Hettinger (1966) revealed that for strength training, intensities less than 30% of maximum do not provide a training effect. For endurance sports (cross-country

Zone 5 activities are low intensity but use a great volume of energy

TABLE 4.3 Four Zones of Intensity Based on HR Reactions to Training Load

Zone	Type of intensity	Heart rate/min.
1	Low	120-150
2	Medium	150-170
3	High	170-185
4	Maximum	>185

Nikiforov 1974

skiing, running, rowing, swimming), the threshold HR beyond which the cardiorespiratory system will experience a training effect is suspected to be 130 beats per minute (Harre 1982). This threshold varies among athletes due to individual differences; thus, Karvonen, Kentala, and Mustala (1957) proposed that it should be determined by the sum of the resting heart rate plus 60% of the difference between maximum and resting heart rates.

$$HR_{threshold} = HR_{rest} + .60(HR_{max} - HR_{rest})$$

Thus, the threshold HR depends on the resting and the maximum HR. Furthermore, Teodorescu (1975) advocates that an athlete should employ stimuli in excess of 60% of his or her maximum capacity to achieve a training effect.

Low-level loads or exercises in training lead to slow development, but ensure sufficient adaptation and consistency of performance. High-intensity exercises result in quick progress, but lead to less stable adaptation and a lower degree of consistency. Using only intensive exercises is not the most effective way to train, and alternating training volume and intensity is necessary. The high volume of low-intensity training athletes experience during the preparatory phase provides a foundation for high-intensity training and enhances performance consistency.

In training theory, there are two types of intensities: (a) absolute intensity, which measures the percentage of maximum necessary to perform the exercise; and (b) relative intensity, which measures the intensity of a training lesson or microcycle, given the absolute intensity and the total volume of work performed in that period. The higher the absolute intensity, the lower the volume of work for any training lesson. Athletes may not repeat exercises of high absolute intensity (greater than 85% of maximum) extensively in a training lesson. Such training lessons should be no more than 40% of the total lessons per microcycle, with the remaining lessons using a lower absolute intensity.

Relationship Between Volume and Intensity

Athletic exercise usually involves both quantity and quality; therefore, it is difficult to differentiate between them in training. For instance, when a swimmer sprints, the distance and time of the event represent volume, and the velocity of performance indicates intensity. Placing different relative emphasis on these components in training yields different effects on the body's adaptation and training status. The higher the intensity and the longer it is maintained, the higher the energy requirements and the more stress on the CNS and athlete's psychological sphere.

Swimming long distances may be possible if intensity is low, but the athlete may not maintain maximum velocity beyond competition distance. Decreasing a sprinter's training intensity by 40% may allow him or her to increase work volume by 400 to 500%. Consequently, it appears that the efficiency with which the athlete can perform work of reduced intensity may substantially elevate the volume (i.e., number of repetitions). Of course, such a drastic increase in volume capacity would not prevail for an endurance athlete (long-distance runner, skier, swimmer) if the intensity decreases from his or her maximum since this already scores low on the absolute scale. Rather, to facilitate an equivalent (400-500%) increase in volume, measure the 40% decrease in intensity from the highest supermaximum load the athlete can handle.

Ozolin (1971) exemplifies accurately the relationship between the volume and intensity of training during one year for sports with varied intensity requirements. High jumpers spend approximately 2 hours on jumps with a full approach; pole vaulters 3 hours; triple jumpers 10 to 12 minutes; gymnasts (high bar combinations) 6 hours; and long-distance runners 70 to 100 hours (for repetitions close to the competition's speed). The remaining time they dedicate to other exercises that develop the abilities required by that particular event. You can use a completely different approach for team sports, boxing, wrestling, and martial arts, in which a standard duration of competition determines the relationships between volume and intensity.

Determining the optimal combination of volume and intensity is a complex task and usually depends on the specifics of the sport. It is simpler in sports with objective assessment methods. For instance, in canoeing the volume is based on the distance covered in training, and the intensity is expressed by the velocity at which the athlete performs a given distance. In other sports, such as team sports, gymnastics, and fencing, consider the total number of actions, elements, repetitions, their distance, and the speed at which the athlete performs them in defining the accurate proportions between the training components. Often, however, you can use the duration of a training lesson or the number of repetitions of certain skills to calculate the volume. Although not accessible to most coaches, computing the energy expenditure may be a more accurate method of assessing the weight you place on either the volume or intensity.

Heart rate (HR) is often used as an indicator of the level of work. This method may suffice for beginners; however, elite athletes do not benefit as much from it because training involves all body functions, and change in HR is just one of many reactions. Using HR as the only method could, therefore, restrict athletes from employing the optimum training stimuli, and consequently affect the improvement rate. Using HR as a method of assessing the recovery rate between training lessons may be of more assistance in estimating the work and the athlete's reaction to it.

Dynamics of Increasing the Volume and Intensity

The amount of work current international-class athletes perform was inconceivable in the 1970s or 1980s. Eight to twelve or even more training lessons per week of 2 to 4 hours each are considered normal. Most coaches are concerned with maximizing the athlete's free time for training. As suggested in chapter 2, add components progressively and individually. Elevate training sessions in steps. A session that was optimal in one training cycle may be inadequate in the next, because its intensity does not reach the threshold and provoke the required training effect. An optimal session produces optimal body adaptation. Thus, an optimal session must relate to the index of effort capacity;

otherwise, it may be either too weak or too powerful. The athlete accumulates the index of effort capacity in qualitative steps as a result of quantitative accumulations of work and his or her adaptation to it. During training, the athlete's adaptation and the index of work capacity increase periodically in steps and not in a straight line. Coaches need a great deal of patience to wait for the expected improvements from their training programs.

The best progression for increasing the volume and intensity of training is as follows:

Volume of Training

- Increase the duration of a training session. If 3 sessions of 60 minutes is your present volume of work per week, then increase it to 3 × 90 minutes and later to 3 × 120 minutes.
- Increase the number of training sessions per week. Take the 3 × 120 minutes to 4 × 120, 5 × 120, and so on.
- Increase the number of repetitions, drills, or technical elements per training lesson.
- Increase the distance or duration per repetition or drill.

Intensity of Training

- Increase the velocity to cover a given distance, the rhythm (quickness) of performing a tactical drill, or the load in strength training.
- Increase the number of repetitions the athlete performs with this intensity.
- Decrease the rest interval between repetitions or tactical drills.
- Increase the number of competitions per training phase (only if this is not at a desirable level for your athletes or sports).

The dynamics of intensity used in training depend on the following three factors: the characteristics of the sport; the training environment; and preparation and the athlete's performance level.

The characteristics of the sport. For sports in which maximum effort determines performance (weightlifting, throwing, jumping events, and sprinting), the intensity level during the competition phase is usually high, between 70 and 100% of the total amount of work in training. For sports in which skill mastery defines the performance (figure skating, diving, synchronized swimming), athletes rarely use high intensity. According to Ozolin (1971), the average intensity such sports use is a medium level. On the other hand, the intensity of training in team sports is complex, because the rhythm of the game is fast and the intensity alters continually between low and maximum. To meet such requirements, a training program should include some high and a continuous variety of intensities.

The training environment. For example, increase training intensity by cross-country skiing on wet snow, running on sand or uphill, or dragging an object while swimming or rowing. Rivalry between athletes or the presence of spectators may elevate the intensity as well.

Preparation and the athlete's performance level. The same training content for athletes of various preparation levels or performance capabilities may represent a different intensity for each. What may be medium intensity for an elite athlete may be maximum intensity for a prospective athlete. Although athletes of various preparation levels may train together, the coach's program must differ to meet each athlete's needs.

Elevate intensity by increasing the intensity during a lesson or phase of training, or by increasing the density of a training lesson. Obviously, the coach should emphasize the first mode because it increases the individual's potential according to the specifics of the sport or event. The coach should use the second method mainly to increase the total means of training, aiming at developing intensity, general physical preparation, or cultivating specific endurance.

As suggested, the HR method can help calculate training intensity. By using the HR method as an objective measure, a coach may be able to compute overall intensity (OI) in training as an expression of the total demand an individual experiences during a lesson. You can calculate the OI by using the following equation proposed by Iliuta and Dumitrescu (1978):

$$OI = \frac{\Sigma(PI \cdot VE)}{\Sigma(VE)}$$

PI stands for percentage of partial intensity and VE for the volume of exercises. Because we must calculate the percentage of partial intensity first, we can use the following equation:

$$PI = \frac{HR_p \cdot 100}{HR_{max}}$$

HR_p is the heart rate resulting from performing the exercise for which we are calculating partial intensity, and HR_{max} stands for the maximum heart rate the athlete achieves in performing the sport.

The dynamics of volume and intensity are also a function of the dominant biomotor ability in a sport. For sports dominated by either speed or strength, emphasize intensity for progress, especially during the competitive phase. For endurance sports, volume is the main element of progression in a given phase, with intensity playing a much lesser role. Thus, it appears that volume and intensity are inversely proportional. Intensity increases only as volume decreases.

For training content, a high absolute intensity should prevail for exercises of less than 2 minutes. At 2 minutes, the ratio between the anaerobic and aerobic energy systems is equal, or 50:50 (Astrand and Rodahl 1970). For sports that last approximately 2 minutes, emphasize volume and intensity equally. The importance of the aerobic energy system, however, is evident even in the first minute of a race (Mader and Hollmann 1977). Therefore, events of less than 2 minutes still require emphasis on volume in training, especially during the preparatory and early competitive phases. Over the 2-minute zone, aerobic power is evidently dominant; therefore, athletes should emphasize volume of training for sports that last longer than 2 minutes. I discuss the volume and intensity of training further in part II, chapter 8 (the annual plan).

Rating the Volume and Intensity

The human body adapts and improves in direct relationship to the type of stimuli it experiences. The work the athlete performs in training is the cause, and the body adaptation is the effect. The optimal stimuli results in an optimal training effect. To achieve an optimal training effect, plan training programs specific to the sport and prescribe them in an appropriate dose. Set the quantity of work the athlete performs in a training lesson according to individual abilities, the phase of training, and a correct ratio between volume and intensity. If you properly administer the training dosage, correct athletic development will result, leading to an adequate degree of training (the physical and psychological level in a training phase). In training there are two forms of dosage: external and internal (Harre 1982).

The *external* dosage, or load, is a function of training volume and intensity. To construct a correct training program, correctly assess the intimate characteristics of the external rating, which includes volume, intensity, density, and frequency of stimuli. Because these components are simple to measure, you can rate them easily. The external dosage usually elicits physical and psychological reactions from the athlete. These individual reactions are the *internal* dosage, or load, and they express the degree and magnitude of fatigue the athlete experiences. Each component of the external dosage affects the size and intensity of the internal dosage.

Applying the same external dosage does not always produce similar internal reactions. Since the internal dosage is a function of the individual's athletic potential, you can estimate its reaction in general terms only. An adequate training diary and periodic testing may facilitate reading internal reactions. The external dosage may be affected by circumstances such as the opponent's athletic caliber, equipment, facilities, environmental conditions, and social factors.

Relationship Between Volume and Adaptation

Application of the correct dose of training results in anatomical, physiological, and psychological changes in the athlete. Positive changes from systematic training show adaptation to various stimuli. A high correlation exists between adaptation and dosage in training.

The adaptability processes occur only when the stimuli reach an intensity proportional to the individual's threshold capacity (Harre 1982). A high volume of work without a minimal intensity (for example, less than 30% of maximum) does not facilitate adaptation, because a higher level is required to initiate such adaptation. It is possible, however, to exceed optimal stimulation by demanding too much work from the athlete or by miscalculating the volume-intensity ratio. In this case, adaptation decreases, leading to performance stagnation or even regression. Adaptation results from a correct alternation between stimulation and regeneration, between work and rest.

The process of adequately adapting to training and competitions increases the athlete's degree of training, correct peaking, and physical and psychological improvement. The effects of a standard dosage and stimulus diminish after a while, resulting in modest performance; therefore, increase the external dosage periodically (as suggested by the principle of progressive increase of the load in training). Furthermore, if you reduce the stimulus, the training effect diminishes, resulting in an involution phase. The benefits of training may also diminish if you interrupt training too long. For instance, if the transition phase is too long or if it includes totally passive rather than active rest, all improvements obtained from the preparatory and competitive phases disappear. This requires the athlete to start training for the next preparatory phase at a low level.

Density

The frequency at which an athlete participates in a series of stimuli per unit of time is called the density of training. Density refers to the relationship, expressed in time, between working and recovery phases of training. An adequate density ensures training efficiency and prevents the athletes from reaching a state of critical fatigue or exhaustion. A balanced density may also lead to achieving an optimal ratio between training sessions and recovery.

The rest interval between two training sessions depends directly on the intensity and duration of each session, although you may also consider factors such as the athlete's training status, the phase of training, and the specifics of the sport. Sessions higher than submaximum intensity require long rest intervals to facilitate recovery before the following session. Sessions of lower intensities require less recovery time because the demand on the athlete is lower.

An objective way to calculate a rest interval is the HR method. Harre (1982) and Herberger (1977) suggest that, before applying a new repetition, HR should slow to 120 to 140 beats per minute. Harre (1982) proposes an optimal density ratio between work and rest. For developing endurance, the optimal density is 2:1 to 1:1 (the first digit refers to the working time and the second to the rest interval). A ratio of 2:1 means that the rest interval is half as long as the work interval. When using highly intensive stimuli for developing endurance, the density is 1:3 to 1:6, meaning the rest interval may be 3 to 6 times the duration of the work. For strength training, especially for developing maximum strength or power, the rest interval should be 2 to 5 minutes, depending on the percentage of load and the rhythm of performance.

You can also compute density by using other parameters. You can calculate relative density (RD), which refers to the percentage of work volume the athlete performs compared with the total volume per training lesson, using the following equation:

$$RD = \frac{AV \cdot 10}{RV}$$

AV stands for absolute volume, or the volume of training an individual performs. RV refers to the relative volume or the duration of a training lesson. For example, let AV be 102 minutes and RV be 120, or 2 hours of training, for the hypothetical boxer discussed earlier in this section. Substituting these two figures in the previous equation will find the following:

$$RD = \frac{102 \cdot 100}{120} = 85\%$$

This percentage suggests an RD of 85%, or the athlete worked 85% of the time. Although the RD has certain significance for both the coach and the athlete, the absolute density (AD) of an athlete's training is of greater importance. AD is the ratio between the effective work an athlete performs and the AV. Find the effective work an athlete performs by subtracting the volume of rest intervals (VRI) from AV using the following equation:

$$AD = \frac{(AV - VRI)100}{AV}$$

Let VRI be 26 minutes and AV 102 minutes, the figures already used. Substituting these figures into the formula results in the following:

$$AD = \frac{(102 - 26)100}{102} = 74.5\%$$

Thus, our hypothetical boxer has an AD of 74.5%. Because training density is a factor of intensity, the index of absolute density is medium intensity (please refer to the scale of intensities in table 4.1). This approach can assist a coach in conducting effective training lessons, especially for sports such as gymnastics in which training density is often unsatisfactory.

Complexity

Complexity refers to the degree of sophistication of a training exercise. The complexity of a skill, its coordination demand, could increase training intensity. A complex technical skill or element may cause learning problems and therefore extra muscular strain, especially during the phase when neuromuscular coordination is inferior. The exposure of a group of individuals to complex skills discriminates quickly between well and poorly coordinated individuals (provided that none previously experienced the skills). As Astrand and Rodahl (1970) advocated, the more complex an exercise, the greater will be the individual differences and mechanical efficiencies.

Even previously acquired skills of high complexity may be a source of volitional and nervous stress; therefore, you should also associate the complexity of a skill or tactical maneuver with stress in the psychic sphere. Korcek (1974) claims that tactical complexity in team sports represents an important stressor and that the athletes are often affected by such circumstances. Players' reactions to complex tactics were signified through the elevation of the HR by 20 to 30 beats per minute. The coach must, therefore, consider the complexity of a task in the planning process of training so that athletes do not overwork. Similarly, for arranging game schedules, the coach should consider highly demanding games not only from a physical point of view, but also from the complexity of the tactics involved. Under such circumstances, the coach should allow sufficient recovery time following the game, or plan demanding games at longer intervals.

Volume, intensity, and density mainly affect the demand athletes encounter in training. Although these three components may complement each other, an increased emphasis on one may cause an increased demand on the athletes. For instance, if the coach intends to maintain the same demand in training, and the needs of the sport require developing endurance, then he or she must increase volume. The coach then has to decide how this will affect density and how much to decrease intensity. If the coach decides to evaluate overall demand in training by varying intensity, then he or she needs to forecast how this new situation will affect the volume or density of training.

The planning and direction in training is a function of the three main components. The coach must guide the evolution of the curve of these components, especially volume and intensity, in direct relationship with the athlete's index of adaptation, phase of training, and the competition schedule. Furthermore, the science of knitting the training components may facilitate a correct peaking for the main competition.

You can calculate the index of overall demand (IOD), which expresses the level of demand in training, with the equation proposed by Iliuta and Dumitrescu (1978):

$$IOD = \frac{OI \cdot AD \cdot AV}{10,000}$$

Summary of Major Concepts

The amount of work, the volume of training, represents a key variable in training. A large amount of work that is physical, technical, and tactical is consistently important for a high level of adaptation, which normally translates into better performance. Although training volume is often adequate in individual sports, in most team sports, especially basketball, volleyball, soccer, and hockey, there is still room for improvement.

The athlete could easily double the volume of training from the traditional 6 to 10 hours per week for several team sports by doing more work outside of the gym, field, or ice arena. When this happens, improvements will be clearly visible in these sports.

Training intensity, on the other hand, fares much better for most sports in which both speed and power or specific drills tax the neuromuscular systems.

To better handle training volume and intensity, examine the progression of increasing them. It is essential to know how to apply progression in training and how to use it to avoid overtraining.

Pay maximum attention to training density, the number of drills or exercises performed in a certain time. The more drills per time unit, the higher the intensity, and the more stressful the training. To better control the undesirable effects of too much intensity per time unit, examine the restoration time for energy fuels the athlete uses in training (chapter 1). This will help you calculate the rest interval following an activity accurately and avoid critical levels of fatigue.

Chapter 5

Rest and Recovery

Most athletes, especially elite athletes, participate in demanding training, often two or more times a day. Under such circumstances, athletes may push beyond physiological and psychological norms. In addition, they experience other professional and social stressors that increase the overall stress encountered during training and competitions. To overcome this, athletes should maintain a good equilibrium between training, social life, and recovery.

Athletes are fatigued after training, and the greater the fatigue, the greater the aftereffects, such as low recovery rate, poor coordination, and decreased speed and power of muscle contractions. Strong emotional fatigue often accentuates normal physiological fatigue, especially following competitions, from which it takes longer to recover.

Coaches and training specialists should continually look for methods that allow athletes to overcome the limits of training and increase performance. One of the most effective ways is recovery techniques. Coaches should understand and actively enhance recovery so it becomes a significant training component. A coach seldom parallels increased training demand or higher intensity stimuli with similar regeneration efforts following training and competition. Similarly, research is lacking in this extremely important area. Proper recovery accelerates the regeneration rate between training lessons, decreases fatigue, enhances supercompensation, and facilitates using heavy loads in training. It can even decrease the number and frequency of injuries, because fatigue impairs coordination and concentration, leading to poor movement control.

Training and rest are unique, necessary training components, and the drive for high success must assign similar importance to both. Because athletes seldom fully recover between training lessons, consider using various recovery methods. Athletes should be equally concerned and realize that training time when the coach is not supervising them is important. The athlete's conscience for a well-balanced life plays an important role in success.

Recovery techniques must become habitual and be synchronized with the biological adaptation to a training demand and the correct alternation of work with regeneration. Recovery must be a daily concern and not follow only isolated training lessons and main competitions. This way, athletes regenerate following the training session and prevent acute exhaustion and overtraining.

Recovery Theory

Recovery or regeneration is a multidimensional process that depends on intrinsic and extrinsic factors. A coach aware of these factors who understands the physiological makeup and discipline of the athlete can apply selected recovery techniques. Consider the following factors.

The athlete's *age* affects recovery. Athletes older than 25 require longer recovery periods after training than younger athletes. Athletes younger than 18 require longer rest periods between workouts to facilitate overcompensation (Nudel 1989; Rowland 1990; Schöner-Kolb 1990).

Athletes with more *experience* will recuperate sooner because they have a much faster physiological adaptation and perhaps more efficient movement (Noakes 1991).

Gender can affect recovery rate. Female athletes tend to have a slower rate of regeneration due primarily to endocrinological differences, particularly less of the male hormone testosterone (Noakes 1991; Nudel 1989; Rowland 1990; Vander et al. 1990; Zauner, Maksud, and Melichna 1989).

Environmental factors will also affect regeneration time. These include competing at high altitudes (usually higher than 3,000 meters), where the partial pressure of respiratory gases is low (Berglund 1992; Fox 1984), or training in extremely cold weather. Training in cold temperatures affects the production of specific regenerative hormones, in particular human growth hormone (HGH) and testosterone (Levine et al. 1994; Stokkan and Reiter 1994; Strassman et al. 1991). Exercising in cold climates increases the rate of lactate production at submaximal loads and lowers the rate of lipid metabolism. This drop in fat metabolism may be due to vasoconstriction in adipose tissue and adrenergic vasoconstriction (Doubt 1991).

Freedom of movement influences recovery rate, because a decreased range of motion from either tight myofascial tissue or localized adhesions (i.e., knots) can affect athletic performance and regeneration. Poor blood supply to knots limits their chance of receiving adequate nutrients and oxygen, thus compromising overall muscle activity (Andrews 1991; Kuipers and Keizer 1988).

The *type of muscle fiber* used in training can affect recovery. Fast-twitch fibers tend to fatigue much faster than slow-twitch fibers due to their contractile properties (Fox 1984; Noakes 1991).

Type of exercise and hence the *type of energy system* the athlete is taxing (i.e., dominant aerobic versus dominant anaerobic) influences recovery rate. An athlete training endurance will have a lower recovery rate than one performing sprint training (Fox 1984; Noakes 1991).

Psychological factors influence recovery. Throughout training, the coach should avoid expressing any negative feelings such as fear, indecisiveness, or lack of determination, because it may stress the athlete. Also, the stress on one athlete can affect others. An athlete's perception of such emotions will trigger the release of cortisol and other stress-related hormones. This causes a variety of physiological problems that can inhibit muscle tissue growth and repair, increase muscle tension, depress the inflammatory response, depress the immune response, and affect timing and neuromuscular coordination (Bloomfield et al. 1996; Nordfors and Harvig 1997). The coach should ensure that athletes do not physically or psychologically exhaust themselves following the first trials of competitions with several races or games. Avoid early exhaustion by using modeling in training and psychological relaxation techniques.

Freedom from acute localized trauma and overtraining is important for recovery. An injured athlete will have a difficult time recuperating due to increased levels of catabolic hormones (e.g., cortisol) and ammonia (Berg 1994; Kuipers 1994).

Availability and replenishment of micronutrients (vitamins and minerals) and fuel at the cellular level impact recovery. Proteins, fats, and carbohydrates are constantly in demand for cellular metabolism, either in forming ATP-CP or for reconstructing damaged muscle tissue (Colgan 1993; Noakes 1991; Wardlaw et al. 1992).

Efficient energy transfer and removal of waste products influence recovery rate. Athletes in superior physical condition exhibit a much faster rate of recovery due to how efficiently they metabolize food and how effectively their bodies discard waste. Both factors depend on the circulatory system to provide each working cell, first, with the exchange of respiratory gases and, second, with nutrients from the digestive system (Fox 1984; Noakes 1991; Vander et al. 1990).

When athletes compete in different countries, *time differences* of 3 to 10 hours or more will effect the bodies' circadian rhythms. Some symptoms include malaise; appetite loss; tiredness during daylight hours; desynchronization of renal function (excess potassium and sodium are excreted causing muscle cramps, exhaustion, headaches); digestive disorders (a disturbance in cycles of blood amino acid levels, waste elimination, and other visceral activities); suppressed human growth hormone (HGH) levels (HGH plays an important role in elevating metabolism, increasing appetite, maintaining immune function, and integrating other hormones that regulate carbohydrate, protein, lipid, nucleic acid, water, and electrolyte metabolism); and disturbed sleep. The severity of these symptoms depends on the ability to preset the body rhythms before traveling, the number of time zones crossed, the direction of travel, the type of individual (extrovert or introvert), age, social interaction, activity, diet, and prescribed use of chronobiotic pharmaceuticals (Loat and Rhodes 1989; O'Connor and Morgan 1990). Loat and Rhodes recommend the following when traveling through small and large time zone shifts:

Small Time Zone Shifts

- Preset sleep and wake cycles to the time of the destination.
- If possible train or compete in the morning after westward flights and in the evening after eastward flights.
- Travel in one direction when competing at different cities on extended road trips.
- Eat meals at regular times after arriving at the new destination.
- Alter light and heavy meals before the flight. Eat a high-protein breakfast and a low-protein, high-carbohydrate dinner following a time zone advance.
- Avoid alcoholic beverages before, during, and after the flight.
- Indulge in light social and physical activity approximately 2 hours after the flight.
- Intestinal gas expands at high altitudes so avoid gas-producing foods (i.e., beans, carbonated beverages).
- Take a vitamin B complex along with vitamins C and E.

Large Time Zone Shifts

- Arrive at your destination a least 1 day early for each time zone crossed. For flights crossing more than 6 time zones, allow 14 days for resynchronizing.
- For flights crossing more than 10 time zones, always take westward flights.
- Attempt to partially synchronize sleep and wake cycles and mealtimes to the time of the destination.
- Indulge in light social and physical activity approximately 2 hours after the flight.
- Maintain regular sleeping times (i.e., anchor sleep) and eating times after you arrive at the destination.
- Alter light and heavy meals 3 days before flight. Eat a high-protein breakfast and a low-protein, high-carbohydrate dinner following time zone increases.
- Avoid alcoholic beverages before, during, and after the flight.
- Intestinal gas expands at high altitudes, so avoid any gas-producing foods (i.e., beans, carbonated beverages).
- Take a vitamin B complex along with vitamins C and E.
- Programmed use of prescribed chronobiotic drugs (i.e., melatonin) helps alleviate the symptoms of circadian dysrhythmia. Take 1 milligram of melatonin for every hour difference 1 to 3 hours before the new, desired bedtime (Claustrat et al. 1992; Petrie et al. 1993).

Recovery Curve

The dynamics of the recovery curve are not linear (Florescu, Dumitrescu, and Predescu 1969) but curved. The line drops dramatically by 70% during the first third and less drastically during the second and last third by 20% and 10% respectively (see figure 5.1). To move from the first third to the last third may take from several minutes to several months depending on which energy system is taxed and whether the athlete is recovering from short-term fatigue and exhaustion or long-term overtraining, which involves the neuroendocrine system.

For peaking purposes, use invasive and noninvasive monitoring techniques to establish which phase of the recovery curve the athlete is in. Different monitoring methods enable the coach to establish baseline values for the athlete and accurately determine if the athlete has peaked. The physiological and psychological responses to work help the coach conclude how much work the athlete can tolerate to achieve supercompensation and also determine individual recovery rate for specific forms of training before short-term fatigue or overtraining result.

Recovery of various biological parameters and substances occurs sequentially. First, heart rate and blood pressure return to normal 20 to 60 minutes following the work. Restoring glycogen takes 10 to 48 hours after aerobic work and 5 to 24 hours following anaerobic intermittent activity. Proteins take 12 to 24 hours, and fats, vitamins, and enzymes take more than 24 hours.

For peak physiological and psychological regeneration, use recovery techniques at specific times before, during, and after training or competition. Allow time for restorative measures. When athletes take special recovery measures within 6 to 9 hours or sooner, they facilitate supercompensation and increase working capacity (i.e., the first 2-4 hours for restoring muscle glycogen) following work (Noakes 1991; Talyshev 1977). Ignoring adequate regeneration can have a negative influence on supercompensation by making it nonexistent or by delaying it.

The choice of recovery techniques depends on residual fatigue accumulated from past training sessions, which energy system has been taxed, and the time of day. For example, if training or competition concludes late in the evening, use only techniques that will not interfere with the athlete's sleep. The next morning, you may use techniques that were impractical the night before.

Before using regeneration techniques, work closely with physicians and other medical personnel (i.e., massage and physiotherapists) to avoid misconceptions and maximize the effectiveness of the athlete's regeneration through certain techniques.

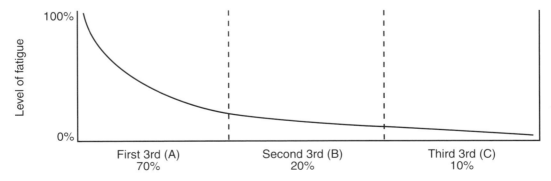

Figure 5.1 Dynamics of the recovery curve. A is initial muscle fuel replenishment (~30 min to 6 hr); B is full replenishment of fuels in the entire organism (~6 hr to 24 hr); and C represents recovery of neural sphere CNS + A + B, or 24 hr

Natural Means of Recovery

Natural recovery methods do not require any special devices or modalities. Some widely used methods are kinotherapy or active rest and complete rest or passive rest.

Kinotherapy or Active Rest

Kinotherapy refers to rapidly eliminating waste products (i.e., lactic acid) during moderate aerobic exercise or stretching. Athletes can use stretching alone or with active rest. Although its effects are transient (up to 3 hours), the benefits are well documented (Noakes 1991).

The scientific basis of kinotherapy was revealed at the beginning of the century. Setchenov (1935) and Weber (1914) demonstrated that a fatigued muscle can increase its recovery rate and consequently its working capacity if another muscle group, preferably antagonistic, performs low-intensity work during rest rather than being inactive. This is explained by the compensatory effect that physical exercise has on the fatigued centers of the CNS. Focusing on another center enhances the recovery of the previously excited nervous center. Recovery occurs faster and more effectively than through total rest. Apply kinotherapy during the transition phase as well as during times of emotional fatigue when deflective exercises (Asmussen 1936) are appropriate.

The intensity of the aerobic exercise used during kinotherapy should be no higher than 60% of the athlete's maximum heart rate, or 220 minus the athlete's age (Hultman and Sahlin 1980). Light, continuous jogging removes about 62% of the lactic acid during the first 10 minutes and an additional 26% between 10 and 20 minutes. It seems advantageous, therefore, to maintain an active recovery period for 10 to 20 minutes after strenuous exercise to produce an 88% reduction in lactic acid; only a 50% reduction occurs during the 20-minute rest period (Fox 1984).

Complete Rest or Passive Rest

Complete rest is the main physiological means of restoring working capacity. Athletes require 9 to 10 hours of sleep, 80 to 90% of it during the night (the balance may be completed by naps during the day). Naps should be guided so they do not affect work or the training schedule. A psychologist may help athletes who have difficulty napping at available free times. For night sleep, athletes should follow a strict schedule and go to sleep no later than 10:30 P.M.

An athlete can use several methods to promote relaxed sleep. Relaxation techniques, a massage, or a warm bath before bedtime are all helpful. Herbal preparations are helpful, such as fragrant valerian root, St. John's wort, chamomile, peppermint, lavender flowers, hops, dill seed, anise seed, fennel seed, passion flowers, lemon balm, linden flowers, and primrose flowers (Balch and Balch 1997). A dark, noise- and stress-free, oxygenated (fresh air) room is necessary. Exposure to early morning light tends to shorten the sleep cycle, so it is easier to sleep in the evening (Deacon and Arendt 1994; Lemmer 1994; Myers and Badia 1993). Eat a small, high-carbohydrate meal (avoid a high-protein, high-fat meal as it might cause insomnia). Go to bed when tired. Use earplugs if the environment is noisy, and turn off the phone. Consider wearing eyeshades to prevent any light reaching the eyes. Awake at the same time each morning.

STRETCH THERAPY

Nikos Apostolopoulos

Nick Apostolopoulos, a recovery regeneration specialist in therapeutic stretching, is the founder and director of the Serapis Stretch Therapy Clinic in Vancouver, British Columbia, Canada. This is the only clinic of its kind in the world and pioneers therapeutic stretching. Many athletes and individuals suffering from musculoskeletal disorders have been treated at the clinic.

Recovery is an important concept in training. To achieve high levels of performance, athletes train longer and harder than ever before. No shortcuts can abbreviate the workout process. However, athletes can work more if they properly recover, speeding the process by which they attain maximum performance levels. Stretching is an often neglected aspect.

Recovery is the process, or processes, that result in restoring muscles and key physiological processes stressed in an activity. Stretching has both rehabilitative and prophylactic qualities. Stretch therapy, the means by which you apply stretching therapeutically, can accelerate recovery from workouts or competition and increase work capacity.

Stretch therapy's potential for assisting in the recovery process is extensive. The constant demand of competition invites an increased risk of injury. Excessive strain of the spinal column, ligaments, tendons, and muscles, if not addressed early in an athlete's career, can lead to permanent damage. Stretch therapy can assist the athlete and coach in preventing damage. Most coaches are interested in developing the athlete's response to the following three elements.

- Quick adaptation to training stimuli
- Good recovery rate between training sessions and competitions
- Protection from injuries

The aims of stretch therapy are as follows:

- To enhance physical performance by making muscles more flexible. The athlete achieves this by removing or quickly disposing the waste products of fatigue that cause stiffness.
- To promote the healing of microinjuries, injuries not initially visible, but which manifest themselves after years of training and improper recovery. Implementing stretch therapy during the formative years of training lays the groundwork for preventing microinjuries.
- To increase the elasticity and strength of muscles and their resistance to damage. This also transcends into the joints, tendons, and ligaments.
- To develop a balance between agonist and antagonist muscles.

Because you cannot train tired muscle, although it is susceptible to injury, the need for a proper recovery program is vital. The program should focus mainly on the systems that require more recovery time, particularly the avascular connective tissues (tendons, ligaments, and fascia) and the supportive tissues (ligaments and bone). Direct any attempts to accelerate adaptation to the training stimuli and recovery primarily to these structures. How you accomplish this ultimately varies with the intensity, density, and duration of the training load.

Continuous or strenuous effort affects the athlete physically and mentally. Fatigue reduces the body's ability to sustain high levels of activity because it depletes glucose levels, affecting the muscles, central nervous system (CNS), and peripheral nervous system (PNS). The nervous system depends on the glucose level. Stretch therapy increases circulation, particularly venous blood return to the heart which aids in removing waste products from the body and restoring oxygen to oxygen-depleted areas. Replenishing glucose to the body also occurs, which promotes relaxation, calmness, and a sense of well-being. If the athlete has a high-intensity workout or a competition the following day, he or she will be both physically and mentally prepared.

(continued)

(continued)

This brings us to the next concept of why stretch therapy is vital to the recovery process. One concept I tried to develop in myself as an elite athlete and for my athletes as a coach was spatial awareness, the sensation of muscle and body internally and in regard to the environment (training or competitive). This is enhanced with stretch therapy, as athletes learn to sense their bodies and to assess the state of their muscles and their injuries. Awareness aids in developing a greater sense of control and confidence, ultimately determining peak performance.

Incorporating stretch therapy into your training program is important. The capacity of muscles, tendons, ligaments, and fascia to stretch; the range of motion in the joints; and the ability of the muscles to contract and coordinate all define how we move. Heavy competitive schedules stress our capacity for movement. With a systematic approach to training, we are able to help an athlete fully recover mentally and physically. A proper approach implements stretch therapy within the annual training plan, during general training, the preparatory phase, and the recovery phase.

Phase 1: General Training Phase

- Aims at improving the general physical and psychological condition of the athlete and providing regular and immediate relief from fatigue.
- Because the training hours, volume, and intensity of training have increased, the athlete must stretch with special care.
- The intensity of stretching depends on the sport, the athlete's makeup, and his or her ability to recover. The athlete should use passive, active-passive, and active stretching.
- The most important goal is the recovery of the entire organism, especially the nervous system. The constant stimulation of nerve cells, whose high working capacity cannot be maintained for long without proper recovery, affects muscular action and ultimately athletic performance.

- To accommodate the effects of the high training load and the increase in the athlete's working potential, stretching has to be intense, rhythmical, and sequential.
- Generally, stretching before a training session should last 40 to 60 minutes. Athletes should also stretch after morning training, paying attention to the muscles that exercised the most, especially during explosive movements.

Phase 2: Preparatory and Competitive Phase

- Apply immediately before competitions to enhance the athlete's physical level and psychological readiness.
- Active stretching should be performed 15 to 20 minutes before a main competition. This can either increase or decrease the nerve cell's excitability depending on the intensity and duration of the stretch and the nature of the sport.
- A properly implemented stretch program can cause shortening or lengthening of the muscular contraction time. This is vital to achieve a peak performance.
- Stretching can help warm up the athlete (muscles, joints, ligaments) before competition or during a break. Stretching heightens the muscles' ability to contract more quickly, improving the nerve reflex time as well as the blood supply.
- Stretching is important when competing in cold conditions, when the start is delayed, or breaks are longer than expected.

Phase 3: Recovery Phase

- After major competitions and hard training, the main objective of this form of stretching is to facilitate optimal recovery of the entire organism, especially the (CNS).
- Fatigue sets in when the period of training or competition has a high rate of fuel consumption. Because blood glucose is depleted from the system, the CNS

fatigues. Properly applied stretching techniques stimulate venous return, promoting circulation of blood and lymph. This increase in circulation removes metabolic waste products and increases oxygen and nutrients to the muscle-tendon region (diminishing stiffness and hastening recovery). Muscles you stretch during the recovery period regain vigor and are able to do more work.

• The emphasis of stretching during this phase is on the musculo-tendon-ligament system. As the training and competitive season progress and muscle increases its ability to generate force, the tendon receives great stress. Tendons are often the weakest link in the chain, accounting for more than 90% of injuries, particularly at the musculo-tendon junction. Because tendons are avascular compared with muscle, they do not receive as much oxygen and nutrients and, therefore, are in greater need of recovery. This is also heightened with the development of scar tissue.

• Use stretching as a therapeutic means for recovery and regeneration. An athlete unable to adhere to a proper stretching program slowly develops involuntary contractions. The first sign of this involuntary contracted system is pain and the consequent decrease in range of motion (ROM) about a joint. Associated with this decrease is muscle atrophy, beginning a vicious cycle.

• Along with the vicious physical cycle, the athlete develops a vicious psychological cycle. Because an athlete's identity is related to properly executing movement, any delay or detriment results in stress, which releases stress hormones that tighten muscles, further accentuating

the loss of ROM. This state often presents itself as a great challenge to coaches and therapists. Stretch therapy is able to break these loops and speed the athlete's recovery.

When you apply stretch therapy immediately after training or competitions it

• increases local blood supply to joints and the musculo-tendon system;

• hastens drainage from the region of involved joints, thereby decreasing swelling;

• produces muscular relaxation;

• increases lymphatic and venous return, thereby detoxifying the body;

• prevents fibrosis and adhesions in muscles, decreasing the tendency toward muscular atrophy;

• improves, loosens, and stretches tight tendons, thereby increasing or maintaining ROM; and

• stimulates and soothes the CNS and PNS.

Competitive sports often impose great volumes of intensive training, involve frequent movement repetitions, and place heavy loads on the motor activities of the skeletal and muscular systems. This produces inevitable wear and tear in the body tissues. Knowledge about such conditions assists in developing a proper recovery program throughout the annual training plan. Stretch therapy can accelerate the body's natural healing processes. You should realize, however, that a recovery specialist needs to design such a program. The experience of this consultant leads to more effective recovery assessment, treatment, and evaluation.

Physical disorders such as restless leg syndrome, sleep apnea, arthritis, chronic pain, cardiac problems, emphysema, and asthma can impair proper rest. Exercising 3 hours before bedtime can lead to other physical disorders (Van Reeth et al. 1994). Psychological difficulties such as nightmares, depression, stress, anxiety disorders, emotional discussions or arguments before bed, or chronic stress can also interrupt sleep (Monteleone et al. 1993). An improper sleep environment due to noise, temperature too high or too low, bed too hard or too soft, blankets too light or too heavy, or a snoring or restless bed partner can make sleeping difficult. Athletes with inadequate sleep habits caused by too much time in bed reading or watching TV, daytime naps (longer than 1 hour after 4:00 P.M.), irregular schedule, or not eliminating bodily waste before bedtime may wake during the night. Finally, avoid overuse or misuse of nicotine, caffeine (no coffee, tea, chocolate, or caffeinated carbonated beverages after 7:00 P.M.), alcohol (which inhibits melatonin production [Ekman et al. 1993]), and sleep medications.

Time and exposure to darkness affects the release of the sleep hormone melatonin. Melatonin is released according to the circadian rhythms of our body clocks (Stokkan and Reiter 1994). Sleeping in a bright room or not having a consistent sleep schedule may compromise its release.

Lifestyle usually affects recovery rate. Poor relationships with a spouse, girl- or boyfriend, siblings, parents, teammates, or coaches can negatively influence recovery. Narcotics and alcohol use can negatively affect rest. If necessary, a sport psychologist may assist athletes with deep emotional problems that affect the development of a strong will and character.

Physiotherapeutic Means of Recovery

Physiotherapeutic methods have special modalities and include massage, the use of heat (thermotherapy) or cold (cryotherapy), contrast baths, oxygenotherapy, aerotherapy, altitude training, reflexotherapy (acupuncture, acupressure), vagal-reflexotherapy, and chemotherapy.

Massage

Massage is the systematic manipulation of soft body tissues and assists in removing toxic energy metabolism by-products and residual fluid buildup resulting from structural damage of muscle tissue. Massage has been used for thousands of years, long before the advent of modern medicine. Massage uses specific maneuvers (manual, mechanical, or electrical) for therapeutic purposes and can be either localized, focusing on a specific area, or therapeutic, the conventional approach in which relaxation is a primary goal. We can divide massage into surface massage or deep massage, depending on the muscles' proximity to the skin or bones.

An athlete can receive a massage for 15 to 20 minutes before training (following a general warm-up), 8 to 10 minutes following a shower and at the end of a training lesson, and 20 to 30 minutes or longer immediately after a hot bath or sauna.

Kuprian (1982) addresses the need for massage before, during, and after training. He categorizes four types of massage: intermediary, preparatory, training, and warm-down. Each has a distinct purpose and uses a particular technique to achieve specific means.

The role of massage in preparation for and recovery from exercise has been well documented (Weinberg et al. 1988). Massage can positivly affect an athlete's mood by reducing tension, anger, fatigue, depression, anxiety, and confusion. Athletes who exhibit positive moods as a result of the relaxation effects from massage will have a lowered perception of stress. Massage contributes all-around benefits to the body, such as the following.

Increased blood circulation. If the muscles are relaxed, squeezing the muscle bellies with simple mechanical pressure helps to empty veins in the direction of the applied pressure. This results in opening up to 35% of the small capillaries (at rest, 4% of capillaries are open). The net result is an increased availability of fresh blood to the massaged area, making possible greater interchange of substances between capillaries and tissue cells (Bergeron 1982; Cinque 1989).

Increased lymphatic circulation. Lymphatic circulation assists venous circulation in returning fluids (waste products) from the tissues. Massaging specific sites on the body that correspond to certain muscles is the most effective external means of moving excess vascular fluid into the lymph vessels, then into the circulatory system. We describe this as a cleaning out.

Stretching for muscle adhesions, knots, or microtrauma. The mechanical pressure and stretching of the tissue mobilizes muscle adhesions for removal by the circulatory system. Knots are inflexible areas of muscle caused by a combination of factors, such as lack of oxygen and nutrients (calcium and protein) to a specific area and scar tissue buildup from microtrauma associated with heavy loads or repetitive, overuse-type work. If untreated, the cumulative effect of consistent microtrauma can result in muscle strain. Treating knots requires 5 to 10 sessions of deep, cross-friction massage lasting 5 to 10 minutes.

Relief of muscle fatigue. The mechanical effects of massage on the bloodstream promote the removal of metabolic by-products and the entry of fresh blood to the working area (Bergeron 1982; Cinque 1989).

Removal of excessive swelling. This is especially beneficial when treating certain types of inflammation and will promote the removal of edema (Bergeron 1982; Cinque 1989).

The sensory effects of massage are not fully understood, but according to Bergeron (1982), Cinque (1989), and Vander et al. (1990), they have a positive effect on pain relief, muscle spasm relief, and increased metabolism.

Heat or Thermotherapy

The circulatory system serves two purposes, to deliver nutrients to the skin and tissues and to conduct heat from inside the body to the skin, allowing the dissipation of heat from the surface of the skin (Prentice 1990; Vander et al. 1990). Two major types of vessels carry out these functions: nutritive arteries, capillaries, and veins; and vascular vessels for heating the skin.

Vascular structures can be broken down further into subcutaneous venous plexus (SVP) and arteriovenous anastomosis (AA), which are blood vessel junctions. Both serve important functions. SVPs hold large volumes of blood that heat the surface of the skin, and AAs provide vascular communication between arteries and venous plexuses. Heat's analgesic effect is due to the release of norepinephrine from sympathetic vasoconstrictor nerve fibers that innervate venous plexuses close to the surface of the skin. The greatest concentrations of these fibers are found in areas such as the volar or palmar surfaces of the hands and feet, the lips, the nose, and the ears. When body temperature is normal (36.8° Celsius, 98.3° Fahrenheit), the sympathetic vasoconstrictor nerves keep AAs closed. When heat moves to the superficial tissue, the number of sympathetic signals diminishes, causing the AAs to dilate and allow the flow of warm blood into the veins of the surrounding heated tissues. This process promotes heat loss from the body and increases blood flow (hyperemia) by about twofold (Prentice 1990).

Indications for Use

Heating modalities come in several forms, such as saunas, heat lamps, steam baths, and moist heat packs (Hydroculator). Localized heat tends to affect only the skin and not deep tissues. The skin may become too hot before any muscle tissue has been heated and may be traumatized by excessive heat. Remedy this problem when using moist heat packs by placing a towel between the heat pack and the skin (Arnheim 1985; Prentice 1990).

Steam baths and saunas affect the nervous and endocrine systems and locally influence organs and tissues (Zalessky 1977). Saunas and steam baths stimulate the release of growth hormone. Direct heat or hot showers or baths (36° to 42° Celsius) for 8 to 10 minutes relaxes muscles and improves local and general blood circulation.

The penetration depth of low-level thermal radiation (saunas) is about 4 centimeters, sufficient to stimulate perspiration without producing feelings of suffocation or discomfort. This sets up a vibratory resonance between the infrared emissions of the sauna and the body. This emission, and not necessarily the heat, produces the benefits associated with saunas. Saunas reduce the likelihood of neurotic reactions, improve sleep, and normalize metabolic processes. This promotes excretion of toxins (cadmium, lead, zinc, nickel, sodium, sulfuric acid, and cholesterol) through perspiration via the vasodilatation of sweat glands (Prentice 1990; Serban 1979). If the toxins are not eliminated, fatigue lingers and affects CNS stimulation (Dragan 1978).

Heat also "warms" the CNS, easing nervous transmission within the muscle and facilitating more efficient and powerful communication between the muscle and brain. Usually 5 to 20 minutes is sufficient (in contrast to a 1- or 2-minute cold shower), starting with the extremities, then the core. The total time spent using heat can vary from 15 to 40 minutes in intervals of 5 minutes, interspersed with 1- to 2-minute cold showers (Francis and Patterson 1992).

The athlete should lie down with a towel that has been immersed in cold water on his or her face. Most heat loss comes from the head and, when in a hot environment, the head is particularly sensitive to excessive heat, due to its high blood circulation and heat regulatory mechanisms in the brain (Vander et al. 1990).

Contraindications of Heat

Do not apply concentrated heat therapy immediately after training or in cases of acute trauma. For trauma, introduce heat 3 or 4 days after the initial injury, by which time the edema should be reduced significantly if you applied cold during the first 3 days. Pregnant athletes should restrict use of sauna or steam baths (Arnheim 1985; Prentice 1990). Wait 6 to 8 hours before introducing any form of heat after a training session or competition (Gündhill 1997).

Thermotherapy increases the sensitivity of muscle fibers to the actions of calcium. Thus, when you activate calcium, you also influence the muscles involved (Paha 1994). Perhaps this is why warming up increases the activation and force production of muscles. Although thermotherapy has a positive effect on muscles before training, it has a contrasting effect after training. At this time, it increases the sensitivity of damaged muscle tissue to calcium and increases blood flow to the traumatized area. The excessive temperature can cause the same effects as a fever. Extremely high body temperature, above normal 37° Celsius, will cause the body to catabolize muscle tissue. Hot saunas or steam baths (greater than 90° Celsius) after intense weight-training sessions, therefore, is not advisable (Baracos 1984).

Cold or Cryotherapy

Perhaps the most sought benefit of cold therapy is the analgesic effect (reduced pain) it has on localized tissue, without any pharmacological products. Extreme temperature changes affect nerve fiber conduction responding to pain.

Cold therapy immediately increases blood flow, raising the level of oxygen, increasing metabolism, and significantly reducing muscle spasm.

Indications for Use

Lievens (1986) suggests that, for optimal results, apply the cold immediately following training and no longer than 2 hours after for 15 to 20 minutes, depending on the desired tissue depth. In the case of microtrauma, Arnheim (1985) and Prentice (1990) suggest using contrast baths to facilitate a capillary response. The initial exposure, however, should be cold; then you can use contrast baths for 1 or 2 hours after the initial cold treatment.

The best areas for cold therapy are those requiring the longest time to regenerate, such as weak muscles, muscles with predominantly fast-twitch (FT) fibers, and tendinous units.

Take care when using direct ice-to-skin contact. The length of time needed to achieve the desired effect is usually half as long as for other cold therapies. The depth of penetration, however, is limited to the skin's tolerance to cold.

Techniques for applying cold include ice massage using cups, cold packs, a bag filled with crushed ice placed and contoured around the injured limb, and cold whirlpools. Studies have indicated that the effects of this form of therapy have a reflex vasodilatation of up to 2 hours.

Contraindications for Cold

There are only a few contraindications for cryotherapy, some of which athletes need not concern themselves. These include cold allergies that bring about hives, joint pain, nausea, and rheumatoid conditions such as pain and joint stiffness.

Contrast Baths

The theory is that contrast baths induce a pumping action within the muscle. Alternating vasoconstriction and vasodilatation penetrates muscle tissue to a superficial depth. Irrespective of this, contrast baths are effective in treating localized muscle spasm and providing pain relief.

Contrast baths are best suited for injuries when they are in the subacute phase. It is not the treatment of choice by many therapists during the acute phase because of the heat, despite it being coupled with cold. For localized microtrauma associated with training, contrast baths are effective for reducing stiffness and soreness (Arnheim 1985; Prentice 1990).

The temperature of the cold and hot treatments should be between 10° to 15° Celsius and 35° to 37° Celsius (up to 40° to 43° Celsius) respectively. The treatment should last at least 20 to 30 minutes, with the longer treatment resulting in a better conclusion. Athletes should keep in mind, however, that smaller and more superficial muscles require less time. Although the ratio between the two modalities is variable, it is recommended that you apply heat three to four times longer than cold. It is also suggested that the treatment begin and end with cold, especially after training and competition (Arnheim 1985; Prentice 1990).

Techniques for using cold and heat exist in a variety of modalities. We can label combinations of the varieties from each modality as contrast. For instance, athletes could combine infrared heat, such as a sauna, with a cold whirlpool or shower, a form of contrast bath. They could start with one form of a modality, then halfway through use another form. For example, use hot and cold showers followed by a dry sauna to relax the neural sphere and keep in line with the contrast treatment. Many combinations exists, and athletes should become aware of each modality's function and when is the best time to introduce it (Arnheim 1985; Prentice 1990).

Oxygenotherapy

Athletes often experience O_2 debt because of the high O_2 consumption inherent in training. Dragan (1978) implies that when the O_2 saturation diminishes to 85% of normal, it decreases concentration. Also, athletes experience a decrease in strength at 75% and may experience depressive states at 70%. To overcome the reduction in O_2 saturation and replenish the body, use yoga and respiratory exercises, as well as artificial O_2 inhalation, before and after competitions and training and during intermissions. The continuous refreshing of the air in locker rooms and gymnasiums to ensure a rich proportion of oxygen is important to athletes.

Aerotherapy

In atmospheric air, particles are positively and negatively charged (positive or negative aeroions). The air around mountains, sea shores, waterfalls, and after rainstorms is negatively charged due to the presence of water vapor. Water is negatively charged, and when in the atmosphere it creates a negatively ionized atmosphere. Positive ions occur when air moves over dry, arid surfaces like a desert, metal, or a weather disturbance. Fossil fuel combustion, synthetic fibers, and electronic equipment positively charge the environment. Such an environment may increase lethargy, depression, irritability, and headaches in a training situation. According to Dragan (1978), negative ions facilitate fast recovery of the circulo-respiratory systems, relax the neuropsychic system (releasing large amounts of serotonin), and increase working capacity. Negative ions also stimulate production of immunoglobulin A, one of the five major classes of antibodies. Aerotherapy can be naturally and artificially generated. Active rest at subalpine altitudes or walking through parks and forests are some natural means. You can produce ionized air artificially by placing instruments in locker rooms that produce negative aeroions.

Altitude Cure

Training or active rest for 1 to 2 weeks at subalpine altitudes (600-1,000 meters) can enhance recovery. At this altitude, atmospheric pressure is reduced; humidity and temperature are low; and solar rays, especially ultraviolet rays, are of higher intensity and longer duration than at lower elevations. Such favorable circumstances help lighten the functions of the main organs, allowing quicker regeneration and improved working capacity (Dragan and Stanescu 1971). Between 1,300 and 1,650 meters, athletes begin to feel the effects of altitude-induced hypoxia (Fox 1984). After returning from a higher altitude, competition is not recommended for 3 to 5 days while readaptation takes place. Fox even suggests that athletes postpone any competitions for at least 2 weeks upon returning from a high altitude. The positive changes in the athletes' bodies following an altitude cure may last 1 to 2 months (Berglund 1992).

Training at moderate altitudes (1,800 to 3,000 meters) can increase hemoglobin concentration in the blood by about 1% per week. Training higher than 4,500 meters can significantly increase the risk of altitude sickness. Adaptation may take up to 2 months or longer; adaptation time is much shorter at moderate altitudes, usually 2 or 3 weeks (Berglund 1992).

Reflexotherapy—Acupuncture and Acupressure

Reflexotherapy comes from an ancient form of Chinese medicine based upon the energy flow, or "chi", along channels called meridians in the body. Disruption in the energy flow due to improper diet or too much stress can lead to serious medical problems. Acupuncture and acupressure help restore proper energy flow, promoting healing and harmony within the body.

Indications for Use

Athletes can use acupuncture before, during, or after training (Bucur 1979; Dragan 1978). Due to the localized and overall effects it can have on the body, acupuncture is a useful modality. Treatment can last from 1 to 5 minutes up to 20 minutes, depending on its complexity. Usually pain relief and reduced muscle spasm are almost immediate, although it can take a few weeks to fully benefit from treatments. Needles are not entirely necessary. Low-intensity, direct pressure on specific points using the middle or index finger, thumb, or even an elbow can be as effective. Apply pressure in small, frictionlike circles. The amount of pressure should be enough to allow effective treatment but not enough to bruise or cause discomfort. Effects last from a few minutes to several hours depending on the athlete (Ohashi and Monte 1992; Prentice 1990).

Contraindications for Acupuncture and Acupressure

Acupuncture is known by Chinese practitioners to treat various forms of diseases, although Westerners are still unsure. As research grows, however, more Western physicians are recommending it as a legitimate form of treatment for certain medical conditions. Treating acute injuries is best done with acupuncture. Researchers suggest that the athlete consult a trained physician before beginning treatment on traumatized tissue (Arnheim 1985; Prentice 1990).

Vagal-Reflexotherapy—Pertaining to the Vagus Nerve

This technique stimulates the parasympathetic vegetative system (autonomic nervous system), which governs the recovery process of the whole organism (Popescu 1975). This is done through exciting or inhibiting effector cells or innervating smooth and cardiac muscle, glands, and gastrointestinal neurons (Vander et al. 1990). To increase recovery, Popescu suggests techniques that stimulate peripheral reflexes. Ultrathoracic pressure, or the Valsalva maneuver (named after an Italian physician from the Middle Ages), performed by a physician, may calm the heart's agitated function, which could be pronounced by the end of intensive work. Similarly, slight pressure with the fingers above the eyes can be calming. Finally, using acupressure on both temporal arteries calms the circulatory system, especially cerebral circulation.

The athlete may also achieve a good sense of regeneration and functional balance by placing a hot cloth on the face or blowing warm air (i.e., with a hair dryer) on the back of the neck, which has vagus nerve innervation at a superficial level. You can experience the same effect by taking a warm shower and positioning the shower head so the water aims to this area.

Chemotherapy

Vitamins have been suggested as an important asset to athletic performance (Bucur 1979; Dragan 1978; Sauberlich, Dowdy, and Skala 1974). Take them to supplement energy needs, especially for those with a low tolerance to work (Zalessky 1977), and to enhance regeneration.

The word *vitamin* was introduced by Funk, a Polish biochemist, in 1912 who applied it to a group of compounds called *amines* that are *vital* to life (Van der Beek 1985). Vitamins are a class of essential organic molecules required for energy-yielding reactions in the body, which also function as antioxidants. They cannot be manufactured via metabolic pathways, nor do they yield any energy; therefore, you must obtain them from everyday food sources. The body requires trace amount of vitamins for normal health and growth (Van der Beek 1985; Wardlaw et al. 1992).

Vitamins are classified as water soluble (vitamins C and B complex) and fat soluble (vitamins A, D, E, and K). Water-soluble vitamins serve as enzymes and coenzymes vital for metabolizing fats and carbohydrates but are not stored by the body. The body stores fat-soluble vitamins in adipose tissue (Colgan 1993; Noakes 1991; Van der Beek 1985; Wardlaw et al. 1992).

Minerals are inorganic (without carbon) substances in food. The body uses several types of minerals, such as calcium, phosphorus, potassium, sulfur, sodium, iron, fluoride, chloride, manganese, magnesium, copper, chromium, selenium, iodine, and zinc. Specific vitamins and minerals work synergistically (e.g., vitamin C and B complex, vitamin C and iron, vitamin E and selenium) and are best taken together for better absorption by the gastrointestinal tract.

A certain amount of mysticism surrounds vitamins. The belief that they have special properties that enhance health and human performance has led to the creation of vitamythology. Thus, many coaches and athletes feel that supplementation above the recommended daily allowance (RDA) will improve performance. Through their ignorance or arrogance, they feel "if a little is good, more is better" (Brotherhood 1984; Colgan 1993; Wardlaw et al. 1992).

Discourage megadosing or megachemical therapy, especially with fat-soluble vitamins and minerals, as these substances can accumulate in the body and cause harm. Often, excessive amounts of these vitamins lead to gastrointestinal distress and expensive urine. Either way, excessive oral supplementation of vitamins and minerals can be toxic and are not a substitute for real food or physical training. To ensure better absorption of these nutrients, consume them with real foods (Balch and Balch 1997).

Use vitamin and mineral supplements under the watchful eye of the team physician and dietitian. In most cases, you can obtain a majority of the RDA for specific micronutrients through eating a well-balanced diet (Van Erp-Baart et al. 1989; Wardlaw et al. 1992).

Some elite athletes can consume two to five times more kilocalories than sedentary individuals. Consuming such large quantities of food to keep pace with energy expenditure requires a large number of calories from food sources typically known as empty calories (refined carbohydrates). Because the nutrient content in these foods is minimal, oral vitamin supplementation, in particular B vitamins (B1, B6), might benefit the athlete.

Loss of minerals such as iron, zinc, calcium, potassium, and magnesium is common among athletes training in hot, humid climates. Endurance athletes in particular are more susceptible to mineral losses either through insufficient caloric intake or heavy sweating during prolonged training sessions.

For sports in which $\dot{V}O_2max$ is a limiting factor, iron and zinc loss will not only affect regeneration but also performance (Colgan 1993; Couzy et al. 1990). The expansion of blood volume in endurance athletes can contribute to low hemoglobin concentrations in the blood not resulting from a drop in hemoglobin. Iron status in endurance athletes is also affected by dietary intake (if lower than RDA), sweat loss, iron absorption, menstrual blood loss in female athletes, and intravascular haemolysis in runners due to increasing physical training and the constant pounding they put on their bodies (Brown and Herb 1990; Noakes 1991). Brotherhood (1984) found that when the body experiences a decrease in minerals, there is greater absorption from meals. As long as athletes consume foods containing these minerals, a deficiency is unlikely.

Lack of trace minerals, such as zinc, copper, chromium, magnesium, and potassium, can affect performance if the athlete is consuming a diet poor in nutrient quality and quantity. Usually a diet high in simple sugars (i.e., candy, pop, pastries) or highly processed food will be deficient in trace minerals (Balch and Balch 1997).

Athletes who consume a balanced diet cannot obtain all the micronutrients they metabolize during heavy training or intense competition (Colgan 1993). Vitamin and mineral supplements can, therefore, be a great asset especially for endurance athletes.

The coach and athlete should pay particular attention to the types of food being consumed and in what proportions. This will support the maintenance of a well-balanced diet.

Psychological Means of Recovery

Fatigue is located in the CNS. Because the regeneration of a nervous cell is seven times slower than muscle cells (Krestovnikov 1938), pay attention to neuropsychological recovery. When the athlete restores the CNS, which leads and coordinates all human activity, he or she can concentrate better, perform skills more correctly, react faster and more powerfully to internal and external stimuli, and subsequently maximize working capacity. Prevent psychological fatigue by understanding the foundation of motivation; fatigue as a normal training outcome; how to cope with stress and frustration; how to use training models to adapt to various competitive stressors; and the importance of a sound team atmosphere. Efficient means of treating fatigue include coach suggestion, self-suggestion, and psychotonic training. A coach unfamiliar with psychological methods of recovery and relaxation should consult a sport psychologist.

Both physical and psychological stress affect performance (Levy et al. 1987; Mace and Eastman 1986). Athletes who have high fitness levels cope with psychological stress much better than those with low fitness (Perkins et al. 1986; Tucker et al. 1986). The increased tolerance toward stress was identified by Cooper et al. (1986), who stated that athletes with increased stroke volumes, lower resting blood pressures, and decreased adrenal secretions during stressful situations were physiologically better able to handle stress.

Training stress increases adrenal hypertrophy; however, Bohus et al. (1987) and Lysens et al. (1986) state that psychological stress could result in the same sort of hypertrophy. Excessive amounts or prolonged secretion of adrenaline and noradrenaline, although touted by most coaches as excellent for competition, influence performance (Mace and Carroll 1986) by affecting timing, neuromuscular coordination, and increasing muscle tension, which could lead to injury (Ekstrand and Gillquist 1983). A drop in neurotransmitters, a consequence of perceived psychological stress, lowers production of somatocrinin (growth hormone-releasing hormone), resulting in a reduced production of human growth hormone and other hormones secreted by the anterior pituitary (Guyllemin et al. 1983).

Researchers have postulated that psychological stress and stress-related syndromes augment age-related physiological changes. Some suggest that psychological and physical stress promote anatomical and biochemical changes. These changes affect the neuromuscular junction by reducing the amount of available neurotransmitter chemicals (i.e., acetylcholine, norepinephrine in the brain), impairing communication between muscle and nerve cells. This reaction could lead to chronic fatigue and reduced physical strength (Bloomfield et al. 1996; Thibodeau 1987).

An athlete's personality type, whether type A (hard driving, competitive) or type B (relaxed, easygoing) can affect physiological stress (Thibodeau 1987). Identical psychological stressors do not always elicit the same response in different people partly because some individuals possess better autonomic responses to psychological stress than others.

Muscle Tension

Muscle tension is the force or energy produced by muscle contraction. Perception of psychological stress elevates muscle tension, which could affect performance (Kraus 1975; Reynolds 1984). According to Kraus, muscle tension caused by psychological stress can override some natural tension reduction experienced by physical activity. Elevated muscle tension has been linked to an increased incidence of injury and accelerated depletion of muscular fuel stores (Astrand and Rodahl 1977; Lysens et al. 1986; Sandman and Backstrom 1984).

Fatigued muscles subjected to stress for a prolonged time do not exhibit high recovery rates from elevated muscle tension (Kessler and Hertling 1983) and show the greatest injury potential.

In addition, higher than normal muscle tension levels impair physical skills by simultaneously tensing opposing muscles and reducing flexibility (Ekstrand and Gillquist 1982). Athletes can reduce muscle tension by maintaining flexibility. Stretching disengages the cross bridges, which allows blood to flow to this area, removing accumulated metabolic by-products from heightened muscle tension (Glick 1980; Sandman and Backstrom 1984).

Relaxation Physiology and Techniques

Stress is the product of each athlete's perception; therefore, response will vary. No two athletes exhibit identical responses to the same stressor. Stress management techniques are highly individual.

Keep in mind that the reaction to stress is multidimensional, involving physiological, environmental, social, behavioral, and cognitive areas (Kessler and Hertling 1983; Landers 1980). Relaxation techniques are highly individual, because what works for one athlete may not work for another. The diverse techniques and the timing of each technique according to training needs may offer the coach and athlete the best approach to relaxation management.

Relaxation increases sympathetic tone, lowering the heart rate; dropping muscle tension, which allows freedom of movement and less cramping; and dropping oxygen consumption, indicating a reduction in cellular metabolism and better emotional control (Cooper et al. 1986; Schutt and Bernstein 1986). Biomechanically, athletes who were more relaxed had more control of their movements, thus were able to maintain optimal technique (good technique = high efficiency).

Relaxation techniques have been well documented as beneficial to athletes and can involve several methods: relaxation response, progressive muscle relaxation (PMR), stress inoculation training, biofeedback, transcendental meditation (TM), counseling by sport psychologist, yoga, deep

Stretching helps maintain flexibility by reducing muscle tension

muscle relaxation autohypnosis, visual imagery, breath control, Trager, and time management (Knox et al. 1986; Lippin 1985; Patel and Marmot 1987). Not all techniques may benefit the athlete. Keeping this in mind, be selective and choose techniques that will evoke optimal positive arousal for athletic competition.

Stress inoculation refers to the athlete learning to apply a variety of self-statements that lead to a graduated reduction in stress (Mace and Carrol 1986).

Autogenesis or guided imagery has been effective in some athletes (Barolin 1978). A particular brain wave is associated with being in a TM state, along with decreased oxygen consumption and heart rate (Vander et al. 1990). Mental and physical tension were significantly reduced, and reaction time, which is important to sprinters, was significantly lower (Wallace 1970). Benson (1975) and Knox et al. (1986) outline the use of biofeedback training and how it can help the athlete control specific biological functions (i.e., heart rate, blood pressure, respiration rates), once believed to be governed solely by the autonomic nervous system.

Yoga, which involves controlled breathing with specific stretching exercises, elicits benefits in muscle relaxation along with reduced peripheral sympathetic activity (Deabler et al. 1973).

Trager involves physiological, cognitive, and behavioral means to lower muscle tension and increase relaxation by communicating the physical feeling of relaxation to the mind (Trager 1982; Trager and Guadagno 1987). Both passive movement (movement reeducation) and mentastics (mental gymnastics) create a feeling of relaxation. The treatment is generally 1 hour, with each session consisting of two parts, passive and active.

During the passive section, the subject lies on a table. The movements encompass several kinematics, such as traction, rotation, and compression, which the practitioner gently and rhythmically administers using the subject's own tension. Through the treatment, the practitioner is aware of heavy body parts or difficult movements. These areas may require additional treatment. The movement sequence begins with the neck, then progressively moves down to the shoulders, legs, feet, abdomen, chest, and finally the arms. The practitioner applies the opposite sequence, with the addition of the back area, when the subject is on the stomach (Trager 1982).

During the active section, the subject remembers the feeling of relaxation. The subject moves in the mind and body, otherwise referred to mentastics, but this time with a programmed memory from the passive movements; therefore, the movement should feel less resistive (Trager 1982).

PMR involves tightening specific muscle groups for a short time (5 to 10 seconds), then relaxing. This technique enables the athlete to identify muscle tension and relaxation specific to each region of the body. Practiced regularly, it can become an effective tool in controlling muscle tension. PMR can be especially beneficial during (only if the athlete is tense) or at the end of a training session or just before bedtime.

Sport-Specific Recovery

During training and competition, systems can be impaired to the extent of compromising future working capacity and athletic performance. Unless the body recovers quickly, the athlete may not be able to train adequately, perform the planned workload, or achieve expected performance. Consequently, take preventive measures. Dragan (1978) and Bucur (1979) suggest that athletes ritualistically adhere to the following recovery techniques.

- For the neuropsychological sphere, consider psychotonic relaxation, yoga exercise, Trager, acupressure, oxygen therapy, aerotherapy, balneotherapy, massage, and chemotherapy.
- For the neuromuscular system, consider balneo-therapy, massage, psychotonic relaxation, yoga, Trager, acupressure, a diet rich in alkaline foods and minerals, and chemotherapy.
- For the endocrine-metabolic sphere, consider oxygen therapy, psychotonic training, massage, acupressure, kinotherapy, chemotherapy, and a diet rich in minerals and alkaline substances.
- For the cardiorespiratory system, consider oxygen therapy, balneo-therapy, massage, psychotonic relaxation, acupressure, chemotherapy, and a diet rich in alkaline substances.

The coach and qualified personnel may choose adequate recovery techniques by knowing the systems and spheres that are more strongly solicited for several sports, based on the characteristics of each sport and the training demand (see table 5.1).

Recovery From Exercise

The coach and athlete must be aware of the time necessary for restoring energy-releasing fuels like ATP-CP, intramuscular glycogen, and other metabolites.

TABLE 5.1   Biological Parameters Solicited in Training for Various Sports

Sport	Parameters
Athletics	
Sprinting	Neuromuscular, endocrine-metabolic, neuropsychological
Mid-distance events	Cardiorespiratory, neuropsychological, neuromuscular
Distance events	Endocrine-metabolic, cardiorespiratory, neuromuscular
Jumping events	Neuromuscular, neuropsychological
Throwing events	Neuropsychological, endocrine-metabolic, neuromuscular
Basketball	Neuropsychological, endocrine-metabolic, neuromuscular
Canoeing	Cardiorespiratory, endocrine-metabolic, neuromuscular
Fencing	Neuropsychological, neuromuscular, endocrine-metabolic, cardiorespiratory
Gymnastics	Neuropsychological, neurometabolic, neuromuscular
Handball	Neuropsychological, endocrine-metabolic, neuromuscular
Rowing	Endocrine-metabolic, cardiorespiratory, neuromuscular
Rugby	Neuropsychological, neuromuscular, cardiorespiratory
Soccer	Neuropsychological, neuromuscular, endocrine-metabolic
Swimming	Cardiorespiratory, endocrine-metabolic, neuropsychological
Table tennis	Neuropsychological, neuromuscular
Volleyball	Neuropsychological, endocrine-metabolic, neuromuscular

Extenuating circumstances (i.e., severe glycogen depletion, dehydration, or disease) can hinder the restoration of these fuels and the clearance of their by-products. Under normal training situations restoring fuels and removing metabolic by-products requires a certain length of time, depending on the energy system the athlete uses during training or competition (i.e., aerobic, anaerobic lactic, or anaerobic alactic). Table 5.2 indicates the time necessary for each energy system.

Restoring Phosphagen (ATP-CP)

Restoring ATP stores requires energy, derived from the oxygen system through the metabolism of carbohydrates (CHO) and fats. Some authors suggest that part of the restoration comes from recycling lactic acid. Some of the ATP the body generates breaks down to form the CP portion of ATP-CP, and the other portion is stored directly into the muscle (Fox 1984).

Phosphagen is restored rapidly, with 50 to 70% restored during the first 20 to 30 seconds and the remainder in 3 minutes. Activities with intermittent bursts of high-energy metabolism (e.g., basketball, hockey) require different restoration times since some the energy is anaerobic. Brief events such as sprinting (i.e., 100 meter, 200 meter) demand different times for restoring phosphagen. If the effort lasts less than 10 seconds, the phosphagen used is minimal. For 30 seconds 50% is used, for 60 seconds 75%, for 90 seconds 87%, for 120 seconds 93%, for 150 seconds 97%, and for 180 seconds 98% (Hultman et al. 1967, cited in Fox 1984). Although phosphagen restoration demands little time, PC replenishment requires up to 10 minutes for full

TABLE 5.2 Recommended Recovery Times After Exhaustive Exercise

Recovery process	Minimum	Maximum
Restoration of muscle phosphagen (ATP and PC)	2 min	3-5 min
Repayment of the alacticid O_2 debt	3 min	5 min
Restoration of O_2-myoglobin	1 min	2 min
Repayment of the lactacid O_2 debt	30 min	1 hr
Restoration of muscle glycogen		
a. After intermittent activity	2 hr to restore 40% 5 hr to restore 55% 24 hr to restore 100%	
b. After prolonged, nonstop activity	10 hr to restore 60% 48 hr to restore 100%	
Removal of lactic acid from the muscles and blood	10 min to remove 25% 20-25 min to remove 50% 1 hr-1:15 hr to remove 95%	

Compiled based on data from Fox 1984.

recovery. Generally, it takes 2 minutes for 85%, 4 minutes for 90%, and 8 minutes for 97%.

Restoring Intramuscular Glycogen (IMCHO)

Several factors affect the rate and concentration of muscle glycogen synthesis during recovery from exercise. As mentioned, the manipulation of dietary nutrients, in particular CHO, has been positively correlated with increased intramuscular CHO storage. Other factors include the intensity and duration of the exercise performed (i.e., prolonged versus intermittent) (Fox 1984).

Hultman and Berstrom (1967), cited in Fox (1984), provided the following guidelines for glycogen replenishment for prolonged exercise.

- Only consuming a high CHO diet will accommodate full muscle glycogen restoration depending on the nature of the activity (i.e., speed- or power-dominant; anaerobic vs. aerobic).

- If the individual does not consume a high CHO diet, only partial intramuscular glycogen restoration will occur.

- Complete CHO replenishment requires 48 hours, despite a high CHO diet.

- Muscle glycogen restoration occurs rapidly within the first 10 hours. The muscular glycogen replenishment for intermittent exercise follows a slightly different protocol (Fox 1984).

- Intramuscular glycogen is restored within 2 hours after ceasing exercise in the absence of CHO intake. The restoration, however, is not complete. Some restoration can occur within 30 minutes.

- Muscle glycogen stores are completely replenished within 24 hours with a normal diet.

- The first 5 hours after ceasing exercise exhibits the most rapid restoration of muscle glycogen.

Several factors influence muscle glycogen restoration. The amount of glycogen depleted during exercise will govern some replenishment requirements (i.e., the greater the exercise time, the greater the CHO metabolized). During intermittent exercise, blood glucose levels are hardly affected due to greater involvement of FT fibers that do not rely on blood glucose or liver glycogen stores for fuel. Instead, these fibers lean heavily on intramuscular glycogen and CP.

Coaches should advocate high CHO diets several days before competitions to ensure complete glycogen restoration. If for some reason the athlete cannot eat a high CHO diet for several days, then dietary modification could begin within 10 hours before the competition (Fox 1984). This methodology only applies to endurance athletes. Athletes involved in intermittent exercise can afford to modify their dietary intake of CHOs within 5 to 24 hours of their competition.

Removing Lactic Acid (LA)

Removing LA requires two phases: removing it from the muscle and removing it from the blood. The activity performed during the rest interval will influence these factors (Fox 1984).

It takes roughly 2 hours to remove LA from the blood and muscle if the athlete undertakes a regime of passive rest and recovery. This refers to completely stopping activity following intense anaerobic exercise. The active recovery or active rest method (walking, light jogging) removes LA from muscle and blood much faster (about 1 hour).

Recovery for Training and Competition

Recovery related to training and competition is a multidimensional endeavor requiring various modalities, such as relaxation techniques, micronutrition (vitamins, etc.), macronutrition (protein, CHO, fats), and hydration. Consider three phases of regeneration to ensure optimum results: before, during, and after competition and training.

Before Competition

One to two days before competition, neuromuscular and psychological relaxation are prime concerns. For complete regeneration, try the following techniques: psychotonic training, balneo-hydrotherapy, massage, active and passive (10 hours of sleep) rest.

Consuming a small amount of food before competition allows the diaphragm to ascend better. High amounts of protein or greasy foods, however, require at least 5 to 6 hours to digest. This type of meal might cause gastrointestinal cramping during competition.

Wenger (1980) recommends the following nutrient consumption as a function of time before competition: no less than 4 hours before for fat and animal proteins; no less than 3 hours before for fish proteins; and no less than 1 to 2 hours for CHOs.

The diet has to balance qualitatively with 60% CHOs (low glycemic CHOs), 20% lipids, and 20% protein. Fruits, liquids, and vegetables should ensure a diet rich in minerals, alkaline substances, and vitamins. Do not use too much bread and vegetables, as this could lead to excessive intestinal gas. Athletes should also refrain from alcohol or carbonated beverages.

During Competition

Between events, games, during intermissions, you can use recovery techniques to calm the neuropsychological sphere and various psychological functions. During intermission, athletes may drink previously prepared liquids (fruit juices) with some glucose (20 grams) and salt added, to replenish what they lost during the first half of the competition. Self-massage of 5 minutes is also advisable to relax the main muscle groups involved in performance.

Between events or games, consider a slightly different approach. Athletes should rest in a quiet place where the excitement of competition cannot reach them. During this time, use both psychological and neuromuscular means of recovery. Massage, acupressure, oxygen therapy, and psychotonic relaxation are useful. Athletes should wear dry, warm clothing. Use additional blankets to cover the athletes to facilitate perspiration, which may eliminate metabolic wastes and enhance recovery. Throughout the resting time, the athlete should drink alkaline liquids, which may counterbalance the acidosis state. If the interval between events is less than 4 hours, take only liquid nutrients because they will not overtax the digestive system.

Following Competition

If only a few coaches and athletes pay attention to recovery, even fewer worry about psychophysiological regeneration following competition. Various recovery techniques make this process thorough and fast so that training effectiveness may begin within the next day or two.

The athlete does not have to stop physical activity at the end of competition. It is essential to continue moderate exercise to eliminate excessive metabolites from muscle cells. For sports dominated by anaerobic processes, the athlete replenishes the O_2 debt built during competition in the minutes following the activity. In such cases, in addition to light exercise of 10 to 15 minutes, neuromuscular recovery is necessary. Try hydrotherapy (15 minutes), massage, aerotherapy, and psychological relaxation. For sports in which aerobic processes dominate, the first concern is to reach homeostasis (to stabilize the body's internal functions). You can facilitate this by 15 to 20 minutes of light, physical activity, during which time the body flushes toxins. Also, use recovery techniques such as aerotherapy, hydrotherapy (15 minutes), massage, and psychological relaxation. In both cases, ingest liquids to replenish what was eliminated through perspiration. Dragan (1978) highly recommends alkaline beverages (milk, fruit juice) enriched with minerals, glucose, and vitamins. Adequate relaxation, especially through psychotonic training, which may remove stress and eventual frustration, facilitates a desirable deep and resting sleep.

During the first 1 or 2 days following competition, follow a recuperation diet rich in vitamins and alkaline substances (salads, fruits, milk, vegetables). Protein-rich meals are not advised (Bucur 1979). Use other recovery techniques (massage, acupressure, psychotonic relaxation, chemotherapy), and restrict alcohol, smoking, and sexual activity.

Permanent Means of Recovery

Effective training requires employing constant, permanent means of recovery. Recovery facilitates fast recuperation following training and maintains a state of high physical and psychological capacity. Permanent means of recovery should include the following:

- A rational alternation of work with regeneration phases
- An attempt to eliminate all social stressors
- A sound team atmosphere of calm, confident, and optimistic players
- A rational and varied diet according to the specifics of the sport and the phase of training
- Active rest and involvement in pleasant, relaxing social activities
- Permanent monitoring of each athlete's health status

Fatigue and Overtraining

When the homeostatic balance of the body is upset, the human organism attempts to adjust itself to restore balance. It is obligatory that the training regime stresses the athlete to provide the stimuli for adaptation, alternating rest periods with work periods. After administering an appropriate training stimulus, complete regeneration of the organism takes place within 12 to 24 hours. To recover from training that is within the adaptation limits of the athlete, specific regeneration techniques and a properly planned training load progression must be in place.

Avoid large increments in training loads. Exposing athletes to physical stress levels beyond their capabilities or providing inadequate rest results in a drop in the ability to adapt to the new stress. Failing adaptation or overreaching is characterized by fatigue and nonrecovery from training sessions. Monitor athletes' reactions to training as presented in table 5.3.

For the coach and athlete to understand overtraining, a few terms must be defined (Fry, Morton, and Keast 1991; Kuipers and Keizer 1988; Lehmann et al. 1993). Acute fatigue with muscular overstrain results from a single training session. This fatigue is short, lasting 1 to 2 days or less, usually accompanied by muscle soreness, disturbed sleep, and heightened response to allergens.

Overload stimulus with muscular overstrain is induced by a shock microcycle and is similar to acute fatigue. However, symptoms last longer than 2 days. Symptoms include a reluctance to work, disturbed sleep, lack of appetite, irrational use of energy, and emotional disturbances.

Overreaching is induced by one or more intense microcycles or too few regeneration periods. This fatigue is usually transient, lasting a few days up to 2 weeks. There may or may not be muscular overstrain associated with this state. Symptoms are similar to overload stimulus. They are, however, a little more severe, including increased resting heart rate; increased heart rate and lactic acid concentration during submaximal workloads; premature fatigue; a considerable drop in performance; and increased thirst, especially during the night.

TABLE 5.3 Symptoms of Fatigue Following Stimuli

	Low-intensity stimuli	Optimal stimuli	Stimuli up to one's limits	Stimuli at or slightly in excess of one's limits
Fatigue level	Low	Great	Exhausted	Exhausted
Sweating	Light to medium in upper body	Heavy sweat in upper body	Heavy sweat in lower body	Some sweat
Quality of technical movement	Controlled movements	Loss of precision, inconsistency, some technical faults	Poor coordination, technical uncertainty, many technical faults	Motor inconsistency, lack of power (24 hr), precision/accuracy impaired
Concentration	Normal, athletes react quickly to coach's remarks, maximum attention	Low ability to acquire technical elements, reduced span of attention	Low concentration span, nervousness, inconsistency	Mindlessness, unable to correct movements (24-28 hr), unable to concentrate on intellectual activities
Training and health status	Perform all training tasks	Muscular weakness, lack of power, low working capacity	Muscle and joint soreness, headache and stomach upset, vomiting sensation, and feeling of malaise	Sleeping difficulties, muscle soreness, physical discomfort, high heart rate for up to and even longer than 24 hr
Training willingness	Eager to train	Desire for longer rest and recovery phase but still willing to train	Desire to stop training, need for complete rest	Abhorrence to train next day, carelessness, negative attitude to training requirements

Adapted from Harre 1982.

Overtraining syndrome results from successive overreaching microcycles with insufficient regeneration. This fatigue is long term, lasting several weeks to several months. There are significant organic changes occurring during this phase of overtraining, mostly in the form of pronounced dystrophic processes. This state may or may not accompany muscular overstrain.

The severity and complexity of these symptoms progress as the symptoms increase in number. The symptoms associated with the stimuli will vary depending on the intensity. Table 5.4 illustrates the causes of fatigue for several sports. By understanding them the practitioner may avoid severe fatigue and overtraining by manipulating training methods and alternating intensities.

Three main areas influence overtraining. Although each system is independent, they are all part of the human body and correlate to one another: neuromuscular, metabolic, and neuroendocrine.

Neuromuscular Fatigue

Increasing evidence suggests that the CNS may be involved in limiting performance to a greater extent than once assumed. Fatigue may involve different processes associated with CNS command or peripheral mechanisms. CNS fatigue (long-term overtraining) causes a drop in motivation, impaired transmission down the spinal cord, and impaired recruitment of motor neurons. Peripheral fatigue (short-term overtraining) may involve impairment in the function of the peripheral nerves, neuromuscular junction, electrical activity of muscle fibers, or the process of activation within the muscle fiber (Gibson and Edwards 1985; Lehmann et al. 1993).

Peripheral fatigue can be divided into two types: high-frequency fatigue (electromechanical fatigue) and low-frequency fatigue (mechanico-metabolic fatigue) (table 5.5, p. 123).

High-frequency fatigue usually occurs in sports lasting less than 60 seconds to slightly longer than 60 seconds. Force output drops as a result of action potential failure (the ability of a muscle membrane to conduct an electrical signal) along the surface membrane (sarcolemma) of the muscle cell. The sarcolemma helps transmit electrical signals into the porous openings on

TABLE 5.4 Causes of Fatigue for Various Sports

	Neural factors	ATP-CP depletion	Lactic acidosis	Glycogen depletion	Blood glucose depletion	Hyperthermia
Archery	X					
Athletics (track & field)						
100, 200m	X	X				
400m		X	X			
800, 1,500m		X	X			
5,000, 10,000m			X	X		
Marathon				X	X	X
Jumps	X					
Throws	X					
Badminton		X	X			
Baseball		X	X			
Basketball		X	X			
Boxing		X	X			
Cycling						
Sprint 200m	X	X				
4,000 pursuit		X	X			
Road racing				X	X	X
Diving	X					
Driving (motor sports)	X					
Equestrian	X					
Fencing	X	X				
Field hockey		X	X			
Figure skating		X	X			
Football	X	X	X			

(continued)

TABLE 5.4 *(continued)*

	Neural factors	ATP-CP depletion	Lactic acidosis	Glycogen depletion	Blood glucose depletion	Hyperthermia
Gymnastics	X	X	X			
Ice hockey		X	X			
Judo		X	X			
Lacrosse		X	X			

Kayaking-canoeing
  500, 1,000m
  10,000m
		X	X
			X
				X		

Rowing		X	X			
Shooting	X					

Skiing
  Alpine
  Nordic
	X	X	X
			X
				X		

Soccer		X	X			

Speed skating
  Short/medium
  distances
  Long distance
		X	X
			X
				X		

Squash/handball	X	X	X			

Swimming
  50m
  100-200m, 400m
  800-1,500m
	X	X
		X
			X
			X
				X		

Synchronized swimming		X	X			
Team handball		X	X			
Tennis		X	X			
Triathlon				X	X	X
Volleyball		X	X			
Water polo		X	X	X		
Weightlifting	X					
Wrestling		X	X			
Yachting	X					

TABLE 5.5 Symptoms Associated With CNS Fatigue

Fatigue	Characteristics	Mechanisms
Central	Force or heat generated by voluntary effort less than that by electrical stimulation	Failure to sustain recruitment or frequency of motor units
Peripheral	Same force loss or heat generation with voluntary and stimulated contractions	
a. High frequency	Selective loss of force at high stimulation frequencies	Impaired neuromuscular transmission or propagation of muscle action potential
b. Low frequency	Selective loss of force at low stimulation frequencies	Impaired excitation/contraction

From Gibson and Edwards 1985.

the muscle cell's surface (T-tubules) and on the individual actin and myosin filaments within the contractile mechanisms. The failure of electrical signals (action potentials) to propagate is due to potassium (K+) buildup in the T-tubules and the spaces between the actin and myosin filaments. This fatigue occurs readily in cold muscles, muscles that have not been warmed up properly.

Low-frequency fatigue is caused primarily by cellular damage, especially associated with eccentric contractions. Cellular damage leaves the muscle cell in a state of disarray. The tearing of cellular structures that carry the electrical signals resembles torn or frayed wires. As a consequence, the electrical signals are weak.

The events leading to voluntary muscular contraction involve a controlling chain of command from the brain to actomyosin cross bridges (figure 5.2). Each link has been separately analyzed in different physiological systems, ranging from whole animal preparations to isolated cells or subcellular fractions. Fatigue may be due to impairment at any one or more links in the chain.

The CNS has two basic processes, excitation and inhibition. Excitation is a favorable stimulating process for physical activity; inhibition is a restraining process. Training constantly alternates the two process. For any stimulation, the CNS sends a nerve impulse to the working muscle ordering it to contract and perform work. The speed, power, and frequency of the nerve impulse depends on the state of the CNS. When (controlled) excitation prevails, the nerve impulses are the most effective, evidenced by a good performance. When as a result of fatigue the nervous cell is in a state of inhibition, the muscle contraction is slower and weaker. Thus, the force of contraction and the number of motor units (muscle fibers) recruited directly relates to the electrical activation the CNS sends. Nerve cell working capacity cannot be maintained for long. Under the strain of training and competition, working capacity decreases. If the athlete maintains high intensity, the nerve cell assumes a state of inhibition to protect itself from external stimuli. Once in this state, the nerve cell does not respond with the same activation. The force generated by the working muscle diminishes because some nerve cells lower their firing rate well below threshold level. This decreases the number of motor units recruited.

Should the coach disregard the needs of alternating high- with low-intensity training days, the new intensive stimuli will result in exhaustion, when the nerve cell is in a state of inhibition of protection. While in this state performance is below normal. Emotional disturbances are associated with such behavior of the nervous system. In the end, continuing training beyond this level results in overtraining, when the athlete is completely out of shape (see figure 5.3).

Fast-twitch fibers, fast glycolitic (FG), and fast oxidative glycolitic (FOG) are more susceptible to fatigue than slow-twitch fibers (ST). Fast-twitch fibers have a high potential for fast turnover of Ca++ ions and ATP-CP in connection with muscular contraction and for ATP-CP production via anaerobic processes. However, ST fibers have a higher aerobic potential evidenced by a higher myoglobin and mitochondrial enzymatic activity level (Edgerton 1976; Ruff 1989).

Possible Fatigue Mechanisms

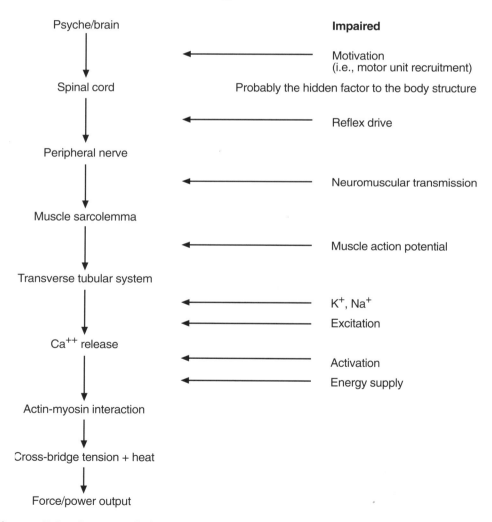

Figure 5.2 Command chain for muscular contraction (Gibson and Edwards 1985).

Several weeks	Normal level of fatigue that does not inhibit supercompensation.
2 weeks	Capacity to tolerate fatigue is increased. Adaptive responses are created.
1-2 weeks	Acute level of fatigue. Rest intervals inadequate for compensation.
1 week	Athletes appeal to motivation to defeat the strain of fatigue.
1 week	Inhibition. Inadequate nerve activation to external stimuli. Performance starts to decrease.
1 week	Pressure to continue from coach, peers, family, and competition schedule.
2 weeks	Inhibition of protection. Nerve cell protects itself from further stimuli. Performance decreases. Prone to injuries.
1 week	Athletes appeal to last resort of willpower, and continue to train.
2 weeks	Overtraining. Athletes out of shape. Emotional problems. Injuries.

Figure 5.3 Progression of the stages of acquiring fatigue and overtraining

Skeletal muscle produces force by progressively activating its motor units and regulating their firing frequency, which is progressively increased to enhance force output. Slow-twitch muscle fibers are recruited for the size of their motor-neuron cell body and their predominant aerobic metabolism. As the demand for force increases, FOG fibers are recruited, followed by FG, which can generate the most force (Edgerton 1976; Finnbogi et al. 1988; Rose and Rothstein 1982).

You can neutralize fatigue, which inhibits muscle activity, some by a modulating strategy, responding to it through the ability of the motor units to alter firing frequency. The muscle can maintain force more effectively under a certain state of fatigue. However, if the duration of sustained maximum contraction increases, the frequency of motor units firing decreases (Bigland-Ritchie et al. 1983; Hennig and Lomo 1987), signaling that inhibition will become more prominent.

Marsden, Meadows, and Merton (1971) demonstrated that, compared with the start of a 30-second maximum voluntary contraction, the end firing frequency decreased by 80%. Similar findings were reported by Grimby et al. (1992), who stated that as the duration of contraction increased, activation of large motor units decreased, lowering the firing rate below threshold level. Any combination of contraction beyond that level was possible through a short burst (phasical firing), but not appropriate for a constant performance.

These findings should caution those who promote the theory (especially in football and bodybuilding) that you can improve strength only by performing each set to exhaustion. The fact that as a contraction progressed, the firing frequency decreased discredits this highly acclaimed method. As contraction progressed, fuel reserves depleted, resulting in longer motor unit relaxation time and a lower frequency of muscle contraction. Because the source of such neuromuscular behavior was assumed to be fatigue, practitioners should be warned that short rest intervals, the standard 2 minutes between two sets of maximum contraction, are not sufficient to relax and regenerate the neuromuscular system to achieve high activation in the subsequent sets.

When analyzing the functional capacity of the CNS during fatigue, consider the athlete's perceived fatigue and past physical capacity in training. When physical capacity is higher than the level of fatigue experienced in testing or competition, the athlete's motivation and capacity to overcome fatigue are enhanced. Motivation relates to past experience and conditioning.

Metabolic Fatigue

Overexertion at the muscular level can mean muscle fiber damage or metabolic fatigue, such as the depletion of fuel, the accumulation of Ca++ flux in the muscle, or the buildup of intramuscular hydrogen ions (pH) (Allen et al. 1992; Appell et al. 1992; Sahlin 1992).

Metabolic mechanisms of overexertion usually occur during prolonged submaximal or repetitive, short-term intensive exercise. The complex cycle of muscle contraction is triggered by the nerve impulse that depolarizes the surface membrane of the muscle cell, resulting in an action potential (electric charge), which then propagates down to the muscle fiber. This is followed by a series of events in which Ca++ is bound with protein filaments (actin and myosin), resulting in contractile tension (Allen et al. 1992; Clarkson et al. 1992).

The functional site of fatigue is the link between excitation and contraction, resulting either in reducing the intensity of these two processes or in decreasing sensitivity to activation. Changes in the flux of C++ ions affect the operation of excitation and contraction. Researchers found the elevation of lactic acid level in the blood and muscle negatively affect performance of medium and longer duration, suggesting a cause-effect relationship between local muscle fatigue and lactate accumulation. Increased acidosis or lactate fatigue, which seems to determine the point of exhaustion (Armstrong et al. 1991; Sahlin 1986), could impair the mechanical processes involved in muscular contraction by four possible means.

Hydrogen ion accumulation interferes with the production of energy (ATP) by inhibiting phosphofructokinase (PFK), the rate-limiting enzyme in aerobic glycolysis. The activities of other enzymes, such as lactate dehydrogenase (LDH), phosphorolase, and myosin-ATPase, are also limited (Armstrong et al. 1991).

Increased acidosis decreases the affinity of O_2 to bind to hemoglobin. However, to counteract the eventual low level of O_2 at the muscle cell level, during its transport through the capillaries, the hemoglobin will release even more oxygen (Brooks and Fahey 1985).

Increased acidosis competes with troponin for binding sites, inhibiting the binding of Ca++ to troponin. Because troponin is an important contributor to muscle cell contraction, its relative inactivity may explain the connection between fatigue and exercise. The depression of Ca++ also makes cardiac muscle more sensitive than skeletal muscle, which probably explains why it has a more pronounced depression on contractability during acidosis. Increased hydrogen ion concentration inhibits the release of Ca++ from the sarcoplasmic reticulum (Allen et al. 1992; Fabiato and Fabiato 1978).

Accumulating hydrogen ions create discomfort, which could be a limiting factor in psychological fatigue and tolerance (Brooks and Fahey 1985).

From an energy system standpoint, fatigue occurs when creatine phosphate is depleted in the working muscle, muscle glycogen is consumed, and carbohydrate stores are exhausted (Sahlin 1986). The obvious result is that the work the muscle performs decreases, possibly because in a glycogen-depleted muscle ATP is produced at a lower rate than it is consumed. Studies show that carbohydrate is essential to the ability of a muscle to maintain high force (Conlee 1987). Also, endurance capabilities during prolonged moderate to heavy physical activity directly relate to the amount of glycogen in the muscle before exercise. This indicates that fatigue occurs as a result of muscle glycogen depletion (Bergstrom et al. 1967).

For activities of high intensity but short duration, the immediate sources of energy for muscular contraction are ATP and CP. Complete depletion of these stores in the muscle would certainly limit the ability of the muscle to contract (Karlsson and Saltin 1971).

With prolonged submaximal work, free fatty acids and glucose provide energy, the latter supplied in significant amounts by the liver. Inhibition of free fatty acids (by beta-receptor blockade) can increase the rate of glycogen degradation, affecting performance (Sahlin 1986).

Oxidation depends on the availability of oxygen, which, in limited quantity, oxidizes carbohydrates instead of free fatty acids. Maximum free fatty acid oxidation is determined, therefore, by the inflow of the fatty acids to the working muscle and by the aerobic training status of the athlete, because aerobic training increases both the availability of oxygen and the power of free fatty acid oxidation (Sahlin 1986).

Metabolic events such as hypoxia (reduced O_2 delivery to the working muscle), which results in altered ion concentration, ATP deficiency, and lactic acid accumulation, may clarify muscle damage. However, evidence shows that greater structural damage occurs when the muscle is subjected to repeated eccentric or concentric loading. Between the two types of mechanical loading, eccentric contractions cause greater muscle fiber damage. Eccentric contractions produce more tension per cross-sectional area of active muscle than concentric contractions. Although eccentric contractions produce greater structural damage, there must be sufficient tensile stress in repeated contractions to cause a breakdown of the tensile strength of the muscle fiber. Only then will the structural components of the muscle fiber rupture (see figure 5.4).

A model from the field of material fatigue can show why repeated contractions are more effective. Material subjected to alternating tension and compression or relaxation will eventually fail. The rate or velocity of the alternations, determines how quickly the material fatigues. For most ductile materials, the relationship between stress and the number of cycles of alternating forces to failure is exponential; therefore, as stress increases, the number of cycles to failure decreases. We can also apply this approach to muscle fibers that are constantly subjected to bouts of work that slightly exceed the tensile strength of the structural components of the muscle (Appell et al. 1992; Armstrong et al. 1991; Clarkson et al. 1992; Fahey 1991).

Heat enhances muscular contractions by increasing the sensitivity of the muscle fibers to the actions of Ca++ (Paha 1994). This is why athletes should not neglect warming up before physical activity. Some evidence, however, suggests that heat production during muscular contractions contributes to muscle damage. Eccentric contractions generate more thermal energy than concentric muscular work. The increase in heat production during eccentric contractions is probably due to the muscle's decreased ability to remove the heat, rather than a higher rate of heat production within the muscle cell. The elevation in intramuscular temperature also accounts for an 18% higher rate of structural lipid and protein degradation. This appears more with negative than with positive contractions. The rate at which the contractions take place also directly affects heat production (Armstrong et al. 1991; Baracos 1984; Fahey 1991).

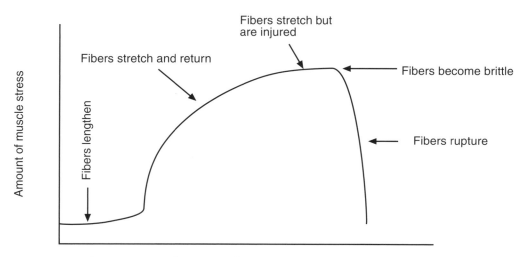

Figure 5.4   Change in shape of muscle tissue (Fahey 1991)

The disruption of structural muscular components often leads to microtrauma. The discomfort does not begin immediately, but peaks in 24 to 72 hours. Figure 5.5 shows soreness ratings of the forearm flexor muscles based on a scale from 1 = normal to 10 = very, very sore. Measures were taken before eccentric exercise of the forearm flexors (pre) and for 5 days after exercise. The sport scientific community refers to this discomfort as delayed-onset muscle soreness or DOMS. The sensation the athlete experiences is often a dull, aching pain, combined with localized tenderness and stiffness. These sensations diminish within 5 to 7 days after the initial bout of exercise (Appell et al. 1992; Armstrong 1986; Clarkson et al. 1992; Fahey 1991).

During muscular work, force is transmitted from the muscle through the tendon onto the bone. The fibers just proximal to the musculotendinous junction, which form the tendinous tissue, are orientated in a wavy but oblique manner, making them most vulnerable to the high tensions of eccentric exercise. These fibers are also less elastic than muscle tissue, another reason they are more susceptible to injury and localized pain from DOMS (Armstrong 1986; Armstrong et al. 1991; Clarkson et al. 1992; Ebbing et al. 1989).

The wavy configuration will disappear on a tendon stretched by 4% of its resting length. Four to eight percent of the collagen fibers will slide past one another as small ruptures appearing within the matrix fibers. If the tendon is stretched to 8 to 10% of its resting length, considerably more fibers will become damaged. The damage occurs at the weakest point in the tendon (Renström and Johnson 1985). Damaged tendons can result from any of the following conditions:

- Tension is applied too quickly. This can be the result of explosive movement.
- Tension is applied obliquely.
- The tendon is under tension before loading.
- The attached muscle is maximally innervated. The hamstring muscle group is highly innervated, making it more susceptible to injury.
- The muscle group is stretched by external stimuli (i.e., partner-assisted stretching).
- Tension is from eccentric movements.
- The tendon is weak compared with the muscle.

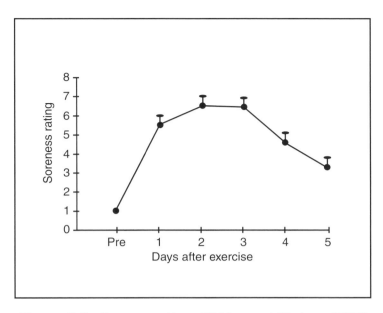

Figure 5.5   Soreness ratings (Ebbing and Clarkson 1989)

Damaged tendons require a long time to regenerate. Researchers attribute this to a limited blood flow to this part of the muscle (Renström and Johnson 1985).

For several years, lactic acid was cited as the cause for DOMS. Through sophisticated chemical tests and electron microscopy, researchers discovered that DOMS was actually caused by muscle fiber damage resulting from an influx of Ca^{++} ions into the muscle cell (see figure 5.6).

Slow-twitch and fast-twitch fibers are susceptible to exercise-induced muscle damage. There appears, however, to be greater damage in fast-twitch fibers, primarily during eccentric and maximum concentric force outputs. Although no clear explanation exists for this difference, we may attribute it to the type of contraction, the intensity of the activity, the motor recruitment patterns, or the structural differences that exist between the two sets of muscle fibers (Armstrong et al. 1991; Clarkson et al. 1992; Friden and Lieber 1992).

Neuroendocrine Fatigue

The nervous system divides into afferent and efferent. The latter breaks into the somatic and the autonomic nervous system. The somatic nervous system innervates skeletal muscle and always leads to muscle excitation; the autonomic nervous system innervates smooth and cardiac muscle glands and GI neurons, leading to excitation or inhibition of effector cells.

Training athletes may experience two forms of overtraining. We associate the first type, Basedowoid overtraining, with either sympathetic or parasympathetic dominance. It results from sympathetic overexcitation or overstressing the emotional process. The second type, Addisonoid overtraining, is due to parasympathetic inhibition. Of the two, parasympathetic or Addisonoid overtraining is more difficult to detect; the sympathetic form predominates in sporting events (Altenberger 1993; Fry, Morton, and Keast 1991; Israel 1963; Kuipers and Keizer 1988; Lehmann et al. 1993).

Under normal conditions, sympathetic nervous activity increases as a result of exercise and the levels of several hormones, such as adrenaline (epinephrine),

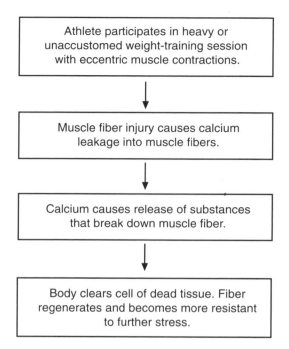

Figure 5.6 How muscles get sore (Fahey 1991)

noradrenaline (norepinephrine), HGH, cortisol, and thyroid stimulating hormone. Researchers have found these hormones in elevated concentrations in the blood and consider several of these changes to be components of a normal stress response to exercise.

However, when the body is physically and psychologically overstressed for several weeks, without adequate regeneration, it no longer supercompensates. If the stress comes from too much high-intensity training stimuli or a sudden increase in training load, the body produces symptoms that resemble those of Basedow's disease (hence the term Basedowoid overtraining syndrome). The symptoms of this disorder have been closely linked to athletes who participate in nonendurance activities of high intensity (e.g., sprinting). Symptoms (Kuipers and Keizer 1988) include increased resting heart rate, decreased appetite, retarded recovery after exercise, disturbed sleep, increased resting blood pressure, retarded return of blood pressure to basal levels after exercise, increased incidence of infections, decreased maximal power output, decreased performance, weight loss, increased irritability and emotional instability, loss of training and competitive desire, postural hypotension, increased incidence of injuries, and decreased maximal plasma lactate levels during exercise

Biochemically, the testosterone to cortisol ratio is disrupted. Researchers have proven that down-regulation of cortisol production is primary for the onset of testosterone elevation, required in the anabolic process. Decreased testosterone levels inhibit testicular secretion, possibly through elevated cortisol levels or other hormonal mechanisms. The testosterone level may be slow to return to normal basal levels following severe physical training, possibly requiring several days to return to normal. Because the testosterone to cortisol ratio has implications for switching on the anabolic process for recovery, and as this can require more than 1 day to occur, the ratio may be associated with the catabolic state reported in Basedowoid overtraining syndrome (Israel 1963; Kuipers and Keizer 1988; Lehmann et al. 1993; Parry-Billings et al. 1993).

Parasympathetic overtraining resembles symptoms associated with Addison's disease. The adrenal glands fail to properly regulate hormonal concentrations; consequently, hormone levels drop, particularly cortisol hormones such as thyroid hormones, HGH, and free testosterone.

Addisonoid overtraining results from too much high-volume training and is more common in endurance athletes. Like Basedowoid overtraining, the CNS's ability to work is markedly decreased. Some symptoms associated with Addisonoid overtraining are progressive anemia; decreased hemoglobin; decreased hematocrit; the need for more quality sleep despite no apparent insomnia; low blood pressure; low resting pulse rate; decrease in free testosterone level; mood state disturbances; and digestive disturbances, which ultimately decrease performance (Israel 1963; Kuipers and Keizer 1988; Fry, Morton, and Keast 1991; Parry-Billings et al. 1993)

Monitoring, Treating, and Preventing Overtraining

Most research and information available on fatigue and overtraining concern what to do after athletes experience these negative effects of demanding training programs. Little is done to prevent overtraining and avoid deterioration of performance before important competitions.

Establishing unity of work and recovery is an essential element in creating an effective training program for athletes. Adaptation to greater training loads will come to fruition only with the correct compromise between loading and recovery. Proper training loads create a degree of fatigue that temporarily lowers the functional ability of the athlete. The athlete adapts to the training stimulus during the recovery process, which renews energy sources and may regenerate them beyond the original levels. The progressive application of an appropriate training stimulus during the supercompensation phase, therefore, will enhance the peaking process. Ideally, subsequent training should not take place until supercompensation has occurred.

Practically, this is a complicated matter. It is difficult to define the moment of recovery and the phase of supercompensation. Individuals recover and respond to training at various rates, even with identical training loads. Adaptation programs, therefore, should be tuned to the subtle differences of the individual athlete. Personal training diaries and scientific testing can produce data to help coaches and athletes tailor the program to the individual.

Some have access (geographical and financial) to invasive testing (i.e., laboratories) in which they can receive sophisticated physiological, psychological, and biomechanical testing. Such tests evaluate improvements, current biological status, performance efficiency, technical effectiveness, and psychological status. Coaches without such opportunities can employ noninvasive techniques to monitor training. By systematically monitoring recovery, the coach and athletes can verify recovery following training. This practice should continue throughout the training year, providing constant physiological and psychological feedback for the intensity and volume prescribed at specific times in the training calendar.

Causes of Overtraining

Several factors can influence the rate of recovery and overtraining. Usually these factors are the result of a disparity between load, load tolerance, and regeneration. Some authors, however, feel it is a combination of the intolerance to adverse physical and psychological stimuli (see table 5.6). Athletes continuing to train under these conditions might be setting themselves up to fail adaptation or overtrain. The coach and athletes must plan adequately to reach positive conclusions, especially if they are also monitoring reactions to training.

Detecting Overtraining

Overtraining decreases working capacity and performance. Symptoms are usually preceded by insomnia, poor appetite, and profuse sweating during the night and day. The coach can identify the symptoms by observing the daily remarks athletes make in their training journals. For a more descriptive identification of fatigue, view the symptoms in table 5.7.

We can divide monitoring by two techniques. The first uses noninvasive techniques, and the second uses invasive techniques. Noninvasive monitoring does not require expensive or sophisticated laboratory testing. However, invasive testing is far more accurate and can provide physiological, psychological, and biomechanical evaluations. You can use the data from these tests to increase performance efficiency, technical effectiveness, and mental power.

Biochemical testing should encompass seven physiological systems to properly diagnose overtraining syndrome or to distinguish it from overreaching, which is short-term overtraining. The areas are (a) neuromuscular, (b) cardiovascular, (c) metabolic-endocrine, (d) immunological, (e) kinanthropometric, (f) physiological performance, and (g) psychological.

Authors have outlined various physiological and psychological parameters that, if monitored, can effectively assess training adaptation. Fry, Morton, and Keast (1991) developed a list that outlines the hierarchy of procedures for monitoring training to prevent the symptoms of overtraining (table 5.8). Select which tests to use based on the sport. Conduct tests at regular intervals under standardized conditions in which some variables are ongoing and others are more infrequent, but habitual. Some variables, however, may not be valid indicators of overtraining, as they may be due to outside negative social-psychological stimuli rather than training load.

Some of these indices are only anecdotal, thus their validity and practicality for testing on athletes remain questionable. For a diagnosis of overtraining to be valid, Nieman and Nehlson-Cannarella (1991) and Van Erp-Baart et al. (1989) suggest six factors to consider:

1. Achieve a better understanding of the mechanisms involved in the appearance of overtraining.
2. Hone the elements of diagnosis.
3. Establish conditions to prevent overtraining.
4. Develop simple but effective means to diagnose that do not require sophisticated and expensive laboratory testing.
5. Establish baseline values several weeks before commencing a training. During this time, reduce the training load significantly, but not drastically. Otherwise, mood disturbances from the diminished training load might induce withdrawal (Hollmann 1993).
6. Schedule the biochemical testing for specific times in the day under standardized conditions (i.e., morning, before training, during training, after training, or before bed).

Using biochemical markers to monitor adaptation is fruitless unless the coach and athletes learn the basic physiology behind them, such as creatine phospho kinase (CPK), methylhistadine (3-MH), ammonia, urinary nitrogen excretion, serum urea, serotonin, steroid hormone binding globulin (SHBG), catecholamines excretion, urinary ketosteroids, uric acid, and cortisol. Biochemical markers that indicate overtraining when in depressed concentrations are basal catecholamines and cortisol concentrations (morning and evening); plasma free testosterone to cortisol ratio greater than 30%; red blood cell count (RBC); serum ferritin; blood hemoglobin (Hb); plasma glutamine; immunoglobulins (IgA, IgG); and electrolytes (Zn, Mg, Na, etc.) (Altenberger 1993; Banister 1985; Berglund 1992; Booth 1993; Dishman 1992; Fry, Morton, and Keast 1991; Karvonen 1992; Kuipers and Keizer 1988; Legros 1992; Reiter 1991).

Monitoring and Preventing Overtraining

Athletes should actively monitor recovery daily and weekly. Daily monitoring includes keeping a training diary; eating; stretching; and using saunas, contrast baths, and relaxation techniques (PMR, breathing exercises, visualization). Weekly monitoring includes having at least one active recovery day a week, massage 3 times a week, and practicing time management.

Although there are many variables to monitor, practicality exceeds any method requiring sophisticated and elaborate means of assessing adaptation. Although some methods appear simplistic, the interpretation of these methods can be more beneficial than going to a laboratory. In most instances, laboratory testing merely confirms in detail what was determined by simple monitoring charts and tests. The cost of such elaborate testing can sometimes

TABLE 5.6 Activities That May Cause Overtraining

Training faults	Athlete's lifestyle	Social environment	Health
Overlooking recovery	Insufficient hours of sleep	Overwhelming family responsibilities	Illness, high fever
Higher demand than capacity	Unorganized daily program	Frustration (family, peers)	Nausea
Abrupt increase of training load following long pauses (rest, illness, etc.)	Smoking, alcohol, coffee	Professional dissatisfaction	Stomachaches
High volume of high-intensity stimuli	Inadequate living facilities (space)	Stressful professional activities	
	Quarrel with peers	Excessive emotional activities (TV, noisy music, etc.)	
	Poor diet	Quarrel with family re sports involvement	
	Overexciting and agitated life		

Adapted from Harre 1982.

TABLE 5.7 Symptoms of Overtraining

Psychological	Motor and physical	Functional
Increased excitability	Coordination	Insomnia
Reduced concentration	Increment in muscle tension	Lack of appetite
Irrational	Reappearance of mistake already corrected	Digestive disturbances
Sensitive to criticism	Inconsistency in performing rhythmical movements	Sweat easily
Tendency to isolate oneself from coach and teammates	Reduced capacity for differentiating and correcting technical faults	Decrease in vital capacity
Lack of initiative	Physical preparation	Heart rate recovery longer than normal
Depression	Decrease in speed, strength, and endurance	Prone to skin and tissue infections
Lack of confidence	Slower rate of recovery	
Willpower	Decrease in reaction time	
Lack of fighting power	Prone to accidents and injuries	
Fear of competitions		
Prone to give up a tactical plan or desire to fight in a contest		

Based on data from Bompa 1969, Ozolin 1971, and Harre 1982.

outweigh the worth of the data obtained. Ideally, each athlete should do monitoring charts each day. The coach can employ simple methods to verify the athletes' recovery state following training. Observe athletic shape expressed through the effectiveness of training, accomplishment of training objectives, or achievement of testing standards. Be aware of the athlete's attitude. A conscientious, optimistic attitude during training, adequate relationships with teammates, and a positive reaction to training indicates that the training load is proportional with the recovery rate for that athlete.

Feedback can sometimes present itself in the simplest ways, for example, direct communication with the athlete. Ask him or her at the beginning of training lesson, "How do you feel today?" If the response is, "My legs feel heavy and stiff" or "I don't feel good," this indicates that the athlete has not adapted from the previous day's training load. Body language, such as facial expressions, bending over to recover after an effort, a new or recurring training fault, and just looking into their eyes (eyes are the window to a person's inner world) can provide effective feedback. Become aware of any emotional problems the athlete might experience (i.e., quarrel with peers, girlfriends or boyfriends, parents, stress from school or work). Implement steps to help the athlete remedy these problems before they become negative factors in performance.

The athlete's health status, monitored by a team physician and subjectively sensed by the athlete, indicates recovery. An exhausted, unregenerated individual may diminish the normal functioning of the circulatory system.

TABLE 5.8   Symptoms of Overtraining as Indicated by Their Prevalence in the Literature

Physiological/performance	Psychological/information processing
Decreased performance	Feelings of depression
Inability to meet previously attained performance standard/criteria	General apathy
Recovery prolonged	Decreased self-esteem/worsening feelings of self
Reduced toleration of loading	Emotional instability
Decreased muscular strength	Difficulty in concentrating at work and training
Decreased maximum work capacity	Sensitive to environmental and emotional stress
Loss of coordination	Fear of competition
Decreased efficiency/decreased amplitude of movement	Changes in personality
Reappearance of mistakes already corrected	Decreased ability to narrow concentration
Reduced capacity of differentiating and correcting technical faults	Increased internal and external distractibility
Increased difference between lying and standing heart rate	Decreased capacity to deal with large amount of information
Abnormal T wave pattern in ECG	Gives up when the going gets tough
Heart discomfort on slight exertion	**Immunological**
Changes in blood pressure	Increased susceptibility to and severity of illness/colds/allergies
Changes in heart rate at rest, exercise, and recovery	Flu-like illnesses
Increased frequency of respiration	Unconfirmed glandular fever
Profuse respiration	Minor scratches heal slowly
Decreased body fat	Swelling of lymph glands
Increased oxygen consumption at submaximal workloads	One-day colds
Increased ventilation and heart rate at submaximal workloads	Decreased functional activity of neutrophils
Shift of the lactate curve toward the x axis	Decreased total lymphocyte counts
Decreased evening postworkout weight	Reduced response to mitogens
Elevated basal metabolic rate	Increased blood eosinophil count
Chronic fatigue	Decreased proportion of null (non-T, non-B lymphocytes)

(continued)

TABLE 5.8 *(continued)*

Physiological/performance *(continued)*	Immunological *(continued)*
Insomnia with and without night sweats	Bacterial infection
Feels thirst	Reactivation of herpes viral infection
Anorexia nervosa	Significant variations in CD4 : CD8 lymphocytes
Loss of appetite	**Biochemical**
Bulimia	Negative nitrogen balance
Amenorrhea/oligomenorrhea	Hypothalamic dysfunction
Headaches	Flat glucose tolerance curves
Nausea	Depressed muscle glycogen concentration
Increased aches and pains	Decreased bone mineral content
Gastrointestinal disturbances	Delayed menarche
Muscle soreness/tenderness	Decreased hemoglobin
Tendinostic complaints	Decreased serum iron
Periosteal complaints	Decreased serum ferritin
Muscle damage	Lowered TIBC
Elevated C-reactive protein	Mineral depletion (Zn, Co, Al, Mn, Se, Cu, etc.)
Rhabdomyolysis	Increased urea concentrations
	Elevated cortisol levels
	Elevated ketosteroids in urine
	Low free testosterone
	Increased serum hormone binding globulin
	Decreased ratio of free testosterone to cortisol of more than 30%
	Increased uric acid production

From Fry, Morton, & Keast 1991.

Note the athlete's willingness, desire to surpass personal performances, appetite, sleep habits (poor sleep for more than 2 days in succession indicates a problem), and balance of emotions (Profile of Mood States [POMS] in Dishman 1992) to determine recovery (Calder 1996).

Weight variations of plus or minus 1 kilogram (or greater than 3%) over a 24-hour period show normal recovery. Gains or losses beyond this suggest either a light training load (weight gain) or a load that prevented proper regeneration (weight loss) (Calder 1996; Dishman 1992).

Measure morning resting heart rate, an important physiological indicator of recovery. Dragan (1978) suggests that a difference larger than 8 beats per minute between resting HR supine and standing represents low recovery, indicating you should alter training (see figure 5.7).

Classifying muscle soreness enables the coach to plan training loads for the following lessons. Knowing how the athlete is responding to current training loads via residual soreness can be an effective tool in monitoring recovery (table 5.9).

When palpating the athlete's muscles, be aware of any knots or adhesions that may hinder optimal range of movement and ultimately affect performance. If these adhesions go undetected, the athlete may risk tearing the tight muscle tissue (Andrews 1991; Francis and Patterson 1992).

Observe CNS excitability using a handgrip dynamometer (see figure 5.8). Study field and laboratory physical performance testing after a regeneration period, for example, blood LA analysis during submaximal exercise, time trials, or previous personal records (e.g., 1,500 meters), skill, and strength and power tests.

Observe the ability to respond to relaxation or meditation techniques (Calder 1996).

Watch for a drop or increase in the response to allergic substances and an increase in susceptibility to infections, especially in the mouth and on the lips (i.e., cracked, swollen, peeling, dryness, blisters, or redness) (Fleck et al. 1982; Keast et al. 1988). Inspect the tongue to see whether it is yellow, red, or swollen. Eyelid twitches, caused by an increase in intraoccular pressure, can indicate tiredness. When gently pressing down on the eyeballs with the eyes are closed, the athlete should feel no pain on initial depression. Only after applying more pressure should the eyes begin to hurt (Francis and Patterson 1992).

Ensure proper intake of macro- and micronutrients (Balaban 1992; Wardlaw et al. 1992).

Be aware of sleep reactions to time zone changes, which disrupt the athlete's normal circadian rhythms (Newsholme et al. 1992; Pierrefiche et al. 1993; Totterdell et al. 1994).

Monitor planned volume and intensity of training lessons and compare it with what was achieved during training. Develop a well-structured and organized training plan, in which you methodically outline the volume and intensity according to the needs of the athlete and the sport.

Look for mechanical overtraining or overuse injuries (Kuipers 1991; Lehmann et al. 1993).

The intensity of training contributes more to overtraining than the duration; therefore, dropping the intensity of training or maintaining the same volume will minimize the overtraining effect.

Training Monitoring Charts

At the end of this chapter, on pages 143-146, are sets of charts. The first two pages show examples, and the third and fourth pages show blank charts to be copied for use. At the top of each page there is space to write the name of the athlete and month of training. Place these charts in the locker room or include them in each athlete's training log.

Look at each athlete's charts before the training session and modify the training program according to the athlete's psychological state and level of fatigue. For instance, if the heart rate chart indicates a high level of fatigue, or the sleep data chart shows four hours of restless sleep, make the daily program easier, with no high intensity (which normally increases fatigue).

Figure 5.7 Effects of training and overtraining on early morning lying and standing heart rates

From "A Simple Method to Control Fatigue in Endurance Training" by W. Csajkowski in *Exercise and Sports Biology*, International Series on Sports Sciences (Vol.12, p.210) edited by P.V. Komi, 1982, Champaign, IL: Human Kinetics. Copyright 1982 by Human Kinetics. Adapted by permission.

The heart rate chart monitors the athlete's reaction to the previous day's training program. Before an athlete uses the chart, he or she should know the base heart rate (BHR), the heart rate taken in the morning before stepping out of bed. Time the heart rate for 10 seconds then multiply by 6 to give a value in beats per minute. On the blank chart, place a dot representing the BHR in the lower third of the chart, and write the value of the heart rate in the space. Complete all the spaces of the chart. As the athlete continues to take the BHR daily, he or she places the dots on the chart, linking them together with a line to form a curve.

BHR illustrates the athlete's physiological state and reaction to training. Under normal conditions, the curve does not have too many deflections. The dynamics of the curve could, however, change according to the phase of training and the athlete's adaptation to the training program. The BHR curve will drop progressively as the athlete adapts. The better the adaptation, the lower the curve. The curve may often depend on the chosen sport. Usually, athletes from endurance sports will exhibit lower resting heart rates.

The BHR also reacts to the training intensity of the previous day. A BHR increase of 6 to 8 beats per minute in one day (see p.143) over the standard curve could mean that the athlete did not tolerate the training program well or that he or she did not observe a normal athletic lifestyle. The coach should find out the reason from the athlete. In either case, change the planned training program so it does not add to an already high level of fatigue. When the curve returns to its standard levels, the normal program can resume.

BHR can monitor training for short term; use the body weight chart (BW) for long term. A well-trained athlete whose diet correlates to training volume and intensity should have a steady BW. BW can fluctuate, especially during the transition phase, in which some athletes gain weight. During the preparatory phase, however, it quickly drops to the normal levels. On the other hand, a changeable training program with volume and intensity beyond the athlete's threshold of tolerance for a long time can result in a high level of fatigue. Loss of appetite is a symptom of acute fatigue and the athlete starts losing weight.

BW loss is not abrupt; on the contrary, it is a long-term process (see p.143). Constant drops in BW can signal a critical level of fatigue and possible over-

TABLE 5.9 Classification of Muscle Soreness

Grading	Symptoms	Indication
0	No discomfort.	Continue training.
1	Some discomfort on feeling muscle.	Reduce training for 7 days. No racing for 2 weeks.
2	Discomfort on walking. Unable to squat without discomfort.	Reduce training for 14 days. No racing for 1 month.
3	Severe pain. Walking with difficulty.	Reduce training for at least 1 month. No racing for 2 months.

From Noakes 1991.

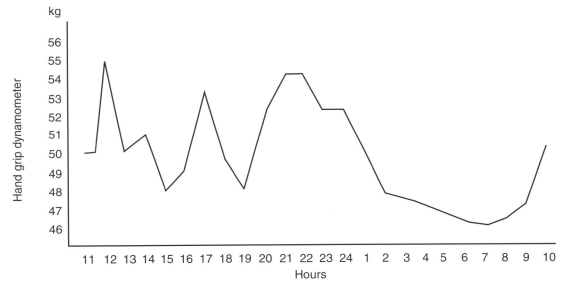

Figure 5.8 Variations of CNS excitability over a 24-hour span
(data based on handgrip dynamometer techniques from Ozolin 1971)

training. In such a case, a physician should examine the athlete, a nutritionist should check the diet, and the coach should decrease the training load until the athlete fully recovers.

The chart that monitors psychological traits and appetite shows a high correlation between them. A high degree of fatigue disturbs sleeping patterns and depreciates appetite. These correlate with tiredness and training and competitive willingness. All decrease with fatigue or overtraining.

The chart on page 144 shows a real situation of an athlete training for the Olympic Games. By adequately changing the training program and improving the diet, including supplements, the athlete recuperated and competed as expected in the games, finishing in fourth place.

These proposed simple, practical charts for monitoring training are useful for the serious athlete. You can prevent many undesirable situations by completing them every day and having a coach examine them before every training session. It may help an athlete avoid overtraining.

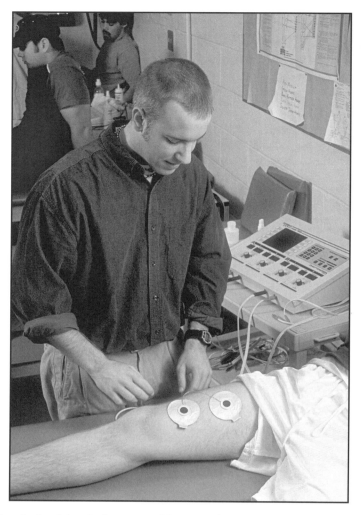

Consult a trained physician before an athlete receives treatment on traumatized tissue

Treatment of Overtraining

The treatment of overtraining is linked with two nervous processes, excitation and inhibition (Israel 1976). Once you identify overtraining, reduce or cease training immediately, irrespective of the cause. If overtraining is severe, in addition to complete training abstinence, the athlete should also avoid negative social stimuli. Consult a physician and training specialist to determine the cause. In mild overtraining, when you need only reduce training, the coach should not expose the athlete to any testing or competitions. Consequently, completely eliminate high-intensity stimuli from both training and lifestyle. Consider active rest (mild exercise in a completely different environment) even for an athlete in a severe overtraining state, because an abrupt interruption of training may be harmful to an athlete accustomed to extensive physical involvement (Hackney et al. 1990; Hollmann et al. 1993).

Use specific regeneration techniques to enhance recovery. Dietary modification might also be appropriate. Increasing or manipulating one or more macronutrients and micronutrients can influence regeneration. For example, extra CHOs with proteins and essential fats elevate nighttime melatonin levels, which in turn can provide the athlete with optimal rest (Gazzah et al. 1993) and assist in regenerating exercise-induced muscle damage (Horrobin 1994; James 1996; Wu 1996). In all cases, strict adherence to the various forms of regeneration will be fundamental to bringing the athlete out of this undesirable training state.

In sympathetic overtraining, use regeneration techniques to overcome excitation (table 5.10). Use different recovery methods to overcome inhibition processes or parasympathetic overtraining.

TABLE 5.10 Techniques for Treating Overtraining

To overcome the excitation processes (sympathetic overtraining)	To overcome the inhibition processes (parasympathetic overtraining)
Special diet	Special diet
Stimulate appetite through alkaline foods (milk, fruit, fresh vegetables)	Favor acidifying foods (cheese, meat, cake, eggs)
Avoid stimulatory substances (coffee), small quantities of alcohol permitted	Vitamins (B group and C)
Increased quantities of vitamins (B group)	
Physiotherapy	Physiotherapy
Outdoor swimming	Alternate hot and cold showers
Bathing 15-20 min at 35°-37° (but no sauna)	Sauna at medium temperature, alternated with short, cold showers
Cold showers in the morning and brisk toweling	Intensive massage
Light and rhythmical exercises	Active movements
Climatic therapy	Climatic therapy
Moderate ultraviolet irradiations, but avoid intense sun radiations	Sea and sea-level altitude
Change the environment, if possible alternate areas of various altitudes	Preferred bracing climate
Chemotherapy	
Sedatives	
Vitamins (C, D, E, A)	
Beta-carotene	

Based on information from Israel 1963, Ozolin 1971, and Bucur and Birjega 1973.

Summary of Major Concepts

Traditionally, coaches see their jobs as how to better train athletes. Although they often do many elements of training well, most coaches neglect recovery methods and techniques yet recovery techniques are as important as training. The faster athletes can recover following training or competition, the more work they can do. Increased training levels normally translate into performance improvement. Everyone involved in training should therefore change their mentality regarding the importance of rest and recovery.

Many methods can be used to recover from the fatigue of training and competition. The better you understand and use these techniques, the better you control fatigue and prevent overtraining.

Many athletes and training specialists are, and rightfully so, concerned about the negative effects of overtraining on athletic performance. When signs of overtraining appear, they pay maximum attention to the treatment technique but not to its *prevention*. To prevent overtraining, pay maximum attention to supercompensation, the restoration time of energy fuels used in your sport, and methods of monitoring training. Later in this book you will learn about planning and how to plan training to avoid critical levels of fatigue and overtraining.

Name _____ Month _____

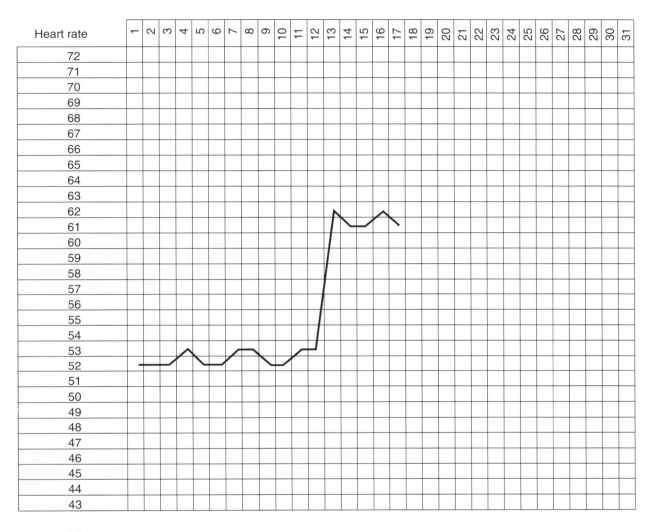

Heart rate

| | 1 | 2 | 3 | 4 | 5 | 6 | 7 | 8 | 9 | 10 | 11 | 12 | 13 | 14 | 15 | 16 | 17 | 18 | 19 | 20 | 21 | 22 | 23 | 24 | 25 | 26 | 27 | 28 | 29 | 30 | 31 |

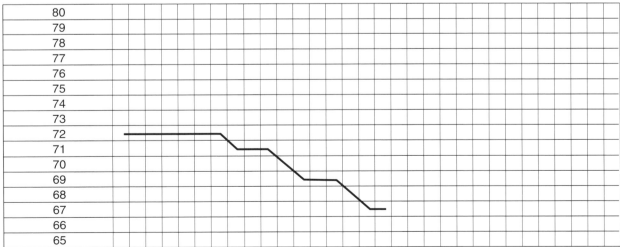

Weight

Name _____   Month _____

Length of sleep	1	2	3	4	5	6	7	8	9	10	11	12	13	14	15	16	17	18	19	20	21	22	23	24	25	26	27	28	29	30	31
12+ hours																															
11																															
10																															
9																															
8																															
7																															
6																															
5																															
4																															
No sleep at all																															

Quality of sleep

Very deep	
Normal	
Restless	
Bad with breaks	
Not at all	

Tiredness sensation

Very rested	
Normal	
Tired	
Very tired	
Painful tiredness	

Training willingness

Very deep	
Good	
Poor	
Unwilling	
Did not train	

Appetite

Very good	
Good	
Poor	
Eat because should	
Did not eat	

Competitive willingness

High	
Average	
Low	
Not at all	

Muscle Soreness

No pain	
Little pain	
Moderate pain	
Severe pain	

144

Name ——————————————————————————— Month ———————————————————

Heart rate	1	2	3	4	5	6	7	8	9	10	11	12	13	14	15	16	17	18	19	20	21	22	23	24	25	26	27	28	29	30	31

Weight

Name _____   Month _____

Length of sleep	1	2	3	4	5	6	7	8	9	10	11	12	13	14	15	16	17	18	19	20	21	22	23	24	25	26	27	28	29	30	31
12+ hours																															
11																															
10																															
9																															
8																															
7																															
6																															
5																															
4																															
No sleep at all																															

Quality of Sleep																															
Very deep																															
Normal																															
Restless																															
Bad with breaks																															
Not at all																															

Tiredness sensation																															
Very rested																															
Normal																															
Tired																															
Very tired																															
Painful tiredness																															

Training willingness																															
Very deep																															
Good																															
Poor																															
Unwilling																															
Did not train																															

Appetite																															
Very good																															
Good																															
Poor																															
Eat because should																															
Did not eat																															

Competitive willingness																															
High																															
Average																															
Low																															
Not at all																															

Muscle soreness																															
No pain																															
Little pain																															
Moderate pain																															
Severe pain																															

PART II

Periodization Training

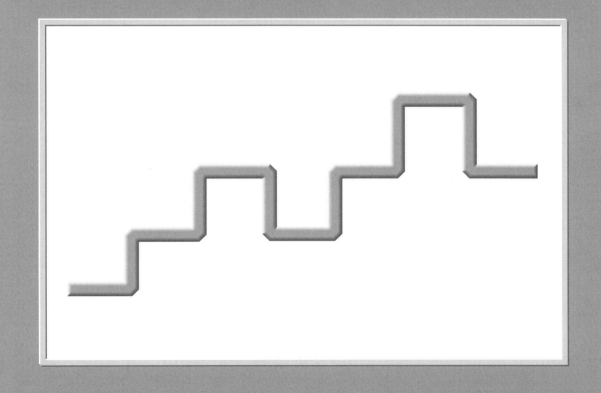

Chapter 6

Workout Planning

Planning is not a novelty, and neither is it a Russian discovery as some enthusiasts proclaim. In simple forms, planning has existed since the ancient Olympic Games. Flavius Philostratus (A.D. 170-245) wrote several manuals on the planning and training of the Greek Olympians, most of which have been destroyed. His surviving manuals, *Handbook for the Athletics Coach* and *Gymnasticus*, teach how to train for competitions including the importance of recovery. He also mentioned the type of knowledge a coach should have: "He should be a psychiatrist with considerable knowledge in anatomy and heritage."

This is why I have said that planning is not a novelty. The expertise we have represents the progress from ancient times to today. Many authors, sport scientists, and coaches from several nations have contributed to this evolution. They all deserve credit for what we know now.

Importance of Planning

The planning process is a methodical, scientific procedure to help athletes achieve high levels of training and performance. It is the most important tool a coach has in conducting a well-organized training program. A coach is only as efficient as his or her organization and planning.

An organized, planned training program eliminates the random, aimless approach still used in some sports. A well-structured plan gives guidance, direction, and scope to everything done. Good planning removes any relevance from those who still proclaim "no pain no gain" and "intensity all the way." Replace such rhetorical claims with intelligent training. Why? Because planning is the art of using science to structure a training program! In training nothing happens by accident, but by design.

In training, you don't plan work, you plan the physiological reaction to your training plan. You should not be concerned with what you plan for today or tomorrow. Rather you should predict what the body's reaction will be to what you plan. Will the athlete be maximally challenged and be in a state of fatigue? Will he or she replenish the energy sources and supercompensate for the next training session? View the process of planning as a medium for manipulating the athlete's training, according to the specifics of the sport, to reach the highest performance possible.

A coach must have a high level of professional expertise and experience for planning endeavors to be effective. A plan reflects methodical inference and knowledge in all areas of physical education. It must consider the athlete's potential and rate of development, and the facilities and equipment available. A training plan must be objectively based on the athlete's performance in tests or competitions, progress in all training factors, and consider the competition schedule. A training plan has to be simple, suggestive, and flexible, so you can modify it according to the athlete's rate of progress and your improvement in methodical knowledge.

Planning Requirements

When an instructor develops a training plan, he or she must follow certain requirements, the foundation of the planning process.

Long-Term Plans

Blend long-term plans with current plans. A long-term plan is an important requirement of the training process. The coach uses it as an objective means to guide the athlete's training. Such a plan requires that skills and performance are continuously improving. The coach must consider the improvement rate, foresee levels the athlete will achieve, and direct the athlete's programs toward these objectives. After forecasting future developments, the coach elaborates the appropriate means to accomplish the athlete's performance and training objectives.

A coach solves individual problems, physical and psychological

The objectives of a long-term plan rely on the parameters and content of training included in the annual plan's macro- and microcycles, providing a continuity between the present and future. This continuity also reflects the index of performance and test standards, which the coach must plan and achieve progressively. This approach, although desirable for elite athletes, is especially important for children and teenagers as a guarantee of appropriate guidance.

Establish and Emphasize the Main Training Factor

During training, always emphasize equally, or according to the athlete's needs, each training factor and the underlying importance of volume or intensity. However development is seldom proportional. Often an athlete will improve more rapidly in skill mastery or in certain biomotor abilities. During competitions and testing, assess the athlete's improvement and compare the achieved levels with the objectives planned for that phase. This process allows conclusions about gains in a training factor, and more important, areas in which the athlete did not gain or may have lost ability. Training factors that fall behind the mean development rate are the weakest links in training. After establishing the weakest links, readjust the training program, shifting more emphasis to the appropriate areas in the following training phases. Often technical improvements (i.e., in gymnastics) depend on a high degree of strength development. Should a coach realize that a gymnast cannot perform a technical element because of inadequate strength, then emphasize strength (the weakest link) in the following phase of training.

Periodical Achievement of Plans

At the beginning of every training phase, note the performance objectives or test standards to achieve during or at the end of that cycle. Accomplish the objectives of each phase periodically. This indicates a gradual increase of training level and performance ability and ensures the continuity of a sound, qualitative training program.

Establishing performance objectives, training factors, and test standards for each training phase eliminates the random approach still used. It is not uncommon to find some coaches ignoring this important component of an organized training program, proceeding to dramatically increase the volume or intensity of training. Such actions may decrease an athlete's performance ability and well-being. Coaches must, therefore, employ the concept of periodical achievement and strive for set standards or performance objectives to maximize the potential for success.

Types of Training Plans

A coach's effectiveness reflects his or her ability to organize and employ appropriate planning tools. An organized coach may use all or some of the following training plans: training lesson plan, microcycle, macrocycle, annual plan, and the quadrennial (4-year) plan. Longer plans (8-16 years) are often also necessary for children who aim for high performance.

Plan terminology is not the same all over the world. The terminology used in this book is shared by several countries, including Germany and a few other Anglo-Saxon countries. The Russians call an annual plan a macrocycle, and a training phase of 4 to 8 weeks a mesocycle. Because of my deep admiration for Philostratus' work on yearly planning, I have decided to use the term "annual plan" to describe a yearly training program.

In my opinion, the most important, practical, and functional plans are microcycles and annual plans. An instructor understanding these plans will be efficient. I do not emphasize the Russian messocycle because such a plan is a formality.

A coach usually begins by setting up long-term training parameters to achieve by the end of a long cycle, such as the quadrennial plan. In a quadrennial plan, the coach sets performance and training factor objectives for each year of the plan, then prepares the annual plan for the current year. The objectives of the annual plan and the competition schedule establish macro- and microcycles. The shortest term plan is the training lesson. Though this approach is methodically sound, for simplicity and progression I will reverse the description of the planning chapter, starting with the training lesson.

Training Lesson

Methodically, the training lesson is the main organizing tool used. The coach shares knowledge with the athletes, whose task it is to develop one or more training factors. In the methodology of training, training lessons are classified based on the tasks and form of the lesson.

Types of Lessons

Based on its tasks, training lessons types are learning, repetition, skill perfection, and assessment. The main task of a learning lesson is to acquire new skills or tactical maneuvers. The coach organizes this lesson simply: after the coach explains the objectives and warm-up, the remaining time is used for skill acquisition. The last few minutes will include remarks about whether the athlete achieved the task. A repetition lesson refers to further learning, during which the athletes try to improve their skills. Learning and repetition lessons are more frequent for beginners, whose limiting factor of improvement may be technique.

Plan training lessons for skill perfection only for athletes who have reached an accepted skill level. Such lessons prevail in high-performance training, in which athletes strive to master technique, tactical maneuvers, or physical preparation. According to your plan, conduct assessment lessons periodically. Either test athletes or have an exhibition competition to estimate the preparation level achieved in a training phase. The tasks of such a lesson may be to make final team selections, homogenize it, or simply test one or more training factors.

Forms of Lessons

The coach may organize training lessons in several forms to accommodate groups of athletes and individuals.

Group Lessons

The group lesson is organized for several athletes, not necessarily in team sports since athletes from individual sports may train together. Although such a lesson may disadvantage individualizing training, the main attributes are developing team spirit (effective especially before important competitions) and psychological qualities.

Individual Lessons

Individual lessons allow the coach to stress and solve individual physical or psychological problems. During such a lesson, the coach may rate the workload individually, adjust skills according to the athlete's characteristics, and give room for individual creativity. Such workouts are best during the preparatory phase; before competitions the coach may also use other forms.

Mixed Lessons

As the term suggests, mixed lessons combine group and individual lessons. During the first part, athletes warm-up together, after which, they pursue individual objectives. At the end of the lesson, athletes gather for a cool-down and the coach expresses his or her conclusions.

Free Training Lessons

Limit free training lessons almost exclusively to advanced athletes. Although such a lesson minimizes a coach's control over the athlete's training, it develops a common trust and confidence between coach and athlete. Such a lesson develops the athlete's conscientious participation in training and stimulates the individual's independence and maturity in solving training tasks which is extremely beneficial during competitions when the coach is not available.

Lessons commonly last 2 hours, although they could run 4 to 5 hours. There are short (30-90 minutes), medium (2-3 hours), and long (more than 3 hours) training lessons. Individual sports have the most length variety; team sports generally have greater consistency. The duration of a lesson depends on its task, type, kind of activity, and the athlete's physical preparation. For type of training, for example, during the competitive phase a sprinter trains approximately 1 hour and a marathon runner 3 hours. If training was broken two or three short training lessons per day, the sum of all lessons would be longer than 2 or 3 hours. The length of a lesson also depends on the repetitions the athlete performs and the length of the rest between repetitions.

Structure of Lessons

According to methodical and physio-psychological rationales, a training lesson is divided into smaller parts, allowing the coach and athlete to follow the principle of progressive increase and decrease of work. The basic structure consists of three or four parts. In three parts, the lesson is divided into preparation (warm-up), the body of the workout, and a conclusion. A four-part lesson includes an introduction, preparation, the body, and the conclusion.

Use of these structures depends on the training task and content, the training phase, and the athlete's training level. For group lessons during the preparatory phase and for beginners, the four-part structure is advisable. In the introduction, the coach explains training objectives and how to achieve them. The three-part method is used mostly for advanced athletes, especially during the competitive phase. Such athletes need less explanation and motivation; the coach can condense the introduction and preparation into one part. The only major difference between the two structures is that the four-part structure has an introduction.

Introduction

Begin training lessons by gathering the athletes, taking attendance (especially for team sports), and explaining the objectives. Detail how the objectives should be accomplished (i.e., the means and methods to use). Try to increase the athletes' motivation for the challenging portion of the lessons, because a higher degree of excitement may assist in fulfilling the objectives. Next, organize the team into small groups according to each athlete's specific goals. The introduction should last 3 to 5 minutes (often a little longer for beginners), depending on the length of the explanation. As the athletes' knowledge or expertise improves, you may reduce the duration.

The coach should always be well prepared. While explaining the objectives, use the training lesson plan or audiovisual aids. Post the plan so that the athletes become acquainted with it. Often a coach may have small handouts regarding portions of the plan, outlining what the athletes should do on their own. This enhances training organization and shares the responsibility of the lesson with the athletes. Similarly, the athletes may feel that the coach has confidence in their ability and maturity, assisting them to develop dependability and willpower.

Preparation

The warm-up is a physiological and psychological preparation for the training tasks to come. Asmussen and Boje (1945) were among the first to study the merits of a warm-up; following investigators often yielded questionable conclusions. Inconsistent investigation methods, type, duration, intensity, and the subject's levels of physical preparation makes comparing results difficult. Most investigations, however, seem to conclude that a warm-up facilitates performance, which is what practitioners have adhered to for a long time. Ozolin (1971) claims inertia and the efficiency of the athlete's functions may not elevate immediately. There is a certain time required to reach a state of high physiological efficiency. The purpose of a warm-up is to reach or approach this state before training or competing.

A warm-up raises body temperature, which appears to be a main factor facilitating performance (Asmussen and Boje 1945; Binkhorst, Hoofd, and Vissers 1977; Kaijser 1975; Martin et al. 1975). A warm-up stimulates CNS activity, which coordinates the athlete's systems (Gandelsman and Smirnov 1970), reduces the time of motor reaction, and improves coordination (Ozolin 1971), improving motor performance. During the warm-up, the athlete either self-motivates or is motivated and encouraged by the coach to overcome challenges and be psychologically ready. A good warm-up also helps prevent injuries.

Although the warm-up appears to be an integral whole, it should consist of two parts, the general and special warm-up. During the general warm-up, progressively increase the working capacity by increasing the functions of the body, following which the whole metabolic process occurs more rapidly. Blood flow increases, elevating body temperature. This stimulates the respiratory center, leading to an increase in oxygen supply. The increased oxygen and blood flow augment the working potential, assisting the athlete to perform more effectively.

Physical activity is the most common means of warm-up, in which the athlete performs several exercises, preferably wearing a dry, warm uniform. The most effective warm-up seems to be of low to moderate intensity of long duration. To determine optimal duration, measure the body temperature. Usually, however, the beginning of perspiration, which signifies an increase in internal body temperature, marks the termination of the warm-up. Most athletes perform an adequate warm-up, especially those in endurance sports, but figure skaters, divers, fencers, and ski jumpers often perform only a partial one.

The warm-up should be 20 to 30 minutes or longer, with the final 5 to 10 minutes dedicated to specific warm-up activities. Physical preparation, general

The most effective warm-ups are low to moderate intensity and of long duration

endurance, and environmental temperatures can influence the duration. For athletes in long-distance events, a 10-minute warm-up run is not demanding enough, but for a sprinter, a 10-minute warm-up run might suffice. The temperature of the environment affects warm-up duration, its intensity, and certainly the time required for the individual to perspire. Perspiration may commence after 12 to 13 minutes of uninterrupted work when the external environmental temperature is 8° Celsius, 9 minutes at 10° Celsius, 6-1/2 minutes at 14° Celsius, and 5-1/2 minutes at 16° Celsius. An intensive, uninterrupted warm-up may yield the same results after 2 or 3 minutes but may not ensure that functional potential has reached an adequate level.

Consider guidelines and progression during a warm-up. However, it is more important for the performance speed to be lower than that of training or competition and for most exercises to be specific (similar or identical to the skill the athlete will perform). Adjust the frequency and repetitions according to environmental temperature, specifics of the sport, and the athlete's level of physical preparation. A warm-up should always start with slow running of various forms (sideways, backward, but mostly forward). This accelerates blood flow, generating a higher temperature in the whole body as well as in the muscles. Such an approach is also suggested by Barnard, Gardner, Diaco, MacAlpern, and Hedman (1973), who claimed that strenuous exercises at the beginning of a warm-up may be associated with inadequate blood flow. Although Mathews and Fox (1976) share this reasoning, their recommended sequence starts with stretching, apparently contradicting this physiological reality. Stretching exercises would hardly be regarded as generating blood flow. The athlete should perform exercises that pull the muscle toward the end of the warm-up because a warm muscle stretches more easily.

Following 5 minutes of slow-paced running (skating, skiing), the athlete may perform calisthenic exercises starting with the neck, then moving toward the arms, shoulders, abdomen, legs, and back. By now the athlete may be ready for more strenuous exercises. The next group can be flexibility exercises, and if the sport requires it, the athlete can follow these by some light jumping or bounding exercises. A few short sprints (20-40 meters) may complete the whole range of exercises for general warm-up. Include resting and muscle relaxation (shaking the limbs) between all these exercises to ensure a quiet and untaxing warm-up. During this phase, athletes prepare psychologically for the main part of the lesson or competition by visualizing the skills and motivating themselves for the difficult aspects.

The objective of the special warm-up is to tune the athlete to the predominant type of work he or she will perform during the main part of the lesson. Tuning does not refer only to mental preparation or coordination of certain exercises. It also refers to CNS preparation and elevating the body's work capacity. The athlete realizes the latter by repeating technical elements and exercises of a certain intensity. Selecting exercises for the special warm-up depends strictly on the type of exercises the athlete will perform in the main part of the lesson or competition. A gymnast, wrestler, figure skater, thrower, or jumper may perform certain technical elements or parts of a routine. A swimmer, runner, or rower may repeat starts, or wind sprints, with rhythm and intensity close to what they will perform later. Using this approach for average-class athletes may reduce the intensity of the critical phase of the adaptation processes (accumulating lactic acid that can impede performance). This, in turn, would facilitate the second wind, a sudden feeling of release following the distress of the early part of a prolonged exercise or race.

Every athlete must perform the tuning phase of the warm-up, especially those whose sports require complex skills. The more complex the skill, the more repetitions of technical elements included. As a rule, the higher the volume of work or the longer the duration of the competition, the longer the warm-up should be (long-distance athletes warm up for 45 minutes). To warm up properly, the athlete requires good physical preparation and endurance. Only fit athletes can perform a 20- to 30-minute warm-up. Athletes use long warm-ups especially during the preparatory season to develop general physical preparation.

Active, natural athletic means and passive means, such as hot showers, heated sleeping bags, electric infrared rays, chemicals, and massage have been used elevate body temperature. Although there are claims that local heating, electrical means (Ozolin 1971), and massage (Bucur 1979) elevate body temperature, their effect on performance is limited. An active warm-up, sometimes preceded by local massage, seems to be the most beneficial for the athlete.

Main Body of the Lesson

The objectives of the training lesson are fulfilled during the main or third part. Following an adequate warm-up, an athlete learns skills and tactical maneuvers, develops biomotor abilities, and enhances psychological qualities.

The content of the main body depends on many factors, dominated by the degree of training, kind of sport, sex, age, and training phase. Interval training is widely used. The coach may stress technique and develop specific biomotor abilities and psychological traits at the same time. Lesson content for less advanced athletes should follow this succession:

1. First the athlete should exert movement to learn and perfect technical or tactical elements.
2. Next, the athlete should develop speed or coordination.
3. Then, develop strength.
4. Finally, develop endurance.

Include technical and tactical elements first in the main part of the training lesson because learning is more effective when the nerve cell is still rested. Should the athlete learn or perfect a technical element after speed, strength, or endurance exercises, fatigue would impede retention. The reference here is to CNS fatigue, a loss of the capacity to respond to a stimulus. For the composition or sequence of learning or perfecting technical and tactical elements, I advise that the athlete consolidate elements or skills acquired in previous lessons, perfect technical elements or skills of utmost importance for the sport, and apply skills in competition-like conditions.

If perfecting technique requires heavy, fatiguing work, the athlete may perform these exercises later in the lesson, usually following speed exercises. Use this approach in throwing events in track and field and in weightlifting.

Exercises to develop and perfect speed are usually high intensity, though short duration. Such exercises require the athlete's full potential; the athlete must perform them while fresh or relatively rested. This is why they have to precede strength and endurance exercises. When developing maximum speed is the lesson's main objective (i.e., sprinting or starts with full velocity in other sports), such exercises should follow the warm-up. When coordination is the prime objective, place such exercises at the beginning of the main body because a rested athlete can concentrate more easily on his or her tasks.

In an organized lesson, all strength-developing exercises follow movements for developing or perfecting technique and speed. It is not advisable to reverse this sequence because exercises employing heavy loads impair speed development in that particular lesson.

Plan exercises for developing general or specific endurance for the last part of the lesson. After these demanding exercises, an athlete would hardly be in a position to acquire skills or develop speed. Do not confuse this sequencing with practicing certain drills at the end of the main part with a certain level of fatigue, or occasionally even residual fatigue, typically for team sports. In this situation, the goal is not learning but training under specific game conditions.

Because learning is often the dominant objective, training lessons for beginning athletes should always follow this sequence: technical, speed, strength, endurance. The training sequence for elite athletes should be more flexible, although this sequence should prevail. Researchers discovered that a few strength exercises of a moderate load (40-50% of maximum) increase CNS excitability, enhancing the ability to perform speed work. Van Huss, Albrecht, Nelson, and Hagerman (1962) and Ozolin (1971) referred to this effect, although de Vries (1980) suggested that it may be psychological. Whatever the reason, explore the potential for each athlete and apply whatever yields the best results.

Plan the objectives to achieve during the main part before each training lesson. Do not plan more than two or three objectives per lesson, no matter how varied, because they would be difficult to accomplish effectively and would slow the athlete's improvement rate. Link objectives with the micro- and macrocycle plans, the athlete's performance level, and his or her potential. Although it may be advisable to plan objectives derived from different training factors (technical, tactical, physical, which also have a psychological component), choose them according to the needs of the sport and the athlete's abilities.

Following the achievement of daily objectives, plan 15 to 20 minutes of supplementary physical development, often called a conditioning program. Consider this for less-demanding training lessons that do not exhaust the athlete. Supplementary physical development must be specific in accordance with the dominant biomotor abilities of the sport and the athlete's needs. Usually, you should emphasize the limiting factor of the athlete's improvement rate.

Conclusion

Following strenuous work in the body of the training lesson, progressively decrease the workload to approach the athlete's initial biological and psychological rest state. At the end of the main part, most if not all the athlete's functions are operating at close to maximum capacity, and a progressive return to less demanding activity is necessary for two main reasons. First, an abrupt interruption of work may lead to negative physiological and psychological effects (dissatisfaction). Second, the cool-down enhances the recovery rate and rapidly decreases accumulated lactic acid in the blood. Unfortunately, most coaches and athletes do not organize this part of the lesson and fail to optimize the recovery processes. This means that the athlete may not maximize the rate of improvement and efficiency in training.

The structure of the fourth part is simple. Initially, the athlete decreases physiological functions. This can be assisted by 3 to 5 minutes of light exertion, depending on the nature of the sport. For cyclic sports, this takes the form of a low-intensity performance of the skill (run, walk, row, or ski). During this time, the presence of more oxygen than during a passive rest accelerates the elimination of burned foodstuff. For other sports (wrestling, boxing, gymnastics), often a short, low-intensity game of basketball or volleyball has good relaxation benefits. Organize such a game only when the athletes did not experience high emotions during the lesson.

As soon as body's functions decrease, athletes should relax the prime movers, the muscles mostly involved in performing the dominant skills. Only athletes who performed strength exercises during the main part of the lesson should do light stretching. Such exercises artificially bring the muscle heads close to the resting length, during which all metabolic functions are at their highest efficiency. By stretching the muscle, which normally takes 2 or 3 hours to reach its anatomical length following heavy strength training, athletes enhance their physiological recovery rate.

In the last few minutes of the fourth part of a training lesson, conclude whether the athletes achieved the objectives. Although the coach may not state the conclusions every time, they should be an integral part of a lesson. They may make important contributions to solving technical, tactical, physical, and psychological factors of training.

Duration for Each Part of a Lesson

An average training lesson lasts 2 hours (120 minutes), which I will use as a reference point for the duration of its parts. The parts of a lesson and the duration for each part, depend on many factors including age, sex, level of performance, experience, type and characteristics of the sport, and phase of training. Regard the following suggestions as a guideline.

For a four-part training lesson, the allotted time may be the following:

Introduction—5 minutes

Preparation—30 minutes

Main body—75 minutes

Conclusion—10 minutes

Total—120 minutes

The time alloted for a three-part lesson may be the following:
Preparation—25 to 35 minutes

Main body—75 to 85 minutes

Conclusion—10 minutes

Total—120 minutes

Fatigue and Methodical Guidelines for Lessons

After a demanding session, fatigue causes a decrease in working capacity. Recent research indicates several possible causes of physical fatigue, of which energy depletion and CNS fatigue are most commonly accepted. When under severe stress for long periods, the CNS reacts by increasing the amount of stimulation needed to elicit muscular contractions. An individual is less reactive to internal or external stimuli, which deregulates normal nervous function.

Each sport has different physiological characteristics that disproportionately stimulate the CNS causing uneven fatigue. Fatigue is often seen from the beginning of a lesson (when both O_2 intake and gaseous exchanges reach high levels), but the well-trained athlete can cope with it as long as it does not exceed his or her physiological or psychological limit. Only if these limits are exceeded will the body's working capacity decrease.

According to Gandelsman and Smirnov (1970), fatigue has two phases: *latent* and *evident* fatigue. During the early part of the lesson, functional changes occur although work productivity and energy production are not affected. All functions are elevated, and often the nervous system's excitability and metabolism are intense. If this is the case, the athlete has reached latent fatigue. If activity is prolonged at the same level, the athlete may maintain working potential for a while but at the expense of higher energy consumption. Should the athlete still maintain the same intensity to the point that he or she experiences a high degree of tiredness, evident fatigue results. Consequently, the athlete's ability to perform maximum work will progressively decrease.

Diminish latent fatigue by alternating rest intervals; however, do not forget that latent fatigue does have its benefits. Training under conditions of latent fatigue prepares athletes of cyclic-endurance sports for conditions that exist at the end of competitions and enables them to command a stronger finish. Evident fatigue is more easily overcome through an appropriate training lesson conclusion and recovery techniques.

The power with which a stimulus acts on the CNS is determined not only by its intensity and duration but also by its novelty. New, unfamiliar elements stimulate the CNS to a greater degree, intensifying the excitation of the nervous centers and increasing muscular work and energy consumption. This places additional stress on cardiorespiratory functions. During the learning and training processes, therefore, carefully apply a systematic and methodical approach. Nervous system activities require limitations be set on tasks and objectives in a training lesson. Usually, the more intense an activity, the more difficult even simple problems become. Exercises or activities requiring maximum effort necessitate a simply organized training lesson. Habitually, such a lesson would have an adequate warm-up and conclusion, and the athlete would maximally use working and will-power capacities during the main part. On the other hand, if the training lesson is of lesser intensity, the coach could plan two or even three objectives, provided that each focused on a different training factor (i.e., perfecting a technical element, incorporating it into the team's tactical scheme, and doing tactical drills with a high endurance component).

Design training lessons to alternate between exercises aimed at achieving each training objective and between muscle groups. The former minimizes monotony; the latter allows regeneration. In addition, alternation elevates the total volume of low-intensity training lessons. High-intensity training should have a restricted number of objectives. It appears, therefore, that the intensity of training influences the duration of the lesson and its structure. Furthermore, all three parameters influence the physiological changes in an athlete. The easiest way to discover the athlete's reaction to a stimulus is by measuring heart rate. Heart rate varies from the beginning until the end. Its dynamics are a function of the intensity, duration, and character of a stimulus, which when represented in a graph, illustrate the physiological curve of a training lesson (figure 6.1). The heart rate curve often elevates slightly from the normal biological rate an athlete experiences before the lesson, mostly due to psychological factors (excitation, challenge).

Cardiovascular function rises progressively during preparation. The shape of the curve fluctuates during the main body, according to the rate of training stimuli, intensity, duration, and rest intervals. Heart rate drops progressively during the conclusion, illustrating a decrease in the athlete's workload. In the postlesson phase, it is slightly higher than the normal biological level because the body's functions need time to completely recover. Recovery rate and duration are direct functions of the lesson's intensity and the athlete's fatigue and physical preparation.

Supplementary Training Lessons

When every athlete is trying to maximize free time for training, supplementary training lessons are one of the most effective ways of elevating training volume and, thus, improving the preparation level. Supplementary individual training

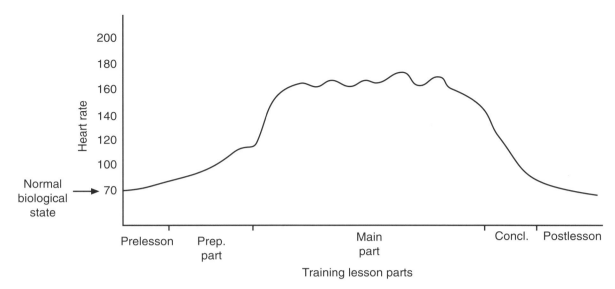

Figure 6.1 Dynamics of the physiological curve of the training lesson

lessons and special group training lessons (i.e., camp) are often organized for the early morning, before school or work. The athlete usually trains before breakfast; however, if the duration exceeds 30 minutes then a small quantity of light food may be desirable. The duration of these lessons varies depending on each athlete's time. If an athlete can afford 30 to 60 minutes each day and accumulate 150 to 300 hours of extra training a year, this volume can influence his or her degree of training and athletic potential.

These training lessons are performed at home, indoors or outdoors. However, they must be part of the training plan the coach makes. The coach suggests the content and dosage of each lesson according to the athlete's objectives, weaknesses, and training phase. Supplementary training lessons of 20 to 40 minutes may improve an athlete's general endurance, general or specific flexibility, and even general or specific strength in certain muscle groups. One goal might be to improve the athlete's weaknesses to accelerate the improvement of certain abilities.

A basic, supplementary lesson consists of three parts, with the time allotted per part as follows: (1) preparation 5 to 10 minutes, (2) main 20 to 45 minutes, and (3) conclusion 5 minutes, which amounts to 30 to 60 minutes. The goal and format of each part follow the same concept as regular training lessons. The main part focuses on no more than two objectives. One objective only is the most realistic and desirable considering the time available.

Sample Training Plan

Training lesson plan format should be simple and functional, meaning that the plan has to be an important tool for the coach's training endeavors. The date and location are at the top left side, and objectives and equipment for the lessons are on the right side (figure 6.2). The coach will briefly specify all exercises or drills to use in each part of the lesson in the first column. The second column shows the dosage; duration of each part, exercise, or drill; distance; and number of repetitions per exercise. You can also specify the intensity and load in this column (figure 6.2, part III). The formation column is for the coach, especially in team sports, to draw the most difficult drills the athletes will perform during the lesson. The last column is for brief notes, remarks that the coach wants to emphasize throughout the lesson.

The length of a plan differs from sport to sport according to the coach's experience. Inexperienced coaches should be as specific as possible, writing down everything they intend to do with the athletes. They must then follow the plan closely to ensure that they miss nothing. A general training lesson outline will suffice for experienced coaches.

The coach can briefly present the plan to the athletes during the introduction. If the coach chooses and the facilities permit it, he or she can post the plan in advance, enabling the athletes to become acquainted with it before training. One advantage of such an approach is that the athletes have time to prepare psychologically for any demanding lessons.

Daily Cycle of Athletic Training

The daily training schedule is heavy, especially in a camp situation. To maximize time, organize the daily schedule carefully and effectively. Athletes want to train hard but also need free time for their own purposes, relaxation, and fun. Training programs and other activities from the daily regimen must be extremely well organized and adhered to. Following are activities for three and four daily training lessons, applicable to elite athletes in a camp situation.

In a camp situation, some coaches and athletes prefer only two lessons per day of longer duration, often 3 to 4 hours. However, based on personal experi-

A daily program with three training lessons:	
6:30	wake up
7:00-8:00	first training lesson (low intensity)
8:30-9:00	breakfast
9:00-10:00	rest
10:00-12:00	second training lesson
12:00-13:00	recovery techniques and rest
13:00-14:00	lunch
14:00-16:00	rest
16:00-18:00	third training lesson
18:00-19:00	recovery techniques and rest
19:00-19:30	dinner
19:30-22:00	free program
22:00	sleep

A daily program with four training lessons:	
6:30	wake up
7:00-8:00	first training lesson
8:30-9:00	breakfast
9:00-10:00	rest
10:00-12:00	second training lesson
12:00-13:00	recovery techniques and rest
13:00-14:00	lunch
14:00-16:00	rest
16:00-17:30	third training lesson
17:30-18:30	recovery techniques and rest
18:30-19:30	fourth training lesson
19:30-20:00	recovery techniques
20:00-20:30	dinner
20:30-22:00	free program
22:00	sleep

Coach: _____

Training lesson plan no. 148

Date   June 14th _____

Place   York Stadium

Objectives   Perfect the start; specific _____
endurance, power training.
Equipment   Starting block, barbells

Part	Exercises	Dosage	Formations	Notes
I	- Describe the lesson's objectives and how to achieve them - What the athletes should stress during training.	3 min		John: pay attention to arm work
II	- Warm-up	20 min		Rita: put on two warm-up suits
	- Jogging	1200m		
	- Calisthenics - Arm rotations	8x (8 times)		
	- Upper body rotations	12x		
	- Hip flexibility	8-10x		Stress hip flexibility
	- Ankle flexibility	8-10x		
	- Bounding exercises	4 x 20m		Stress the weak leg
	- Wind sprints	4 x 40-60m		
III	- Starts	12 x 30m Rest I = 2 min		Stress arm work
	- Specific endurance	8 x 120m 3/4 (14 s)		Maintain a constant velocity throughout all repetitions
	- Power training	$\dfrac{60\text{kg}}{8\text{-}10\text{ reps}}$ 4 sets		Between exercises relax arms and legs
	- Jogging	800m		Light and relaxing
	- Massage	5 min		Work with a partner

Figure 6.2   Training lesson plan for a sprinter

ence and considering the practice most East European specialists use, it seems that the breakdown of 5 to 6 hours of training into 3 or 4 training lessons is more effective. Training lessons of longer than 2-1/2 hours seem to be less effective because of acquired fatigue, which hinders learning and limits the development of certain biomotor abilities.

Summary of Major Concepts

This chapter (and chapters 7 through 9 to follow) emphasize the benefits of organization and planning. Training effectiveness depends on planning, from a workout to a long-term plan.

Although a workout plan is not difficult, a well-structured plan can help you reach all your goals. The warm-up is important, though often neglected or superficially done. In preparing athletes for a workout, nothing replaces a good, properly sequenced warm-up. Try two or three types of warm-ups, but never de-emphasize the cardiorespiratory system, before choosing the one that is most effective and works best for your athletes.

Equally important for training effectiveness is to always set goals for the workout, and constantly tell your athletes whether they achieved these objectives. The feedback you give is essential for training motivation, especially if you turn everything into a positive experience.

Chapter 7

Training Cycles

Customarily, training cycles refer to short-term plans such as micro- and macrocycles. Some authors complicate the study of micro- and macrocycles by suggesting 8 or more types. In this chapter, I simplify planning by concentrating on 5 types (with some variation) of micro- and macrocycles: developmental, shock, regeneration, competition, and tapering.

Microcycle

The term microcycle is rooted in Greek and Latin. In Greek, *mikros* means small, and in Latin, *cyclus* refers to a sequence of phenomena that succeeds regularly. In training methodology, microcycle refers to a weekly training program that succeeds within an annual program, according to the needs of peaking for the main objective (competition) of the year.

In training, a microcycle is probably the most important, functional tool of planning because its structure and content determine the quality of the training process. Not all training lessons of a single microcycle are of the same nature. They alternate according to objectives, volume, intensity, and methods, any of which may dominate a training phase. Furthermore, physiological and psychological demands on an athlete cannot be steady; they must change depending on the working capacity, needs of recovery and regeneration, and the competition schedule.

Constructing Microcycles

As a short-term plan, the microcycle is not unique. Philostratus, the ancient Greek scholar, proposed a short-term plan he called the Tetra System, a 4-day training cycle in this order:

Day 1 Prepare the athlete with a short and energetic program.

Day 2 Exercise intensely.

Day 3 Relax to revive the activity.

Day 4 Perform moderate exercise.

Philostratus suggested that the athletes repeat the tetrads continually. This happened in ancient times. How far have we come? Read on.

The main criteria for a microcycle comes from the general training goal, improving training factors and elevating athletic performance. Improving abilities closely relates to changes in various training factors, so that a correct mix prevails. The efficiency of a lesson to develop a technical element is a function of the type and content of the training performed previously. If the former training lesson focused on endurance or if it used intense stimuli, the following lesson should not aim at perfecting technique since there will probably not be adequate time for the athlete, and particularly the CNS, to recover. The reverse sequence seems to be more effective, in which developing endurance follows a training lesson for developing speed.

The criteria for sequencing training lessons in a microcycle includes the dominant factors or biomotor abilities specific to the sport. According to Ozolin (1971) the optimal sequence is:

- Learn and perfect technique with medium intensity.
- Perfect technique at submaximum and maximum intensity.
- Develop speed of short duration (up to the limit).
- Develop anaerobic endurance.
- Improve strength using a load of 90 to 100% of your maximum.
- Develop muscular endurance using medium and low loads.
- Develop muscular endurance with high and maximum intensity.

- Develop cardiorespiratory endurance with maximum intensity.
- Develop cardiorespiratory endurance with moderate intensity.

Consider this sequence a general guide, and apply it according to the specifics of the sport and the athlete's training needs. Intensity increases progressively and concludes in the middle section; endurance development prevails toward the end.

This sequence has strong similarities to what I advocate during the main part of the training lesson: (a) address technique or tactical elements, (b) develop speed or power, (c) develop strength, and (d) develop general endurance.

Constructing a Microcycle

Often, an athlete must repeat training lessons of similar objectives and content two or three times during a microcycle to have a training effect. Repetition is essential for learning a technical element or developing a biomotor ability. The Romans used to say *repetitia mater studiorum est*, "repetition is the mother of study." However, the athlete must repeat exercises to develop biomotor abilities with varying frequencies during a microcycle. You develop better general endurance, flexibility, or strength for a large group of muscles when you repeat the lessons every second day. Strength training large muscle groups has cardiovascular components, which are more exhaustive and require a longer recovery than localized training for smaller muscle groups. For developing specific endurance of submaximum intensity, three training lessons per week will suffice. However, for specific endurance of maximum intensity during the competitive phase, plan training lessons twice a week, and dedicate the remaining days to lower intensity training. Use two lessons per week to maintain strength, flexibility, and speed. Finally, two or three times per week seems to be optimal for bounding exercises that develop leg power and exercises for speed performance under strenuous conditions such as snow or sand.

Alternate work with regeneration when planning a microcycle. Plan work to an athlete's limits no more than twice a week; plan active rest of low-intensity relaxation once a week. The days for active rest should follow a lesson that demands maximum effort from an athlete.

Repetition may also be valid for microcycles themselves, especially during the preparatory phase. Throughout a macrocycle, you can repeat a microcycle of the same nature (i.e., content and methods) two or three times, following which you may observe a qualitative improvement based on the athlete's adaptation. The nature of the microcycle can be constant, but the volume and intensity of training should increase for each cycle, especially for advanced athletes.

Structural Considerations

Although an organized coach would use long-term plans to extract macro- and microcycle plans, he or she should not prepare a detailed training program more than two microcycles into the future. It is difficult to foresee the dynamics of improvement. The coach could compile an athlete's macrocycle and be flexible in applying it, considering that the last microcycle would be a guideline for making necessary alterations according to the improvement rate.

Consider many factors in constructing a microcycle, among which these are primary:

- Set the microcycle's objectives, especially for the dominant training factors.

- Set the training demand (number of lessons, volume, intensity, and complexity).
- Set the level of intensity for the microcycle—how many peaks and alternations with less intensive training lessons.
- Decide the character of training, referring to the kind of methods and means of training to use per lesson.
- Set training or competition days (if applicable).
- Start a microcycle with low- or medium-intensity training lessons and progress with increasing intensity.
- Before an important competition, use a microcycle with one peak only, which the athlete should reach 3 to 5 days before the competition.

Along with these factors, determine whether an athlete should perform one or more training lessons per day, and the time and content of each lesson. Precede each microcycle with a short meeting between coach and athlete.

During the meeting, discuss objectives for each training factor; performance standards to reach during the microcycle; methods to achieve the objectives; the program details, such as time of each lesson, volume and intensity of training, difficulty and priority of lessons; special notes for individual athletes; and miscellaneous information. If the microcycle ends with a competition, give athletes all the details and motivate them to meet goals for the competition.

Following the last training lesson of a microcycle, conclude with a short meeting. Analyze whether the athletes achieved the objectives and negative and positive aspects of the athletes' training behavior and motivation. Athletes comment on the past microcycle. Outline changes to consider for the future that may appear in the following microcycle.

Meetings where everything is directly and honestly stated are a practical communication vehicle. Coaches and athletes learn about their athletic endeavors, and help each other make changes for future athletic improvements.

Classifying Microcycles

Use these criteria in structuring microcycles; however, particular circumstances could lead to variations. Additionally, the dynamics of a microcycle depend on the training phase and the priority of training factors (whether technical or physical factors prevail). More importantly, they must reflect the athlete's progress and training capacity. Thus, the coach should eliminate standardization and rigidity. Flexibility allows for alterations that include information the coach gathers regarding the progress of athletes and opponents.

You can structure a microcycle according to the number of lessons per week. The number of lessons depends on the athlete's preparation and whether he or she follows a club program or participates in a camp. Training time availability plays an important role. Figure 7.1 illustrates a microcycle with eight training lessons that maximize the athlete's free time on the weekend. The T symbol suggests when training takes place, and the diagonal line illustrates a rest time.

In a camp situation or during holidays, alter the structure according to the time available and the athlete's training potential. Figure 7.2 illustrates a 3 + 1 structure that suggests the athlete train successively in 3 half days, with the fourth half day for rest.

Consider a slightly altered design for athletes whose training potential meets a more demanding microcycle. A 5 + 1 (five lessons followed by 1/2 day rest) and a 5 + 1 + 1 (five lessons plus 1/2 day rest, followed by 1/2 day of work) are illustrated by figures 7.3 and 7.4 respectively.

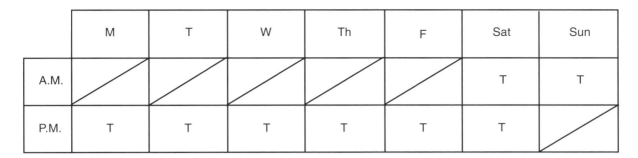

	M	T	W	Th	F	Sat	Sun
A.M.						T	T
P.M.	T	T	T	T	T	T	

Figure 7.1 Microcycle with 8 training lessons

	M	T	W	Th	F	Sat	Sun
A.M.	T	T	T	T	T	T	
P.M.	T		T		T		

Figure 7.2 Microcycle with a 3 + 1 structure

	M	T	W	Th	F	Sat	Sun
A.M.	T	T	T	T	T	T	
P.M.	T	T		T	T		

Figure 7.3 Microcycle with a 5 + 1 structure

	M	T	W	Th	F	Sat	Sun
A.M.	T	T	T	T	T	T	T
P.M.	T	T		T	T		

Figure 7.4 Microcycle with a 5 + 1 + 1 structure

The coach leads the analysis of performance and plans for changes

You may also structure a microcycle according to available time and the kind of training. Figure 7.5 illustrates a supplementary training lesson (ST) organized during early morning, with the main training of the day in the evening, followed by a weight-training (WT) program.

Training dynamics through a microcycle are not uniform, but vary intensity or training demand depending on the training character, type of microcycle, climate, and environmental temperature. For intensity dynamics, there is an alternation between high (H) or 90 to 100% of maximum, medium (M) or 80 to 90%, and low (L) or 50 to 80%, often followed by rest (R) on Sundays. An

	M	T	W	Th	F	Sat	Sun
7:00	ST	ST	ST	ST	ST	ST	ST
17:00	T	T	T	T	T	T	
19:00	WT	WT		WT	WT		

Figure 7.5 Microcycle illustrating various kinds of training

intensive microcycle may have one, two, or occasionally three peaks of high intensity.

Follow the principle of load progression when increasing intensity and planning the number of peaks of intensity and high training demand. Altitude, temperature, long travel, time difference, and climate also influence the intensity and number of peaks in the training program of a microcycle. In high altitudes or after long travel involving 5 to 8 hours of time difference, plan a peak only in the second microcycle; the first is for adaptation. In a hot, humid climate, plan one peak at the beginning of the week when the athlete has more vigor.

Methodically, you should plan only one peak in a microcycle for one of the three middle days of the week, or you could place two peaks toward the two ends of the cycle linked by 1 or 2 days of regeneration. An exception may occur when using model training, in which two peaks may occur on adjacent days to simulate a competitive situation.

Before the examples of microcyles, some comments are necessary. Although the examples refer to intensity, I really mean total training demand. In the past, I made microcycles to show how volume and intensity vary per week (other authors still do the same). However, contemporary sport is more complex, and one sport is very different from the others. Some sports are speed-power dominant (sprints, jumps, and throws in track and field; diving; ski jumping; fencing; and weightlifting); others are endurance dominant (mid- and long distance events in track, speed skating, and cross-country skiing). Some sports, such as most team sports, are too complex regarding skills and strategies to just refer to volume and intensity. Each sport has psychological and social stress, qualities often overlooked in planning. Therefore, figures 7.6 through 7.12 do not refer to volume and intensity as separate identites but rather to *total training demand.*

In the past, I also attempted to classify microcyles and training phases into 22 categories. I have found this to be ridiculously complicated and a source of great confusion to most of my audience. I have tried to simplify these examples as much as reasonably possible. The reader is invited to adapt the examples presented to specific individual situations and training needs.

The microcycle has to be functional and, therefore, as simple as possible. Figure 7.13 shows a plan from the competition phase. The plan should specify

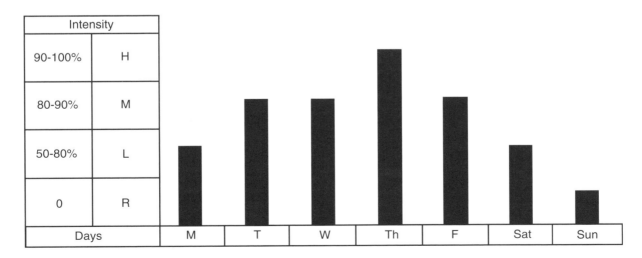

Figure 7.6 Microcycle with one peak

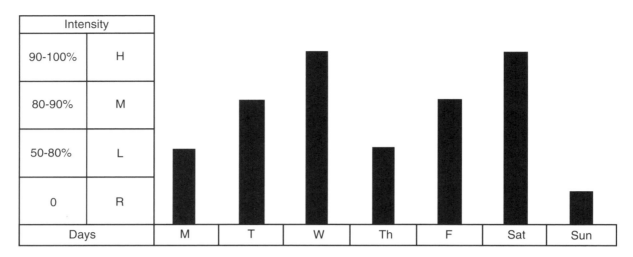

Figure 7.7 Two-peak microcycle

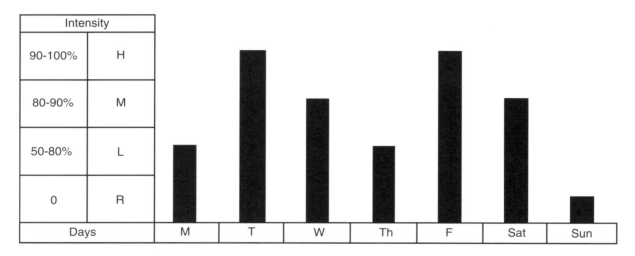

Figure 7.8 Another version of the two-peak microcycle

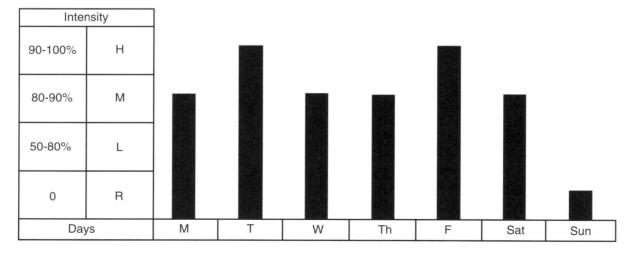

Figure 7.9 Two-peak microcycle with higher demand

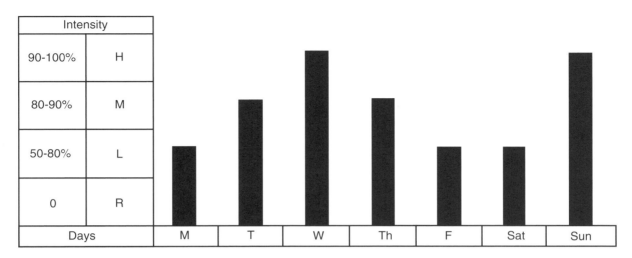

Figure 7.10 Two-peak microcycle, in which the second one is a competition, preceded by two unloading training lessons

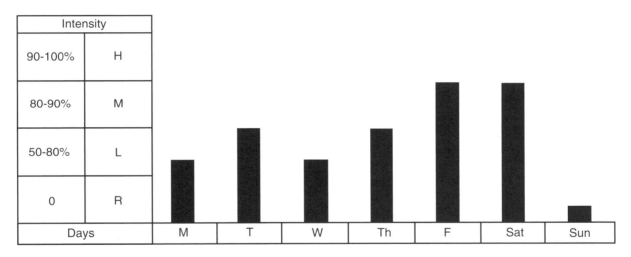

Figure 7.11 Two adjacent peaks of a model training microcycle

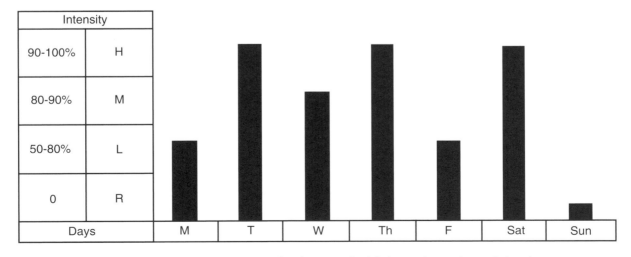

Figure 7.12 Three-peak microcycle alternated with lower intensity training lessons

Sport/event: Javelin

Microcycle No. 29

Date: 20.07-27.07

Objectives - Performance 67:00m
 - Perfect the rhythm of the last three
   strides under higher velocity conditions
 - Develop the ability to concentrate for the
   morning competition
 - Maintain leg and arm power

Time	M	T	W	Th	F	Sat	Sun
A.M. 10:00- 11:00	- Warm-up 15 min - Sprints $\frac{20, 30, 40m}{2/4; \ 3/4}$ 6	- Competition warm-up - 6 throws		Same as Tuesday	- Competition warm-up	- Competition 10.45	
P.M. 17:00- 19:30	- Warm-up 20 min - Sprints $\frac{30m}{4/4}$ 3 - Technique last 3 strides - 30 throws with baseball - 15 medicine ball throws - 2 x 30m bound	- Competition warm-up - 6 throws 4/4 - 15 throws 3/4 with short approach - 7 min spec. warm-up - 30 min wt. training - 5 min flex exercises - 10' game	Basketball game 2 x 15 min	Same as Monday	- Competition warm-up - 15 throws med. appr. - 15 min walk & throw at different spots in the grass - Special exercises for relaxation	Basketball game 2 x 15 min	

Figure 7.13   Competition phase microcycle plan

the date, objectives, and content for each training lesson. Express the content briefly, citing the major items of each training lesson.

The structure of a microcycle depends on the overall training objective, and as such is training phase dependent. From this point of view, we could classify microcycles as follows:

• *Developmental microcycle:* specific to the preparatory phase. The objective is to improve skills and develop specific biomotor abilities. Such cycles could have two or three peaks of high demand. Use either the step- or the flat-loading method, depending on the athlete's classification.

• *Shock microcycle:* suddenly increases training demands beyond those previously experienced. Typical for the preparatory phase, a cycle may have three or four peaks of high training demand. The objective is to break the ceiling of adaptation achieved in a previous phase, so the athlete pushes to a superior homeostasis. A microcycle is taxing physiologically and psychologically. You should not plan it immediately before competitions or testing dates. Also, because the shock microcycle results in a high level of fatigue, it is advisable to follow with a regeneration cycle.

• *Regeneration microcycle:* removes fatigue from the mind and body and restores energy. Low-intensity aerobic compensation training is best suited for these goals. An atmosphere of fun and enjoyment relax the mind in preparation for the taxing cycles to come. Organize regeneration microcycles following a series of important competitions or after a shock training cycle. These cycles restore the athlete's previous potential and prevent overtraining.

• *Peaking and unloading microcycles:* manipulate training volume and intensity to facilitate the best performance for a major competition. Visible decrease in training demands facilitates supercompensation before competition, setting up the body and mind for a good performance.

Quantifying Training

Instructors rarely use objective methods to alternate or plan training intensities. Programs often are based on subjective feelings, or in the best case, alternate heavy training days with easy days throughout the year. Followers of the "no pain, no gain" philosophy constantly overload athletes so that they are already overtrained by the time they participate in a major competition.

Few coaches quantify their training programs. In individual sports, such as athletics, swimming, and rowing, coaches quantify volume using mileage (i.e., the kilometers or miles per microcycle, macrocycle, or year of training). Track and field coaches usually use percentage of maximum speed or throwing or jumping distance to quantify intensity. In strength training, coaches use the percentage of maximum strength to quantify the training load (intensity). Training intensity or volume is seldom quantified in team sports, leaving one to wonder how coaches monitor their athletes' training.

Quantifying training is difficult and cannot be done specifically unless you make a training program for an athlete you know well. This program cannot and should not be used by anybody else, because background, genetics, and training environment are different. This is why I propose guidelines rather than presenting a specific program. When you understand these guidelines, you can put together a specific training program considering an athlete's potential. I feel strongly, however, about using mathematical symbols of intensity for planning a program. The number of times an athlete repeats a given intensity is an individual matter.

In all programs, the coach must change the training intensity throughout every microcycle. This enhances physiological adaptation to the load and regeneration after a demanding workout. A coach may identify three to five intensities based on the physiological characteristics of a sport. Each intensity should correlate with an activity rhythm; training type and method; and heart rate, plus or minus a few beats per minute. A specific ergogenesis, the percentage of each energy system used, must characterize each intensity level. Then the coach must plan the percentage of each intensity of training to use in the microcycle (table 7.1). Allocate the highest percentage of training to developing the dominant ability and the ergogenesis of the sport.

Tables 7.1 and 7.2 show this concept applied in a microcycle. In table 7.1, intensities 3 and 4 dominate and comprise 70% of the total training for the competitive phase of the annual training plan for rowing. The same two intensities dominate the example in table 7.2, which shows the link between the concept and its application in training.

If an objective means to quantify training does not exist, the coach may subjectively divide skills and training into more difficult; pace of game, race, or match; and less difficult. Simulate the pace of the game, race, or match with intensity number 2. Use this intensity for at least 50% of training time per week.

TABLE 7.1 Numeric Intensity Symbols for Rowing.

	INTENSITY SYMBOL				
	1	**2**	**3**	**4**	**5**
Characteristics of training	Endurance of speed	Endurance of strength	Specific (racing) endurance	Aerobic endurance of medium distances	Aerobic endurance of long distances
Rhythm of activity	Maximum	Very high, over the racing rate and rhythm	Rapid, the optimal rhythm and ratios	Moderate, lower than the the racing rhythm	Low
Stroke rate	>40	37-40	32-36	24-32	<24
Type of training	Starts and sprints up to 15 s; rest = 1.5 min	Repetitions of 250-1,000m; rest = 3-10 min	Races and controlled racing; interval training of 3-4 min; rest = 4-5 min	Long repetitions; variable rate and variable power; long-distance rowing intercalated by sprints of 30-60s	Long-distance (steady state) technique
Heart rate/min	>180	170-180	150-170	120-150	<120
Ergogenisis: Anaerobic Aerobic	80% 20%	65% 35%	25% 75%	15% 85%	5% 95%
Total training volume	10%		70%		20%

A better quantification is five intensities, in which 5 is a low intensity to use for compensation between other intensities or to facilitate super-compensation:

1. Maximum intensity
2. Higher than the pace of the game, race, or match
3. Pace of the game, race, or match
4. Lower than the pace of the game, race, or match
5. Compensation

In either case, the intensity higher than the pace of the game, race, or match is dominant anaerobic, and below that the activity will be dominant aerobic.

Whether using objective or subjective methods to quantify training, follow the correct sequence in planning a microcycle. First, plan the intensity values for each day of the week and write the number in the top right corner of the

TABLE 7.2 Numeric Intensity Symbols to Construct a Microcycle for Rowing

Training time	M	T	W	Th	F	Sat	Sun
9:30-11:30	4 24K Long reps 8 × 2K	3 20K I.T. 10 × 3 min R = 3 min	5 24K Aerobic endurance, long distance	4 24K Variable rate, variable power	3 20K I.T. 6 × 3 min R = 5 min	4 24K Aerobic endurance 3 × 1 min	
16:00-18:00	2 20K Model training 1 × 250 m 2 × 500 m 2 × 1,000 m 2 × 500 m 2 × 250 m Weight training, maximum strength	4 24K Variable rate, variable power Weight training, muscular endurance		1 20K Sprints, 500 total strokes R = 1.5 min Weight training, maximum strength	4 24K Long reps 3 × 6K R = 5 min Weight training, muscular endurance	2 20K Model training 1 × 250 m 6 × 1,000 m 2 × 500 m 2 × 250 m	

Note: The intensity symbols in the upper right-hand corner and the sum of the mileage for that ΣK=200.

box (see table 7.2). Choose intensity values for each day of the week so that you alternate intensities, type of work, or the energy systems (please refer to the next section of this chapter). Second, plan the training program. For the best results, have several variables of work for each intensity, irrespective of whether this refers to technical (T), tactical (TA), or physical training. You can plan one to three intensity symbols in each workout, which means that it is possible to train at least two types of work that tax the same energy system.

An example for a team sport will better illustrate this sequence. Table 7.3 is to quantify training, and table 7.4 is for planning intensity values. Note that in some days intensity 5 is between 1 and 2. The scope is compensation, aerobic activity placed between two anaerobic intensities.

Alternating Intensity and Energy Systems

Alternating training demands during a microcycle depends not only on the training phase (preparatory versus competitive), but also on the need to supercompensate an energy system. This will more correctly train an athlete and prevent exhaustion, staleness, and overtraining.

Most sports tax at least two, often all three, energy systems. Fuel restoration is different for each energy system. If a competition exhausts all energy reserves, then training intensity during the postcompetitive days is low, to remove fatigue and facilitate supercompensation.

TABLE 7.3 Quantification of Training for Team Sports.

	INTENSITY SYMBOL				
	1	**2**	**3**	**4**	**5**
Characteristics of training	T Complex skills TA Lactic acid tolerance training	T/TA Suicide drills	TA Max VO_2	T/TA Alactic	T skills Accuracy in passing, shooting, serving, etc.
Duration	30-60 s	20-30 s	3-5 min	5-15 s	10 min (several bouts)
Rest interval	3-5 min	3 min	2-3 min	1-2 min	1 min
Heart rate/min	>180	>180	>170	>170	120-150
Ergogenisis Anaerobic Aerobic	80 20	90 10	40 60	90 10	10 90
Total training volume	40%		20%	20%	20%

Note: During the rest interval, athletes can practice T skills of low intensity (e.g., shooting the basketball).

TABLE 7.4 How to Alternate Intensities During a Microcycle (Team Sport)

M	T	W	Th	F	Sat	Sun
3 1 5	2 5	4 5	3 5 2	4 1 5	5	

Note: Several intensities are planned for given day

Although alternating work and regeneration is important, do not apply it rigidly. During the preparatory phase, when the scope of training is to build a strong physiological foundation, the athlete may not experience supercompensation during two or three microcycles of high demand. Plan developmental and shock microcycles without allowing time to remove accumulated fatigue. As competition approaches, carefully alternate intensities.

Many sports are complex in both energy systems and technical and tactical skills used. Such sports tax the body and mind to refine a skill and to train speed, strength, and endurance. The question is how to plan a microcycle so that you train all the skills and biomotor abilities without overtraining. How can you make sure each energy system has time to restore its energy pools?

The first step is to classify all the skills and types of training according to the energy system they tax. Use the classification in table 7.5 as a guideline. You may make your own systematization of skills and biomotor abilities specific to the sport and use it to plan a microcycle. You can plan all skills and physical

TABLE 7.5 A Suggested Classification of Skills and Physical Training for Alternating Energy Systems

Anaerobic alactic	Anaerobic lactic	Aerobic
Technical skills – 1-10 s	Technical skills – 10-60 s	Technical skills, long duration
Tactical skills – 5-10 s	Tactical skills – 10-60 s	Tactical skills, medium and long duration
Maximum speed	Speed training – 10-60 s	Aerobic endurance
Power training, short duration	Power endurance	Muscle endurance, medium and long duration
Maximum strength – 1-2 sets long rest interval	Muscle endurance	

training under a given energy system in the same day, as they all tax the same energy source. However, for practical reasons, select only some of these training options for one day, leaving the balance for other days.

The second step is to plan a microcycle that alternates the training options from table 7.5 to restore the fuel taxed in a given day. When the athlete fully restores the fuel, supercompensation will occur, with all its physical and psychological benefits.

Before suggesting examples of microcycles that alternate the energy systems, it is important to mention that such training cycles are not planned throughout the annual plan. In deciding when to plan such a microcycle, remember that there are training weeks when you will want the athlete to fully supercompensate, and others when the athlete must push to exhaustion to challenge the adaptation level of a given training phase. Although you can alternate training options even in these microcycles, their volume and intensity are so high that supercompensation does not occur.

The bottom of each chart has a diagram showing the dynamics of supercompensation to give you a better understanding of how the body reacts to alternating energy systems. Training demand leads to fatigue some days and supercompensation in others. The planner manipulates training this way. Certain days challenge the athlete, resulting in a high level or a critical level of fatigue; other days purposefully have a light session to allow the athlete to supercompensate.

Team sports are so complex that the same training session can train multiple energy systems and elements involving the nervous system (technique, maximum speed, strength, and power). Monday's session could be neurological training, a day to tax the anaerobic alactic system (figure 7.14). Speed, power, and maximum strength of short duration rely on ATP-CP as fuel, so replenishment is fast. The athlete can follow Tuesday's training program without much physiological fatigue. However, longer repetitions on Monday may deplete the glycogen stores.

Under a traditional plan, in which the athlete exhausts all energy systems almost every day, demanding training on Monday could nearly deplete the glycogen stores. Under the system I propose, however, this could seldom be the case. Why? Tuesday has tactical and aerobic endurance. Both types of training rely on the aerobic system, facilitating faster replenishment of glycogen stores. The athlete alternates energy systems throughout the week. As

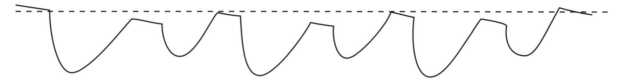

Monday	Tuesday	Wednesday	Thursday	Friday	Saturday	Sunday
- T	- TA	- T	- TA	- T	- T/TA	
- S	- O$_2$ End	- P/MxS	- O$_2$ End	- S	- O$_2$ End	
- P/MxS				- P/MxS		

Figure 7.14 Microcycle for a team sport, end of preparatory phase (T = technique, S = speed, P = power, MxS = maximum strength, TA = tactical training, and O$_2$ END = aerobic endurance)

shown by the supercompensation curve, each day that taxes the aerobic system results in supercompensation.

A similar training philosophy appears in figure 7.15. Speed and power are in the same day as power-endurance (P-E), which refers to repeating power exercises 10 to 25 times per set. Also, tempo training occurs on the days that tax the aerobic system. However, this example has two days of alactic training before a day that taxes the aerobic cardiorespiratory system.

Figure 7.16 considers a sport dominated by the aerobic system. Note that various training options tax the same energy system in the same day. Simultaneously, types of strength training specific to endurance sports occur with the energy system taxed in that particular day. Consequently, muscular-endurance (M-E), referring to many repetitions of strength exercises performed nonstop, follows aerobic endurance training. Alactic and lactic types of strength (MxS/P-E) fall either on days with anaerobic endurance or ergogenesis training.

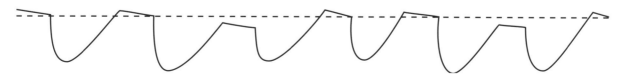

Monday	Tuesday	Wednesday	Thursday	Friday	Saturday	Sunday
- T	- S	- Tempo	- T	- S	- Tempo	
- MxS	- P/P-E	- TA	- MxS	- P	- TA	
					- P-E	

Figure 7.15 Alternating energy systems and types of strength training for a sport in which speed and power dominate (P-E = power endurance, Tempo = repetitions of 2-400m runs at 60-75% maximum velocity)

Monday	Tuesday	Wednesday	Thursday	Friday	Saturday	Sunday
- O$_2$ End	- AN End	- O$_2$ End	- Ergogenesis	- O$_2$ End	- O$_2$ End	
- M-E	- MxS/ P-E	- Comp	- P-E	- M-E	- O$_2$ Comp	

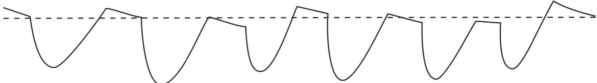

Figure 7.16   Alternating energy systems and types of strength training for a sport in which aerobic endurance dominates (M-E = muscle endurance, or strength training with many repetitions; AN END = anaerobic endurance; O$_2$ END COMP = aerobic endurance light to facilitate compensation/supercompensation)

Figure 7.17 shows another example for endurance sports. Anaerobic endurance is more important since the duration of the activity is 4 to 6 minutes. Days training anaerobic lactic are always followed by aerobic compensation. The scope of supercompensation is to quickly eliminate the lactic acid and facilitate a fast recovery. Days strong on anaerobic lactic training (Monday and Friday) are followed by days of aerobic compensation to reach supercompensation.

Recovery and Regeneration Microcycles

Performance improvement occurs during supercompensation! Such improvements are visible to the coach and felt by the athlete only after the regeneration days when the athlete achieves glycogen restoration and is in a state of supercompensation. To experience the positive physiological and psychological effects of supercompensation, the instructor must plan regeneration

Monday	Tuesday	Wednesday	Thursday	Friday	Saturday	Sunday
- O$_2$ End	- AN LACT	- O$_2$ Comp	- O$_2$ End	- AN LACT	- O$_2$ Comp	Off
- M	- O$_2$ Comp		- H	- AN THRE		or
				- O$_2$ Comp		O$_2$ Comp

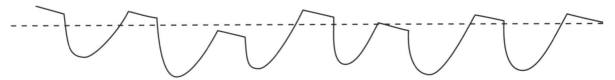

Figure 7.17   Endurance sport in which the duration of the event could be 4 to 6 minutes (M = medium demand; AN LACT = anaerobic lactic training; H = high demand; AN THRE = anaerobic threshold training, around 4mm of lactate)

microcycles at the end of a macrocycle, step 4. In order to facilitate regeneration and supercompensation, some of the training sessions of this cycle may differ from traditional methods.

The format of such a training session could be as follows:

1. Schedule a good, long warm-up (30 minutes).

2. Include 30 to 45 minutes of work completely different from the specifics of the sport (e.g., play soccer for fun). Training of a different kind helps athletes maintain conditioning and relax mentally. Athletes do not achieve this goal if they do not enjoy the activity.

3. Use regeneration activities such as:

   • 10 minutes hydrotherapy in a whirlpool or bathtub with water temperature at 35° to 40° Celsius (95° to 104° Fahrenheit). Hot water opens skin pores and cause perspiration, eliminating waste products from the body.

   • 10 minutes alternating between sauna and hot shower every minute. This relaxes the muscles and facilitates the elimination of waste products.

   • 10 to 15 minutes of massage (e.g., vibro-massage, below water massage or high jet shower).

   • Shower, alternating hot and cold water.

   • 15 to 20 minutes of mental relaxation in bed in a quiet room with soft music.

   • Drink alkaline liquids to buffer the acidic effects of training. Supper should be alkaline (no meat), rich in vitamins and minerals.

The regeneration microcycle plays an important role in the annual plan, especially during the competitive phase. Many sports have a series of competitions scheduled in a block of two or three microcycles. Such a heavy competition schedule results in a high state of fatigue. It would be a grave mistake to immediately start a demanding training program. At such times, I strongly recommend a regeneration and recovery microcycle.

Figure 7.18 illustrates a regeneration microcycle in which the scope of training is energy replenishment, removal of physiological and neurological fatigue, mental relaxation, and supercompensation toward the end of the cycle.

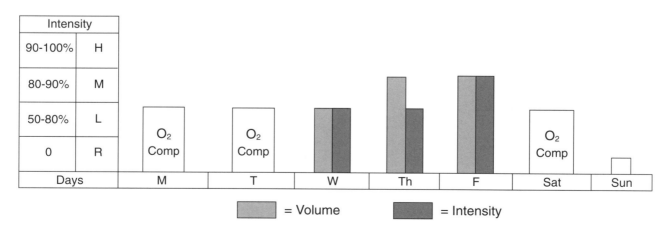

Figure 7.18 Regeneration microcycle, with low-intensity training and two days of medium demand

Microcycle Dynamics During the Competitive Phase

The competition schedule dictates microcycle structure and placement of necessary regeneration and unloading days. The dynamics of a microcycle have their own originality when weekly competitions occur for most of the competition phase as with some team sports, or several weeks in a row for individual sports (figure 7.19). After a weekend competition, athletes must take 1 or 2 days for regeneration. The planner must next decide how many days athletes need for unloading (U) to trigger supercompensation for the next competition. The middle of the week is the only time that you can use for training (a medium - or high-demand training session).

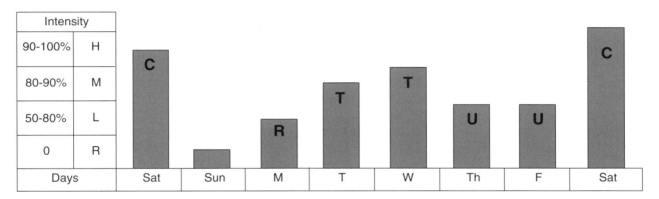

Figure 7.19 Microcycle for weekly competitions

You can alter the activity schedule when the opponent is weaker or of little importance. Such circumstances do not challenge athletes to the maximum so their fatigue level is lower. You can schedule training on Monday and use just one unloading day before competition. The net gain is 4 days of training time, with at least one of high demand. In figure 7.20, note Monday is a regeneration day with a light, short training session. Tuesday has light tactical (TA model) training planned. The training for Monday and Tuesday aims at facilitating supercompensation for the game Wednesday. For this schedule, Friday is the only demanding day.

When a competition is organized over the two days of a weekend (e.g., team sports tournament or several races in track and swimming), the microcycle

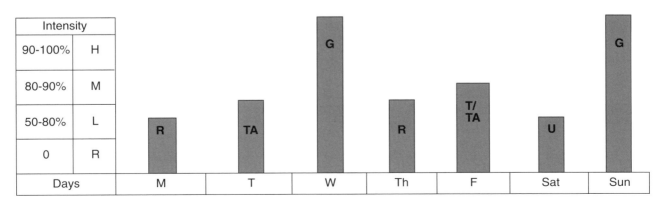

Figure 7.20 Competition microcycle for a team sport with two games a week

can be organized as illustrated in Figure 7.21. Please note that prior to the day of competition (C) there are two days of unloading (Th and F). The only challenging training session is at the beginning of the week (T).

Figure 7.22 presents a microcycle for team sport championships. Following each game, the coach suggests light O_2 compensation training in the morning and afternoon. Such training is more beneficial than no training; light aerobic training of 30 to 45 minutes facilitates better resynthesis of glycogen, replenishing glycogen stores before the next game. In team sports like soccer, basketball, and hockey, glycogen is depleted during the game. Unless the coach plans O_2 compensation, it will not be completely restored before the next game. Consequently, if energy stores are replenished by only 60 to 70%, players will not be able to play to full potential.

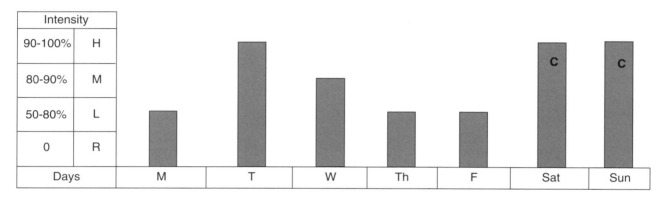

Intensity								
90-100%	H							
80-90%	M							
50-80%	L							
0	R							
Days		M	T	W	Th	F	Sat	Sun

Figure 7.21 Microcycle for a sport in which two competitions (C) are organized in the weekend.

Time	M	T	W	Th	F	Sat	Sun
A.M.		TA		O_2 Comp		O_2 Comp	
	Game	- - - - -	Game	- - - - -	Game	- - - - -	Game
P.M.		TA		O_2 Comp		O_2 Comp	

Figure 7.22 Microcycle for a team sport when playing in a national or international tournament

Model of a Microcycle for Competition

The many microcycles of the annual training program mostly develop skills and specific abilities required by a sport. However, during the competitive phase, the training program focuses strictly on creating a successful performance in the major competition. To facilitate a good performance, modify the last microcycle according to the specific needs of the competition and the athlete's physiological and psychological adjustments to them. Develop the microcycle based on a model of the competition, then repeat it several times before the main contest. This model should incorporate training lessons of various intensities, in which training alternates with active rest and recovery, and the daily cycle is identical to the day of competition.

Major competitions often have qualifying rounds, followed by finals in the same day (e.g., Friday 10:00 A.M. and 6:00 P.M.). This type of program is used in track and field, swimming, tennis, some team sports, and martial arts. In the competition model, regard Friday as the main training day, and plan two intense training lessons at the time of the scheduled competitions. Some sports, such as team sports, boxing, tennis, and wrestling, schedule 3 or 4 days of consecutive contests. Reflect this situation in the competition model and repeat it several times before the tournament starts. However, you cannot repeat the model consecutively; do it at intervals of 2 or 3 weeks and plan developmental microcycles between.

Some tournaments such as the Olympic Games, World championships, or other top international competitions, are organized over 4 to 9 days. You can hardly reproduce this in training because of the time factor and the high demand on the athletes. To gain experience for the larger tournaments, enter your athletes in shorter tournaments of 2 or 3 days, in which they participate in four or five contests. Reflect the characteristics of the future tournament in the developmental microcycles, especially the daily cycle. Familiarize the athletes with the competition schedule by applying the model training concept and simulating the rhythm of alternating contest and free days. Training lessons that fall on the same day as the competition in the upcoming tournament should be demanding, and those that fall on a day of no competition should be lower intensity.

Alternating simulated competitive days with days of rest is important in the athlete's adaptation to the competition schedule. Many athletes do not favor free days between competitions because performance during the second day of competition is sometimes not as good as expected. The decrease in performance seems to be based on postcompetition psychological reactions (i.e., overconfidence, conceit) rather than an accumulation of fatigue. Overcome such negative behavior by introducing model microcycles in all macrocycles for the competitive phase. If the competitive phase is short, introduce the same model during the last part of the preparatory phase. This program develops a stereotype that enhances performance in future competitions.

During the competitive phase, athletes may take part in other competitions on a different day of the week or a different time of day than the main competition. In such cases, do not alter the model microcycle, especially if the competitions pose no serious problem in qualifying the athletes for the main competition.

The athlete must be completely recovered, physiologically and psychologically, from the last training cycles and lessons when competition begins. He or she should feel in optimal physical and psychological condition, and supercompensated. Enhance this state in one of two ways. One is to reduce training volume and intensity during the 5 to 8 days preceding the competition. This ensures that the athlete replenishes all the energy spent during training. The second is to use a double microcycle to unload. In the first cycle, maintain intensity higher than medium, and keep it high for one or two training lessons. It will be much lower during the second cycle, averaging well below medium. Although the first cycle may be demanding, fatigue will disappear during the second microcycle. This should lead to a physiological and psychological state that will favor optimal performance. The first alternative is adequate for sports requiring dynamic performance; the second will meet the needs of sports in which endurance dominates.

Macrocycle

Macro is derived from the Greek word *makros*, meaning something of large size. In training methodology, a macrocycle represents a phase 2 to 6 weeks long or microcycles. Although the coach uses a microcycle to plan a program in the immediate future, a macrocycle projects the guidelines of a training program a few weeks in advance.

Duration of a Macrocycle

Although there may be some similarities, the criteria used to establish the duration of macrocycle often differs from sport to sport.

A long macrocycle of 4 to 6 weeks is usual for the preparatory phase. The main criteria are the training objectives and types in different parts of this stage. Consider a macrocycle as the time necessary to develop or perfect a technical element or certain tactical maneuvers. For developing biomotor abilities, the time the athlete needs to perfect an ability or its components may also be an adequate criterion for the length of a macrocycle (see table 7.6).

Should the coach plan exhibition competitions toward the end of the preparatory phase, the competition dates are also factors in determining the macrocycle length. If the coach is able to select the competitions, they should be scheduled for the end of a macrocycle. This allows the coach to obtain specific information regarding the athlete's progress in that training stage.

A macrocycle is usually shorter in the competitive phase (2 to 4 weeks). Establishing each cycle depends mainly on the competition schedule. For international athletes, the schedule of trials and international competitions is the chief factor in deciding the duration of a macrocycle. Divide the competitive phase so that each competition falls at the end of a macrocycle, especially for individual sports. Often, several competitions occur per month during the competitive phase (possibly 4 to 8), especially for team sports. If this is the case, decide which competition is the most important and prepare the athlete accordingly, giving slightly less attention to the other competitions. Structure the macrocycle so the main competition falls at the end of the cycle.

Another criterion for deciding the duration of a macrocycle is which system of the body the athlete is addressing. Nadori (1989) suggested that there are *metabolic* and *neural* macrocycles. Metabolic pertains to the breakdown of foodstuff into the fuel that supplies the body with energy, and neural pertains to nervous system training. He suggested that metabolic cycles should be longer, and neural cycles should be shorter.

TABLE 7.6   Strength Training Program for a Long Jumper.

Month	Dec.	Jan.	Feb.	Mar.	April
Macrocycle	1	2	3	4	
Number of microcycles	5	6	5	4	
Objectives	- Testing - Anatomical adaptation - Prepare the muscles, tendons, and ligaments for heavy load training	Maximum strength		Power Maintain maximum strength	Power Maintain maximum strength

Note: The objectives of training are the criteria for defining the macrocycles.

Neural training, such as complex skills, fast and powerful drills, or heavy loads, should be short because they heavily tax the CNS. I presume that Nadori reasoned that nervous system recovery from fatigue is much slower than muscular recovery. Consequently, longer neural cycles could result in unwanted nervous system fatigue, which could negatively affect homeostasis and performance improvement.

However, to suggest that metabolic cycles ought to be longer is too generic. Short, fast, and powerful exercises and drills tax the metabolic system (ATP-CP) and the nervous system since athletes need maximum concentration for these tasks. These drills and exercises use fuel that is restored quickly, within minutes.

The only types of training that require longer macrocycles are those that develop aerobic endurance. However, these are not related to the metabolic system and are justified because adaptation of the cardiorespiratory system to endurance work takes much longer. A better criterion for defining the duration of a macrocycle is adaptation to a particular type of training.

Structural Consideration for a Macrocycle

Base the structure of a macrocycle on specific objectives, training phase, and the competition schedule. We could classify the structure of macrocycles per training phase and within each phase have variations depending on the training goal and competition schedule.

Macrocycles for the Preparatory Phase

Training during the preparatory phase is to induce adaptation. Developmental and shock macrocycles are best suited for these macrocycles. The training demand per week of developmental macrocycles (figure 7.23) follows the step-loading method. Figure 7.23a refers to a 4:1 structure in which the load increases in four steps, with one week of regeneration at the end. I recommend such a structure for the early preparatory phase when the athlete is fresh and training demand is mildly challenging. Dedicate this time of the year to learning new technical and tactical skills, correcting old technical habits, and laying the foundation of physical training. I suggest the 3:1 structure (figure 7.23b) for most of the preparatory phase, often alternating with shock macrocycles (figure 7.24). If the fatigue level is higher than expected, as demonstrated by the monitoring techniques, the regeneration week could decrease below the suggested levels.

Plan shock macrocycles (figure 7.24) or a cycle of repeated maximal training demands two or three times during the preparatory phase to break the athletes' ceiling of adaptation. If you notice a plateau in athletes' adaptation, especially in the past year, plan a 3-week shock cycle to further stimulate response to training and force the body to adapt to higher demands. I highly recommend careful monitoring of athletes' physiological and psychological reactions to shock training. Although just 1 week of regeneration is suggested in figure 7.24, athletes may require 2 weeks of regeneration and recovery due to high levels of fatigue.

Macrocycles for the Competitive Phase

The competition calendar dictates the dynamics of a macrocycle during the precompetitive and competitive phase. Loading pattern variations are numerous and sport specific.

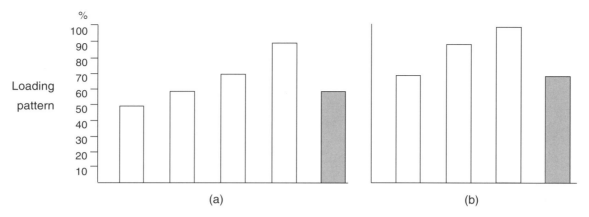

Figure 7.23 Two examples of developmental macrocycles: (a) 4:1 and (b) 3:1

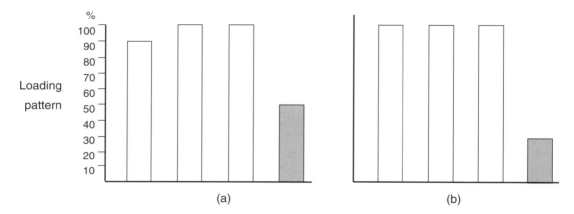

Figure 7.24 Two variations of the shock macrocycle, in which (b) is of much higher demand

Team sports, with one or two games per week throughout the season, maintain a steady loading pattern. Most intensity variations occur inside a microcycle, in which games, regeneration days, and training of low and medium demand are the norm. Therefore, a team sport coach should examine alternating intensities per microcycle.

The structure of a macrocycle for individual sports may vary from 4:1, 3:1, 2:1, 1:1, 2:2, or any other combination. For this reason, it is important to discuss a macrocycle with two peaks, meaning two important competitions, one at each end of the plan (see figure 7.25).

The competitions on July 9 may be qualifying rounds for the main competition on August 14. The coach planned no competitions between these two important dates. After the qualification meet, the coach makes necessary changes in training to ensure that the athletes have the chance to maximize their skills and potential for the main competition. If a coach plans a competition on July 23 or 30, this approach would become impossible. The strain of another competition would focus the athletes and the coach on performing well, rather than training. Also, participation in such an unnecessary competition would create fatigue.

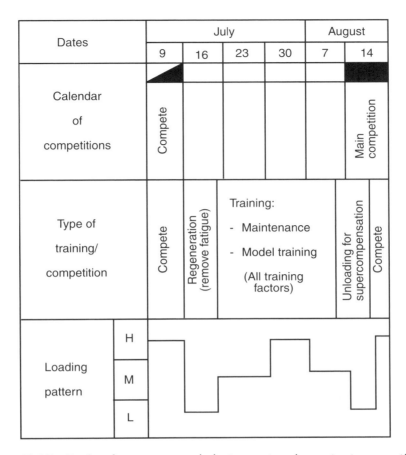

Figure 7.25 Design for a macrocycle between two important competitions

Under normal circumstances, with no competition between July 9 and August 14, the first week would be for regenerating, relaxing mentally, and removing the fatigue accumulated during the July 9 competition. The weeks of July 23, July 30, and August 7 would be for technical, tactical, and physical training. Now is the time to refine everything possible before the championship in a quiet, unstressful environment. Also during this time, the coach builds the athletes' confidence in their abilities and energizes them psychologically for an all-out effort. The coach will use the 7 to 10 days before the August 14 competition for peaking: unloading the training volume and intensity to replenish energy stores, especially glycogen, and facilitate supercompensation. The expected gains from supercompensation will set the stage for a good performance.

Competing at a high altitude creates many problems for athletes and coaches. Interest in high-altitude training started before the 1968 Olympic Games in Mexico City (7,347 feet above sea level). Most research done demonstrated an increased performance efficiency after returning to sea level. These findings, not published in training literature, created interest in high-altitude training to benefit athletes participating in competitions at sea level.

Figure 7.26 illustrates a high-altitude training model followed by Russian swimmers. East German swimmers and other athletes followed a similar model. I created a similar model for wrestlers competing in the world championships in Mexico City and achieved excellent results.

The top of the chart shows the type and number of weeks of training at high altitude and at sea level. The model includes 3 weeks of high-altitude training followed by 2 weeks of sea level training. At the end of the fifth week, the athletes participate in a major competition, usually World or Olympic Games.

This 5-week macrocycle was determined by the fact that high-altitude training results in two waves of increased physiological efficiency, when performance is superior compared to swimmers training at sea level. The first, short wave of physiological efficiency occurs the first day after returning to sea level; the second, much longer wave occurs in days 13 to 17. The model was created so the second wave coincides with a major competition.

The first week at high altitude is aerobic to allow the athletes to acclimate. Anaerobic training prevails in week 2, followed by training based on the ergogenesis of the sport. The first macrocycle after returning to sea level is for regeneration and aerobic training. In microcycle 4 or 5, the athletes travel to the competition, where training is light to facilitate supercompensation.

The main benefit of high-altitude training is increased hemoglobin content, which increases the blood capacity to supply the muscle cell with more oxygen. Sports that have an important aerobic content benefit from following such a training model.

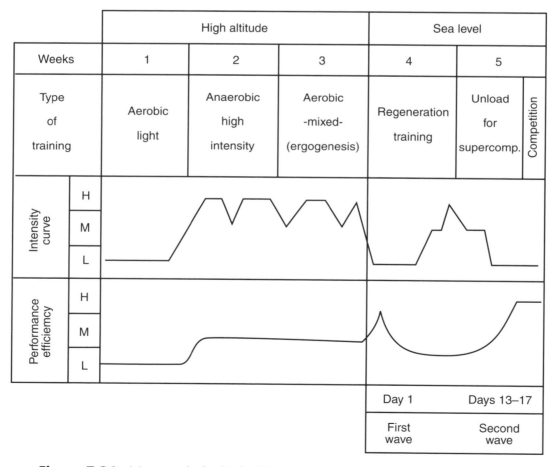

Figure 7.26 Macrocycle for high-altitude training before a major competition

Macrocycle for Unloading and Tapering for Competitions

The main role of an unloading and tapering program is to train specifically for an important competition by closely reproducing the specific conditions under which the athletes will compete. This is model training. The other goals of such a program are to remove fatigue and facilitate supercompensation by unloading.

Although some authors promote a different approach, I believe unloading and tapering should be no longer than 2 weeks (please refer to unloading in chapter 8). I feel this is true for swimming, which traditionally uses a 5- to 6-week tapering macrocycle with the loading pattern decreasing continually. This means lower volume, but an intensification of the work in the pool. I question such an approach, because intensifying the program could mean a significantly higher fatigue level. Only research that tests physiological parameters in these two unloading and tapering techniques could clarify this argument.

Macrocycle for the Transition Phase

The scope of the transition phase is explained in the next chapter. At this point, I will simply illustrate a suggested structure of such a macrocycle (figure 7.27).

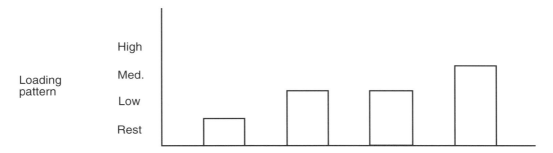

Figure 7.27   A suggested loading pattern for a macrocycle for the transition phase

Summary of Major Concepts

Along with the annual plan, the microcycle is the most important training plan.

The technique you use to alternate intensities during a microcycle is a science. In most cases, it is based on the time necessary to restore the fuel that supplied energy during training.

The better you alternate intensities per week, the easier it is for your athletes to cope with fatigue and avoid overtraining. Equally important is alternating developmental, shock, and regeneration microcycles. Do not abuse the shock microcycles; the result is high levels of fatigue.

Remember the main scope of training is to adapt the body and mind to demanding stimuli in order to duplicate body reactions in competition. For the sake of training efficiency, developmental and shock cycles are constantly repeated.

In your quest to quantify training, consider the numeric intensity symbols. Their alternation per week will help you plan for days when athletes reach supercompensation. Now is the time to use what you have learned about energy systems, especially about supercompensation, and carefully manipulate them to increase the desired training effect.

Annual Training Program

The annual plan is the tool that guides athletic training over a year. It is based on the concept of periodization, which divides the annual plan into training phases, and the principles of training. An annual training program is necessary to maximize performance. In principle, this means that athletes must train continually for 11 months, then reduce the amount of work during the last month. This work should vary from regular training to facilitate physiological, psychological, and CNS rest and regeneration before beginning another year of training.

The main objective of training is to reach a high level of performance at a given time, usually the main competition of the year, based on correct development of athletic shape. Good athletic shape occurs when the degree of training is high and the psychological status enhances a high level of performance. To achieve such a performance, the coach must properly periodize and plan the entire program so the development of skills, biomotor abilities, and psychological traits follow logically and sequentially. Well-organized and planned training is difficult to achieve. In many instances, the highest performance of the year does not occur at the major competition, a result of inadequate knowledge and planning experience.

In training methodology, one of the most challenging and complex problems is peaking athletic shape on the planned date. Often, athletes peak before the main competition due to being pushed to reach a high level without adequately alternating work with short regeneration phases. It is also common for athletes to peak after the top competition, the result of deficient preparation or an inadequate load or demand. A typical example of poor planning occurs in gymnastics when routines are finalized just before an important competition.

The coach must do the planning, especially for inexperienced athletes. Experienced athletes should help the coach set objectives and plan for the following year. This way, they have a say in designing their programs, and the coach can use their feedback in a positive way. Athlete involvement in planning can be an important motivational tool for them and the coach.

Periodization

Periodization is one the most important concepts in training and planning. This term originates from *period*, which is a portion or division of time into smaller, easy-to-manage segments, called phases of training.

The concept of periodization is not new, but not everybody is familiar with its history. Periodization existed in an unrefined form for an unknown time. It is difficult to trace who initiated it. It was used in a simple form by the Greek Olympians. As mentioned, Philostratus was the vanguard of today's planning. Over the centuries, many authors and practitioners added to the process, improving the knowledge to the present status.

Since 1963, I developed many aspects of periodization, copyrighted under the names:

Periodization of Strength

Periodization of Bodybuilding

Periodization of Psychological/Mental Training

Psychological Supercompensation

Periodization of Endurance

Periodization of Nutrition

Integrated Periodization

The Chart of the Annual Plan

Periodization refers to two important aspects. *Periodization of the annual plan* divides it into smaller training phases, making it easier to plan and manage a training program and ensure peak performance for the main competition of the year. *Periodization of biomotor abilities* refers to structuring training phases to lead to the highest level of speed, strength, and endurance.

Many are unaware of the difference between periodization as a division of the annual plan and periodization of the biomotor abilities, which results in confusion. In most sports, the annual training cycle is conventionally divided into three main phases: preparatory, competitive, and transition. The preparatory and competitive phases are divided into two subphases because their tasks are different. The preparatory phase has a general and a specific subphase, based on the different characteristics of training, and the competitive phase usually is preceded by a short precompetitive subphase. Furthermore, each phase is composed of macro- and microcycles. Each smaller cycle has specific objectives derived from the general objectives of the annual plan. Figure 8.1 illustrates the division of the annual plan into phases and cycles.

	The Annual Plan					
Phases of training	Prepatory			Competitive		Transition
Sub-phases	General preparation	Specific preparation	Pre-competitive	Competitive		Transition
Macro-cycles						
Micro-cycles						

Figure 8.1 Division of an annual plan into its phases and cycles of training

Athletic performance depends on the athlete's adaptation, psychological adjustment to training and competitions, and development of skills and abilities. The duration of phases depends heavily on the time the athlete needs to increase training level and athletic shape. The main criterion for calculating the duration of each training phase is the competition schedule. Athletes train many months for competitions, aiming to reach their highest level on those dates. This requires organized, well-planned annual training that facilitates psychological and physiological adaptation. You can enhance the organization of an annual plan by periodizing training and using the sequential approach in developing athletic shape. However, an optimal periodization for each sport and precise data regarding the time required for an optimal increase in the degree of training and athletic shape is not yet exact. Individual characteristics, psychophysiological abilities, diet, and regeneration increase this difficulty. You can facilitate your planning ability by developing a model plan that you can continually improve, based on yearly observations.

Needs of Periodization

Adaptation created the different training phases because athletes progressively develop and perfect functions over a long period. Also consider physiological and psychological potential and realize athletes cannot maintain athletic shape at a high level throughout the year. Athletes should precede any increase in training work with an unloading phase in which they decrease the training level. Develop athletes' physiological foundation during the preparatory phase, and strive for perfection according to the needs of competitions during the competitive phase.

The methodology of developing skills, strategical maneuvers, and biomotor abilities also requires a special approach, unique for each training phase. The athlete learns a skill sequentially throughout training phases over time; this is also true for strategical maneuvers. The closer to perfection a skill becomes, the more sophisticated strategical tools a coach can use. Periodization also influences developing a sequential approach to perfecting biomotor abilities. Enhancing athletic shape requires increasing the volume and intensity of training in an undulatory manner, as proposed by the principle of load progression.

Climatic conditions and the seasons also play decisive roles in the needs of periodizing training. The duration of a training phase often depends on climate. Seasonal sports, such as skiing, rowing, and soccer, are restricted by climate. In sports such as rowing and soccer, winter is always the preparatory phase, and the competitive phase is in the summer or spring and fall. The reverse is true for winter sports such as skiing and hockey.

Competition and intense training specific to the competitive phase has a strong component of stress. A phase of stressful activities, such as maximum concentration and CNS fatigue, should not be long, even though most athletes and coaches may be able to cope. It is important to alternate stressful phases with periods of recovery and regeneration, during which the athletes experience less pressure. Such a phase, usually the transition phase, creates a favorable mood and generates potential, providing a solid foundation for the following period of heavy work.

Classifying Annual Plans

Simple annual plans have been used since ancient Olympic Games. Philostratus referred to a preparatory phase for the ancient Olympic Games with few informal competitions before and a rest period after. A similar approach was used for the modern Olympic Games (1896 in Athens, Greece), and by U.S. college athletes at the beginning of the 20th century. Planning has progressively become more sophisticated, culminating with the German programs for the 1936 Olympic Games, when coaches used a 4-year plan and annual plans. After World War II, the Soviets started a state-funded sports program with the scope of using athletics as the stage to demonstrate the superiority of their political system.

In 1965, Matveyev published a model of an annual plan based on a questionnaire that asked athletes how they trained. He analyzed the information statistically and produced an annual plan divided into phases, subphases, and training cycles. Some enthusiasts called it the classical model, forgetting what had been done before Matveyev from Philostratus onward. The difference between the specialists of the early 1900s and post-World War II is that the Russians, Germans, and Romanians have published books and articles about planning.

Figures 8.2 through 8.5 illustrate models produced by four authors.

Although annual plans differ according to the specifics of the sport, classification depends on the number of competitive phases in a plan. Seasonal sports such as skiing, canoeing, and football, or sports with one major competition during the year, use only one competitive phase. Such an annual plan is a monocycle; since there is only one competitive phase, there is only one peak (figure 8.6). This plan is divided into preparatory, competitive, and transition phases. The preparatory phase includes general and specific preparation. In

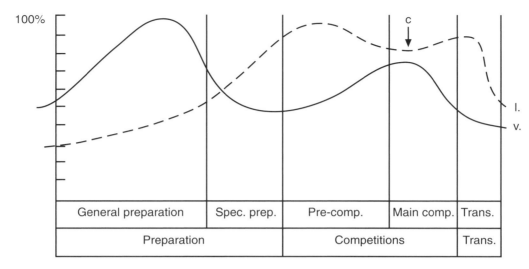

Figure 8.2 Matveyev model (1965)

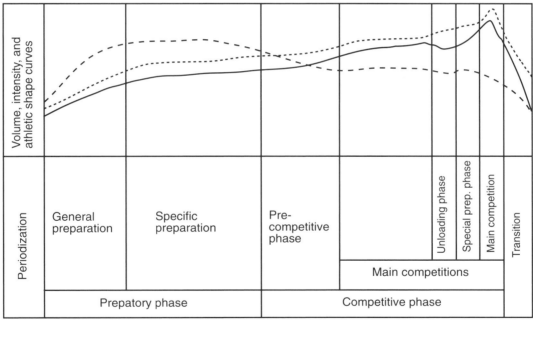

- - - - Volume
·········· Intensity
——— Stress

Figure 8.3 Monocycle annual plan (modified after Ozolin 1971)

figure 8.6, note the relationship between general and specific preparation: as one decreases the other increases substantially.

The competitive phase is divided into smaller subphases. The precompetitive subphase, which usually includes exhibition competitions only, precedes the subphase of main competitions, in which all official competitions are scheduled (C). Before the most important competition of the year, the coach plans

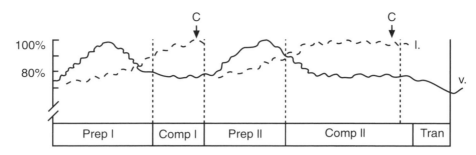

Figure 8.4 Bondarchuk model (1986)

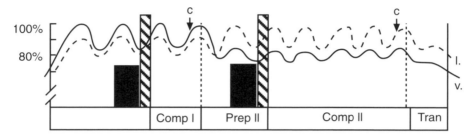

Figure 8.5 Tschiene model (1989)

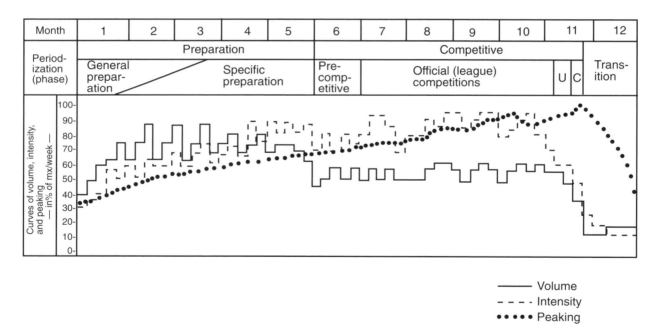

Figure 8.6 Monocycle or single-peak annual plan for a speed-power sport

two shorter phases. The first is an unloading phase (U), or tapering off, of lower volume and intensity so athletes can regenerate and supercompensate before the main competition. A special preparation phase follows, during which the coach may make technical and tactical changes. The coach can organize this phase separately or with the unloading phase and may use it for relaxation and psychological preparation for competitions.

During the preparatory and early competitive phases, emphasize training volume with low levels of intensity according to the specifics of the sport. During this period, quantity of work should dominate, as opposed to the competitive phase when you emphasize work intensity or quality.

Another important point: as the competitive phase approaches, the training volume curve decreases drastically while the intensity curve increases (figure 8.6). Such a monocycle model is typical for sports dominated by speed and power. The volume curve decreases to allow the coach to concentrate on speed and power.

The model illustrated in figure 8.6 is not appropriate for everyone. Training specialists from endurance sports would be mistaken to follow figure 8.6. For sports in which ergogenesis is close to 50-50% or dominant aerobic, the curve of the training volume must be high throughout the competitive phase as well. Otherwise, the development of specific endurance will be insufficient and negatively affect the final performance. For aerobic-dominant sports, I have provided another model (figure 8.7). Please note in figure 8.7, the division of the annual plan in the training phases is based on the type of endurance training the athlete will perform. Also, the volume of training, so important for aerobic sports, is dominant throughout the year.

A completely different approach is taken in sports that have two separate competitive seasons such as track and field, in which indoor and outdoor seasons are common. Because there are two distinct competitive phases, such a plan is called a bi-cycle (*bi* in Latin means two). Figure 8.8 illustrates a bi-cycle that incorporates the following training phases:

- Preparatory phase I, which should be the longer preparatory phase.
- Competitive phase I.
- Short transition (1-2 weeks) linked with a preparatory phase II. The unloading transition phase is for recovery.
- Competitive phase II.
- Transition phase.

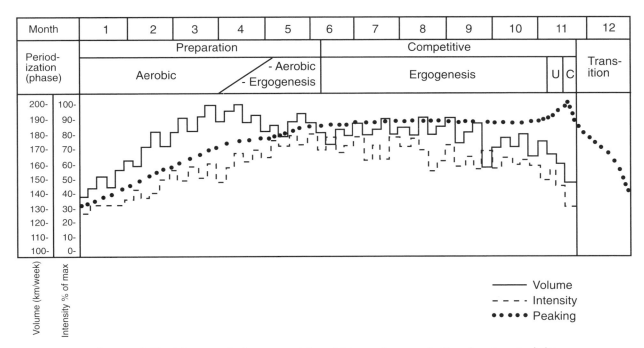

Figure 8.7 Monocycle for a sport in which endurance is the dominant ability

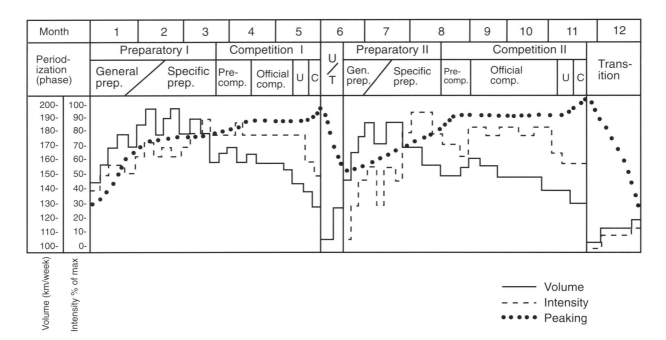

Figure 8.8 Bi-cycle for a sport (track and field) in which speed and power dominate

A bi-cycle consists of two short monocycles linked through a short unloading/transition (U/T) and preparatory phase. For each cycle, the approach may be similar except for training volume, which in preparatory phase I is of much higher magnitude than in preparatory phase II. Also, the level of athletic shape may be lower in competitive phase I. (In our example of track and field, the outdoor championships are usually more important.) This is illustrated by the curve of the athletic shape, which reaches the highest values during competitive phase II.

Again, for endurance sports, the volume curve must always be higher than intensity, even during the competitive phase. This approach will ensure proper emphasis on the dominant energy system, which in the end (competitive phase II) will translate into better performance.

It is not unusual for sports like boxing, wrestling, and gymnastics to have three big competitions during the annual plan (for instance, national championships, a qualifying meet, and the competition itself). Assuming each competition is 3 or 4 months apart, an athlete would have three competitive phases, and the plan would be a tri-cycle (Latin *tri*, meaning three).

As illustrated by figure 8.9, a tri-cycle incorporates the following sequence of training phases:

- A long preparatory phase I
- Competitive phase I
- A short unloading, transition, or preparatory phase II
- Competitive phase II
- Unloading, transition, or preparatory phase III
- Competitive phase III
- Transition

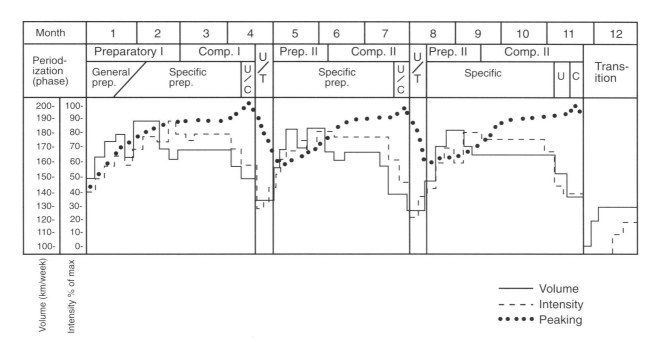

Figure 8.9   Tri-cycle or triple periodization

When planning a tri-cycle, the most important competition of the three should occur during the last cycle. The first of the three preparatory phases should be the longest, during which the athlete builds the technical, tactical, and physical foundations that will foster the following two cycles. Because such a plan is conventionally used with advanced athletes, the general preparation subphase is only in the early part of the first cycle. Also the curve of volume is the highest, reflecting the relative importance of training volume in the preparatory phase I, as opposed to the following two preparation phases.

The curve of intensity for each cycle follows a pattern similar to a monocycle. Both the volume and intensity curves drop slightly for each of the three unloading phases preceding the main competitions. For the curve of athletic shape, the coach would plan the highest peak for the third cycle, which corresponds with the main competition of the year.

Finally, sports such as tennis, martial arts, and boxing have four or more competitions when peak performance is desirable (figure 8.10). In such cases, the structure of the annual plan differs in that the preparatory phase, so important for developing skills and biomotor abilities, is short. Although international athletes with a good foundation of training during the early years of athletic development may find it easy to cope with such a heavy schedule, children and teenagers do not. This is why many young tennis players burn out before they have a chance to experience the satisfaction of winning major tournaments.

A multicycle of four or more competitive phases is a challenging task. This is especially true if the athlete skips a quiet preparatory phase in which to regenerate and focus on improving biomotor skills in an unstressful environment. We see this situation in tennis, in which many players are injured or withdraw from tournaments because of physical and mental exhaustion.

Month	1	2	3	4	5	6	7	8	9	10	11	12
Type of training	1	2	3	4	1	2	3	4	1	2	3	4	1	2	3	4

Figure 8.10 Multipeak annual plan (four main peaks) in which 1 = preparatory; 2 = intensification, or concentrated specific training for a competition; 3 = unloading for supercompensation; and 4 = recovery-regeneration

Selective Periodization

Programs for young athletes often follow those specifically produced for mature and advanced athletes. I would like to propose that everyone concerned look at periodization from the point of view of athletes' readiness for heavy schedule competitions. Irrespective of whether you are in a sport of multipeaks, consider the following sequence of types of annual plans.

- A monocycle is for novice and junior athletes. The advantage of such a plan is that it has long preparatory phases, free from the stress of competitions. This allows the coach to concentrate on developing skills and a strong foundation of physical training.

- A bi-cycle is for experienced athletes who can qualify for national championships. Even then, the preparatory phase should be as long as possible, to allow time to train fundamentals.

- A tri-cycle and multipeak plan are recommended only for advanced or international athletes. Presumably, these athletes have a solid foundation and their background allows them to handle an annual plan with three or more peaks with greater ease.

Although the duration of training phases depends on the competition schedule, table 8.1 could be a good guideline for distributing weeks per training phase

Stress—Planning and Periodization

Stress is a significant by-product of training and competition, which if not properly manipulated may affect athletes' performance and behavior. Because training deals primarily with biological and psychological components, stress is considered the sum of these phenomena, elicited by internal and adverse external influences.

Throughout training and competition, athletes experience biological, psychological, and sociological stressors. Stress is additive and is produced by competition, the audience, peers, family, coach's pressure to perform well, and training intensity. A wise coach deals with these athletic by-products by training athletes to cope and by planning the stress properly throughout the annual plan. Again, the concept of periodization is an important tool in properly planning stress. As shown in figure 8.11, the curve of stress does not have the same magnitude throughout the annual plan, a distinct advantage of periodization.

Please note in figure 8.11 that the curve of stress parallels the curve of intensity—the higher the intensity, the higher the stress. The shape of the curve is low during the transition phase, progressively elevates through the preparatory phase, and fluctuates during the competitive phase because

TABLE 8.1 Distribution of Weeks for Each Training Phase for the Classical Types of Annual Plans

Annual plan	Preparatory	Competitive	Transition
Monocycle: 52 weeks	32 or more	10-15	5
Bi-cycle: 26 weeks	13 or more	5-10	3
Tri-cycle: 17-18 weeks	8 or more	3-5	2-3

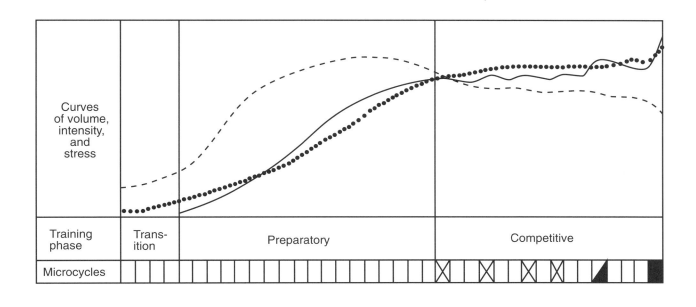

- - - - Volume
●●●●●● Intensity
—— Stress

Figure 8.11 Stress curve during a monocycle

of alternating stressful activities (competitions) with short regeneration periods. During the preparatory phase, the magnitude of the stress curve is the outcome of the relationship between training volume and intensity. While the volume or quantity of training is high, the intensity is lower, because it is difficult to emphasize a high amount of work and an elevated intensity simultaneously (with the probable exception of weightlifting). Training intensity is a prime stressor. Because the coach emphasizes it less than training volume through most of the preparatory phase, the curve of stress is also low. One exception to this may be testing dates, which could stress some athletes, especially those who find it difficult to meet the standards. Similarly, because coaches in team sports select the team during the preparatory phase, the days before selection are often stressful as well.

The stress curve throughout the competitive phase has an undulatory structure because of alternating competitive with developmental and regeneration microcycles. It appears evident, therefore, that the number of competitions and their frequency cause an elevated stress curve. When top competitions are more frequent, athletes experience more stress. In these

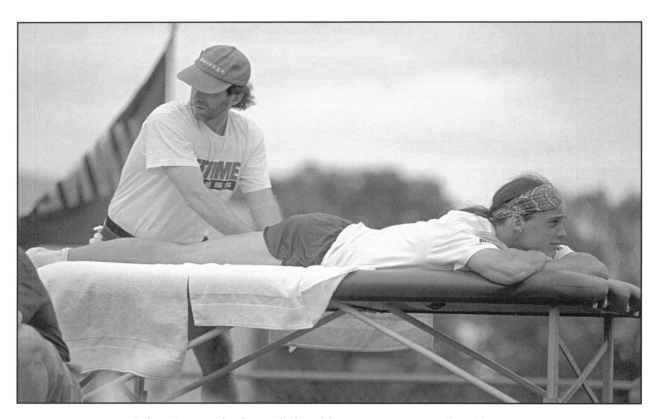

Relaxation methods can help athletes cope more easily with stress

cases, the coach must plan a few days of regeneration following competitions, and only when athletes are almost recovered do they participate in intensive training lessons again. Similarly, the coach would be wise to plan a short unloading period (2-3 days) before important competitions.

Apart from alternating high and low stressful activities, the coach may also use relaxation techniques to help athletes cope. Some athletes cope well, and others have more difficulty. Those who have difficulty dealing with stress may need more than motivational and relaxation techniques. When selecting athletes, the coach should consider psychological tests that sort the candidates according to the needs of high-performance athletics.

The ability of athletes to cope with stress depends, to a high degree, on the coach. The coach has to plan the program to allow phases of regeneration and relaxation and introduce athletes to mental training and its specific techniques.

I strongly believe that athletes' psychological behavior depends on their physiological well-being. In other words, athletes' mental state is a by-product of their physiological condition. This is why I believe that, "Perfect fitness results in the best psychology!" A well-planned periodized program will ensure superior psychological readiness, stress management, and mental training.

While creating a periodized training program, the coach should produce a psychological periodization (please also refer to Integrated Periodization later in this chapter). Canadian psychologists were among the first to realize the necessity of psychological periodization. Following are the mental training phases as suggested by Bacon (1989).

Psychological Supercompensation

Physiological supercompensation has a critical impact on the psychological well-being of athletes. Long-term observations of athletes' behavior during all the segments of the supercompensation cycle led me to conclude that, during training and competition, athletes also experience a *psychological supercompensation cycle.*

Psychological supercompensation starts before physiological supercompensation, during the early days of tapering-peaking for a competition. As illustrated by figure 8.12, the psychological supercompensation cycle has the following segments.

Phases	Mental Training Objective
General	• Evaluate mental skills. • Learn basic mental skills in a quiet setting.
Specific Preparatory	• Adapt and practice mental skills in sport-specific situations. • Maintain basic mental skills.
Precompetitive	• Develop and practice focus plan. • Use focus plan in simulations. • Maintain basic mental skills.
Competitive	• Evaluate and refine focus plan. • Use mental skills to prepare for specific opponents and competitions. • Use mental skills for stress management.
Unloading	• Use mental skills to aid regeneration and lower stress.
Transition	• Maintain fitness and prevent staleness through recreational activities.

Precompetitive Arousal

About 2 to 3 weeks before an important competition, the psychologist or coach should create a mental strategy to help athletes handle stress related to the event, opponents, and hostile audiences. Athletes should reach a psychological readiness to cope with stress, allowing them to behave and compete successfully under pressure. Maximize focusing techniques and use visualization to prepare athletes for stressful situations. Set goals for mental habits needed to cope with the stressors before, during, and after competition. The most effective visualization techniques are imagery, mental rehearsal, positive suggestion, and psychological relaxation.

The precompetitive days are as important as the competition itself. An inappropriate unloading phase can compromise physiological supercompensation because of mental and physiological fatigue. To avoid this, design an energy-management strategy so that athletes avoid extreme intensities. Properly control the pace, speed, and power of activities. Successful energy management should result in optimal arousal for competition. Facilitate mental arousal for

Perfect fitness results in the best psychology

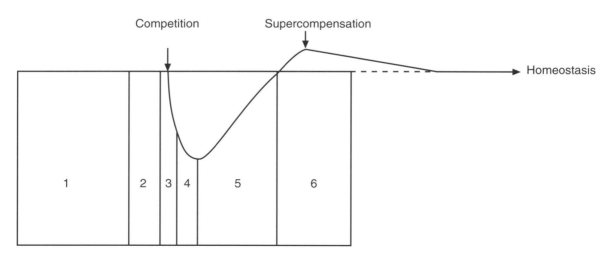

Figure 8.12 Components of psychological supercompensation: 1 = Precompetition arousal—2-3 weeks; 2 = Precontest motivation—day/hours before competition; 3 = In-contest motivation—duration of competition; 4 = Postcontest fatigue—hours/days; 5 = Compensation—3-7 days; 6 = Psychological supercompensation—when compensation is complete

the contest by using psychological techniques, such as psychic energy management, visualizing energizing scenes, self-regulation, and relaxation in a dark room with music.

Precontest Motivation

Organize precontest motivation during the hours before competition. Eliminate negative thoughts, and use positive thinking and cue words to increase self-confidence. Remind athletes of the good workouts of the past few days or good results achieved in a past competition or in testing. Build athletes' confidence on tangible, practical cues to which they can relate.

In-Competition Motivation

In team and contact sports, where the coach can directly communicate with athletes, he or she should use cue words to energize and motivate them for a superior performance. The coach should do this through encouragement and creating an optimistic feeling about the athletes' chances to achieve the competition's goal. Similarly, using cue words can motivate the athletes for an all-out effort and playing their chances to the end of the competition.

Postcontest Fatigue

The stress of competition results in physiological and psychological postcompetition fatigue. Fatigue of the mind results from mental exhaustion caused by the athletes' concentrating maximally during the competition to achieve the goals. This maximum concentration wears down the nervous system in general and the nerve cell in particular. It also seems that if the nervous system is in prestart excitation before the competition, it is in poststart inhibition after the competition to protect itself from further stimulation. Relaxation techniques, such as autogenic training, meditation, and stress management, may speed recovery from fatigue.

Compensation

Compensation starts as soon as the competition ends, with the goal of quick recuperation so athletes can train for the next competition. Physiologically, compensation means replenishing the fuels used by using various techniques for recovery and regeneration explained in chapter 5. Specific nutrition plans that enhance the replenishment of energy fuels are also important.

If athletes will begin training soon, pay equal attention to removing stress and mental fatigue. Relaxation and autogenic training techniques are indicated for removing mental fatigue and recharging the battery of mental energy.

Physiological compensation can take 1 to 3 days, the time to fully restore glycogen stores, rest, and relax the muscles. Psychological supercompensation is longer (3 to 7 days) because the nervous cell relaxes five to seven times slower.

Psychological and Mental Supercompensation

Psychological and mental supercompensation occurs when athletes have totally removed mental fatigue, released stress, and replenished energy stores. Replenishment of energy stores is the key element that triggers psychological

A precontest pep talk increases motivation and self-confidence

supercompensation. At this point of psychological supercompensation, athletes are full of optimism and confidence and demonstrate positive thinking. In other words, athletes have been able to rebound psychologically.

One main role of a sport psychologist is using specific techniques to assist athletes to pass the present athletic potential. Such a goal is always easier to achieve if athletes are in a state of psychological supercompensation at the time of competition.

Periodization of Biomotor Abilities

Using periodization is not limited to the structure of a training plan or the type of training to use in a given training phase. On the contrary, this concept also applies to the methodology of developing the dominant biomotor abilities of the chosen sport.

Some sports, mostly individual, have a loose structure of periodization, especially of endurance. However, in most team sports the periodization of dominant abilities allows room for improvement. Similarly, when we compare the periodization of endurance with strength, we often see that strength training does not properly follow the concept of periodization.

In many sports, the dominant biomotor ability is power. Recognizing this, some coaches employ exercises aimed at developing power throughout the

year, from the early preparatory phase to the beginning of the competitive phase. Such an approach may be from misunderstanding the concept of periodization and the principle of specificity some physiologists suggest. Power is the product of maximum strength and maximum speed. This product could reach a much higher level when athletes really need it, namely before the main competitions, if they develop the strength component separately, then convert it into power (figure 8.13).

	Preparatory		Competitive		Transition
	General preparatory	Specific preparatory	Pre-competitive	Main competition	Transition
Strength	Anatomical adaptation	Maximum strength	Conversion - Power - Muscular endurance - Both	Maintenance C	Compensation
Endurance	Aerobic endurance	- Aerobic endurance - Specific endurance (ergogenesis)	Specific endurance (ergogenesis)		Aerobic endurance

Speed	Aerobic and anaerobic endurance	- Alactic speed
		- Anaerobic endurance (ergogenesis) - Specific speed
		  • Alactic
		  • Lactic
		  • Speed endurance
			- Specific speed
			- Agility
			- Reaction time
			- Speed endurance		

Figure 8.13 Periodization of main biomotor abilities

Periodization of Strength Training

The objectives, content, and methods of a strength-training program change throughout the phases of an annual plan. Such changes occur to reflect the type of strength a sport, event, or individual athlete requires to enhance optimum performance improvement (figure 8.13).

Anatomical Adaptation

After a transition phase, when most athletes do little strength training, it is scientifically and methodically sound to begin a strength program to adapt the anatomy to a new program. The main objective of this phase is to involve most muscle groups, preparing the muscles, ligaments, tendons, and joints for the following long, strenuous training phases. A general strength program with many exercises (9-12) performed comfortably, without pushing the athletes, is desirable. A load of 40 to 60% of maximum, 8 to 12 repetitions in two or three sets, performed at a low to medium rate with a rest interval of 60 to 90 seconds between exercises, over 4 to 6 weeks will help achieve the objectives for this first phase. Consider a longer anatomical adaptation (9-12 weeks) for junior athletes and for those without a strong background in strength training.

Maximum Strength Phase

Most sports require either power (e.g., long jumping), muscular endurance (e.g., 800- to 1,500-meter swimming), or both (e.g., rowing). Both power and muscular endurance are affected by the level of maximum strength. Power cannot reach high standards without a high level of maximum strength because power is the product of speed and maximum strength. First develop maximum strength, then convert it into power. The goal during this phase is to develop maximum strength to the highest level of an athlete's capacity. The duration of this phase (1-3 months) depends on the sport and the athlete's needs. It may be long (3 months) for a shot-putter or football player; an ice hockey player may need only 1 month for this type of development.

Conversion Phase

Convert maximum strength into power, or muscular endurance, or both according to the needs and characteristics of the sport or event. Gradually convert maximum strength by applying the adequate training method for the type of strength and using methods specific to the selected sport (e.g., speed training). During this phase (1-2 months), the athlete must maintain a certain level of maximum strength or power may slightly decline at the end of the competitive phase.

The appropriate method of power or muscular endurance must prevail in training according to the sport. When the sport requires both power and endurance, an adequate training time and method should reflect the optimal ratio between these two abilities. For instance, the ratio must be almost equal for a wrestler, but power should dominate in a canoer's (500 meter) program, and muscular endurance should prevail for a rower (race duration of 6-8 minutes).

Although maximum strength training is specific to the preparatory phase, the conversion period begins toward the end of preparatory and continues into the beginning of the competitive phase (precompetitive phase).

Maintenance Phase

As the term suggests, the main objective for this phase is to maintain the standards achieved during previous phases. Again, the program for this phase is a function of the specific requirements of the sport. The ratio between maximum strength, power, and muscular endurance has to reflect such requirements. For instance, a shot-putter and football lineman may plan two sessions for maximum strength and two for power; a jumper may consider one for maximum strength and three for power. A baseball player, football wide receiver, or a 100-meter swimmer may plan one session for maximum strength, two for power, and one for muscular endurance; a 1,500-meter swimmer may dedicate the entire program to perfecting muscular endurance.

Two to four sessions should be dedicated to maintaining the required strength, depending on the athlete's performance level and the role strength plays in the skill (e.g., pole vault) and performance. Considering the objectives of the competitive phase, the time given to maintaining strength is secondary. Therefore, the coach must develop an efficient, specific program. Two to four exercises involving the prime movers may suffice to maintain previously reached levels.

Cessation (C) Phase

The strength-training program ends 5 to 7 days before the main competition so the athlete can reserve all energies for a good performance.

Compensation Phase

The compensation phase completes the annual plan and coincides with the transition phase. One objective of the transition phase is to remove fatigue and replenish exhausted energies through active rest. Another is overall regeneration, which is more complex. For injured athletes, the relaxation phase also means rehabilitating and restoring injured muscles, tendons, muscle attachments, and joints. Trained personnel should design rehabilitative programs.

Whether parallel with rehabilitating injuries or afterward, all athletes should follow a program to strengthen the stabilizers before the end of this phase. Stabilizers are the muscles that secure a limb against the pull of the contracting muscles through a static contraction. Not developing stabilizers means injury-prone athletes whose level of maximum strength and power could be inhibited. Strengthening these important muscles ensures a higher probability of injury-free athletes for the next season. This is also the time to work on compensation of other muscle groups, the muscles that are not primarily used during other phases of the year.

Periodization of Endurance

During an annual plan, endurance develops in several phases. Using an annual plan with one peak as a reference, an athlete accomplishes endurance training in three main phases: aerobic endurance, aerobic endurance and specific endurance (ergogenesis), then specific endurance.

I suggest a similar approach for long-term training. Assuming an athlete begins training at the age of 12, the development of endurance would follow the phases suggested: 12 to16 years old for aerobic endurance; 17 to 18 years old for aerobic endurance and specific endurance; and 19 and over years old for specific endurance. Each phase has its own training objectives.

Aerobic Endurance

Aerobic endurance develops throughout the transition phase and early preparatory phase (1-3 months). Although each sport requires slight alterations, aerobic endurance could be achieved through the uniform and steady state method, with moderate to medium intensity. As a consequence of such a program, the athlete's cardiorespiratory system progressively improves. Parallel with the adjustment to training, the workload must increase, especially training volume.

Aerobic Endurance and Specific Endurance

Aerobic endurance and specific endurance are extremely important in achieving the goals for endurance training. Through this transition from aerobic endurance to sport-specific endurance, continue to emphasize aerobic endurance. Introduce elements of anaerobic activity, depending on the specifics of the sport and the ergogenesis of each activity. The rhythm of activity and the pace of specific drills are progressively becoming sport specific particularly for team sports. Intense training specific to the competitive phase may fail unless you develop solid foundations of endurance during the second phase. The prevailing methods are uniform, alternative, and long- and medium-interval training (toward the end of this phase). The volume of training reaches the highest levels during the aerobic phase and this phase of the annual plan.

Specific Endurance

Specific endurance coincides with the precompetitive and competitive phases. The appropriate training method depends on the ergogenesis of the sport and the needs of the athlete. For many sports, the coach must emphasize training intensity so it often exceeds racing intensity. Alternating various intensities facilitates recovery between training lessons, leading to a good peak for the final competition.

Periodization of Speed

The periodization of speed depends on the characteristics of the sport, performance level, and competition schedule. Training for team sport athletes will differ from that for sprinters. Team players usually follow a monocycle annual plan, but sprinters, who usually participate in an indoor and an outdoor season, follow a bi-cycle plan. Whether for individual or team sports, the periodization of speed may follow these training subphases.

Aerobic and Anaerobic Endurance

Consider aerobic and anaerobic endurance as the training base for the phases to come. Whether through tempo for sprinters or steady state training for other sports, this first subphase of the preparatory phase builds the aerobic foundation on which speed training has to rely. Training progressively incorporates more specific activities of the sport. At the beginning of this subphase, use fartlek (speed play), followed by various intervals and repetition training, to build a strong anaerobic base, which is one step closer to specific speed.

Alactic Speed and Anaerobic Endurance

As the competition phase approaches, training becomes more intensive, event-specific, refined, and specialized. Specificity of training prevails in both methods and specific exercises. Emphasize maximum velocity, progressing from 10 to 15 to 30 to 60 meters.

Specific Speed

Specific speed could incorporate some or all the speed components (alactic, lactic, and speed endurance), depending on the specifics of the sport. Also, you can now introduce drills for developing agility and reaction time.

Specific Speed, Agility, and Reaction Time

Specific methods and drills are dominant for developing specific speed and refining related abilities, such as agility and reaction time.

During the competitive phase, training intensity elevates from specific training methods and participation in competitions. Although exercises specific to the sport prevail, you should also incorporate general training such as games and play for fun, relaxation, and active rest. A correct ratio between these two exercise groups lowers training stress and strain. Many sprinters and team athletes are prone to injuries as a result of high-intensity training; therefore, alternating various means and intensities, although a training deterrent, is an important requirement.

Figures 8.14 through 8.18 illustrate periodization of training for various sports.

Dates	Sept.	Oct.	Nov.	Dec.	Jan.	Feb.	Mar.	Apr.	May	June	July	Aug.
Competitions					Detroit	L.A.	Toronto	Prov. Orillia		Nat. Ch. Vancouver		
Period-ization	Preparatory				Competition						Transition	
	General prep.		Specific prep.		Pre-comp.		Main competition				Transition	
Period of strength	Anat. adapt.	Maximum strength		Convers. to power		Maintenance (maximum strength and power)					Regeneration	

Figure 8.14 Periodization of strength training for gymnastics (monocycle)

Dates	June	July	Aug.	Sept.	Oct.	Nov.	Dec.	Jan.	Feb.	Mar.	Apr.	May
Competitions								Div. champ.	Nat. champ.	World champ.		
Period-ization	Preparatory				Competition						Transition	
	General prep.		Specific prep.		Pre-comp.		Main competition				Transition	
Period of end.	General end. (run, bicycle)		Specific endurance (run, skate)				Specific endurance				General endurance	
Period of strength	Anat. adapt.	Maximum strength		Convers. to power		Maintenance (maximum strength and power)					Regeneration	

Figure 8.15 Periodization of dominant abilities for figure skating (monocycle)

Dates	Sept.	Oct.	Nov.	Dec.	Jan.	Feb.	Mar.	Apr.	May	June	July	Aug.
Competitions						Prov. champ.		Divis. champ.		World champ.		
Period-ization	Preparatory				Competitive						Transition	
	Gen. prep.	Specific prep.			Pre-comp.		Main competition				Transition	
Period of endurance	Anaerobic endurance	Specific endurance (swim, apnea)			Specific endurance						General endurance	
Period of strength	Anatomical adaptation	Maximum strength		Conversion –Musc. end. –Power		Maintenance					Regeneration	

Figure 8.16 Periodization of dominant abilities in synchronized swimming (monocycle)

Dates	Nov.	Dec.	Jan.	Feb.	Mar.	Apr.	May	June	July	Aug.	Sept.	Oct.
Competitions								League games				
Periodization	Preparatory						Competitive					Transition
	Gen. prep.		Specific prep.				Prec.	League games				Transition
Period of strength	Anatomical adaptation	Maximum strength			Conversion –Musc. end. –Power		Maintenance Power Musc. end.				Regeneration	
Period of speed	Aerob. end.	Anaerob. end.	Specific speed				Specific speed, reaction time, and agility				————	
Period of endurance	Specific endurance						Perfect specific endurance				Aerobic endurance	

Figure 8.17 Periodization of dominant abilities for a baseball team (monocycle)

Dates	Nov.	Dec.	Jan.	Feb.	Mar.	Apr.	May	June	July	Aug.	Sept.	Oct.
Competitions					Winter champ.						Summer champ.	
Periodization	Prep. I			Comp. I		T	Prep. II			Comp. II		Trans.
	Gen. prep.		Spec. p.	Prec.	Main. c.	T	Gen. p.	Spec. prep.		Prec.	Main. c.	Trans.
Period of strength	Anatomical adaptation	Maximum strength	Conv.: –Power –M–E	Maintain: –Power –M–E		Anat. adapt.		Max strength	Conv.: –Power –M–E	Maintain: –Power –M–E		Regen.
Period of speed	Aerobic endurance		Anaero. end. and ergogenesis	Specific speed and ergogenesis		Aerobic endurance			Anaer. end. and ergogenesis	Specific speed and ergogenesis		Games

Figure 8.18 Periodization of dominant abilities for swimming (200m) with winter and summer national championships (bi-cycle)

Integrated Periodization

For too long sport scientists and practitioners focused on certain aspects of the periodization process without integrating all the elements into a whole. Although coaches have been overwhelmed by everything they have to do or by keeping up with the complexities of training, sport scientists have produced more knowledge in their field.

Sport psychologists, physiologists, and nutritionists have often increased their knowledge without being too concerned about the planning-periodization process and the specific objectives for each phase of the training plan. Mental and psychological training considers the athlete its main focus, often in connection with the competitive environment. This is also true for nutrition. However, seldom are these sport scientists aware that athletes and coaches need their help throughout the annual or long-term training process and not just before competition.

Integrated periodization combines all the training components into a whole and matches them according to the periodization of the biomotor abilities. Periodization of the biomotor abilities dictates the diet and the psychological skills best suited for a given training phase. Therefore, it is critical for an instructor to learn what diet to use and which psychological skills are best when training aerobic endurance, maximum strength, or other abilities. Armed with such information, the coach will be able to improve athletes' abilities and, as a result, their performance.

Figure 8.19 illustrates integrated periodization for a sport dominated by speed and power.

Months	1	2	3	4	5	6	7	8	9	10	11	12
Training phases	Preparatory					Competitive					Ch.	Trans.
Sub-phases	General	Specific		Pre-comp.		Official/league competitions					Unl.	Trans.
P e r i o d i z a t i o n — Periodization of speed	–Anaerobic/ aerobic endurance	–Max. speed short –Maint. an. endurance		–Max. speed short, medium, long		All in sport-specific proportions					Unl.	Play/ fun
Periodization of strength	AA	MxS	P	MxS	Conv. P.	Maintenance power/MxS					/	Comp.
Mental (m)/ psychological	–Eval. m skills –Learn new m skills –Quiet setting	–M skills to attain training objectives –Visualization –Imagery –Relaxation –Energy management		–M rehearsal –Energize –Positive self-talk –Visioneering –Focus plans –Simulation –Coping		–M skills to cope with specific opponents –Stress management/relaxation –Energizing –Focus plans –Mental rehearsal –Motivation. Positive thinking/optimism –Positive thinking/optimism					* See below	–Active rest –Regen. de-stress
Periodization of nutrition	Balanced diet	–High protein –Carbs	High carbs	–High protein –Carbs	High carbs	Fluctuates according to the schedule of competitions					High carbs.	Balanced diet

* –M skills to aid regeneration, relaxation, stress management
   –Positive talk
   –Visualization

Figure 8.19 Integrated periodization for a speed-power sport

Annual Plan Training Phases and Characteristics

An annual plan has three training phases: preparatory, competitive, and transition. The objectives and characteristics of these phases remain the same whether you do them once or repeat them several times, as in a bi- or tri-cycle. It is important to the athlete's success that you follow the suggested duration, sequence, characteristics, and emphasis on each training phase. This ensures that the highest athletic shape is reached for planned competitions.

Preparatory Phase

The preparatory phase is enormously important to the entire training year. Throughout this period, the athlete develops the general framework of physical, technical, tactical, and psychological preparation for the competitive phase. Inadequate training during this period will have visible repercussions during the competitive phase. A significant amount of training based especially on increased volume would, in the long run, result in a low fatigue level after training and may enhance recovery. Through the phase, particularly during the initial part, a high training volume is essential for adequate body adaptation to the specifics of training.

In general terms, the specific objectives of training in this phase are as follows:

- To acquire and improve general physical training
- To improve the biomotor abilities required by the sport
- To cultivate specific psychological traits
- To develop, improve, or perfect technique
- To familiarize athletes with the basic strategical maneuvers in the following phase
- To teach athletes the theory and methodology of training specific to the sport

The preparatory phase lasts 3 to 6 months, depending on the climate, the sport, and the type of annual plan. For individual sports, it should be one to two times as long as the competitive phase. For team sports, it may be shorter, but not less than 2 or 3 months. For methodological purposes, I divide the preparatory phase into two subphases: general and specific preparation.

The *general preparatory* subphase develops working capacity and general physical preparation and improves technical elements and basic tactical maneuvers. However, the foremost objective is to develop a high level of physical conditioning to facilitate future training. This is necessary for all sports. General exercises as well as those specific to the sport should have a higher priority than just the specific skills of the sport. For instance, a gymnastics coach should dedicate the first two or three microcycles to developing general and special strength of the muscles that will be learning or performing certain technical elements in the following cycles. The same is valid for other sports in which certain physical components may limit technical progress. Often coaches wonder why their athletes do not acquire a skill according to their expectations. These coaches are well advised to test athletes to determine whether they posses adequate physical support for the technical performance of that element or skill.

Throughout this subphase, emphasize a high training volume by incorporating exercises that require extensive general or specific effort. Such a program improves working capacity and psychological drive (determination, perseverance, willpower), progressively adjusting athletes to the specific effort requirements of the sport. Developing aerobic endurance is the main objective for sports in which endurance is the dominant ability or makes an important contribution to the final performance, as in running, swimming, rowing, and cross-country skiing. According to Harre (1982), 70 to 80% of the total training time should be devoted to developing aerobic endurance, evidenced by the kilometers covered in training. General and maximum strength development should be the main objectives of the subphase for sports in which strength is an important attribute, as in weightlifting, gymnastics, wrestling, and throwing events. Increasing the weight the athlete lifts in training would be an objective means of increasing working capacity and specific adaptation to the needs of the sport.

While developing the physical basis of training, athletes in team sports must give substantial time to developing technical and tactical skills. However, they should not neglect endurance, strength, and speed improvement as the physical groundwork for performance accomplishments.

In most sports, the type of training used in the preparatory phase, especially in the general subphase, influences the competitive phase and the quality of results. Insufficient emphasis on training volume during this subphase may account for poor performance, lack of consistency, and a decrease in performance during the last competitions. Consequently, at least one-third of the preparatory phase should be allocated to this subphase (with the rest being specific). The duration of the general preparatory phase reduces constantly for advanced athletes.

As seen previously, training intensity is of secondary importance throughout the preparatory phase, especially during the general preparatory subphase. You may use intensive training continually: however, its ratio should not exceed 30 to 40% of the total amount of training, particularly for juniors and beginners. Gandelsman and Smirnov (1970) suggest that during intense exercise, muscle impulses are strong and irradiate in the CNS, burdening the perception and reaction to a stimulus. This leads to imprecise and uncontrolled movements. A less intensive rate of performing and exercise allows the CNS to be more selective in the type of reply to a stimulus, enabling athletes to have better control over their skills.

Considering the objectives of this subphase, it is inadvisable to compete during this period of heavy work, because athletes will not be ready to test their skills or abilities against opponents. Usually technique is unstable, and poor results often affect the psychological sphere of athletes. In addition, competitions may adversely affect whole training programs, or more specifically the amount of work athletes must perform.

The *specific preparatory*, the second part of the preparatory phase, represents a transition toward the competitive season. The objectives of training are similar to those of the general subphase, but training becomes more specific. Although the volume of training is still high, most work (70-80%) is directed toward specific exercises related to the skills or technical patterns of the sport. Toward the end of this subphase, the volume drops progressively, allowing an elevation of the training intensity. For sports in which intensity is important, as in sprinting, jumping, and team sports, you could lower the volume of training up to 20 to 40%.

For sports in which technique and perfect coordination dominate, such as figure skating, diving, and gymnastics, athletes should continue to improve, perfect, and combine technical elements, so that by the end of the preparatory phase they have at least a rough routine prepared.

Improving and perfecting technique and tactical elements should be the main goals of this subphase. Fulfilling these goals requires specific exercises involving the prime movers—exercises that simulate or are similar to the

Training intensity increases as volume decreases

technical pattern of the skill. Every exercise must be high quality and have a maximum training effect. This way, an optimal link grows between skills and biomotor abilities, leading to developing techniques and abilities required to compete successfully. The coach should maintain only a few indirect exercises in the program (a maximum of 30%) to alternate exercises of various patterns, avoid boredom, and enhance multilateral development, active rest, and fun. Increasing the proportion of specific exercises of direct effect helps an easy transition to the competitive phase.

Following this shift in the proportion of specialized training, athletes should progressively improve their test scores and performance. At the end of this subphase, a competition of secondary importance or an exhibition game will provide important feedback. Training during the preparatory phase is specific for each sport and distinctive for each subphase. Table 8.2 illustrates distinctive training objectives for the general and specific preparatory subphases.

Competitive Phase

Among the main tasks of the competitive phase is perfecting all training factors, enabling athletes to improve their abilities and compete successfully in

TABLE 8.2 Training Objectives for Each Subphase of the Preparatory Phase

Sport	Dominant training factors	General preparatory	Specific preparatory
Gymnastics	Physical	General and maximum strength	Specific strength and power
	Technical	Technical elements	Elements, half and skeleton of full routine
Rowing	Physical	Aerobic endurance General and maximum strength	Aerobic endurance Muscular endurance
Swimming (100m)	Physical	Aerobic endurance General and maximum strength	Anerobic and aerobic endurance Maximum strength and power
Swimming (800m)	Physical	Aerobic endurance General and maximum strength	Aerobic and anaerobic endurance Muscular endurance
Team sports	Technical	Technical elements	Apply technical elements in game situation
	Tactical	Individual and simple team tactics	Team tactics
	Physical	Aerobic endurance General and maximum strength	Anaerobic endurance Power

the main competition or championship. Among the general objectives of the competitive phase are the following:

- Continual improvement of sport-specific biomotor abilities and psychological traits
- Perfecting and consolidating technique
- Improving performance to the highest possible level
- Perfecting tactical maneuvers and gaining competitive experience
- Maintaining general physical preparation

Physical preparation remains the basis of performance. It was the dominant training factor during the preparatory phase for developing a foundation for future training. Through the competitive phase, the athlete must maintain physical preparation at the level achieved by the end of the preparatory phase, as a continuous support for other training factors and performance. From the total amount of physical preparation planned in training, 90% has to be with direct action, and only 10% at most is for exercises with indirect action. The athlete may use the last group of exercises especially for active rest and fun (games and team sports).

The athlete achieves the objectives of the competitive phase through specific skills, exercises, and competitions. Focus on specificity of training to ensure improvement, stabilization, and performance consistency. Consequently, training becomes more intensive while training volume decreases. For sports dominated by speed, power, and maximum strength (sprinting, jumping and throwing events, and weightlifting), training intensity increases dramatically while the volume progressively lessens. In endurance sports (distance running, swimming, cross-country skiing, canoeing, and rowing), training volume may be constant or slightly lower than during the preparatory phase. An exception is the competitive microcycle in which intensity drops according to the number of races and the level of the opponent.

Obviously, performance must improve during the competitive phase as a result of well-planned training. Improvement stagnation or decrease, however, may signal that the coach reduced the amount of work excessively in the second part of the preparatory phase while increasing the intensity. It is an art to discover the correct ratio between intensity and volume.

The competitive phase should last 4 to 6 months, depending on the sport and the type of annual plan. Team sports usually have a longer competitive phase. An excessively long competitive phase requires proportionately longer preparatory and transition phases, which might shorten the duration of the next preparatory period.

Another important factor is to determine the date on which the competitive phase is to begin. A guideline proposed by Harre (1982) includes the following parameters.

- The number of competitions required to reach the highest performance. Gandelsman and Smirnov (1970) claim that, on average, it takes 7 to 10 competitions to achieve high results.
- The interval between competitions.
- The duration of eventual qualifying meets.
- The time required for special preparation before the main competition of the year.
- The time needed for recovery and regeneration.

For methodical and organizational reasons, you may divide the competitive phase into two basic subphases: the precompetitive phase and the main competition phase.

The objective of the *precompetitive phase* is participation in various unofficial or exhibition meets, so the coach can objectively assess the athletes' training level. All technique and tactical skills and physical and psychological training accumulated during the preparatory phase ought to be tested in athletic competition. Competition should not significantly change the training program, especially for elite athletes, because these meets represent a testing ground for the next phase of official contests. Make necessary alterations to training as early as possible during the precompetitive phase, to maximize performance improvements for the main competition.

The *main competition phase* is dedicated strictly to optimizing potential, thus facilitating superior performance in the main contest. The number of training lessons should reflect whether athletes are participating in a loading or a regeneration (unloading) microcycle. A loading microcycle may have 10 to 14 lessons per week. An unloading microcycle will have fewer lessons to permit unloading before competition. Training content for the vast majority of training programs ought to be specific, including exercises directed at physical development. Athletes may use indirect exercises (games) once a week, especially during an unloading phase.

Although training volume may still be high for endurance sports, you may reduce it by 50 to 75% of the level of the preparatory phase for sports requiring perfect coordination, speed, or power. You can increase intensity continually, reaching the highest level 2 or 3 weeks before the main competition, then dropping progressively through the unloading phase. Training lessons of maximum intensity should not occur more than 2 or 3 times per microcycle during the subphase.

The stress curve is also elevated during the competitive phase as a result of the increased intensity of training and participation in competitions. The stress curve should be an undulatory form, reflecting the alternation of stressful activities (competitions and intensive lessons) with short phases of regeneration. The harder and more stressful a competition, the higher the stress curve, and the longer the necessary compensation phase during which the curve decreases.

If possible, arrange competitions progressively in order of importance, concluding with the main competitions. Or introduce hard competitions with a few lighter ones, in which athletes compete without drastic alterations to their training. Though this may be feasible for individual sports, an official game schedule exists for team sports that the coach cannot change.

Six to eight microcycles before the main competition, model the whole training program and daily cycle to the specifics of that competition. Under these circumstances, physical, technical, tactical, and psychological preparation for the main competition is thorough. Predicting and developing every habit of the athletes according to competition specifics will prevent any surprises. During the preparation of the periodization concept, the main competition is preceded by an unloading phase and followed by a special preparation phase.

The *unloading tapering* is the best way to reach supercompensation and improve performance during competition. The objective is to eliminate all training fatigue possible to regenerate body functions, especially the CNS and the psyche, before the main competition of the year. Reduce training volume and intensity so athletes may rest, replenish their energy reserves, and let their bodies rebound and be fresh before entering the annual plan's top competition.

Enhancing psychological supercompensation, which generates positive emotions toward competition, is a major reason for the unloading phase. The time needed for physiological and psychological regeneration must dictate its duration. Krestovnikov (1938) suggested that, following an intense stimulus, the CNS suffers the most fatigue and nervous cells recover seven times slower than skeletal muscle cells. This finding is the foundation of further demonstrations in the area of the needs and techniques of psychological regeneration before, during, and after competition periods (Bompa 1969). However, the duration of this phase should not exceed 2 weeks, during which the coach should lessen the impact of every stress, especially psychological stresses. The approach differs according to the characteristics of the sport. For sports in which the dominant ability is endurance, reduce intensity, the main stressor (figure 8.20).

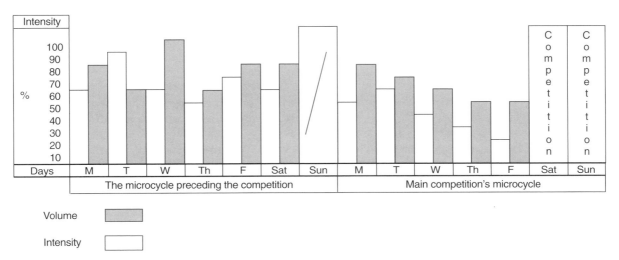

Figure 8.20 Dynamics of volume and intensity during the unloading phase for sports in which endurance dominates

In the first week of unloading, reduce training intensity and the number of daily training lessons to a maximum of two. The number of high-intensity lessons may not exceed two per microcycle, and their duration should be minimum. Outside of the three parts of the training lesson, eliminate all other activities, so athletes can use their free time for recovery. Reduce weight training to two sessions per cycle. Training volume may be as in previous microcycles or slightly reduced. Training content, however, should include mostly medium- and low-intensity methods clearly dominated by the aerobic component. Such a program has dual importance. It produces the least stress, but satisfactorily maintains physical preparation. In the second week, the main competition's microcycle, completely remove both training intensity and weight programs from the schedule. In a camp situation, athletes should still perform two lessons a day, mostly to keep them preoccupied with training rather than worrying about the competition.

Use the same approach for sports dominated by speed, power, or coordination. In the first microcycle, reduce training volume to approximately 50% of the previous level (figure 8.21). You can use a two-peak microcycle, but the intense lessons should have long rest intervals between repetitions to diminish stress. Most exercises performed during the intense lessons should be dynamic, of short duration, and lightly loaded. The dominant intensities, outside of the

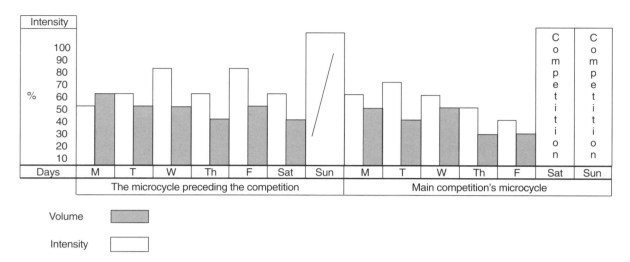

Figure 8.21 Dynamics of volume and intensity for the unloading phase of sports in which speed or power dominate

two intense lessons, ought to be submaximal alternating with moderate- or low-intensity lessons. Exclude weight training completely so the athletes save all their energy for the competition.

During the competition's main microcycle, training volume continues to fall. At the same time, intensity, which also progressively reduces, has one peak in the first part of the cycle, though not of high intensity. This microcycle, even in a camp situation, may be of the 3 + 1 format, meaning after every 1-1/2 days of work there is 1/2 day of rest when psychological relaxation is a priority.

Figure 8.22 suggests the approach for sports in which both training volume and intensity have equal importance (i.e., team sports). In the first week, produce unloading by reducing the work volume. Only one peak may be necessary during the week. Progressively reduce tension, yet keep two intense training sessions of 60 and 50% of maximum. In the second week, the curves of intensity and volume both taper. Volume falls to a lower point than intensity; however, even during this week you may plan a microcycle with two peaks. The first peak should be 30 to 40% of maximum and the second 25 to 30%. Two days before the main competition, schedule short training sessions of low intensity (see figure 8.22). Strive for enjoyment, confidence building, optimism, and team spirit during these sessions.

The *special preparation* period, organized separately or with the unloading phase, refers to activities to facilitate successful participation in an important competition. It could last 3 to 7 days, depending on the specific needs and characteristics of the competition. During this phase, alter certain training aspects, especially tactical aspects, according to the latest information on future opponents or the competition schedule. Most training lessons follow the model training concept, with the purpose of enhancing preparation for the competition to come. An aspect with important implications for the final result is the special psychological preparation that considers relaxation, promoting confidence, and motivating athletes for the contest. However, be careful in how you use psychological techniques, because overemphasis often leads to negative results. Each athlete is different, and you must apply all training aspects individually. Some athletes do not require any psychological preparation and a casual approach might be the most successful.

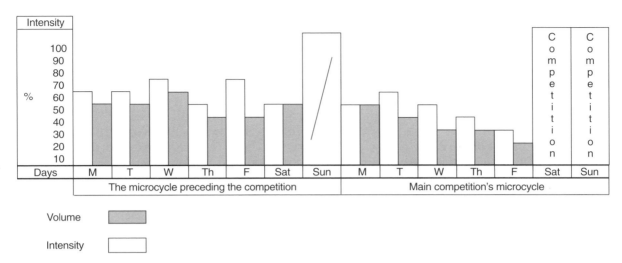

Figure 8.22 Dynamics of volume and intensity for the unloading phase for team sports in which the aerobic and anaerobic energy systems have an almost equal contribution

Transition Phase

After long periods of preparation, hard work, and stressful competitions, when determination, motivation, and willpower are often challenged and tested, athletes have a high level of physiological and psychological fatigue.

Although muscular fatigue may disappear in a few days, CNS fatigue can remain for a much longer period. The more intense the training and the greater number of competitions, the higher the fatigue level. It is hard to believe that any athlete could immediately commence a new annual training cycle under these circumstances. Rest is necessary to refresh athletes physically and psychologically before training starts again. When the new preparatory phase begins, athletes should be completely regenerated and ready to train. In fact, athletes should feel a strong desire to train again after a successful transition phase. Removing CNS fatigue is considered by Hahn (1977) the major goal of the transition phase. To minimize fatigue, athletes should take special psychological preparation and treatment (see chapter 5 on rest and recovery) throughout the annual program, especially during the transition phase. If you cannot eliminate the stress of the previous season and identify and compensate for its negative elements, the athlete may experience the negative elements of stress again throughout and following the preparatory phase.

The transition phase, often inappropriately called the off-season, links two annual plans. It facilitates psychological rest, relaxation, and biological regeneration and maintains an acceptable level of general physical preparation (40-50% of the competitive phase). The transition phase lasts 3 to 4 weeks, sometimes longer. Under normal circumstances it should not exceed 5 weeks. Athletes train 2 to 4 times a week, depending on their level of athletic involvement.

There are two common approaches to the transition phase. The first and incorrect approach encourages complete rest with no physical activity; the term off-season fits perfectly. The abrupt interruption of training and the resulting passive rest or complete inactivity leads to detraining, dissipating most gains from the hard work of the previous 11 months. In addition, the sudden shift from intense work to complete passive rest may be harmful to the body, possibly causing insomnia, loss of appetite, and eventual perturbations of the digestive system.

The symptoms are not pathological and can be reversed if training resumes within a short time. If the cessation of training is prolonged, athletes can display these symptoms for some time, indicating the inability of the human body and its systems to adapt to inactivity. The time needed for these symptoms to incubate will vary from athlete to athlete, but in general they can appear after 2 or 3 weeks of inactivity and vary in severity. Decreased or diminished training can leave the athlete vulnerable to the detraining syndrome (Israel 1972) or exercise-dependency syndrome (Kuipers and Keizer 1988). As a result of detraining, there is a marked decrease in the athlete's physiological well-being and work output (Fry et al. 1991; Kuipers and Keizer 1988).

When training proceeds as planned, the body uses protein to build and repair damaged tissues. Disuse, however, causes the body to increase the process of protein degradation. It starts to break down some gains made during training and catabolize protein, increasing the degradation of protein (Appell 1990; Edgerton 1976).

Testosterone level, which is important for gains in strength, decreases as a result of detraining; this may have a diminished effect on the amount of protein synthesis (Houmard 1991).

Psychic disturbances, such as headaches, insomnia, exhaustion, tension, mood disturbances, lack of appetite, and psychological depression, are among the usual symptoms associated with total abstinence from training. Each athlete may develop any of these symptoms or a combination of them. All these symptoms rise from lowered levels of testosterone and beta-endorphin, a neuroendocrine compound that causes euphoric postexercise feelings (Houmard 1991).

The decrease in the muscle fiber cross-sectional area is apparent after several weeks of inactivity. These changes result from protein breakdown and reduction in the recruitment pattern of the working muscle. The increased levels of some chemicals ($Na+$ and $CL-$) in the muscle play a role in the breakdown of muscle fiber (Appell 1990).

Reduction in speed tends to be the first effect of detraining, because protein breakdown and degenerating motor units decrease the power of muscle contraction. Another reason is perhaps the sensitivity of the nervous system to detraining. Because the motor unit is the first thing to deteriorate, the muscle fiber has a reduction in the nerve impulses to make it contract and relax at rapid rates. The strength and frequency of these impulses can also be affected by lowering the number of motor units recruited during repeated contractions (Edgerton 1976; Hainaut and Duchatteau 1989; Houmard 1991).

As a result of diminished motor recruitment patterns, the loss in power becomes more prominent. The body fails to recruit the same number of motor units it once could, resulting in a net decrease in the amount of force it can generate. For an inactive athlete, the rate of strength loss per day can be 3 to 4% for the first week (Appell 1990). For some athletes, especially in power-speed dominant sports, this can be a substantial loss.

Endurance capacity is also affected by inactivity, some 7% in the first 7 to 12 days. At the same time, there is a 30% decrease in the level of hemoglobin (a complex molecule found in the red blood cell that carries oxygen at cell level) and therefore oxygen supply. Blood volume and mitochondria (subcellular structure found in all red cells) decrease by 5%. With diminishing mitochondria density (50% the first week and another 25% the following week), the result is decreasing function of oxidative (aerobic) and glycolitic (anaerobic) enzymes. The consequence is increased lactate production because the muscle's ability to buffer the buildup of lactate diminishes, which directly affects aerobic capacity (Appell 1990; Terjung and Hood 1986).

Passive rest may also prevent the athlete from beginning the new training cycle at a higher level than the previous year, an important requirement for continuous performance improvement. Astrand and Rodahl (1970) assert that less effort is required to maintain a certain level of preparation than to develop it in the first place. If complete inactivity prevails throughout the transition phase, the first macrocycle of the new annual plan will be wasted to reach a level which the athlete could have easily maintained through active rest.

From a methodical point of view, a second approach is desirable. Emphasize activities of a different nature than those used during regular training. This will enhance active rest, or more specifically psychological relaxation and rest, and maintain a level of physical activity proportional with a good fitness level. Athletes who follow this concept are psychologically vigorous and physically prepared for the new preparatory phase (Harre 1982; Ozolin 1971).

Plan the transition phase well. Throughout this period you should follow athletic ethics. Being physically active does not mean lifting bottles of beer. Overindulgence of alcohol is harmful even during the transition phase. A correct athletic regimen also means an adequate diet. Weight gain of more than 2 to 4 kilograms is undesirable.

Transition phase activity should begin immediately following the main competition. During the first week, progressively reduce both work volume and intensity, and emphasize exercises of a different nature from those regularly used in training. If athletes want to completely postpone physical activity, either because of special medical treatment or a high degree of nervous exhaustion, it should be done the week after the first week of detraining. After total rest, the following 2 or 3 weeks should consist of active rest, fun, and general enjoyment including physical involvement. Plan the activities for this phase, or allow elite athletes to plan it and then approve their plans. The athletes must perform all activities without the coach present. Athletes have to be comfortable to do what they want and have fun, and in some cases the coach might be an impediment. Besides, the coach also needs a relaxation period.

Changes in environment and training means during active rest positively affect CNS relaxation. Gymnasts should go outdoors since they train indoors for 11 months. Athletes in water sports should find some land. Other athletes, such as weightlifters, wrestlers, and gymnasts, should go to the seashore or swim some. In addition to these activities, athletes may perform other means of training, such as exercises for flexibility and general strength, to maintain the general level of physical training. As part of the general activities, Hahn (1977) suggests that the athlete practice his or her hobby, which is often neglected during times of intense training.

Use the transition phase to analyze past programs and compile the following annual cycle. The most appropriate time for analysis is the first week of the transition phase, when many aspects of past activities are still fresh. The coach and athletes should focus on positive criticism in the analysis. The idea is that everyone involved learns from past mistakes and avoids repeating them. A medical control examination would be appropriate during this time, when the physician could make precise assessments regarding health status and possible treatment. The coach should outline the training plan for the following year through the transition phase so it's ready on the first day of the new preparatory phase.

Chart of the Annual Plan

By now you should be familiar with the periodization concept and the main objective of each training phase and subphase. The time has come to make the chart of the annual plan. Compiling a chart requires adequate knowledge of the relationships among the training components and to what degree they represent an important stress on athletes. You must also know the ratio between training factors and the appropriate emphasis to place on each during every macrocycle. An adequate training planner handles all these aspects correctly. The process of making an annual plan represents the highlights of your knowledge in this area.

Compiling an annual plan differs from sport to sport. Its synthesis is expressed in graphical forms in the following charts. You will see various forms of charts and should use the chart that suits you best. Experienced coaches may find that just the chart, without the other factors in the section on compiling an annual plan, is an effective planning tool.

Chart of a Monocycle

The first chart is one of the simplest forms presented (figure 8.23). It is a monocycle intended to be used by the Canadian Rowing Team for the Moscow Olympic Games. Using this chart as a reference, I will explore the methodology of producing the chart of an annual plan.

The top part of the chart lists the athletes' names, followed by a brief statement of objectives set (sometimes in consultation with the athletes). The first objective set is for performance. This should be a measurable performance (i.e., 11.8/100-meter dash), a ranking to achieve, or both (i.e., winning six games and placing fourth in the junior championships). Also, present tests and standards briefly, suggested in the section on training parameters, number 6. Next, set the main objectives for each training factor. Strongly relate objectives of tests, standards, and performance. Achieving the standards for each test and objectives for each training factor should represent a strong guarantee that the athlete will achieve the performance objectives. The objectives of each training factor must aim at improving all weaknesses. If the objectives are listed separately, it may be redundant to specify them again on the chart.

Below the objectives are the dates and competition schedule. The latter is the most important training parameter in planning. The coach cannot begin a planning program for the year without knowing the precise dates of competitions. Therefore, it is necessary that each sport governing body or national sport federation inform clubs of the competition schedule for the following year immediately after the current year's championships.

Construct the chart from right to left around the competition dates. Place the main competition, be it provincial, national, world championships, or Olympic Games, on the right-hand side of the chart, allowing room (3-4 weeks) for the transition phase. That date (July 20 in our example) determines how to list the months and weekends in their boxes. There are 52 boxes, one for each weekend when, in most cases, competitions are organized. In our example, the Olympic finals were on July 20. To the right of that date, the month of August was planned as a transition phase. All other months and weekends were then listed from right to left, suggesting that under normal circumstances the preparatory phase may commence in September. To the left of the main competition of the year the coach should list all the other contests in which he or she plans to enter the athletes. The symbols used to illustrate a competition should enable the coach to discriminate between the main, important, and exhibition competitions. Use the most visible symbol or color to illustrate the main championships of the year.

Should the athletes only participate in domestic competitions, place all the symbols on that line. Otherwise, use the international line to show when such

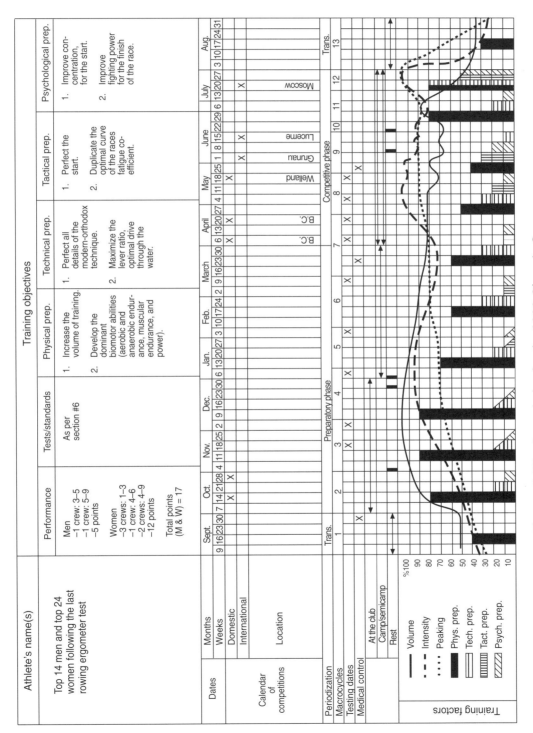

Figure 8.23 Annual plan for the 1980 Olympic Games

competitions are planned. Below the dates of competitions, a space is provided for the location of each competition.

Now the coach knows the dates and locations of competitions, paramount to the process of dividing the year into training phases. Again, work from right to left. The line for periodization is divided into three classic training phases. In our example, August was planned as a transition phase. Incorporate all competitions in the competitive phase. Figure 8.23 suggests a competitive phase 16 weeks long, from April 6 to July 20. The remaining time is a long preparatory phase. Color separately the space left for each phase or divide it by a line, indicating the phase.

To divide the annual plan into macrocycles, use the schedule of competitions, the objectives of training, and the similarities of the methods used to achieve the objectives.

As illustrated in our example (again from right to left), the transition is a separate macrocycle. Although the main competition or tournament is of short duration, athletic preparation, especially psychological preparation, during the days or week before is sufficiently unique to warrant a separate macrocycle. Furthermore, the period preceding the main competition (in our example three microcycles) is another macrocycle, because the coach wants to elevate athletic shape to the highest levels through specific means and methods.

Another short macrocycle is specified for the week following the two competitions in Europe, namely Grünau and Lucerne. After these competitions against some of the finest competitors in the world, athletes will be fatigued and need a few days of recovery before starting an important cycle of training for the Olympics. The two international races are approached in a cyclic manner, each time having one microcycle for training and one for unloading and competition.

Because there is such similarity between these four microcycles, they are incorporated into a single macrocycle. The following cycle is again 4 weeks long, culminating with a time trial race in Welland, preceded by three microcycles of special training for the competition. The longest macrocycle, composed of six microcycles, precedes the special training. Aerobic endurance is the main objective. During this cycle, the athletes participate in two long-distance regattas in British Columbia (BC). The macrocycle for most of February and March is also long and has the main objective of converting maximum strength to muscular endurance. Both cycles before have some similarities (developing maximum strength and aerobic endurance). A small difference leads to the decision to divide these nine microcycles into two macrocycles, through which athletes will develop aerobic endurance. During the cycle, which includes most of December, athletes achieve this objective through running and cross-country skiing. General development, general strength, and aerobic endurance are among the main objectives of both cycles.

Finally, after dividing the year into macrocycles, the coach numbers them from the first to the last. Whenever refering to a macrocycle, the coach specifies its number. These numbers are also useful to refer to when compiling a project.

Next, set dates for testing and medical control. Plan the first test at the beginning of the first macrocycle of the preparatory phase, especially for prospective athletes. Use the data collected to compute the optimal load, number of repetitions, and the amount of work for training. For top athletes with adequate information from past years, you can plan the first testing date later, toward the end of the general preparation subphase. It is advisable, however, to test all athletes at the beginning of a new training program to know their starting points. For other testing dates, I suggest you test at the end of each cycle to find out if athletes achieved the objectives since each macrocycle has specific objectives. This refers mostly to the preparatory phase since the optimal means of testing, the competition itself, is available during the competitive phase. As in our example, consider certain competitions as testing dates, especially during the precompetitive phase, because their goal is to obtain objective information about the athletes.

Three or four dates of medical control are sufficient. Organize the first before the preparatory phase so you know the health status of each athlete. Unhealthy individuals should not be considered or, if necessary, should be committed to a prolonged regeneration and resting phase. Set other dates for medical control before and after the competitive phase. A long competitive phase may require at least one extra date to monitor health status. A good physician with some sports background should thoroughly perform all the medical controls. Medical information collected during the last control may influence the length and type of transition phase for each individual. Some athletes require special treatment before a new annual training program, and the physician should indicate what care is appropriate.

The next heading indicates forms of preparation during the annual plan. Either use different colors or, as in the sample chart, draw an arrow to point out the training time at the club or in camps and semicamps. Indicate rest, including the transition phase. Sundays are not necessarily shown on the chart if they are the only days off. Indicate 2- to 3-day holidays or rest days (for example, Christmas or after an important competition) by a narrow stick in the appropriate box.

The coach has now noted most of the athletes' activities in the chart. What remains is to express the percentage of each training factor per macrocycle. Following this, the coach will draw the curves of the training components and peaking. To distinguish quickly between each training factor, the coach may use different colors or symbols.

The emphasis placed on each training factor depends on the specifics of the sport, the strengths and weaknesses of the athletes, and the phase of training. For the first macrocycle, emphasize physical preparation for most if not all sports. If you stress general physical preparation during the first cycle, then specific physical preparation directly related to the demands of the sport should prevail in the second. This is more valid for individual sports since team sports would include the objective of technical improvement. Physical preparation dominates all training phases for sports in which technique is simple, especially cyclic sports. In any case, regardless of the type of sport, during macrocycles that emphasize physical preparation, gear training toward hard work and a positive attitude. Such an approach strengthens psychological preparation and improves perseverance, tenacity, and determination. These psychological traits can convert into willpower, combativeness, and fighting power during the competitive phase.

Another important factor in deciding what weight to place on each training factor is performance level. The limiting factor of improvement for beginners and prospective athletes is technique, especially for team sports. For elite athletes, physical preparation, particularly specific physical preparation seems to be a limiting factor in performance improvement. Each year, therefore, the coach should emphasize the factors that restrict athletic advancement.

Athletes start the new annual training program with a percentage of work between 30 and 50, depending on their performance levels. Those who allow themselves lower training parameters to start with should not expect more than a low level of improvement. Therefore, the curve of the training volume should not drop below these values. In a year following the Olympic Games, participating athletes may allow themselves a longer rest period; therefore, the curve of volume for the new plan may start between 20 and 30%. An annual training program preceding the Olympics should begin with the curve around 40%. This curve then elevates progressively through the preparatory phase, reaching its summit at the end of general preparation and the beginning of specific physical preparation. During the competitive phase, the endurance curve lowers progressively to below intensity. The intensity curve trails the training volume curve through the preparatory phase, then surpasses it by the middle of the competitive phase. Both curves undulate more during macrocycles with many competitions. The intensity is higher in the microcycle preceding a competition and decreases in the competitive cycle to allow athletes to rest and regenerate before the competition. As a rule, when volume is high, intensity is lower, because athletes can hardly perform many repetitions at a fast pace.

During the macrocycle before the main competition, volume increases, reflecting an emphasis on the quantity of work. The volume lowers again in the last two microcycles before the next macrocycle. Training intensity behaves differently. At first it is slightly lower than training volume for a short period, then elevates progressively as the competition approaches. During unloading, however, both curves may drop slightly depending on the sport. Intensity does not elevate much for endurance sports, allowing the coach to stress volume and intensity almost equally. Contrary to this, intensity may elevate higher than the training volume curve in sports characterized by dynamic performance. As for the short subphase of competitions, volume is down and intensity up, signifying that most competitions are intense.

The peaking curve, a direct result of the interplay between volume and intensity, trails both curves through the preparatory phase and elevates substantially during the precompetitive and competition subphases. The magnitude of the peaking curve depends on the psychological preparation that the coach undertakes with the athletes before important competitions.

In simple charts of an annual plan, as in our example, the magnitude and not the percentage of each curve signifies the emphasis placed on volume and intensity. Their expression in percentage form rather than in relation to each other is more complicated; therefore, experienced coaches training elite athletes may use it. Similarly, the curve of stress was not included in the chart, because habitually its shape is affected by (and therefore similar to) the curve of intensity, as well as the vicinity of and participation in a competition.

Figure 8.24 illustrates a monocycle for a hypothetical volleyball team. One of the main goals is to qualify for and win the finals of the provincial or state championships. The team must qualify for the national championships and place in the top three teams (third being a more realistic objective). Before the league games there are three exhibition games, which are a means of specifically testing the team abilities.

The periodization section has integrated all the elements of periodization from strength to nutrition, unlike the previous chart. Because this is just an example, the reader can insert other elements of periodization of psychological, mental, and nutrition.

The ratio between the training factors is different from the previous chart because of the specific requirements of a team sport. In this example, technical and tactical preparation are more important. In the first macrocycles, physical preparation is the dominant factor, as it should be with most sports, especially when there is a long preparatory phase, because the athletes first must develop a physical foundation. Without solid physical support, they may not perfect certain technical maneuvers. For example, without powerful legs an athlete should not expect adequate spiking and blocking. The relationship between

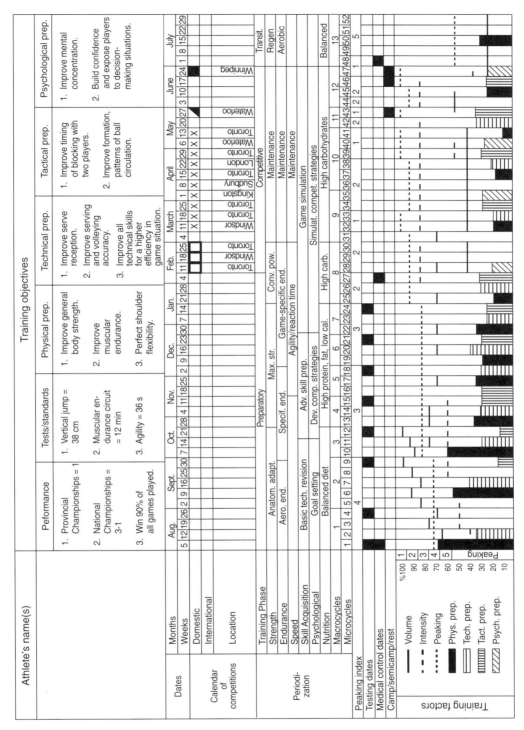

Figure 8.24 Monocycle annual plan for a volleyball team

the curves of volume and intensity, both presented in horizontal lines (step-loading pattern), illustrates their percentage compared with figure 8.23 where I used curves to show the need to stress the intensity component at a much earlier stage in the team's preparation. The volume of training prevails in the first four macrocycles. From the fifth macrocycle, the intensity curve elevates higher than in adjacent cycles. This reflects the development of maximum strength, as well as emphasis on game-specific endurance and agility and reaction time. Throughout the competitive phase, intensity remains higher, which suggests the activity in training and the stress of competitions.

Peaking Index

Figure 8.24 introduces a new parameter, the peaking index. This reflects state of mind, physical, technical, tactical, and psychological readiness at a given time. The peaking index thus refers to prioritizing competitions. The coach should place varying emphases on competitions, according to the level of the team or athlete, the importance of the competition, and the opponents' abilities. Except for high-priority competitions, the competitors (especially elite athletes and teams) do not have to push themselves with equal drive for each competition or peak evenly for every competition. In sports in which the competitive phase is long or there are many competitions, it is stressful and difficult to peak equally for each competition. Athletes must not be worn out by the date of the championship, which occurs at the end of the competitive phase. Elite athletes, especially those in team sports, may approach certain competitions with less drive, resulting in a lower peak and less stress. Peaking for a competition is usually preceded by unloading and special psychological and mental training. Repetitive unloading (say for 40 games) significantly lowers training volume and intensity in the competitive phase, which may result in an inadequate level of physical preparation for the final games. Recurrent psychological preparation for each game may lead to the inability to concentrate until the end of the competitive phase. The peaking index means that, although athletes still focus on each game, they will approach some differently, with a much shorter unloading phase and less tension.

Use peaking index 1 when your team meets one of the three strongest opponents. For such games, the team must reach its highest physical and psychological potential. Equate peaking index 1 with 100% of the athletes' physical and psychological potential. Use peaking index 2 when playing opponents in the top two-thirds of the league, excluding the top three to five teams. It equates to 90% of maximum potential. Reach peaking index 3 when playing much less threatening teams in a league game or during the precompetitive games. For the precompetitive games, however, emphasize certain technical or tactical objectives rather than victory itself. It may be necessary to achieve this level of physical and psychological potential in the special preparation subphase of a bi- or tri-cycle. Peaking index 3 suggests 70 to 80% of potential. Peaking index 4 represents the preparatory phase, when athletes do not compete, and is 60% of maximum. Peaking index 5, the lowest, refers to the transition phase, when the competitive potential is 50% of maximum.

I used this approach in figure 8.25 in which the peaking index line symbolized the appropriate index for each macrocycle. At the bottom of the chart is a special column for the peaking indices, which was a guideline to draw the curve of the peaking index. The curve is symbolically expressed through a straight horizontal line to signify the curve index and magnitude for each macrocycle. However, in reality, the peaking curve should undulate.

Chart of a Bi-Cycle

Figure 8.25 illustrates a bi-cycle for a hypothetical team or athlete for which technical and tactical preparations are both important in training. The annual plan has two main competitions. The first is on August 26. The other major competition, February 25, is also important although not as much so. The first

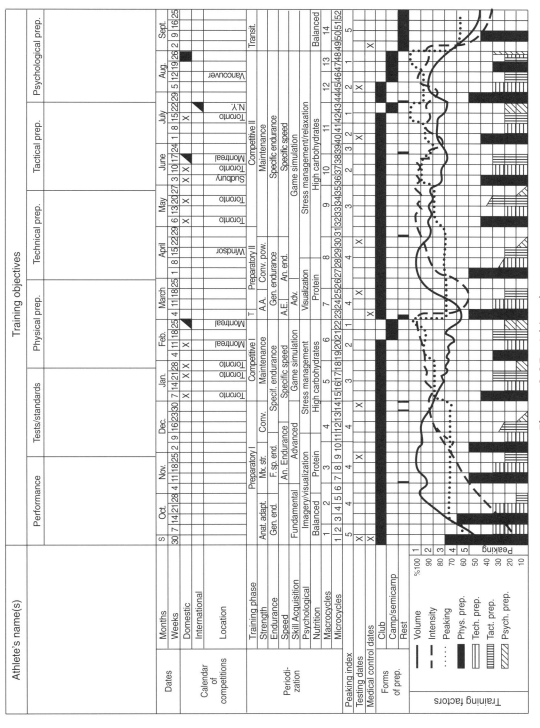

Figure 8.25 A bi-cycle

preparatory phase is longer, and volume is the most significant training component. Less emphasis is placed on training intensity compared with the second preparatory phase, allowing the athletes to acquire a solid base of endurance and strength. The competitive phase is much shorter during the first cycle. Its duration and number of competitions suggest that the coach does not overemphasize outstanding performances for the first half of the training year. The coach expects gains in physical preparation, with technical and tactical improvements in the first cycle, to measure favorably on the athletes' potential during the second competitive phase.

During the second cycle, training volume is dominant for six microcycles and slightly less important for the remaining 19 microcycles due to a longer competitive phase, throughout which the intensity is the most emphasized component of training. Again, the undulatory shape of training volume and intensity signifies the stress during each microcycle and the short unloading phases before each important competition. It is evident that during competitive phase I, the coach organized the competitions in a cyclic manner, and for the second cycle used the grouping approach. This allows the coach to divide competitive phase II into periods of training and competitions. After the first competitions (June 3, 10, and 17), the coach might make observations regarding the athletes' preparation and may then attempt to correct shortcomings during the following three microcycles, which precede the two competitions in July. A similar approach may be appropriate for the last part of competition phase II.

An additional line is included in the chart for periodization, specifying the 52 microcycles of the year. This new parameter is significant, especially during the analysis of the previous year's program. Analysis of the previous year's program can help determine in which microcycle the athletes achieved the best performance and how many cycles they needed to reach it. Then, the coach can design the following year's program to accommodate this finding or can alter the program to reach the highest performance earlier or later as necessary.

Chart of a Tri-Cycle

Figure 8.26 illustrates a chart of a tri-cycle, or an annual training plan with three main competitions. Use a program with three peaks for sports such as boxing, wrestling, and swimming when competitions are spread evenly throughout the year.

The chart shows a hypothetical example without reference to a specific sport. Consequently, the coach set no training objectives and assumed that all training factors played an almost equal role. The first main competition (April 26) was a qualifying meet for the following two international competitions (say Pan American Games on August 2 and World Championships on December 13). In this hypothetical case the athlete or team will qualify for the first competition without any difficulties (probability 90%); therefore, the coach assumed peaking index 2 was adequate. For the following two competitions, the coach plans to reach peaking index 1.

The coach organized an adequate periodization for each competition with the classical training phases and subphases. A transition phase was not necessary after the qualifying meet (April 26), because the peaking index 2 for the first competition did not stress athletes. Instead, after 2 days of active rest the athletes began a new preparatory phase for the August 2 international competition. A short transition phase, or full microcycle, followed this competition, and again the athletes participated in new preparatory and competitive phases. Before the December 13 competition (World Championships), the participation in an invitational international meet (Frankfurt, November 8) was essential for the athletes to gain European experience.

Of the three preparatory phases, the first is slightly longer, when the coach stresses training volume over the longest period. The coach considers the foundation of physical preparation developed in this phase and in

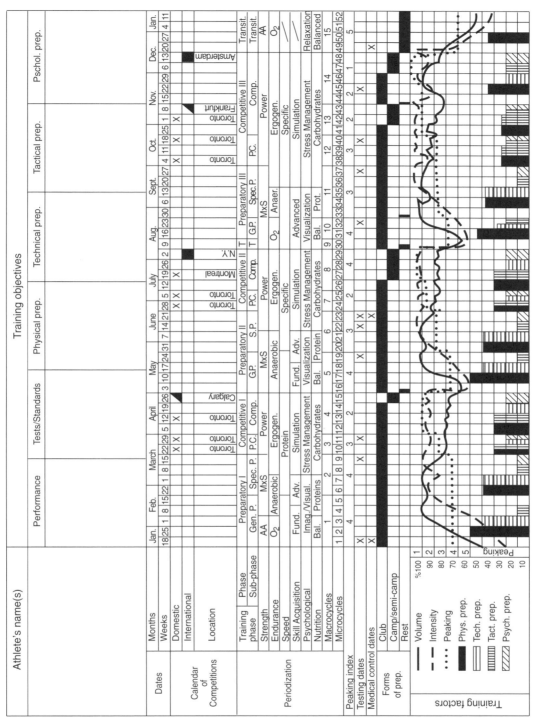

Figure 8.26 A tri-cycle

the following two preparatory phases to be adequate. It provides a base and stresses training intensity through the three competitive phases. The ratio between the training factors illustrates the same concept. Physical preparation appears to be dominant for each preparatory phase. In the following macrocycles, especially during the competitive phase, the ratio changes to illustrate a more balanced interplay between the four training factors.

Figure 8.27 illustrates the training program for an Olympic sprinter in which the coach can specify skill acquisition and psychological periodization in addition to periodizing the dominant abilities. The latter brings forth the year-round concern for psychological preparation, which often is misinterpreted as being essential only before important competitions.

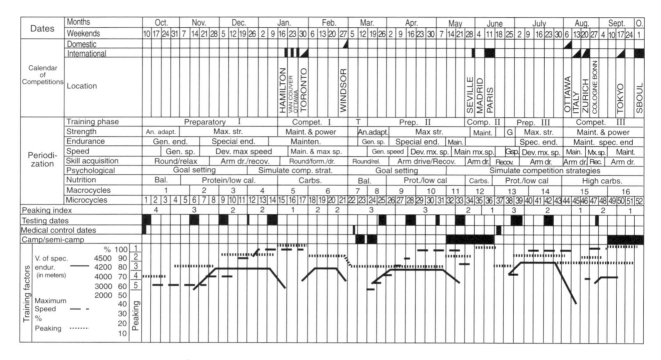

Figure 8.27 Annual plan for an Olympic sprinter

Another substantial addition is incorporating the volume of specific endurance in meters per week. The curve of this activity evolves according to the training phase, following the concept of periodization. Similarly, because you express the volume of specific endurance per week in precise amounts, it adds the critical element of objectively planning the training load.

A similar element of objectivly defining training volume and intensity is exemplified by figure 8.28. This plan, a bi-cycle, illustrates the volume in number of kilometers swum per week, and intensity, in this case speed, is calculated in percentage of maximum.

Such an example works for sports in which training load can be objectively measured, as in running, skiing, canoeing, rowing, cycling, and weightlifting. Sports like gymnastics could also quantify training load by specifying the number of half and full routines performed per week.

Annual Plan for Artistic Sports

You can use a slightly different chart of the annual plan for sports in which perfect artistry, coordination, and skills are prime objectives. Such a plan could be a mono-, bi-, or tri-cycle, depending on the number and distribution of competitions. The middle of the chart is unique. You can specify the time when the gymnast should learn, repeat, and perfect half or full routines. Figure 8.29 exemplifies a chart of an annual plan for gymnastics; however, I suggest the

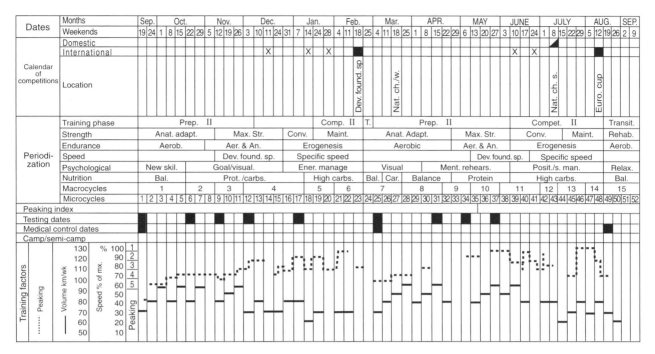

Figure 8.28 Annual plan of a 100-m swimmer with objectiely planned volume (in km/week) and intensity (in % of maximum velocity)

same approach for other sports, such as figure skating, diving, and synchronized swimming.

The plan illustrated in figure 8.29 hypothesizes a bi-cycle with two major competitions, the Olympic Games (July 20) and the World Cup (October 24-26). Before both contests, the coach organizes a competition to select the team or individual gymnasts. As a normal progression, the coach also plans a few exhibition meets during the precompetitive subphase, one of which may be an international meet (May 25). Following the Olympics, the coach plans a short transition phase of total rest for 3 or 4 days followed by light work.

The objectives and the compilation of the chart are based on hypothetical data; therefore, the phase and data when the athletes must learn technical elements, exercises, and routines are also supposition. Obviously, athletes acquire new elements and routines a year before a meet such as the Olympic Games or World Cup. For skill acquisition, where perfecting an element starts, the coach should retain only elements that will be in the final routine. As a rule, the coach should not look for or teach the gymnast any new technical elements from this point, as it may be too late to perfect them before the major competition. The coach should mentally confirm at least one year in advance which elements the athlete will learn and potentially include in a routine. Only under special circumstances should the coach introduce a new skill close to a major competition. Such an instance might be inventing a new element or discovering a new skill that does not pose a learning problem or stress the athlete. Strangely enough, some coaches are poorly organized, and it has happened that a routine is finalized only days before a major competition. Obviously, under such circumstances the responsibility should not be put on the gymnast's shoulders.

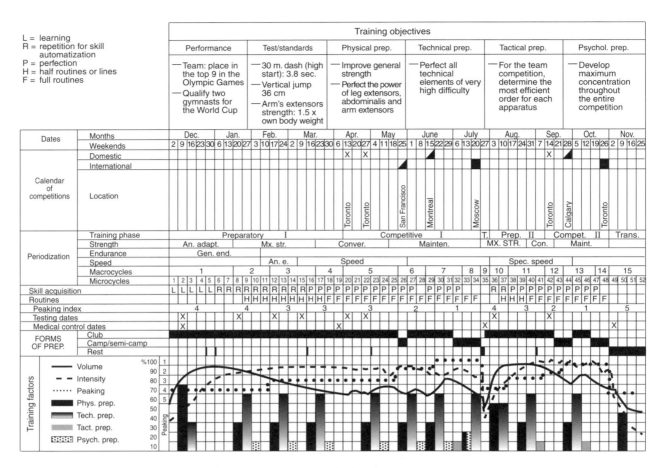

Figure 8.29 Annual plan for gymnastics

The ratio between training factors is unique for gymnastics (as may be the case for other artistic sports) in the sense that tactical training plays a minor role and rarely appears on the chart. In the first macrocycle, physical training should be by far the dominant training factor. During this cycle, the coach seeks to develop or improve the dominant biomotor abilities required, placing special emphasis on specific strength. The gymnast who does not develop strength appropriately will not be able to acquire certain technical elements. From the second macrocycle on, technical training assumes the leading role along with appropriate physical preparation. This is valid for all cycles of training except the 10th, which marks the beginning of the second part of the annual plan. Regard the transition phase as a maintenance phase for physical preparation.

Individual Annual Training Plan

Most annual plans I have presented could be used for either individual athletes or teams. They represent in specific terms the guidelines to follow in preparing a year of training. However specific they may be, such a plan cannot provide for individual quantities of work each athlete will perform, a significant factor in training. Therefore, you may consider using the individual annual training plan outlined in figure 8.30. Such a plan will assist the coach in

Training load for a runner is measured objectively

monitoring each athlete's training plan in precise terms, because it incorporates all the means of training an individual athlete would use and the number of repetitions or mileage for a year of training.

The competition schedule must be known when compiling such a plan. Based on this data, the coach sets the periodization of the plan and the objectives for each macrocycle, expressed according to the training phase for each training factor. In figure 8.30, a hypothetical individual program for a high jumper, general strength (G.S.), power (P.), and maximum strength (M.S.) were developed during the first subphase of training. As the program advances or approaches the competitive phase, other factors such as technique (T.) receive more emphasis. General physical preparation (G.P.P.) prevails during the transition phase.

The coach must state training intensity, which governs the amount and quality of work for each macrocycle. You could simply express the intensity of training on a scale of low (L), medium (M), or high (H) as in our example. You

Year

Athlete's Name _____

Event _____

Performance Obj. : 2.10 m.   Coach _____

		Nov.	Dec.	Jan.	Feb.	March	Apr.	May	June	July	August	Sept.	Oct.
Dates	Months / Weekends	4 11 18 25	2 9 16 23 30	6 13 20 27	3 10 17 24	2 9 16 23 30	6 13 20 27	4 11 18 25	1 8 15 22 29	6 13 20 27	3 10 17 24 31	7 14 21 28	5 12 19 26
Calendar of competitions	Domestic				X X ◢			X X X X	X		☐ ■		
	International												
	Location				Toronto / Edmonton / Montreal			Toronto / Toronto	Regina / Quebec city / Vancouver	Toronto	Sudbury		
Periodization	Training phase	Preparatory I			Compet. I	T. Preparatory II			Competitive II				Transition
	Sub phase	Gen. prep.	Spec. prep.		Comp.	T. G.P.	S.P.	Pre-c.	Competitive		C.		Transition
	Macrocycles	1	2	3	4	5 6	7	8	9	10	11	12	13
Training	Objectives	A.A. / P M.S.	M.S.; T	M.S.; T P.	T.; P.; M.S.	A.A.	M.S.; T	M.S.; T P.	T.; M.S. P.	T.; P.	T.; P.	T.; P.	G.P.P.
	Intensity	M. / M.	M.	H.	H.	L. M.	M.	M.	H.	H.	H. M.		L.
Performance objectives					2.06			2.06		2.08	2.10		
Forms of preparation				Club	CMP.			Club			Camp		Holiday

Means of training													
Jumps 600		15	30	35	60		40	50	100	150	100	20	
Technic. drill 800		25	70	50	85		60	60	130	200	100	20	
Weight train. (kgm):													
—Leg press 342,000	22,000	30,000	60,000	30,000	60,000	20,000	50,000	20,000	30,000	20,000			
—Jump 1/2 squat 90,000	3,000	6,000	12,000	10,000	15,000	5,000	15,000	5,000	6,000	7,000	5,000		
—Power lift 266,000	15,000	20,000	45,000	20,000	40,000	15,000	50,000	14,000	14,000	15,000	7,000		
—Ankle flex. 109,440	4,000	7,220	15,000	10,000	16,220	8,000	20,000	6,500	8,000	10,500	4,000		
Bounding ex. 35,000		2,200	3,800	3,200	3,400	1,850	5,000	2,400	4,200	5,200	3,600	850	
Exer. benches 3,340		280	480	360	360	500	800	560					
Exer. gym box 1,280		160	200	140	200 2	140	260	180					
Exer. med. balls 4660	260	300	1,400	600		200	1,600	300					

Tests and standards													
—30 M. dash 3.3 sec.	3.7		3.5	3.5		3.4		3.5	3.4			3.3	3.3
—Stand. high j. 62 cm.	54		58		60		60	60		62			
—Stand. pent. j. 15.20 m.	14.00			14.80			14.80			15.20			
—Leg press 260 kg.	200	220		240	260	230	250		260				
—Power lift 90 kg.	65	70		75	90		90						
—Back flex. 70 cm.	60		65			68		70					

Figure 8.30 Individual training plan for a high jumper

could do this more precisely using the following scale: 1—up to the limit, 2—maximum, 3—submaximum, 4—great, 5—medium, 6—low.

One practical highlight of the plan is the area that lists the means of training. In this section, the coach lists the dominant technical skills, drills, and exercises to develop specific biomotor abilities. Adjacent to each means of training the coach specifies the repetitions, distance or time, or kilogram force meters (kgm) the athlete will perform during the whole training year. These figures are then divided per macrocycle, depending on the objectives and importance of each in the succeeding macrocycles. Some exercises are part of the entire year of training (i.e., ankle flexions), and others (exercises with medicine balls) are specific for the preparatory and precompetitive phases only. All weight-training exercises are expressed in kgm. Other exercises for developing power are expressed in number of repetitions. For instance, power lifting was calculated as follows: 3,800 repetitions per year × 1 meter, or distance traveled by the barbell × 70 kilograms, or the average load = 266,000 kilogram force meters. The bottom of the chart lists tests and corresponding standards with the progression to achieve those standards.

I advocate the individual annual training plan for both individual and team sports. Although in some instances it may appear that this plan is more suitable for individual sports, especially those with objective means of measurement, you should use it for team sports as well. A coach can easily plan the number of repetitions of specific skills or tactical maneuvers. For physical preparation, tests, and standards, there should not be any discrepancies.

Practicality of the Annual Plan Chart

The chart of the annual plan represents the basic guidelines for most of the training activities organized throughout a training year. The coach builds a plan around the competition schedule, the ratio between training factors, and the curves of the training components and peaking. It is a specific tool that governs the athlete's program. The coach can extract from the chart where to emphasize each training factor in a given training cycle. With this basis, the coach can set priorities for a macrocycle, for example, 50% physical, 40% technical, and so on. The coach can precisely plan the training program for a macro-, then a micro-cycle by concerting this with the magnitude of volume and intensity and the quantity of work planned per cycle in the individual annual training plan.

Criteria for Compiling an Annual Plan

Compiling an annual plan is important because it is the guideline the coach will use to conduct training for the following year. The ideal time to compile the plan is at the end of the transition phase. Following the main competition of the past year, the coach can reflect and analyze the program and review the athlete's improvement, progress rate in competitive performance and tests, and psychological behavior during training and competition. The conclusions drawn from this analysis should influence the objectives for the next year's plan. These observations and the competition schedule are used in compiling the next annual plan.

The following year's competition schedule, including national and international events, is set by the national federation. Based on this schedule, each regional organization sets their competition dates. All coaches should know these dates by the transition phase of the previous annual plan; otherwise they cannot objectively compile the following year's plan. The quality of an annual plan reflects the coach's methodological knowledge, experience, and latest theoretical gains in the field of training. Over time you must improve your first plan to include all these aspects. You will progressively develop a model of an annual plan that, yearly, will reflect your progress in knowledge and gains in experience. After making the annual plan, compile training programs for individuals or small groups based on specific needs. All formulation and language must be clear, concise, and technical. There is no room for rhetoric in an annual plan.

Every organized coach should compile his or her own annual plan. A coach is only as efficient as he or she is organized. The national sports association or funding organization may ask coaches at the national level to submit a model (project) of the program to follow in the next year. Such a program has to be well compiled, justified, and must comprise the main parameters of training. Following is a model of an annual plan or project that consists of all the needed elements.

Introduction

In the introduction, specify the duration of the plan (i.e., September 15 to August 16) and personal or team information: sport, sex, age, height, weight, and somatotype (body type). You may list this data without specific comments. Then, especially for a project, explain some of the scientific and methodological characteristics of the sport from which you determine the training needs. For example, as an individual sport, women's gymnastics is characterized by coordination with great demand for maximum strength, power, muscular endurance, and flexibility. Rhythm and muscial sense are also significant. The duration of activity ranges from 4 to 5 seconds in vaulting to 1:30 minutes in a balance beam routine; consequently, the ergogenesis in gymnastics is 80% anaerobic and 20% aerobic. Major energy sources include the ATP-CP stored in the muscle for activities lasting less than 30 seconds and the anaerobic metabolism system, which produces lactic acid, for parts, half routines, and routines 30 seconds to 1:30 minutes long.

Retrospective Analysis

To properly elaborate the performance predictions and objectives for the following year, thoroughly analyze performance and behavior in the past year. Performance achievements refer to the performance as well as tests and standards, and you could present them as in table 8.3.

TABLE 8.3 A Hypothetical Analysis of Test Results for a Female Javelin Thrower

	Performance	Planned 51.50m	Achieved 52.57m
	Test		
Objectives	1. 30m dash 2. Standing long jump 3. Chin-ups 4. Basball throw	4.8 s 2.40m 8 60.00m	4.7 s 2.36m 7 61.36m

After analyzing the past year's performance objectives and the tests and standards, determine the athlete's state of preparation by analyzing each training factor separately. For physical preparation, analyze whether the indices of general, specific, and biomotor ability development did correspond with the specific needs of the sport and whether they adequately supported the technical, tactical, and psychological preparation. Collect such information from competitions and test results. Link any improvement or decline in technical or tactical performance with the athlete's rate of progress or regress as reflected in test scores. Often it may be that improvement prevails during the preparation phase, but regression occurs during the competitive phase as a result of inconsistent and inadequate physical preparation. Thus, continue specific physical preparation throughout the competitive phase, and test it consistently in each macrocycle to collect objective data regarding the dynamics of physical preparation.

Focus the analysis of technical preparation on the fineness of technical elements and to what extent they affected overall performance. Assess the effectiveness of past technical elements to determine whether to use them in the future. The time dedicated to improving technical elements directly reflects the athlete's level of technical proficiency and the fineness of skill acquisition.

An analysis of tactical preparation should mirror whether tactical maneuvers used were properly chosen, suited to the characteristics of the team, and led to the solution of game problems. As a conclusion of the retrospective analysis, the coach should indicate which, if any, of the past year's strategical tools should be eliminated, maintained as part of the team's strategies, or kept for perfecting, so that the team's efficiency will improve in the following year.

Finally, the coach also has to investigate the athlete's psychological preparation and behavior and how it manifested in the final performance. He or she has to consider positive and negative aspects of the whole process and whether they led to optimizing competition performance. To assess the athlete's behavior, consider what happened during training and all other times, because often the unseen training has important implications in training and competitions.

The coach also reflects on collaboration with training specialists and psychologists to determine what will improve the athlete's performance. The conclusions of the retrospective analysis are the basis for predicting future progress and performance, and for setting the specific objectives for the new annual plan.

Performance Prediction

One of the coach's important abilities is forecasting the progress rate and the skills, abilities, and general performance to be achieved between the date of planning and the main contest. Then, with the performance prediction as a reference, you can draw the objectives and test standards. Achieving these objectives and standards is a guarantee that the athlete will reach the highest possible level of performance. For instance, a gymnastics coach scores routines and technical elements to see whether they are difficult enough to warrant the 9.4 average score needed for a gymnast to place in the top six at the women's national championships. Following such an analysis, the coach decides what technical elements to incorporate in the following year's routines to score as predicted, based on the gymnast's realistic abilities.

Performance prediction of team sports is more difficult than for individual sports. Among the few aspects that the coach may predict are the technical elements, tactical maneuvers, or level of ability the players must acquire to achieve a higher performance the following year.

For sports in which performance is objectively and precisely measured, performance prediction is easier. The coach contemplates the best results achieved in the past year and, based on the rate of performance improvement, predicts the level the athlete will reach the following year. The performances for men rowing in a major regatta were predicted using such a basis (table 8.4).

Considering the athletes' realistic abilities and potential for improvement, the coach can set the standards for his crews and the placing expectation for this regatta (table 8.5). On the basis of performance prediction, the coach sets realistic objectives for each training factor and prepares the chart of the annual plan.

Objectives

In both the annual plan and the planning project, the coach must state the objectives in precise and concise language and in methodological sequence. Objectives are based on past performances, test standards achieved, the improvement rate of skills and performance, and the dates of the main competition. In setting objectives, consider the dominant training factor and the factors that are poorly developed and thus limit the athlete. Then decide the methodological order of priorities in training according to the limiting factors (i.e., is the physical preparation the main limiting factor or is technical or psychological preparation?).

The methodological sequence and presentation order of each training factor is as follows:

TABLE 8.4 Performance Predicted for the Places of Men Rowers in the Olympic Games (Events Listed in Speed Order)

	Performance (minutes) and place			
Event	I	II-III	IV-VI	VI-IX
Eight	5:38	5:41	5:45	5:50
Quad	5:51	4:55	5:59	6:04
Coxless four	6:05	6:09	6:13	6:17
Coxed four	6:13	6:17	6:21	6:26
Double scull	6:23	6:27	6:31	6:36
Coxless pair	6:43	6:46	6:50	6:55
Single scull	7:03	7:07	7:11	7:16
Coxed pair	7:08	7:12	7:16	7:21

TABLE 8.5 Minimum Performance Prediction and Placing Expectation in a Major Regatta

Event	Performance	Place
Eight	5:45	VI-VIII
Quad	5:58	VI-VIII
Coxless four	6:12	III-V
Coxed four	6:20	VII-IX
Double scull	6:30	III-V
Coxless pair	6:50	V-VI
Single scull	7:10	VII-IX
Coxed pair	7:15	VI-IX

1. Performance objective
2. Physical preparation (strength, speed, endurance, flexibility, coordination)
3. Technical preparation (offensive and defensive skills)
4. Tactical preparation (offensive and defensive individual and team tactics)
5. Psychological preparation
6. Theoretical preparation

This does not mean that the coach should stress each factor in this sequence. Give priority to those factors in which the athlete is proportionately underdeveloped and those that are primary to all athletes participating in the sport.

While setting objectives, consider and state the probability (percentage chance) of achieving them, especially the performance objective. Although this process relies on concrete, objective facts, you may consider subjective assessments, such as the athlete's reserves, improvement potential, and psychological traits. Objectives for a hypothetical volleyball player follow.

Performance

- Take first place in the national junior championships. Probability of achievement is 80%.
- Place in the top six in the senior national championships. Probability of achievement is 50 to 60%.

Training Factors

- Physical preparation.

  Strength—improve leg strength for higher and more contested jumps.

  Speed—improve speed to facilitate quicker footwork for blocking and defense.

  Endurance—improve muscular endurance required in long games and tournaments.

  Flexibility—perfect shoulder and improve ankle flexibility.

- Technical preparation.

  Improve serving consistency.

  Improve spiking accuracy.

- Tactical preparation.

  Offense—improve spiking variety in a 6-0 system.

  Defense—improve timing and quickness of blocking.

- Psychological preparation. Develop the ability to play calmly and with confidence following a mistake.

- Theoretical preparation. Know all penalties that the referee may call.

Competition Calendar

The following chapter has a detailed presentation of competitions and their importance in athletics. Certain relevant aspects ought to be mentioned here, however, because this section deals with the methodology of setting up the schedule of competitions for the annual plan.

The coach sets the competition schedule. Choose competitions that suit the athletes, their level of performance and skills, and their psychological traits. Although you may consider the athletes' opinions, especially elite athletes, I advise the coach to assume the decisive role based on his or her experience. Asking athletes to make the final decision seems inappropriate.

The determining factor in periodization and setting up the competition schedule is the major championship, sometimes referred to as the main objective of the year. Other official and unofficial competitions are of secondary importance but provide an opportunity to assess athletes' preparation level. They are spread over the competitive phase and are most prominent during the precompetitive subphase. Do not schedule competitions early in the preparatory phase. During that time, focus on acquiring physical preparation and skills rather than performance. Consequently, you should integrate major competitions with secondary competitions. Alternating such competitions is ideal, though not often possible. Unlike team sports in which there are many leagues or official games, competitions are scarce in some individual sports. To maintain the unity of the annual plan throughout the competitive phase, I advise that you organize preparatory competitions as an integral part of the training plan.

The arrangement of competitions in an annual plan has to consider the principle of progressive increase of training load, in which preparatory competitions of secondary importance must lead official challenging ones. This is not always possible, especially in team sports for which sport governing bodies set the calendar.

A determining factor in achieving the performance objectives is the number of competitions. A heavy, demanding competition schedule, as often occurs in team sports, may speed the process of reaching a high level of athletic shape and may decrease the team's efficiency for important competitions at the end of the competitive phase. A reduced number of competitions may also lead to lower athletic shape for the main objective of the year. Two important criteria for determining the number of competitions are the characteristics and the nature of the demand of the sport, and the athlete's performance level. For sports in which the effort is intense and for athletes with low performance capabilities, 15 to 25 competitions per year may suffice. You may plan more contests (30) for elite athletes involved in most other sports.

Once you make the competition schedule, consider no changes, especially for the major competitions, because the periodization of the entire annual plan is based on this schedule. Plan no competitions, especially important ones, during examination periods for high school and university students. Similarly, engage in no official or demanding contests during the last macrocycle before the main competition. During this last cycle, train in a quiet atmosphere, making a few changes according to the conclusions drawn from the previous competition. Each contest taxes an athlete physically, mentally, and psychologically. The athlete needs time to rest, relax, and rebuild mental toughness and concentration for the main competition of the year. Not respecting such psychological and physiological needs will lead to a poor showing in the last contest of the competition schedule.

Tests and Standards

Knowing more about the athletes and their potential requires organized, systematic, and consistent evaluation. A sound training methodology requires athletic evaluation to be an intrinsic part of the planning process. Aim all evaluation procedures and means of testing at objectively quantifying the athletes' evolution, stagnation, or eventual performance deterioration.

A test requires performance by the individual being tested. Evaluation refers to the process of determining the status of that person relative to a standard. The evaluator should always be the coach and not an athlete, although the latter may often be an important assistant.

A test has to be objectively measured to guarantee comparable results. According to Meyers (1974), the functions of measurement are to ascertain the status or capacity in a given ability or skill and to provide the basis for (a) determining achievement or progress, (b) diagnosing particular weaknesses, and (c) predicting further improvements.

Meyers also implies that a test and measurement program should serve the following functions:

- To determine skill status and ability level, which you can use to plan a training program
- To determine the athlete's training content
- To determine specific strength, weaknesses, and limitations of the athlete's abilities
- To measure improvement in motor skills and tactical maneuvers to use in the future
- To guide to better body mechanics and the development of specific psychological traits
- To establish appropriate standards in all training factors
- To motivate effective learning, develop specific skills, and evolve psychological traits

Tests must be diverse to measure and, therefore, provide information regarding the status of each training factor. Testing one factor, say the strength of a wrestler, would be insufficient and limit the whole process. Consequently, the coach has to measure all the determining training factors. Most of all, a test must detect the limiting factors of the athlete's improvement.

Throughout the training process, a coach should be concerned with two basic categories of tests. The first category includes tests for athletic selection, aimed at tracing genetic abilities specific and dominant in a certain event or sport. The second category provides information about the athlete's adaptability, his or her evolution of skill acquisition, and performance improvement.

Testing for selection ought to be simple, without requiring any technical sophistication or high degree of coordination from the testee (except coordination tests). There should be no official training for such tests, except the time required to learn the simple technique of performing them. Select or design tests to discover an athlete's adaptability and performance evolution specifically to provide valid and useful information to the coach. Design tests that duplicate and possibly develop abilities at which the coach aims through the training program. Ideally, you would use some exercises or means of training as a testing tool. For instance, most jumpers in athletics and most athletes from team sports should use bounding exercises to develop leg power. Penta (5) and deca (10) triple-jump steps are common exercises. These exercises lend themselves nicely as testing devices. Use them throughout the annual training cycles. Such a test is trainable and is specific to the event or sport. What is more important, it motivates the athlete to train, because the exercise serves as a testing tool and as a means to develop a necessary ability.

Be selective when developing a battery of tests, choosing only those that incorporate the majority of abilities a particular sport requires. In rowing for instance, the rowing ergometer test is highly regarded, because it measures the athlete's specific endurance, strength, speed, pacing, and willpower in one test. Often the coach does not follow the concept of having only a small number of tests. In some sports (e.g., volleyball), coaches have a battery of tests as high as 18! If the coach has to test 12 to 16 players in each macrocycle, you may wonder if he or she has any time left for training. Considering this, I advise keeping the number of tests to a minimum (4 to 8), while making sure that all tests have a high degree of validity. Ideally, the coach (who could employ the advice of a testing specialist) should compute the correlation between each available test and the specifics of the sport, then select only those tests that have the highest correlation coefficient. This is the most scientific way to select an appropriate test battery.

Also, the test must facilitate a fair discrimination among athletes and must have an objectively measurable standard. For instance, push-ups are still overwhelming used to evaluate the strength of the elbow flexor. The tester, however, omits the fact that arm length varies from person to person. A comparison between individuals is far from adequate. If no other sophisticated tools are available to measure elbow extensor strength, it is more accurate to use bench press and compute the kilogram force meters (kgm) of each testee to make comparisons among athletes (kilogram force meter = limb's length $\times$ load $\times$ number of lifts, i.e., 0.60-meter arm length $\times$ 50 kilograms $\times$ 10 lifts = 300 kilogram force meters). Coaches requiring assistance with evaluations may ask the advice of a testing specialist or consult a test and measurements book.

Testing and training specialists and coaches often question whether an athlete should train for a test; the answer is both yes and no. Yes, an athlete may train for a test if it is one of many exercises or means of training in the training program (i.e., penta jump). Similarly, an athlete may train for a short time for a test for selection purposes to learn the eventual technical pattern of a skill. All other types of tests the athlete must not train, because prior preparation or training for a test distorts its purpose. As I have stated, most tests measure the effect of previous training at a given time. A test is not a formality; it should not limit the scope of the athlete's preparation. In this context, you should understand that an athlete should not train for a VO_2max test, specifically because the athlete would not gain much by doing so. On the contrary, aerobic and anaerobic endurance would improve much more through training methods that stress the general volume of training. The test should not be a scope in itself.

Decide and plan all testing dates in advance for any annual training program or project. Plan the first date of testing for the first microcycle of the preparatory phase. Such a test provides an opportunity to evaluate the athlete's preparation level, which will influence the development of the new annual program. An organized coach should plan to achieve certain training objectives in each macrocycle. He or she must verify the accomplishment of such objectives. Consequently, at the end of each macrocycle the coach should plan 1 or 2 days of testing to collect information regarding the athlete's progress. If the test results indicate consistent improvement, maintain the training program as originally planned; otherwise, alter the program for the next cycle to reflect the athlete's training status. Plan testing dates periodically for the end of each macrocycle, but only during the preparatory phase and precompetitive subphase. You need to evaluate the athlete's preparatory status during these phases to monitor training programs based on objective data. Similarly, regular testing may motivate in the absence of competitions, as well as develop specific psychological traits. During the competitive phase, plan a testing session only if the time between two competitions exceed 4 or 5 weeks. During this phase, the competitions themselves serve as an ideal form of evaluating all training factors.

Although the coach ought to schedule testing dates throughout the annual plan, he or she may occasionally opt for an ad hoc evaluation. The results are often surprising because the athlete does not have time to prepare psychologically for the test. Those who fail to perform adequately do so mostly because of a lack of psychological support. Though such an approach may reveal certain weaknesses in the athlete's preparation, the coach should not abuse this method. Once or a maximum of twice a year would be acceptable. Testing scores should be accurately recorded by each athlete in his or her training journal, as well as in the coach's records.

In the descriptive part of the plan or project, express the test for each training factor using different colors or symbols. Establish standards for each test, especially for physical and technical factors, while compiling the annual plan. Regard the standards of the previous year as a reference point. The planned progression toward achieving each standard ought to reflect the athlete's adaptation to a program and improvement rate. For athletes just beginning an organized program, you could use the scores of the first test as a reference point for further planning.

Be careful when planning the standards. They represent an incentive for preparation and progress. Standards must be difficult enough to present a challenge and realistic enough to be achievable. Standards for athletes aiming at high levels of performance have to resemble other top athletes. There are two types of standards: evolutionary standards with a stimulative character, which are therefore slightly superior to the athlete's potential in a given time; and maintenance standards, which aim at preserving an optimal preparation level. The progression of these standards is such that you can include a maximum of two macrocycles in each step. If the athlete has not achieved the standard by this time, the coach must determine why.

Set tests and standards for each ability, placing more emphasis on the dominant ones. Each ability has to be trained and tested regularly because the coach conducts unspecific evaluation through testing (as opposed to specific), mostly during the preparatory phase; one prime goal of this phase is improving biomotor abilities. For the sake of simplicity, you could present both the tests and standards in chart form, as in table 8.6.

Periodization Model

You can conceive the periodization of the annual plan so it represents a model to follow. Having the competition schedule as a foundation, decide what type of annual plan is most suitable (mono-, bi- or tri-cycle). Following this, designate the phases of training, specifying the duration of each phase precisely. Continuing the process, specify the macrocycles, stating their number, date, location, objectives, and methods to use to meet these objectives. The next step is one of the most difficult tasks in planning: inserting all athlete (team) activities into the chart of the annual plan as explained previously.

TABLE 8.6 Tests and Standards for the Preparatory Phase for a Hypothetical Male Junior Long Jumper.

	Standards			
Test	**Dec. 23**	**Jan. 28**	**March 4**	**April 1**
30m dash with high start	4, 3	4, 3	4, 2	4, 1
Standing long jump	2, 60m	2, 70m	2, 73m	2, 75m
Standing penta jump	13.50m	13.60m	13.80m	14.00m
Leg press (one attempt)	340kg	360kg	370kg	380kg

Preparation Model

The preparation model is a synopsis of the entire annual training program. It comprises the main qualitative and quantitative parameters used in training and the percentage increment per parameter between the current and previous annual plans. The coach must link the preparation model with the whole structure of the annual plan and its objectives. An experienced coach might predict the duration and number of workouts required to develop the necessary skills and abilities to accomplish the objectives. Structure a preparation model as shown in table 8.7.

TABLE 8.7 Preparatory Model for a 400m Swimmer

Training parameters	Symbol/units	Volume %	% change over previous year
The type of annual training plan	monocycle		
Periodization - Duration of annual plan/days - Preparatory phase days - Competitive phase/days - Transition phase/days	322 182 119 21	100 56.5 37 6.5	>8 <5 <3
Macrocycles	9		
Microcycles - At the club - National camp - Travel abroad	46 41 3 2		
Competitions - International - National - Regional	7 2 4 1		
Number of training lessons	554		>6
Number of hours of training	1,122		<8.4
Number of tests	16		
Number of medical controls	3		
Activity milieu - Specific training/days -Swimming/km - Nonspecific training/days - Running/km - Weight training/kgm - Games/hours - Rest/days	266 2,436 14 640 460.000 28 42	82.6 4.4 13	>3 >6 >2 >2 >14 >1 <8

A hypothetical preparation model of a male 400-meter swimmer is presented in table 8.7. It is assumed that to reach a higher performance level the athlete must increase his aerobic and muscular endurance. He will accomplish this through elevating training volume, prolonging the preparatory phase, and increasing the number of training lessons, thus the total hours of training. Also, modifying the ratio between different methods and types of training will enhance muscular development and aerobic endurance.

To improve both aerobic and muscular endurance through weight training and special water exercises, alter training content using the guideline in table 8.8. The breakdown per training phase may be as in table 8.9.

TABLE 8.8 Model of the Training Content for the Annual Plan and the Alteration of Each Element Compared to the Previous Year's Plan

Content	%	% of change
Anaerobic endurance-speed (AE)	2	<6
Muscular endurance (ME)	16	>2
Racing tempo endurance (RTE)	32	=
Aerobic endurance over medium distance (EMD)	24	>2
Aerobic endurance over long distacne (ELD)	20	>2

TABLE 8.9 Alteration of the Training Content and Its Percentage Per Training Phase Between the Past and the Following Annual Plan

Content	% Preparatory phase	% Change	% Competitive phase	% Change
AE	5	<4	8	<2
ME	10	>2	16	>3
RTE	20	<2	36	<2
EMD	30	>3	20	>2
ELD	35	>5	20	>4

In addition to these sections of an annual plan, also consider the team or club's budget when designing the program. A complete outline of a training program may be as follows:

1. Introduction
2. Retrospective analysis
3. Performance prediction
4. Objectives

5. Calendar of competitions

6. Tests and standards

7. Periodization model (including the chart of the annual plan and macrocycles)

8. Preparation model

9. Athlete/team organization and administration model (including budget and equipment needs)

Summary of Major Concepts

Annual planning and the microcycle are the cornerstones of well-structured training programs and plans. The fundamental concept for good annual planning is periodization, especially structuring the phases of biomotor abilities. The periodization of strength, speed, and endurance represents the manipulation of different training phases with specific goals, organized in a specific sequence, with the ultimate scope of creating sport-specific adaptation. When adaptation is complete, the athlete is physiologically equipped to produce better performances.

A good understanding of periodization will help you produce better annual plans, using charts to schedule training activities. Remember to use the competition schedule to guide your training phases. Also, integrate into your chart the periodization of nutrition and psychological training. Periodization is a complex, all inclusive training concept. Use the blank charts supplied in the appendix to exercise and improve your skills for annual planning. You may also create a simpler chart, specific to your needs.

Long-Term Planning and Talent Identification

Long-term planning is a characteristic and requirement of modern training. A well-organized long-term training program greatly increases training efficiency for future competitions. In addition, it encourages a rational use of training means and methods and facilitates a concrete, specific assessment of the athlete's progress. Long-term planning has to rely on scientific and empirical knowledge. Awareness of advancements in the science of sport training and the experience of top coaches and training specialists will perfect your training.

A long-term plan cannot be successful unless the instructor has the most talented athletes. Therefore, a strong component of any long-term plan is talent identification, the process of identifying the most gifted young athletes.

It should be common for a coach to compile a long-term plan of 8 to 16 years for a young prospective athlete. In fact without such a plan the coach could find him- or herself in a random training program that may not meet their expectations. You can facilitate high performance by the following sequential approach to training.

The steps suggested in figure 9.1 are based on the fact that a youngster scientifically selected for a sport based strictly on his or her specific qualities, and who follows a precise long-term training program, will have a higher probability of reaching top performance than those involved in natural programs. Such an approach is not new but is common in most East European countries. Many Western specialists were overwhelmed by rumors stating that the East German swimming miracle, Cornelia Ender (5 golds in Montreal) was, from the beginning, meant to be an Olympic champion. The truth is that Cornelia, like Romania's Nadia Comaneci and many other great athletes, was selected for the sport because of her outstanding abilities. Becoming a champion was the normal outcome of a long-term, well-organized, and scientifically monitored training program. Such an approach should not be the prerogative of certain countries. It is possible to be just as well organized in other countries.

A long-term training plan must establish its direction and its general and specific objectives, which have to be organized over several years. The construction of such a plan has to consider the following four factors:

- The number of systematic training years necessary for a prospective athlete to obtain high performance
- The average age at which an athlete achieves top performance
- The natural ability level with which the prospective athlete starts
- The age at which the athlete starts specialized training

As illustrated by table 2.3 (pages 35-36), the average number of years necessary to reach high performance is 6 to 8. However, the age of the prospective athlete when he or she starts the systematic program and the number of years until athletic maturation occurs in the chosen sport (table 2.3) may affect this number. A 12-year-old athlete beginning a swimming program has just a few years until maturation in swimming. The long-term training program of such an athlete should, therefore, be drastically altered to accommodate his or her needs. Although not impossible, such an athlete, even with this alteration, would have a lower probability of reaching a high performance level than one with equal abilities who started a systematic program earlier.

During an athletic career, the dynamics of physical and psychological involvement alter frequently. Motor and physiological functions reach an optimal level between the ages of 25 and 30 for men and 3 to 5 years earlier for women. We may not claim, however, that this age is optimal for best performance in all sports. For instance, according to table 2.3, athletes achieve optimal performance in sports requiring maximum speed around the age of 20 to 24. Similarly, athletes optimally perform activities requiring great strength and endurance when approaching the age of 30 and often a little older. On the other hand, for sports in which success depends on mastering movement that athletes can acquire at an early age, the optimal age is drastically lower (figure skating at 16-20 and gymnastics at 14-18 for girls and 18-24 for boys). Although athletes older than this have won Olympic medals,

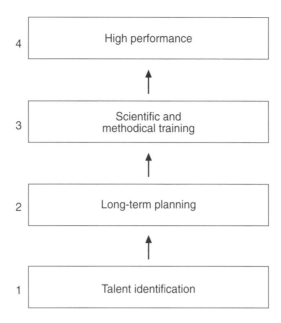

Figure 9.1   Essential steps to achieve high performance

it may be fair to say that victory for older athletes is exceptional rather than common.

A long-term plan should reflect that an athlete's improvement rate, as shown by figure 9.2, is not linear. The dynamics of the athlete's improvement are much higher at the beginning and during the specialization phase, and slow down throughout the phase of high performance. Obviously, the shape of the curve is more undulatory and is the product of correlating physiological and psychological abilities and the type of work, volume, and intensity performed in training. The coach ought to consider this reality when setting long-term objectives, especially performance objectives and standards for tests.

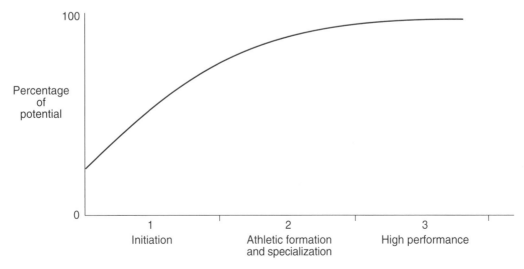

Figure 9.2   Curve of the athlete's improvement from the beginning to the phase of high performance

When developing and constructing a long-term plan, you must consider the athlete's age. For a young athlete, such a plan could be of 6 to 8 years' duration; for a junior (over 16) or elite athlete, I recommend a 4-year plan. Link a long-term plan, especially for a young athlete, to the abilities that were discovered when he or she was selected for the sport.

Figure 9.3 presents comprehensive illustrations of long-term plans for a young prospective athlete (6 years) and a junior (4 years), emphasizing various types of training. Regardless of the duration of the plan, each is solidly based on a multilateral physical preparation, on top of which is built the foundation of specialized training. This facilitates a highly specialized training according to the specifics of the selected sport. You can see that the work increases in steps on a yearly basis. Similarly, as the program progresses, the ratio among the three types of training changes. Whether for an individual or team sport, the coach can make two types of plans: a comprehensive plan for the group and an individual plan for each athlete.

Before constructing either plan, however, set the competition schedule for the whole training period. Obviously, this refers to major competitions only (i.e., national championships, which often have a traditional date).

The comprehensive plan should contain data concerning the whole group and objectives common to all the athletes. On the other hand, the individual plans should focus strictly on the needs, objectives, and specifics of each athlete.

Constructing a long-term plan should entertain the following methodical premises.

• The athlete's performance objectives must relate to factors specific to the sport, and their dynamics should reflect the ascending tendency valid for every sport. Furthermore, the coach should be aware of the dynamics of performance in his or her country and the world.

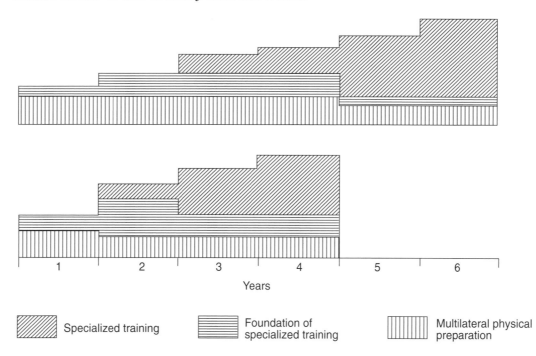

Figure 9.3 Interrelationship of types of training in a long-term plan

- As the athlete progresses, the coach should increase the number of training lessons and training hours per year, and the number and frequency of competitions. The number of competitions, especially major ones, may level off for highly advanced athletes.

- A long-term plan should forecast the annual increase for training volume and intensity according to the dominant component of the sport and the athlete's needs. For artistic sports, speed-power dominant sports, and team sports, increase the intensity of training toward the end of the plan. For most other sports, in addition to increasing the intensity, continually increase volume as the dominant component of training.

- Yearly, especially for the best athletes, the coach must alter the emphasis on various training exercises. At the beginning of the program, I suggest a high variety of exercises, but toward the end, a limited but specific scope (exercises with direct action) should prevail. Such an approach will enhance the athlete's adaptation to the specifics of the sport.

- The plan must specify tests and, if possible, standards the athletes ought to pass every year. This will assist the coach to continually assess and thus discover the strongest and weakest link in the athlete's training. Tests and standards, if correctly selected, represent an important stimulant for athletes. Select a small number of specific tests that reflect the characteristics of the sport. Ensure consistency by employing the same tests over a long time during the same training phases. Demand higher standards every year to reflect the demand and improvement of all training factors. Make medical controls an integral part of the athlete's health and training assessment.

- A long-term plan should incorporate all the particularities of a sport. For instance, in acyclic sports, reflect technical and tactical elements by specific indices, such as the following: the number, level, and variety of technical elements; the number, level of difficulty, and variety of tactical maneuvers; the degree of general and specific physical preparation; the test standards that reflect the physical requirements of a good technique; and performance predictions.

- Finally, show the progression of the number of training lessons and training hours per year in the plan. For the training lessons, start from approximately 200 to 250 per year for the first few years, increasing to around 400 per year toward the end of the plan. For elite athletes, you may increase the number to 500 to 650, especially for those who participate in individual sports. The number of hours of training should follow a similar pattern, between 400 for beginners and 1,000 to 1,200 for world-class athletes.

Stages of Athletic Development

It is essential for coaches to incorporate periodization principles into training children and youth. As demonstrated in figure 9.4, all athletes, regardless of their high-performance potential, should participate in a *generalized* and a *specialized* phase of training. Within the generalized phase, gradually introduce athletes to sport-specific training (initiation), and progressively form their athletic talents (athletic formation). The primary purpose of the generalized phase is to build the foundation on which to effectively develop complex motor abilities, resulting in a smooth transition to the specialized phase.

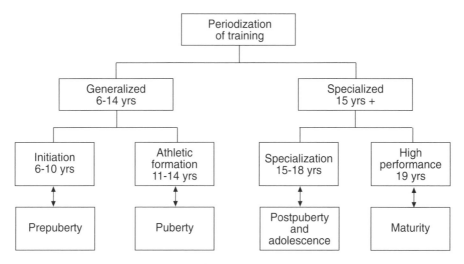

Figure 9.4 Periodization of long-term training

There are two stages within the specialized phase: specialization and high performance. During the specialization stage, athletes choose which sport or event and which position in the chosen sport or event they would like to play. Once athletes have specialized, they can increase the training intensity and volume progressively, resulting in high performance.

Although figure 9.4 outlines the ages associated with each stage, it is important to understand that this model shifts considerably depending on the sport. For example, in sports such as women's gymnastics and women's diving, the age at each stage may be reduced by 2 to 4 years. It is also critical to understand that children and youth develop at various rates. Therefore, you must consider the individual maturation of each athlete, and adjust training and competitive programs accordingly. Familiarity with the physical, mental, and social characteristics of athletes in the initiation, athletic formation, and specialization stages will allow you to better establish training guidelines that will enhance their development and result in high performance.

Generalized Training

Generalized training, which refers to the early stages of development, incorporates both initiation and athletic formation.

Initiation—6 to 10 Years Old

Children in the initiation stage of development should participate in low-intensity training programs. Most young children are not capable of coping with the physical and psychological demands of high-intensity training or high-intensity organized competitions. Focus training programs for young athletes on overall athletic development, not sport-specific performance. The following guidelines will help you design training programs suitable for young athletes.

• Emphasize multilateral development by introducing children to specific drills and exercises that teach fundamental sport skills. Multilateral skills should include running, sprinting, jumping, catching, throwing, batting, balancing,

Emphasize multilateral development in young athletes

and rolling. Also encourage children to learn the skills of activities such as cycling, swimming, skating, and skiing.

• Provide every child enough time to adequately develop skills and equal time playing in games and activities.

• Positively reinforce children who are committed and self-disciplined. Reinforce improvements in skill development.

• Encourage children to develop flexibility, coordination, and balance.

• Encourage children to develop various motor abilities in low-intensity environments. For example, swimming is a terrific environment for developing the cardiorespiratory system, while minimizing the stress on joints, ligaments, and connective tissues.

• Select a suitable number of repetitions for each skill and encourage children to perform each technique correctly.

• Modify the equipment and playing environment to an appropriate level. For example, children do not have the strength to shoot an adult-size basketball into a 10-foot high basket, using the correct technique. The ball should be smaller and lighter and the basket should be lower.

• Design drills, games, and activities so children have opportunities for maximum active participation.

• Promote experiential learning by providing children with opportunities to design their own drills, games, and activities. Encourage children to be creative and use their imaginations.

• Simplify rules so children understand the game. If children cannot understand the rules of the game, they may not develop self-control, which will likely have a negative effect on their self-esteem and their desire to continue participating.

- Lead children in games that introduce them to basic tactics and strategies. For example, if children have developed basic individual skills, such as running, dribbling a ball with their feet, and kicking a ball, they will likely be ready to successfully play a modified game of soccer. During the game, you could introduce the young athletes to situations that demonstrate the importance of teamwork and position play.

- Encourage children to participate in drills that develop concentration and attention control. This will help them prepare for the greater demands of training and competition that take place in the athletic formation stage of development.

- Emphasize the importance of ethics and fair play.

- Provide opportunities for boys and girls to participate together.

- Make sure sports are fun for all children.

Athletic Formation—11 to 14 Years Old

It is appropriate to moderately increase training intensity during the athletic formation stage of development. Although most athletes are still vulnerable to injuries and emotional damage, their bodies and capacities are rapidly growing and developing. However, understand that variances in performance may be the result of differences in growth and development. Some athletes may experience rapid growth spurts, which explains why they lack coordination during particular drills. The emphasis should still be on developing skills and motor abilities, not on performance and winning. The following guidelines will help design training programs that are appropriate for athletes in the athletic formation stage of development.

- Guide athletes through a variety of exercises from the specific sport and from others, which will help them improve their multilateral base and prepare them for competition in their selected sport. Progressively increase the training volume and intensity.

- Design drills that introduce athletes to fundamental tactics and strategies. The drills should reinforce skill development.

- Help athletes refine and automate the basic skills they learned during the initiation stage of development and learn skills that are a little more complex.

- Emphasize improving flexibility, coordination, and balance.

- Emphasize ethics and fair play during training sessions and competitions.

- Provide all children with opportunities to participate at a challenging level.

- Avoid placing young athletes in potentially humiliating situations.

- Introduce athletes to exercises that develop general strength. The foundation for future strength and power gains should begin in this stage of development. Emphasize developing the core sections of the body, in particular the hips, lower back, and abdomen. Athletes should also develop the muscles at the extremities: shoulder joints, arms, and legs. Equipment needs are minimal as most exercises should involve body weight and light equipment, such as medicine balls, rubber (surgical) tubing, wall pulleys, and dumbbells. Low-resistance, high-repetition weight training will also enhance general strength development.

- Continue developing aerobic capacity. Athletes who have a solid endurance base will cope more effectively with training and competition demands during the specialization stage.

- Introduce athletes to moderate anaerobic training. This will help them adapt to high-intensity anaerobic training, which takes on greater importance in most sports during the specialization stage of development. Athletes should not compete in events that place excessive stress on the anaerobic lactic acid energy system, such as the 200-meter sprint or 400-meter dash in track and field. They are usually better suited for short sprints that involve the anaerobic alactic energy system (less then 80 meters, 85 yards) or endurance events that test their aerobic capacities (800 meters, 880 yards, longer distances at slower speeds).

- Avoid competitions that place too much stress on the body anatomically. For example, most young athletes do not have sufficient muscular development to perform a triple jump with the correct technique. As a result, some athletes may experience compression injuries from the shock that the body has to absorb somewhere during the stepping and hopping segments of the jump.

- Introduce athletes to more complex drills to improve concentration and attention control.

- Encourage athletes to develop strategies for self-regulation and visualization. Introduce formalized mental training.

- Introduce athletes to a variety of fun competitive situations. This will allow them to apply various techniques and tactics. Young athletes like to compete; however, de-emphasize winning. Structure competitions to reinforce skill development. For example, base the javelin throwing competition on accuracy and technique, not on how far athletes can throw the javelin.

Specialized Training

During the specialized stage of athletic development, emphasis is placed on exercises and drills from the chosen sport. The foundation laid during specialization will better facilitate good performances during the actual stage of high performance.

Specialization—15 to 18 Years Old

The majority of athletes in the specialization stage of development can tolerate greater training and competition demands. The most significant changes in training take place during this stage. Athletes who have been participating in a well-rounded program that emphasized multilateral development, will now start performing more exercises and drills aimed specifically at high-performance development. Closely monitor the training volume and intensity to ensure that athletes improve dramatically, with few if any injuries. Toward the end of this stage of athletic development, athletes should have no major technical problems. The coach can then move from a teaching to a coaching (training) role. The following guidelines should help in designing training programs that are suitable for athletes who specialize in a particular sport.

- Closely monitor the development of athletes during this stage. They will be developing strategies for coping with the increased physical and psychological

Improving balance, flexibility, and coordination

demands of training and competition. Athletes are vulnerable to experiencing physical and psychological difficulties from overtraining.

• Check for progressive improvements in the dominant motor abilities for the sport, such as power, anaerobic capacity, specific coordination, and dynamic flexibility.

• Increase the volume of training for specific exercises and drills to facilitate performance improvement. The body must adapt to specific training load increments to effectively prepare for competition.

• Then, increase training intensity more rapidly than volume, but increase it progressively. Prepare athletes to perform a particular skill, exercise, or drill with the appropriate rhythm and speed. Training should closely simulate the actions during competitions. Fatigue is a normal outcome of high-intensity training; however, athletes should not reach the state of exhaustion.

• Involve athletes in the decision-making process whenever possible.

• Continue to emphasize multilateral training, particularly during the general preparation phase of the season. However, it is more important to emphasize specificity and use training methods and techniques that will develop a high level of sport-specific efficiency, particularly during the specific preparation phase of the season and the competitive phase.

• Encourage athletes to learn the theoretical aspects of training.

• Emphasize exercising the muscles the athlete uses primarily when performing technical skills (prime movers). The development of strength should start to reflect the specific needs of the sport. Athletes who weight train can start performing exercises that require fewer repetitions and heavier weight. Avoid maximum strength training, in which the athlete performs fewer than four repetitions of an exercise, particularly for athletes who are still growing.

• Keep development of the aerobic capacity as a high priority for all athletes, particularly those in endurance or endurance-related sports.

• Progressively increase the volume and intensity of anaerobic training. Athletes are capable of coping with lactic acid accumulation.

• Improve and perfect the techniques of the sport. Select specific exercises that will ensure the athletes are performing the skills with biomechanical correctness and physiologic efficiency. Athletes should perform difficult technical skills frequently during training sessions, incorporating them into specific tactical drills and applying them in competitions.

• Improve individual and team tactics. Incorporate game-specific drills into tactical training sessions. Select drills that are interesting, challenging, and stimulating and that require quick decisions, fast actions, prolonged concentration, and a high level of motivation from the athletes. Athletes should demonstrate initiative, self-control, competitive vigor, and ethics and fair play in competitive situations.

• Increase the number of competitions progressively, so by the end of this stage the athletes are competing as frequently as senior competitors. It is also important to set objectives for competitions that focus on developing specific skills, tactics, and motor abilities. Although winning becomes increasingly important, do not overemphasize it.

• Guide athletes in mental training. Structure drills and exercises that develop concentration, attention control, positive thinking, self-regulation, visualization, and motivation to enhance sport-specific performance.

High Performance—19 Years and Older

A well-designed training plan, based on sound principles of long-term development, will lead to high performance. Exceptional performance results achieved during the initiation, athletic formation, or specialization stages of development do not correlate with high-performance results as a senior competitor. As demonstrated in tables 9.1 and 9.2, the majority of athletes are most successful after they have reached athletic maturation.

• Increase the training volume and intensity for the specific motor abilities and capacities progressively, relative to the current physical and psychological state of individual athletes. Training should consist primarily of exercises that lead to adaptation in the specific sport. Athletes should maintain multilateral development, especially during the preparatory phase.

• Simulate the rhythm and speed required in competition with specific exercises and drills in training sessions.

• Help athletes perfect and master specific technical skills and tactics and sport-specific mental training strategies.

• Base training programs on sound scientific principles.

Perform comprehensive periodization of long-term plans according to the examples in tables 9.3 through 9.6 for track and field (sprinting), baseball, football, and swimming.

TABLE 9.1 Average Age of the Top Six Finalists at the 1988 Winter and Summer Olympic Games

Sport	Average age
Athletics (all events)	26.3
Sprinting	23.4
Mid-distance running	24.3
Long-distance running	27.3
Walking	29.3
Jumps	23.5
Throws	26.4
Decathlon	25.1
Heptathlon	25.2
Basketball	
Women	23.6
Men	24.6
Boxing	22.4
Diving	
Women	22.2
Men	20.2

Sport	Average age
Gymnastics	
Women	18.6
Men	24.2
Rowing	
Women	24.1
Men	25.2
Skiing (Nordic, cross-country)	27.2
Soccer	24.8
Speed skating	
Women	23.5
Men	25.1
Swimming	
Women	17.5
Men	20.1
Wrestling	25.7

TABLE 9.2 Average Age of Participants at the Olympic Games Between 1968 and 1988

Sport	Average age
Athletics	24.1
Boxing	22.7
Basketball	24.7
Canoeing	24.2
Cycling	23.4
Equestrian	31.2
Fencing	24.1
Field hockey (men)	25.4
Gymnastics	
Women	17.2
Men	22.6

Sport	Average age
Judo	24.0
Rowing	24.2
Sailing	30.3
Shooting	33.2
Soccer	24.1
Swimming	
Women	18.9
Men	21.6
Volleyball (men)	25.2
Water polo (men)	25.3
Wrestling	24.8

TABLE 9.3 Periodization of Long-Term Training Program—Athletics and Sprinting

Training phases			AGE: 6 7 8 9 10 11 12 13 14 15 16 17 18 19 20 21 22 25 30 35				
Training phases			Initiation	Athletic formation	Spec.	High performance	
Skill acquisition		Technical	Basic skills		Auto.	Perfection	
T r a i n i n g		Coordination	Simple		Complex	Perfection	
		Flexibility	Overall		Specific	Maintain	
		Agility			(shaded)	Maintain	
	Speed	Linear			(shaded)		
		Reaction time		Starts		Perfection	
	Strength	Anatomical adaptation		(shaded)			
		Muscular endurance			(shaded)		
		Power			(shaded)		
		Maximum strength			(shaded)		
	Endurance	General		(shaded)			
		Anaerobic			(shaded)		
C o m p.		Fun		(shaded)			
		Local			(shaded)		
		State/provincial				(shaded)	
		National				(shaded)	
		International/ professional				(shaded)	

Shaded area shows the age to start or end the work on that ability.

Initiation = initiation in sport—run, throw, jump.

Spec. = specialization in event.

Auto. = skill automation.

Comp. = competitions.

TABLE 9.4 Periodization of Long-Term Training Program—Baseball

			AGE 6 7 8 9 10 11 12 13 14 15	16 17 18 19	20 21 22	25 30 35
Training phases			Initiation	Athletic formation	Spec.	High performance
Skill acquisition		Technical		Fundamentals	Position specific	Position and game specific
		Tactical		Simple and game strategy	Game strategy	Position/game strategy
T r a i n i n g	Coordination			Simple	Complex	Perfection
	Flexibility			Overall	Specific	Maintain
	Agility					
	Speed	Linear				
		Turns/ changes in direction				
		Reaction time				
	Strength	Anatomical adaptation				
		Power				
		Maximum strength				
	Endurance	General				
		Anaerobic				
C o m p.	Fun					
	Local					
	State/provincial					
	National					
	International/ professional					

Shaded area shows the age to start or end the work on that ability.

Initiation = initiation in sport—run, throw, jump.

Spec. = specialization in event.

Comp. = competitions.

TABLE 9.5 Periodization of Long-Term Training Program—Football

		AGE 6 7 8 9 10	11 12 13 14 15	16	17 18 19 20	21 22 25 30 35
Training phases		Initiation	Mini-football	H.S.	College	Pro
Skill acquisition	Technical		Fundamental	Auto.		Perfection game-specific
	Tactical		Simple rules		Game tactics	Position-specific tactics
Training	Coordination		Simple	Complex		Perfection
	Flexibility		Overall		Specific	Maintenance
	Agility					
	Speed — Linear					
	Speed — Turns/ changes in direction					
	Speed — Reaction time					
	Strength — Anatomical adaptation					
	Strength — Power					
	Strength — Maximum strength					
	Endurance — General					
	Endurance — Aerobic					
	Endurance — Anerobic					
Comp.	Fun					
	Local					
	State/provincial					
	National					
	International/ professional					

Shaded area shows the age to start or end the work on that ability.

Initiation = initiation in sport—run, throw, jump.

H.S. = high school.

Auto. = skill automation.

Comp. = competitions.

TABLE 9.6 Periodization of Long-Term Training Program—Swimming

		6	7	8	9	10	11	12	13	14	15	16	17	18	19	20	21	22
Training phases		Initiation							Athletic form.		Spec.		High perfection					
Skill acquisition	Technical	Basic skills							Auto.		Perfection							
	Tactical						Start				Even splits							
Training	Coordination	Simple							Com.		Perfection							
	Flexibility	Overall							Specific		Maintenance							
	Agility						░	░	░	░	░	░	░					
	Speed — Linear								░	░	░	░	░	░	░	░	░	░
	Speed — Turns/changes in direction									░	░	░	░	░	░	░	░	░
	Speed — Reaction time						Start				Perfection							
	Strength — Anatomical adaptation					░	░											
	Strength — Muscular endurance										░	░	░	░	░	░	░	░
	Strength — Power										░	░	░	░	░	░	░	░
	Strength — Maximum strength										░	░	░					
	Endurance — General				░	░	░	░	░	░	░							
	Endurance — Aerobic							░	░	░	░	░	░	░	░	░	░	░
	Endurance — Anerobic										░	░	░	░	░	░	░	░
Comp.	Fun	░	░	░	░	░	░	░										
	Local									░	░	░	░	░	░	░	░	░
	State/provincial											░	░	░	░	░	░	░
	National											░	░	░	░	░	░	░
	International/professional												░	░	░	░	░	░

Shaded area shows the age to start or end the work on that ability.

Spec. = event/technique specialization.

Auto. = skill automation.

Com. = complex coordination.

Structure practice to simulate the speed and rhythm of the game

Olympic Cycle or Quadrennial Plan

Regard the Olympic cycle or quadrennial plan (comprising 4 years) as a segment of long-term planning. The occurrence of the Olympic Games every fourth year necessitates special planning for sports and athletes in the Olympic program. Although for such athletes the Olympics is the zenith of the Olympic cycle plan, non-Olympians may also use a quadrennial plan as a tool to better organize their long-term training programs.

Classification of Olympic Cycle Plans

There are two methodological approaches for organizing and planning an Olympic cycle. The first is a monocyclic approach, in which all training factors and components increase progressively every year in steps, culminating with the Olympic Games (figure 9.5). Although this approach appears to have a built-in progression, it has the disadvantage of continually elevating stress on the athletes, without a year when you can plan a long unloading phase. The same is not true for the second approach or the bi-cyclic concept. As illustrated by figure 9.6, such an approach allows the coach to increase the load in training in an undulatory way. Often, during the post-Olympic year when a new cycle starts, the intensity and stress of training are lowered so the athlete can achieve a relative regeneration.

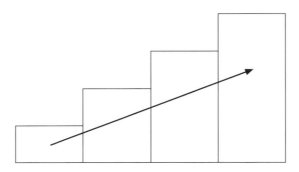

Figure 9.5 Monocyclic approach

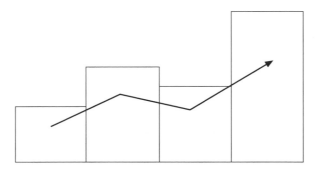

Figure 9.6 Elevation of training load and stress curve in the bi-cyclic approach

During this year, the coach stresses training volume to build the basis for the second year when the intensity will elevate. During the second year the coach may plan demanding competitions, when the athlete must reach high performances, following which the coach makes a thorough assessment (the midquadrennial analysis) of the athlete's ability. Such analysis is valid mostly for Olympic sports, although the concept may be applicable to any sport. The coach should analyze whether the athlete achieved the performance and the objectives for each training factor and make adequate corrections in the plan (objectives, standards of each test, etc.). In the third year, the work level is higher than in the first, as an unloading year, in preparation for the following year when the Olympics will be held. Although the training volume may be high, the intensity and the number of stressful competitions may be less. This would enhance a regeneration phase on which you can build the extremely demanding training program for the Olympics. For the fourth year, the coach attempts to maximize the athlete's performance through wisely using the athlete's talent and knowledge.

Consider the bi-cyclic approach only for athletes who have reached the optimal age for a particular sport and who, based on a strong background, are planning to compete in the Olympic Games. For younger athletes who have not yet reached this level, I advise the monocyclic approach, because their objective is a perpetual improvement up to the maturation age in the chosen sport. For elite athletes who may have intermediate goals, like a successful performance in the world championships, the approach you use in the Olympic cycle plan may be monocyclic (several sports do have world championships annually). In such circumstances, pay careful attention to thorough regeneration periods, usually organized during the transition phase. On the other hand, you may slightly alter the percentage of the total amount of work in the preparatory phase to allow an undulatory approach. Thus, for the post-Olympic year (year 1 in the plan), you may start with a workload equal to 30% of the previous year's most demanding level. In the second year, the total load may begin around 40%, and in the third year, it will be 30% again to allow regeneration. Finally, the plan for the Olympics may commence with a workload equal to 50% of the previous year's most demanding level.

Compiling an Olympic Cycle Plan

An Olympic cycle or quadrennial plan may follow similar headings as the annual plan, such as retrospective analysis, in which the coach analyzes the athlete's dynamics of physical development, the results of competitions, and tests and standards for each training factor.

Make such an analysis with a study of the dynamics of the sport's development at the national and international level. Based on such an analysis, the coach may make the appropriate conclusions and set realistic objectives.

- Performance prediction for each year, concluding with the Olympic year.
- Objectives for each training factor set according to the dynamics and tendencies of development in the world.
- The calendar of major competitions (i.e., National Championships and main international competitions).
- Tests and standards to reflect the conclusion of the retrospective analysis. Link these with the performance prediction and objectives for each training factor.
- The chart of the Olympic cycle plan.
- A basic periodization model for each year of training.
- A preparation model (general outline).

Chart of the Olympic Cycle or Quadrennial Plan

Regard the chart of the Olympic cycle plan as a synopsis of the whole plan, which mirrors the main training objectives you plan to achieve yearly. Also, consider the chart a working tool to be used when the coach extracts the data necessary to construct the current year's annual plan.

Figure 9.7 illustrates a chart of a quadrennial plan for a hypothetical junior athlete, which incorporates the dynamics of all objectives (performance, training factors, and tests and standards), as well as the ratio of all training factors and the curves of the training components.

Assign the objectives separately for each of the 4 years of the plan. Their sequential setup should reflect the overall flow of training from year to year. For instance, with physical preparation, initially emphasize general physical preparation and aerobic endurance, leading to specific physical preparation and anaerobic endurance toward the end of the 4-year period. Use the same approach for technical preparation, most of which (considering our example of a cyclic skill) the athlete must acquire in the first part of the program. Expect that the standards of each test will increase annually, reflecting the growth of the athlete's abilities. For shape of the curves of the components of training and peaking, their magnitude should signify the general ascending tendency from year to year. There is no relationship between the percentage scale (which refers to training factors only) and the curves' magnitude. Furthermore, the interrelationship between the curves of volume and intensity reflects the same

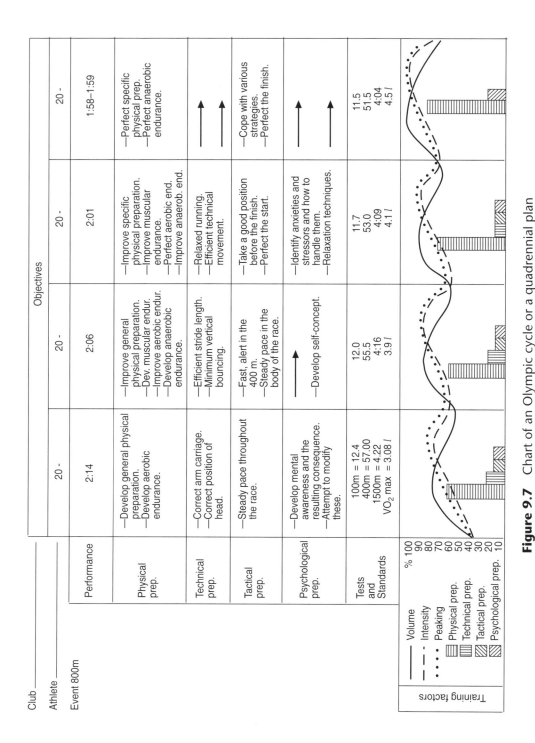

Figure 9.7 Chart of an Olympic cycle or a quadrennial plan

concept as in the annual plan. Volume dominates the preparatory and the beginning of the competitive phase (note the specifics of an event like 800 meters). It is surpassed by intensity in the second part of the competitive phase as a result of the emphasis on anaerobic endurance. The magnitude of the peaking curve also holds an ascendant trend, signifying the athlete's predicted performance evolution.

272

Performance Prediction for an Olympic Cycle Plan

A coach rarely makes a 4-year plan and more rarely uses any normative data to prescribe norms for the athletes to achieve in the future. It is easy to predict trends of performance for individual sports, such as track and field, swimming, and so on, in which performance is measured objectively. In other sports, such as team sports, it is impossible to measure performance objectively. For this group, you can successfully plan superior results by using standards in the tests that monitor training.

Irrespective of whether you are predicting objectively measured performance or test standards, I strongly recommend using normative data. If such information does not exist, the coach can create his or her own. We should give up the habit of using subjectivism in training. Scientific methods that monitor training are available in most college and university laboratories. Although expensive, testing represents a critical element in monitoring athletes' progress. No one should claim to be a reliable coach without using tests and standards or normative data.

Figure 9.8 and tables 9.7 and 9.8, although outdated, are examples of how to create your own normative data.

Talent Identification

The process of identifying the most talented athletes to involve in an organized training program is one of the most important concerns of contemporary sports. Everyone can learn to sing, dance, or paint, but few individuals ever reach a high level of mastery. In sports, as in the arts, it is therefore important to discover the most talented individuals and select them at an early age, then to monitor them continually and assist them to climb to the highest level of mastery.

In the past, and even today in most Western countries, a youngster's involvement in a sport was based mostly on tradition, ideals, desire to participate in a sport because of its popularity, parental pressure, a high school teacher's specialty, the proximity of sport facilities, and so on. For East European training specialists, such methods are no longer satisfactory. They discovered that individuals who, for example, had a natural talent for distance running often ended up as mediocre sprinters. Obviously the outcome rarely led to high performance.

A coach must invest work and time in individuals who possess superior natural abilities otherwise the coach wastes talent, time, and energy, or at best produces mediocrity. The main objective of talent identification is to identify and select those athletes who have the greatest abilities for a sport.

Talent identification is not a new concept in athletics, although not much is formally done about it, especially in the Western World. In the late 1960s and early 1970s, most East European countries established specific methods for identifying potentially high-class athletes. Some of the selection procedures used were discovered and directed by scientists, who then advised the coach which youngsters had the required abilities for a sport.

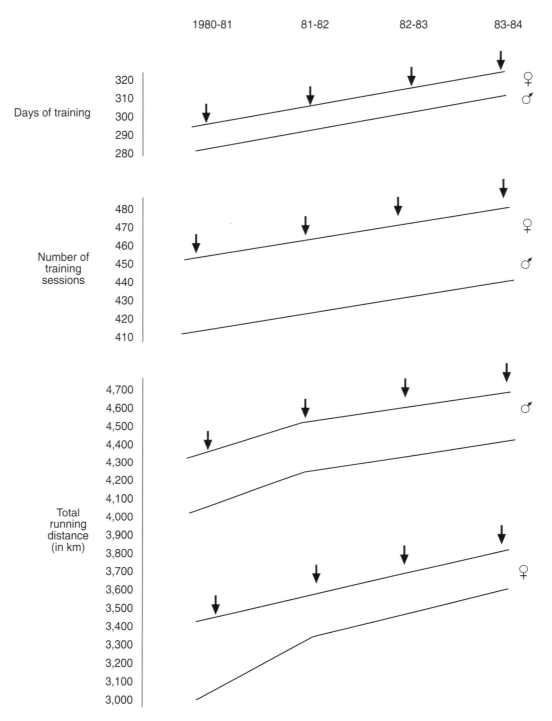

Figure 9.8 Recommended parameters for the candidates of the USSR Olympic Team for 1984 Olympic Games (middle- and long-distance running events)

TABLE 9.7 Four-Year Plan

800m				
	1980-81	**1981-82**	**1982-83**	**1983-84**
Days of training	280-290	290-300	300-310	310-320
No. of training lessons	410-450	420-460	430-470	440-480
Total running distance (km)	4,000-4,300	4,200-4,500	4,300-4,600	4,400-4,700
Aerobic system	2,600-2,700	2,700-2,850	2,800-2,950	2,850-2,950
Mixed zone	710-830	770-860	770-860	780-910
Continuous running	550-650	600-650	600-660	600-700
Repetitions	160-180	170-200	170-200	180-210
Anaerobic training				
Short 200m	180-200	190-200	190-200	200-210
Medium 600m	90-100	95-100	95-100	100-110
Long 3,000m	20-30	25-30	25-30	30-35
Specific strength				
Bounding	220-250	230-260	230-260	240-270
Uphill running	180-190	190-200	190-200	200-215
No. of competitions (No. of starts)				
For selected event	15-20	15-20	15-20	15-20
Other events	8-10	8-10	8-10	8-10
Cross-country	1-2	1-2	1-2	1-2

5,000 - 10,000m				
	1980-81	**1981-82**	**1982-83**	**1983-84**
Days of training	320-330	300-340	330-340	340-350
No. of training lessons	570-580	570-590	570-590	600-620
Total running distance (km)	7,500-7,800	7,800-8,000	7,800-8,000	8,300-8,500
Aerobic system	5,580-5,760	5,780-5,870	5,680-5,770	6,000
Mixed zone	1,600-1,650	1,650-1,750	1,750-1,800	1,850-2,000
Continuous running	1,250-1,300	1,300-1,350	1,350-1,400	1,480-1,600
Repetitions	330-350	350-400	350-400	400-420
Anaerobic training				
Short 200m	20-25	25-30	25-30	35-40
Medium 600m	40-50	50-60	50-60	60-65
Long 3000m	200-220	220-240	220-240	280-300
Specific strength (km)				
Bounding	40-60	40-60	40-60	40-60
Uphill running	20-35	35-40	35-40	40-45
No. of competitions (No. of starts)				
For selected event	6-7	6-7	6-7	6-8
Other events	6-8	6-8	6-8	7-9

Recommended Parameters for the Male Candidates of the USSR Olympic Team for the 1984 Olympic Games (Middle- and Long-Distance Running Events)

TABLE 9.8 Preparation Model for 1984 Olympic Games: USSR Middle, Long-Distance, and Walk

Anthropometric parameters

	Male					Female	
	800-1,500	**5,000-10,000**	**3,000 SC**	**Marathon**	**Walk**	**800**	**1,500**
Age	24±2	25±2	24±3	26±3	27±2	25±2	26±3
Height (cm)	185±2	178±3	182±2	175±3	180±2	168±2	168±2
Weight (kg)	76±3	64±2	66±2	60±3	73±2	50±2	50±2
$\dfrac{\text{Weight (gr)}}{\text{Height (cm)}}$	41.0	35.9	36.2	34.2	40.5	28.7	29.7

Functional parameters

	Male					Female	
	800	**1,500**	**5,000-10,000**	**3,000 SC**	**Marathon walk**	**800**	**1,500**
VO$_2$max	70-75	75-80	80-85	75-85	80-85	65-70	68-73
Heart volume (cm³)	900-1,000	1,000-1,100	1,000-1,150	1,000-1,150	1,000-1,150	700-800	700-800

Physical training (results for various distances)

100m	10.6-11.0	10.9-11.2	11.2-11.8	11.2-11.5	—	11.6-12.0	12.0-12.5
400m	46.0-48.5	46.5-50.0	49.0-52.0	—	—	51.5-52.5	52.0-54.5
800m	—	1.46-1.48	1.47-1.52	1.50-1.51	—	—	1.58-2.01
1,500m	3.36-3.44	—	3.37-3.42	3.38-3.42	—	4.00-4.06	—
3,000m	8.00-8.30	7.50-8.05	7.38-7.48	7.38-7.52	—	9.05-9.20	8.20-9.00
5,000m	—	—	—	13.25-13.35	13.30-13.45	—	—
10,000m	—	—	—	—	28.10-28.30	—	—

The results were more than dramatic. Several medalists in the 1972, 1976, 1980, and 1984 Olympic Games, particularly from former East Germany, were scientifically selected. The same was true for Bulgaria in 1976, when almost 80% of its medalists were the result of a thorough talent identification process.

A group of scientists and rowing specialists in Romania in 1976 selected young girls to participate in rowing. The initial 100 girls were selected from 27,000 teenagers. By 1978 the group had been reduced to 25, and most of these made the team for the Moscow Olympics. The result was 1 gold, 2 silver, and 2 bronze medals. Another group selected in the late 1970s produced 5 gold medals and 1 silver medal at the 1984 Olympic Games in Los Angeles and 9 medals at the 1988 Seoul Olympic Games.

The talent identification process has to be a preoccupation of training specialists and coaches, to further its advances and improve the psychobiological criteria used to discover more talented individuals for high-performance athletics.

Using scientific criteria in the process of talent identification has several advantages:

- It substantially reduces the time required to reach high performance by selecting individuals who are gifted in a sport.
- It eliminates a high volume of work, energy, and talent on the part of the coach. The coach's training effectiveness is enhanced by training primarily those athletes with superior abilities.
- It increases the competitiveness and the number of athletes aiming at and reaching high-performance levels. As a result, there is a stronger and more homogeneous national team capable of better international performance.
- It increases an athlete's self-confidence, because his or her performance dynamics are known to be more dramatic than other athletes of the same age who did not go through the selection process.
- It indirectly facilitates applying scientific training, because sport scientists who assist in talent identification can be motivated to continue to monitor the athletes' training.

Talent Identification Methods

In training there are two basic methods of selection, natural and scientific. Natural selection is the normal approach, the natural way of developing an athlete in a sport. It assumes that an athlete enrolls in a sport as a result of local influence (school tradition, parents' wishes, or peers). The performance evolution of athletes determined by natural selection depends on, among other factors, whether by coincidence they take part in a sport for which they are talented. It may often occur, therefore, that an individual's performance evolution is slow, mostly because the selection of the ideal sport was incorrect.

Scientific selection is the method by which a coach selects prospective youngsters who have proven natural abilities for a sport. Thus, compared with individuals identified through the natural method, the time required for those selected scientifically to reach high performance is much shorter. For sports in which height or weight is a requirement, for instance basketball, volleyball, football, rowing, and throwing events, you should strongly consider scientific selection. The same is true for other sports, such as sprinting, judo, hockey, and jumping events in athletics, in which speed, reaction time, coordination, and power are dominant. You can detect such qualities with the assistance of sport scientists. As a result of scientific testing, the most talented individuals are scientifically selected or directed to an appropriate sport.

Criteria for Talent Identification

High-performance athletics require specific biological profiles of athletes with outstanding biomotor abilities and strong physiological traits. Training science has made impressive steps forward in the past decades, which is one of the main reasons for constant improvements in athletic performance. Other dramatic improvements have also been made in quantity and quality of training.

If, however, an individual involved in sports has a biological handicap or lacks the necessary abilities for a sport, then even excessive training cannot overcome the initial lack of natural ability. Scientific talent identification is, therefore, vital to high-performance athletics.

Individuals not selected for high-performance athletics are not excluded from sports. They can take part in recreational programs in which they can fulfill their physical and social needs and participate in competitions.

Optimal training requires optimal criteria for talent identification. Not necessarily in order of importance, some of the main criteria are as follows.

• Health is an absolute necessity for everyone participating in training. Each youngster must, therefore, have a thorough medical examination before being accepted into a club. The physician should recommend and the coach should select for training only healthy individuals. During the examination, medical and testing specialists should also observe whether a candidate has physical or organic malfunction and make recommendations accordingly. You should not select an individual with a malformation for dynamic sports, for instance hockey, basketball, track and field, swimming, or boxing. On the other hand, such discrimination should be more liberal for sports with static characteristics, such as shooting, archery, and bowling. Similarly, the physiological status of an individual, that is the ability to move arms, legs, and so on, should also play a role in talent identification, because physiological disparities can play a restrictive role. Once again, the eventual discrimination between candidates has to correlate with the physiological needs and specifics of a sport.

• Biometric qualities, or anthropometric measurements, of an individual are important assets for several sports and, therefore, you must consider them among the main criteria for talent identification. Height, weight, or length of the limbs play dominant roles in certain sports. It is, however, difficult to predict the dynamics of an individual's growth and development during the early stage of talent identification, which is performed at the age of 4 to 6 for such sports as gymnastics, figure skating, and swimming. During the primary phase of talent identification, therefore, look mostly for a harmonious physical development. You can do this by examining the leg joint and the hip and shoulder widths and the ratio between them.

At a later age (teens), you may use hand plates (growth plates in the wrist region) and hand radiography (X-ray) techniques to test whether growth is complete. If the tester concludes growth is complete, the coach may make decisions as to whether the height of a given athlete is optimal for a particular sport.

• Heredity, a complex biological phenomenon, often plays an important role in training. Children tend to inherit their parents' biological and psychological characteristics, although through education, training, and social conditioning, they may slightly alter inherited qualities.

The view on the role of heredity in training is neither uniform nor unanimous, but the athlete's genetic potential will ultimately limit the improvements in physiological capabilities. Klissouras et al. (1973) implied that systems and functions are genetically determined: the lactic acid system to the extent of 81.4%; heart rate, 85.9%; and maximal VO_2, 93.4%.

Muscle Fiber Distribution

The proportion of red and white muscle fibers in humans seems to be genetically determined. Similarly, the metabolic function of these fibers also differs. The red, or slow-twitch, fibers have a higher myoglobin (acts as a store for oxygen carried by the blood to the working cell) and are biochemically better equipped for aerobic (endurance) work.

On the other hand, the white, or fast-twitch, fibers have a high content of glycogen (carbohydrate) and are better for anaerobic or short and intensive types of exercises (Fox, Bowes, and Foss 1989; Willmore and Costill 1980). The percentage of muscle fibers cannot be altered, but extensive specific training may increase the capabilities of muscle fibers and change their biochemical structure.

Based on this, an athlete who inherits a high proportion of red fibers may have a high probability of performing successfully in sports in which endurance is a requirement. Similarly, when the white fibers are dominant, the athlete is naturally equipped for sports in which intensity (speed or power) prevails.

Biopsy, the technique of extracting muscle tissue then counting the proportion of two fibers, can determine those groups of sports in which an individual is likely to perform most successfully. The coach can then couple this knowledge with physiological and biometric characteristics to direct the candidate to sports for which he or she is best equipped.

Sport facilities and climate both play restrictive roles in the kind of sports for which you can select athletes. Regardless of an individual's qualities for a given sport, if the natural conditions or facilities do not exist, for instance canoeing and water, then it might be better for an athlete to practice a sport for which he or she is not as talented.

The availability of specialists or the coach's knowledge in the area of talent identification and testing also restricts the selection of candidates. The more numerous and sophisticated the scientific methods you use for talent identification, the higher the probability of discovering superior talents for particular sports. Universities, which are well equipped with testing facilities and scientific specialists, are grossly underused for the scope of selecting and monitoring athletes' training programs. A coach cannot cope with high athletic demands alone. The cooperation among qualified personnel, sport scientists, and coaches is vital if you attempt dramatic progress in training.

Phases of Talent Identification

Comprehensive talent identification is not solved in one attempt; it is performed over a few years in three main phases:

Primary Phase

The primary phase of talent identification, in most cases, occurs during prepuberty (3-10 years). It is dominated mostly by a physician's examination of a candidate's health and general physical development and is designed to detect any body malfunctions or eventual disease.

The biometric portion of this examination could focus on three main concepts:

- Discovering physical deficiencies that may play a restrictive role in a candidate's sport endeavors
- Determining a candidate's level of physical development through simple means, such as the ratio between height and weight

- Detecting eventual genetic dominants (e.g., height) to direct children toward those groups of sports in which they might specialize at a later age

Considering the early age at which this primary phase is completed, it furnishes the examiner with only general information about a child. Definite decisions are premature because a candidate's future dynamics of growth and development are still unpredictable. For sports, such as swimming, gymnastics, and figure skating, in which comprehensive training has already begun at a young age, the primary identification phase should be thoroughly performed.

Secondary Phase

The secondary phase of talent identification is performed during and after puberty, between the ages of 9 and 10 for gymnastics, figure skating, and swimming, 10 to 15 for girls and 10 to 17 for boys for other sports (Dragan 1978). It represents the most important phase of selection. This phase is used with teenagers who have already experienced organized training.

Techniques used in secondary selection must assess the dynamics of the biometric and physiological parameters, because the body should have reached a certain level of adaptation to the specifics and requirements of a given sport. Consequently, the health examination should be detailed and aim at detecting obstacles to performance increase (e.g., rheumatism, hepatitis, acute renal disease).

The critical moment for a child in the puberty phase is when dramatic growth changes occur (i.e., when lower limbs grow visibly). Along with examining general physical development, therefore, consider specialized training on the athlete's growth and development. Popovici (1979) implies that intensive, heavy load, strength training performed at an early age limits growth (height) by hastening the closure of the fibrous cartilage of the bones (i.e., premature closure of long bones).

For sports such as throwing events, rowing, wrestling, and weightlifting, a wide shoulder width (biacromial diameter) is significant. Strong shoulders are closely related to an individual's strength or at least represent a good frame on which to develop strength.

As a guideline, Popovici (1979) suggests that at 15 years, girls should have a biacromial diameter of 38 centimeters, and boys at 18 should have one of 46 centimeters. Popovici also claims that the length of the foot and the arch are important in some sports. For example, a flat-footed individual is limited in jumping, tumbling, or running.

Similarly, joint looseness may affect performance for sports in which strength is critical, such as wrestling and weightlifting. Consequently, consider anatomical and physiological malformations or genetic inadequacies important elements of talent identification.

For athletes going through a training program based on natural selection, all these aspects affect an individual's performance evolution and, therefore, must be of continual concern to a coach.

During the secondary phase of talent identification, sport psychologists start to play a more important role by performing comprehensive psychological testing. Compile each athlete's psychological profile to reveal whether he or she possesses the psychological traits required for a given sport. These tests will also help decide what future psychological emphasis might be necessary.

Final Phase

The final phase of talent identification primarily concerns national team candidates. It has to be elaborate, reliable, and highly correlated with the specifics and requirements of a sport.

The main factors you must examine include the athlete's health; physiological adaptation to training and competing; ability to cope with stress; and most important, potential for further performance improvements.

You can facilitate an objective assessment of these elements by periodic medical, psychological, and training tests. Record and compare data from these tests to illustrate their dynamics from the primary phase throughout an athletic career.

Establish an optimal model for each test and each individual compared with that model. Consider only outstanding candidates for a national team.

Guidelines for Talent Identification Criteria

The criteria for talent identification, including tests, standards, and the optimal model, have to be sport specific. In many sports, especially those in which endurance or a high volume of work is crucial, base the final selection on the athlete's working capacity and the body's ability to recover between training sessions. Dragan (1978) identifies the following testing criteria:

Athletics (track and field)

Sprinting
- Reaction time (and the ability to repeat reactions continuously)
- Neuromuscular excitability
- Coordination and good muscular relaxation capacity
- Ability to cope with stress
- Height to trunk ratio, long legs

Middle-Distance Events
- Anaerobic power and maximum VO_2 per kilogram of body weight
- Lactic acid concentration (the level of excess lactic acid in the blood following heavy exercise) and the O_2 deficit
- Ability to cope with stress
- High concentration span and the ability to maintain it for a prolonged time

Distance Running and Walking
- VO_2max per kilogram of body weight
- Cardiac volume
- High resistance to fatigue, perseverance, motivation

Jumping Events
- Reaction time and explosive strength
- Tall with long legs
- High anaerobic power
- Ability to cope with stress
- High concentration span and the ability to maintain it for a prolonged time

Throwing Events
- Tall and muscular
- High anaerobic power
- Large biacromial diameter
- Reaction time
- High concentration span and the ability to maintain it for a prolonged time

Alpine skiing

- Courage
- Reaction time
- Coordination
- High anaerobic power

Basketball

- Tall with long arms
- High anaerobic power
- High aerobic capacity
- Coordination
- Resistance to fatigue and stress
- Tactical intelligence and cooperative spirit

Boxing

- Great concentration span
- Courage
- Reaction time
- Coordination and tactical intelligence
- High aerobic capacity
- High anaerobic power

Cycling

- High aerobic capacity
- Cardiac volume (medium) and high VO_2 capacity
- Ability to cope with stress
- Perseverance

Cross-country skiing

- High aerobic capacity
- Tall individuals
- Perseverance, staunchness
- Resistance to fatigue and stress

Diving

- Vestibular balance (inner ear)
- Courage
- Coordination
- Great concentration span
- Ability to cope with stress

Fencing

- Reaction time

- Coordination
- Tactical intelligence
- Resistance to fatigue and stress
- High anaerobic and aerobic capacity

Figure skating

- Coordination, aesthetic appeal
- Vestibular balance
- Harmonious physical development
- High anaerobic and aerobic capacity

Gymnastics

- Coordination, flexibility, power
- Vestibular balance
- Perseverance
- Capacity to cope with stress, emotional balance
- High anaerobic power
- Short to medium height

Hockey and lacrosse

- Tall, long arms, large biacromial diameter
- Tactical intelligence, courage, cooperative spirit
- High aerobic and anaerobic capacity
- Strong, robust

Judo

- Coordination
- Reaction time
- Tactical intelligence
- Long reach and large biacromial diameter

Kayaking and canoeing

- Large biacromial diameter, long arms
- Concentration span
- High anaerobic and aerobic capacity
- Resistance to fatigue and stress

Rowing

- High anaerobic and aerobic capacity
- Coordination, concentration span
- Tall, long limbs, large biacromial diameter
- Resistance to fatigue and stress

Rugby

- Tall, robust, large biacromial diameter
- Courage, staunchness
- Tactical intelligence and cooperative spirit
- High aerobic capacity
- Speed and power

Speed skating

Short Distance
- Reaction time, power
- Coordination
- High anaerobic and aerobic capacity
- Tall, long legs

Long Distance
- High aerobic capacity
- VO_2max per kilogram of body weight
- Tall, long legs

Shooting

- Visual-motor coordination
- Reaction time
- Concentration span, resistance to fatigue
- Emotional balance

Soccer

- Coordination, cooperative spirit
- Resistance to fatigue and stress
- High anaerobic and aerobic capacity
- Tactical intelligence

Swimming

- Low body density
- Long arms and big feet, large biacromial diameter
- High anaerobic and aerobic capacity

Volleyball

- Tall, long arms large biacromial diameter
- High anaerobic and aerobic capacity
- Resistance to fatigue and stress
- Tactical intelligence and cooperative spirit

Water polo

- Tall, large biacromial diameter
- High anaerobic and aerobic capacity
- Tactical intelligence and cooperative spirit
- Resistance to fatigue and stress

Weightlifting

- Power
- Large biacromial diameter
- Coordination
- Resistance to fatigue and stress

Wrestling

- Coordination and reaction time
- High anaerobic and aerobic capacity
- Tactical intelligence
- Large biacromial diameter, long arms

Main Factors for Talent Identification

Kunst and Florescu (1971) identified motor capacity, psychological capacity, and biometric qualities (including body somatotype and anthropometric measurements) as the main factors for performance and talent identification. Although these three represent the main factors for all sports, their emphasis differs with each sport. A more effective talent identification system starts with characterizing the sport and its specifics, then isolating the main selection factors based on this analysis.

For sport characterization, express each of the three factors as a percentage to reflect its relative influence on success. For example, good performance in high jumping depends on motor capacity 50%, psychological capacity 10%, and biometric 40%, with the relative emphasis on each expressed as a percentage.

Furthermore, subdivide each factor into the three main elements that incorporate it, expressing their relative importance as a percentage as well. Thus, the main three elements and their emphasis in training for the motor capacity of a high jumper are strength 45%, jumping power 35%, and coordination 20%.

Knowing the characteristics of the sport and their relative importance, it is then important to determine the main factors for talent identification and the emphasis to place on each element. When you express the three elements of each factor, they must be specific and stated in order of importance. Figure 9.9 illustrates the characteristics of wrestling, and figure 9.10 suggests the main factors for talent identification for wrestling. Note the differences between the figures.

By comparing the main factors for performance with those for talent identification (figures 9.9 and 9.10), the reader realizes that sequence and emphasis differ. For the sequence of the performance factors, the motor capacity prevails, but this is not the case for talent identification. In the latter, psychological capacity is the most important.

In talent identification, it is more important for someone uninitiated to wrestling to possess the main psychological traits and the desire to wrestle, because you cannot expect a beginner to have developed the motor capacity. Furthermore, of the three dominant elements in motor capacity, coordination and speed (one of the two components of power) are more likely to have been inherited as natural abilities than endurance. Through training, an athlete can make more dramatic gains in endurance than in coordination or power (the speed component).

Finally, view the importance of biometric qualities relative to the specifics of the sport. For some sports certain qualities may be crucial, for example height in basketball or the ratio between height and weight in rowing. Whereas for other sports, the ratio between various parts of the body and a harmonious development are important but not critical, for instance figure skating.

In each sport, there has to be an accepted ideal model for the main factors of performance and talent identification. During the latter stages of athlete development, a coach, assisted by sport scientists, can test all the candidates and compare their qualities with the ideal model. You can select those who are closer to the model for the high-performance group.

It is possible to develop a more scientific model, although the role of sport scientists is important in this case. An optimal biometric model based on athletes' measurements taken at various Olympic Games and world championships was developed for men's rowing by Radut (1973). Radut found certain biometric measurements correlate highly with an athlete's final standing in top championships. Consequently, the abilities of candidates for elite rowing clubs were compared with the model (table 9.9 and figure 9.11), and those with the highest scores were selected.

The eight biometric tests considered the most relevant for rowing were as follows:

- Standing, back against the wall, arms above the head. The score was the average of the two highest reaches performed with the tips of the longest fingers.
- Standing, back against the wall, arms extended laterally at shoulder height.
- Sitting, legs extended, back against the wall. Measure the distance from the floor to above the shoulder joint (the acromion).
- Sitting, back against the wall, legs extended. Measure the distance from the wall to the flat of the foot.
- Shoulder width, measured as the distance between the two deltoid muscles.
- Standing on a measuring bench, take a crouch position (both heels on the bench) and reach as low as possible. Measure the lowest point reached.
- Specific amplitude, measured by the length of the legs plus the additional length from the knee to the foot.
- The body weight in kilograms.

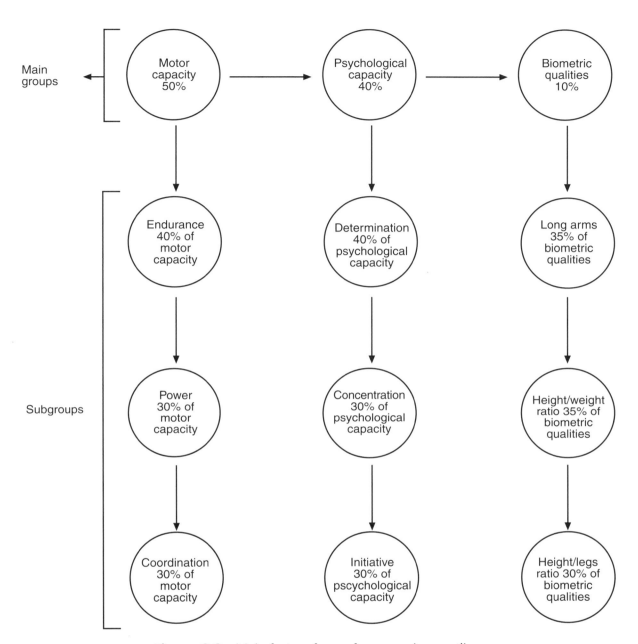

Figure 9.9 Main factors for performance in wrestling (adapted from Kunst and Florescu 1971)

The scores of these tests were plotted in an octagonal shape (figure 9.11), which shows those ranking in the top 12 in the world. Compare the scores of any candidate for an elite program with these, and the closer they come to the outside edge of the octagon the better.

You may also compile optimal models for selection for the physiological and biomotor abilities. Examples of such models are presented in figure 9.12 and table 9.10. The examples represent women's rowing and are based on data from world-class athletes. Once again, a candidate's scores have to be com-

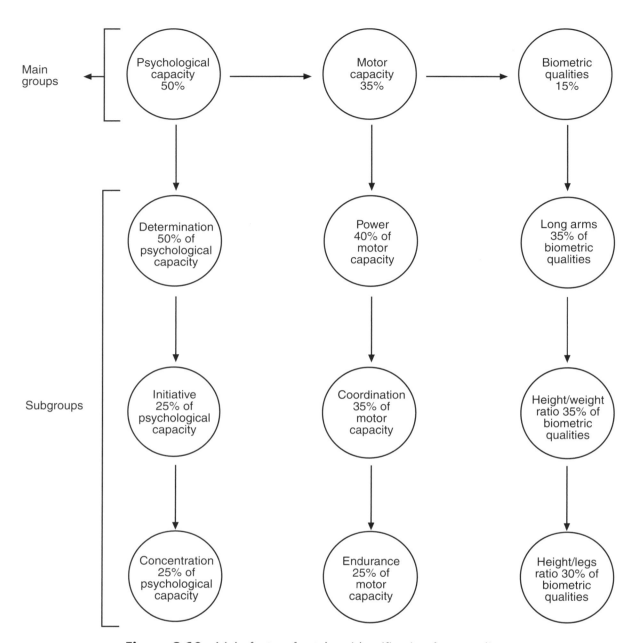

Figure 9.10 Main factors for talent identification for wrestling
(adapted from Kunst and Florescu 1971)

pared with the optimal model, and only those whose scores produce, in this case, an octagonal shape, will be selected for elite class programs.

Close cooperation among coaches, training specialists, and sport scientists can produce such models for each sport. The outcome of such cooperation will obviously be a more scientific talent identification system for elite athletes, which can result in dramatic increases in performance.

TABLE 9.9   Biometric Measurements for Women's Rowing

Ranking	Test 1 Height arms above head (cm)	Test 2 Arm span (cm)	Test 3 Height of upper body (cm)	Test 4 Length of legs (cm)	Test 5 Shoulder width (cm)	Test 6 Reach from crouch position (cm)	Test 7 Specific amplitude (cm)	Test 8 Body weight (kg)
I	249	201	73.5	121	53.5	48.5	169	96
II-III	246	199	70.8	120	52.1	45.5	165	93.5
IV-VI	244	197	68.9	119	51.7	45.0	164	92
VII-XII	242	195	65.7	117	49.9	44.4	161	87.2

Adapted from Radut 1973.

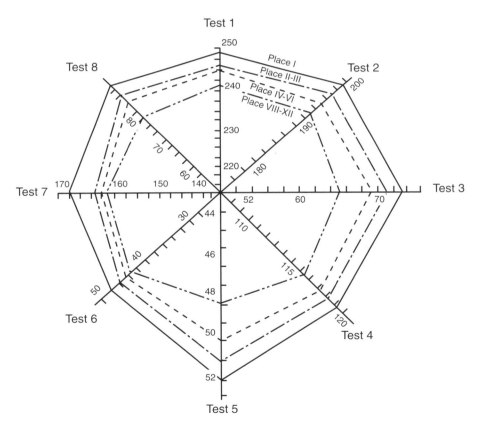

Figure 9.11   Model of biometric measurements for men's rowing (adapted from Radut 1973)

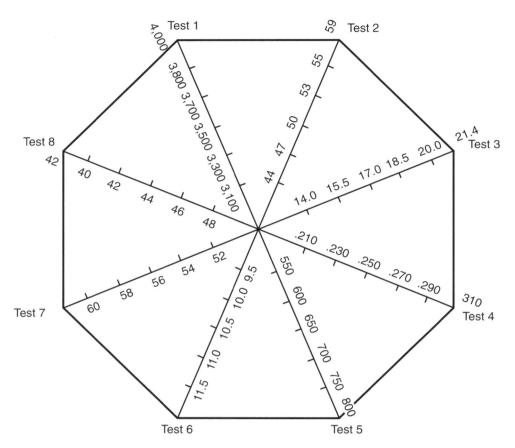

Figure 9.12 Optimal model of talent identification for women's rowing (adapted from Szogy 1976)

TABLE 9.10 Eight Biometric Tests for Women's Rowing

Athlete's name		Club					Date	
Height	Weight		Age		Occupation			

Test#	Tests	Symbol	Units	World ranking			Candidate's scores
				I	II-III	IV-VI	
1	VO₂max	VO₂max	ml	4,100	3,900	3,700	
2	VO₂max/kg	VO₂/kg	ml/kg	59	56	53	
3	VO₂max/HR	VO₂/HR	ml	21.5	20.0	18.5	
4	VO₂max/HR/kg	VO₂/HR/kg	ml/kg	.310	.290	.270	
5	Cardiac volume	CV	ml	800	750	700	
6	Cardiac volume/body wt.	CV/kg	ml/kg	12.0	11.5	11.0	
7	Aerobic metabolic rate	Aerobic	%	62	62	62	
8	Anaerobic metabolic rate	Anaerobic	%	38	38	38	

Although technological sophistication in testing and monitoring athletes' training progress seems to be a constant and essential feature of today's athletic world, talent identification must be considered an attribute of at least equal importance.

The human material—the talent with which the coach works—often makes the difference between international or provincial-level performance. Talented kids are everywhere. You just have to develop the means to identify them; then expose them to well-planned and methodical training. Although the coach recognizes this necessity, he cannot do it alone. It is the job of sport scientists to identify the dominant parameters, develop the model, then apply it to identify talented individuals to recruit for a sport. Only a combined effort can result in better talent identification criteria, superior training methods, and sophisticated testing and training monitoring. The final outcome will be better results in international meets.

Summary of Major Concepts

From the time a talented child starts a sporting program with the intent of reaching the highest performance achievable, he or she should participate in a long-term plan. Guiding young athletes' training programs, both specific and holistic, during the early stages of growth and athletic development is a necessity. You can compile long-term plans, as well as Olympic cycle plans, to guide the young athletes' skills and physical development in conjunction with international standards.

If you train young athletes, try to make your own program, no matter how simple. A plan is always better than no plan. You will surprise yourself by how quickly you will learn these planning skills. Furthermore, you will see how your planning will have a positive impact your athletes' specific and holistic development.

It is important to allocate time in your training activity to identify the most talented children. Use the information in this book or other books to decide the most appropriate tests for identifying anthropometric or physical qualities. The outcome of this work will quickly translate into better training for the most talented individuals.

Beware, however, that there are important differences between the early and late maturers. An early maturer will show the most improvements, but often a late maturer might be a better athlete in the long run. Therefore, don't rush into making decisions. Let children grow at their own pace while you provide the best long-term training programs.

Chapter 10

Peaking for Competitions

$\mathbf{A}$ coach or instructor has to plan a peaking strategy so his or her athletes reach their best performance in time for competitions. Taking into consideration the individual characteristics of each athlete, the training conditions, the athlete's motivation, and other factors that influence peaking, the coach or instructor must design a focused program that leads to ultimate performance when it matters most.

Training Conditions for Peaking

Achieving superior athletic performance is the direct outcome of an athlete's adaptation to various types and methods of training. Training is a complex process organized and planned over various phases and implemented sequentially. Throughout these phases of training, and especially during the competitive phase, an athlete reaches certain training states. Peaking for a competition is complex and the athlete cannot realize it on short notice, but attains it in a sequential, cumulative manner. The athlete must make progress through other training states before the state of peaking occurs.

Figure 10.1 displays the evolution of peaking during a monocyclic annual plan. A detailed explanation of each term will bring better understanding of the concept of training states. Degree of training (see figure 10.1) represents the foundation on which to base other training states. As a result of organized and systematic training, the athlete's working capacity, acquisition of skills, and tactical maneuvers all reach high levels. These are reflected through above average results and thus high standards in all tests toward the end of the preparatory phase. An athlete who has reached a high degree of training is, therefore, someone who has achieved a high level of physical preparation and has perfected all the biomotor abilities required by the sport or event. The higher the degree of training, the higher the athlete's effectiveness. When the degree of training is poor, other training states are adversely affected, which lowers the magnitude of athletic shape and, implicitly, peaking. The degree of training may be general, which signifies a high adaptation to different forms of training and specific, meaning that the athlete has adapted to the specific training requirements of a sport. It is on such a solid base or degree of training during the competitive phase that the athlete attains the state of athletic shape.

During the competitive phase, athletes are often heard to say that they are in good or bad shape. The state of athletic shape is an extension of the degree of training, during which the athletes may perform and attain results close to their maximum capacity. This paramount training state, which is achieved as a result of specialized training programs, may precede or incorporate the process of peaking for the main competition of the year. The state of athletic shape is the basis from which the athlete initiates peaking.

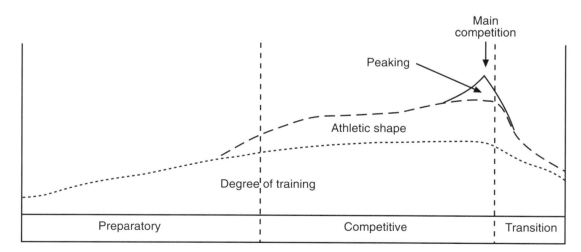

Figure 10.1 Accumulation and elevation of training states throughout training phases in a monocycle

Peaking, as the highlight of athletic shape, results in the athlete's best performance of the year. It is a temporary training state in which physical and psychological efficiencies are maximized and the levels of technical and tactical preparation are optimal. During this state of training, the individual's physiological and anatomical adaptation capacities are also maximum, and neuromuscular coordination is perfect. Peaking is a superior, special biological state characterized by perfect health, an optimal physiological state expressed through quick adaptability to training stimuli, and a good recovery rate following training or competition. The athlete's body reflects a high state of functional synergism (acting together), in which organs and systems channel toward achieving optimum efficiency and the highest possible performance. Concerning the biological characteristics of peaking, they vary according to the specifics of the sport (table 10.1).

TABLE 10.1   Characteristics of the State of Peaking for Various Groups of Sports

Group of sports	Characteristics
Dominant anaerobic	Capacity to involve all the athlete's abilities in a short time with a quick recovery
Dominant aerobic	High working capacity based on a high physiological efficiency
Combined—aerobic and anaerobic	Capacity to handle many repeating moments of maximum intensity on the basis of high physiological efficiency

From the psychological point of view, peaking is a state of readiness for action, with an intense emotional arousal (Oxendine 1968). It is also a state of objective and subjective analyzing of all levels of integration and adaptation for the main competition (Serban 1979). The objective aspects of peaking refer to the nervous system's capacity to adapt quickly and effectively to the stress of competition. The subjective aspects, on the other hand, refer to the athlete's self-confidence, level of motivation, and perception of motor and biological synergism. An important attribute of peaking seems to be the athlete's capacity to tolerate various degrees of frustration that occur before, during, and after competition. To facilitate this, the coach may model many training lessons to create psychological circumstances specific to the main competition. Similarly, taking part in various competitions during the precompetitive and competitive phases enhances the athlete's capacity to cope with frustration. As suggested by figure 10.2, peaking is a special training state characterized by a high CNS adaptation, motor and biological harmony, high motivation, ability to cope with frustration, accepting the implicit risk of competing, and high self-confidence.

Factors Facilitating Peaking

The many complex factors of peaking make it an intricate concept and an ultimate training task. Isolating a singular aspect that would lead to its accomplishment is not possible. You must consider several factors, explained below, and correctly manipulate them to ensure that an athlete is likely to peak adequately for the competition of major interest. It is important to specify that you cannot substitute one factor for another. All factors are essential for optimizing the physical, technical, tactical, and neuropsychological qualities.

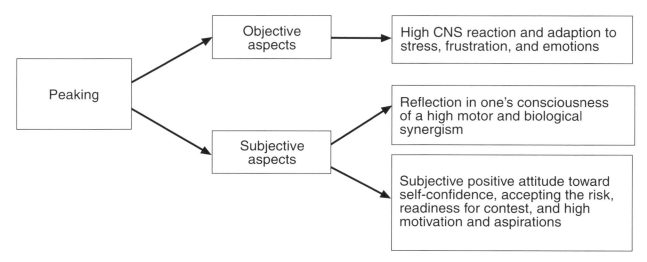

Figure 10.2 Psychological characteristics of peaking

High working potential and *quick recovery rate* are two essential attributes of any athlete who reaches a high training status. An inability to cope with a high volume of work means that high-performance expectations are groundless. Similarly, the athlete's capacity to recover quickly following training symbolizes an optimal adaptability to the specifics of the effort or stimuli in training and competition.

Near-perfect neuromuscular coordination refers strictly to the capacity to perform skills and tactical maneuvers flawlessly, so nothing impairs the performance of a routine or skill. Technical imperfection signifies that a skill was not acquired or automized properly; therefore the probability of a correct technical and tactical performance is low, which degenerates overall performance.

Supercompensation refers to the effects of work and regeneration on the individual, as a biological foundation for physical and psychological arousal for the main competition of the year. Further information can be found in chapter 1 under training adaptation and detraining.

A *correct unloading phase* before the main competition of the year is one of the most important factors to facilitate peaking. Manipulating the training volume and intensity is an important training concept that the coach must carefully consider.

Correct unloading is a significant factor for achieving supercompensation before the main competition (figure 10.3). Figure 10.3 illustrates the last five microcycles before the main competition. During the first three cycles, the load in training progressively and carefully increases; whereas during the last two, the coach unloads the program to facilitate supercompensation.

Recovery and adequate body regeneration following training and competitions is an important factor that enhances peaking. If athletes do not use recovery techniques consistently, they acquire fatigue that can evolve into physical and neuropsychological exhaustion. Under such circumstances, you should drastically alter performance expectations. I present details regarding recovery techniques employed in training in chapter 5.

Motivation, arousal, and psychological relaxation are instrumental factors for peaking as well. I suggest that you refer to topics related to specialized psychological information.

Concerning *nervous cell working capacity,* an athlete whose training factors are properly developed for competitions cannot maximize his or her abilities unless the CNS is in an excellent state and consequently possesses

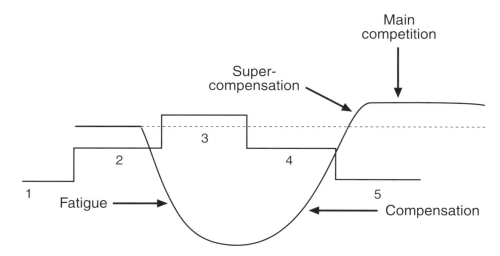

Figure 10.3 Correct unloading before the main competition facilitates supercompensation

a high working capacity. Under optimal conditions, the nervous cell cannot maintain its high working capacity for long. It may be considerably increased only during the last 7 to 10 days before the main competition, which may be the normal outcome of recovery, relaxation, and achieving super-compensation. It is important to mention that an athlete's activities, the performance of skills, are the outcome of muscular activities caused by nervous impulses. As Gandelsman and Smirnov (1970) put it, the force, speed, and maximum number of contractions depend on the nervous cell's working capacity. This capacity depends on the athlete's training state and the cell's level of excitability, which varies dramatically even in a 24-hour span (figure 10.4).

A nervous cell cannot maintain its high working capacity for a prolonged time without being strained or fatigued. When training demands reach the nervous cell's limits, or when the athlete drives him- or herself over such limits, the cell's reaction to training or competition stimuli is impaired. The working capacity decreases abruptly as a result of the cell being fatigued. To protect

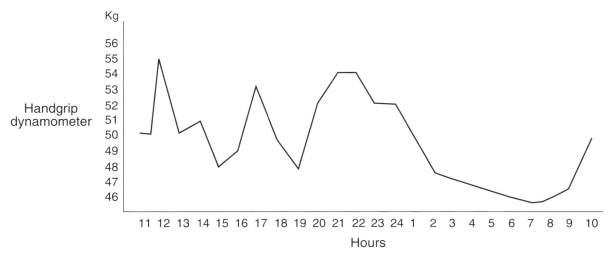

Figure 10.4 Variations of CNS excitability over a 24-hour span (data based on handgrip dynamometer techniques adapted from Ozolin 1971)

itself from further stimuli, the nervous cell assumes a state of inhibition (Pavlov 1927), restraining its processes. The athlete may continue to train by appealing to his or her willpower, but can progressively drive him or herself to the state of complete exhaustion. Performance is far below normal levels under these circumstances. This is why regeneration microcycles and training lessons are so important.

The dynamics of nervous cell excitability alter according to the timing of the competition. It increases progressively during the days before the competition, reaches its maximum peak during the days of contest, and decreases following competition (figure 10.5). In most cases, excitability levels decrease to the normal values, although it may happen that they fall below normal, signifying a high level of exhaustion. When this occurs, the training program should be light to enhance a full regeneration before commencing a normal load.

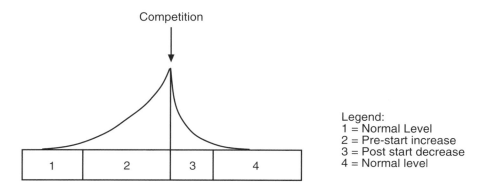

Figure 10.5   Dynamics of CNS excitability level before, during, and after competition (modified from Ozolin 1971)

Athletic peaking, as well as the dynamics of excitability, may be affected by the dynamics of loading the work in training and achieving supercompensation. Figure 10.6a illustrates a situation in which an athlete peaked too early as a result of exaggerated intensive training; a heavy competition schedule during the precompetitive or competitive phase; and specificity of training applied too early in the preparatory phase (exaggeration in the specificity of exercises and training methods). Under such circumstances, the main competition of the year falls in the phase of poststart decrease.

Figure 10.6b illustrates a case in which the athlete achieved the best performance on a later date than the main competition (late peaking). As is often the case, following an important competition, there are several days of relaxation and light training, which enhance supercompensation. The athlete probably did not achieve peaking by the date of the main competition because the coach did not unload properly or supercompensation did not occur.

The competition schedule is an important factor for periodization and, therefore, for peaking. I explain methods of selecting and planning competitions at the end of this chapter.

The *number of peaks* per competitive phase is also determines peaking. The outcome of all factors facilitating or affecting peaking is not a steady, horizontal line. Consequently, the curve of athletic shape, which is a plateau on which peaking builds, is undulatory. The ups and downs of the curve depend on each factor separately. Peaking, or the peak performance of the year, takes place when the coach integrates all these factors properly. Throughout the competitive phase there may be two to four important competitions, which are not spread

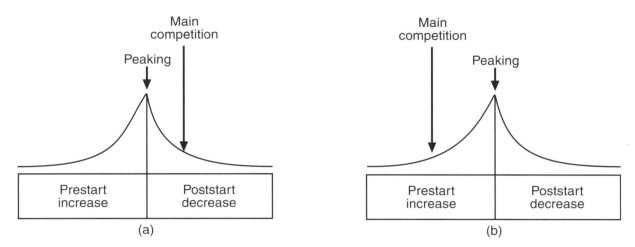

Figure 10.6 Early peaking (a) and late peaking (b)

evenly or in order of importance. The curve of peaking (figure 10.7) may therefore alter according to such a schedule. However, from this figure, you may conclude that peaking was facilitated for only three important competitions and all others were secondary. Although the athlete performed a short unloading phase to enhance supercompensation, the integration of all factors facilitating peaking was performed only for the three top competitions. From the point of view of the nervous cell working capacity and excitability, it would be impossible to peak for most competitions. Such an approach might lead to exhaustion; Pavlov (1927) calls it inhibition of protection. Under such circumstances, the cell protects itself from complete exhaustion by not reacting to external or competition stimuli. Consequently, any expectation of outstanding performance toward the end of the competitive phase may be unrealistic.

Studies regarding means and techniques for long-term planning (Bompa 1968a; Ghibu 1978) revealed some precise data about peaking. Researchers believe that 7 to 10 competitions are sufficient to reach a high state of readiness for major or official competitions. Also, in an annual training plan (monocycle), most elite-class athletes require 32 to 36 microcycles to reach

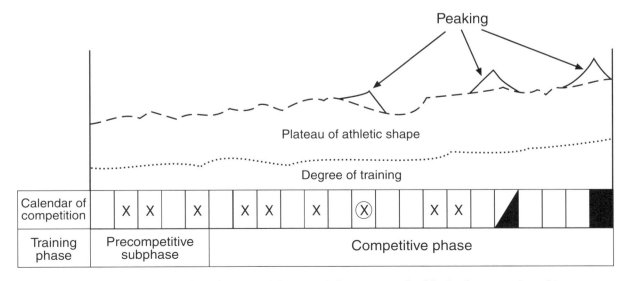

Figure 10.7 Calendar of competitions and the curves of athletic shape and peaking

peak performance of the year. You may use this estimation, though only a general guideline, when planning for the main competition of the year. Similarly, assuming that an athlete participates in a program of daily training lessons, Ghibu advocates that an athlete may reach peaking after enduring 65 to 80% of the total days of training. Athletes may not, therefore, reach peaking quickly, but following a hard and prolonged effort. This claim would indicate that, on the average, an athlete may require approximately 200 days of training before reaching an adequate physical and psychological capacity for peaking. The greater the number of important competitions or peaks per year, the fewer the number of training days. If you properly plan two to four peaks per year, however, this should not represent a hindrance, because athletes may achieve peaking sequentially.

To accomplish high performances every year, you must also increase the degree of training. You could realize this by elevating the physical aspect of training from year to year. With such a solid foundation, an athlete may reach a higher plateau of athletic shape from which to attain higher peak performances. To ignore such an approach leads to a plateau off of an athlete's performances, rather than continual improvements.

Methods of Identifying Peaking

Identifying peaking is difficult and controversial. One of the most objective criteria seems to be the dynamics of the athlete's performances (Matveyev, Kalinin, and Ozolin 1974). Researchers used athletes from sprinting and mid-distance running as subjects (N = 2,300) for a longitudinal study about establishing zones of calculation for peaking. Considering the past year's personal best performance as a reference point (or 100%), the first zone, or the zone of high results, consisted of performances not less than 2.0% lower than the reference point. Medium results were those within 2 to 3.5% deviation of best performance. Low performances within 3.5 to 5% deviation were in the third zone. Finally, the last or fourth zone consisted of poor results, or performances with a deviation of more than 5% from the previous year's best. The authors concluded that when an athlete can achieve performances within 2% (first zone) of best, then he or she is in high athletic shape, close to a peak performance. From this point on, athletes easily facilitate peaking and achieve outstanding performances.

When athletes achieve performances in the first zone, the adaptation to training is complete. The reaction to training stimuli will be consistent and, as a result, the heart rate taken early in the morning will reach consistently low levels. You may consider additional objective data to make a more precise estimation of training states. Ghibu et al. (1978) suggest the following tests: urine biochemical test; tonometry (an indirect estimation of the intraocular pressure from determining the resistance of the eyeball to indentation by an applied force); handgrip dynamometer test; electrocardiography in resting conditions; aerobic or anaerobic power test; and the interval of the systolic tension. Obviously, qualified personnel must perform such specialized tests. Data from various training phases, especially during the competitive phase, are collected and compared. When all scores are superior, the coach is advised that the athlete is in a good training state.

You can also identify peaking by interpreting subjective data, namely the athlete's feelings. These include such things as being alert and optimistic, having a good appetite, getting deep and resting sleep, high willingness in training and competitions, and ease in everything the athlete does.

It is important that the coach also be in good shape. The coach's behavior, optimism, confidence, enthusiasm, encouragement, and cheerfulness are important prerequisites for an athlete's peaking, especially when the relationship between them is close. The coach's role is not only in the training activity, but also in the responsibility of bringing the athlete to high psychological shape. A coach must be psychologically well balanced and calm, with the ability to hide his or her emotions before a competition. Well-controlled behavior has a tremendous impact on the athlete. Similarly, the coach must strive to neutralize all the stressors that might affect an athlete's performance, such as peers, family, job, and intragroup conflicts.

Maintaining a Peak

There exists a high diversity of opinions among coaches and athletes regarding this paramount training aspect, because precise research data scarcely exists. Falsehoods such as "an athlete can peak only once a year" and "an athlete can peak for one day only" are still imprinted in some people's minds. Because the phases of athletic shape and peaking both depend on many physiological, psychological, and sociological factors, it is difficult to make precise statements regarding their duration. It is, therefore, safe to say that the duration of peaking is individualized. The individual training program each athlete follows and the duration and type of training performed during the preparatory phase have substantial influence on the duration of peaking. The longer and more solid the preparatory phase, the higher the probability of prolonging the athletic shape and peaking.

It is difficult to separate peaking from the athletic shape when discussing this topic. As already explained, athletic shape is a high plateau during which the athlete has a high working and psychological capacity. The highlight of this plateau is zone one, in which an athlete's performances are within 2% of the previous peak performance. Assuming that the coach led and organized an adequate training program, the duration of zone one may be between 1 and 2.5 months. During this time, the athlete may facilitate two or three peaks, in which he or she achieves high or even record performances. Researchers suggest that the duration of peaking may be up to 7 to 10 days because the nervous cell can maintain optimal working capacity that long (Ozolin 1971). Following each peaking for a top competition, a short phase of regeneration is strongly desirable, followed by training. Failure to do this will likely reduce the duration of zone one. This approach is a reminder that there is a need to alternate stress with regeneration, an interplay of dramatic importance in training.

The duration of peaking, as well as zone one, may be affected by the number of starts or competitions the athlete experiences. The longer the phase with weekly competitions, the lower the probability of duplicating high results. Many competitions do not necessarily lead to good and progressively higher performances. Often, there is a contrary effect, and results decrease toward the end of a competitive phase, when championship competitions are usually planned. A critical phase often begins after the eighth microcycle with competitions. This does not necessarily mean that performance is compromised toward the end of the competitive phase. On the contrary, it should draw the coach's attention to the need for better alternation of stressful exercises with regeneration activities. In addition, it should bring the coach's attention to the methods and means of selecting and planning competitions during pre- and competitive phases. This should be significant to some college coaches, especially for team sports, in which the competition schedule is loaded with many games, even during the preparatory phase.

An important method to ensure adequate peaking is to prolong zone one and consequently the ability to peak. You can use the peaking index (please refer to chapter 6) to diminish the stress on athletes. Alternating important competitions with secondary one enhances the undulatory shape of the peaking curve, which substitutes stress with regeneration. Similarly, a rational approach to planning competitions is to end a competitive macrocycle with an important competition, which ensures a progression in the arrangement of competitions. For planning the competitions, the grouping approach permits alternating training phases with competition periods and prolongs athletic shape.

The time required to reach zone one is an important factor for peaking. Although this might differ according to each athlete's abilities, the average time an athlete needs to elevate the capacity from a precompetitive level to the aptitude of zone one is four to six microcycles. You may not see dramatic increases during the first three or four microcycles, because hard work that stresses intensity results in a high level of fatigue, which restricts the achievement of good performances. Following the last one or two microcycles, however, when the athlete has adapted to the training load and a slight decrease in the stress of training allows supercompensation to occur, higher performance is feasible. Although the duration of this transitory phase from lower performances to zone one varies according to many factors, it also varies according to the specifics of each sport and the coach's approach to training. Thus, Ghibu et al. (1978) suggest the following duration: gymnastics and water polo, six microcycles; track and field, rowing, swimming and wrestling, approximately four microcycles.

Peaking Obstacles

Peaking is the natural and highly desirable outcome of several months of hard work and a properly planned training program. As described, many factors facilitate training states; however, there are several factors that may adversely affect peaking. It is a coach's responsibility to be aware of these factors and be able to control them, which will eliminate the obstacles and enhance peaking.

Organizing Competitions

Before taking part in a competition, both the athlete and the coach are expecting normal, standard conditions. It may often be that an athlete idealizes everything in his or her mind and expects perfect circumstances. Consequently, every unforeseen change in the conditions the athlete experiences at the competition may affect his or her peaking and performance. Natural factors such as a strong wind or heavy rain may disturb athletes who are not familiar with them. In sports such as cycling, canoeing, and rowing, strong winds could impede an athlete's performance. Big waves developed by the wind substantially affect the performance of rowers and canoers, especially those with improper technique. Heavy rain affects the performance of cyclists and walkers, as well as team sport athletes who find ball control impaired when playing on a wet or muddy field.

The snow's quality influences a skier's final performance substantially. In cross-country skiing, a peak performance depends on the quality of snow and, consequently, the skill and experience of waxing skis according to the terrain and state of the snow. Similarly, all athletes are affected by extreme environmental temperature, climate, and altitude.

The answer to these problems is model training, to prepare and train athletes under such conditions so they do not drastically affect peaking. Of no less impact are changes in the initial draw, biased officiating, and an adverse audience. Exposing athletes to competitions that duplicate the social climate of the main competition is a prerequisite to peak performance, if it differs significantly from what they normally experience.

An Athlete's States

The coach can observe and, therefore, have direct control over an athlete only during training hours. Although it is a coach's responsibility to positively influence an athlete's unseen training or the time an athlete is on his or her own, it is not unusual to find behaviors and lifestyles that contradict athletic moral standards. Negative behavior does affect an individual's working capacity and, therefore, peaking as well. Such things as inadequate sleep, use of alcohol, smoking, and poor diet reduce an athlete's recovery rate, which adversely affects training states. Similarly, social dissatisfaction with family, coach, peers, and school or work, reflects negatively in a person's attitude during training and competitions, resulting in inappropriate performances. In sports that require some risk or strong initiative, a fear of competitions or accidents decreases self-control and leads to an inferiority complex. This can often restrict an athlete's ability to perform. The coach should, therefore, observe an athlete and collect information from close associates to make all possible attempts to correct such negative attitudes and behaviors.

Training and the Coach

Training programs that are improperly planned with too high intensity, quick increases of intensity, or too many scheduled competitions are not only stressing but also impair adequate peaking. This is even more obvious when the competitive phase is long. Under such circumstances, maintaining zone one and a correct peaking for the main competition, which is usually at the end of the phase, is almost impossible. To overlook the needs of alternating work with regeneration may not only reduce the ability to peak but also lead to injuries. If an athlete is continually exposed to many such stressors, the probability of reaching the state of overtraining will increase.

A coach's knowledge, attitude, and behavior, as well as his or her ability to disguise personal emotions and frustrations also affect an athlete's performance. A lack of confidence in the coach's abilities and knowledge, especially if present before the main competition, adversely affects an athlete's performance and, therefore, peaking for that contest. The remedy for such problems is simple: further personal training knowledge, improve self-control, or be honest and advise the athlete to look for a superior coach.

Athletic Competition

It is obvious that the main goals of an athlete's training are to take part in competitions, challenge other athletes for a top spot in the competition hierarchy, and achieve a high level of performance. However, the importance of competitions extends beyond these goals, because they are the most important and specific means of assessing an athlete's progress. Many coaches maintain that participation in competitions elevates an athlete's preparation level. Although this is true to a certain extent, a coach should not expect to achieve a degree of training and correct peaking through competition only, as coaches often attempt in some professional sports. Participation in competitions, especially during the precompetitive phase when exhibition contests are planned, does assist athletes to reach a high state of readiness for the main competition

Negative behaviors can affect an athlete's ability to peak at the right time

of the year. During such competitions, they have the opportunity to test all training factors in the most specific way. To consider the competition as the only means of improvement, however, lessens the philosophy of training and consequently disturbs the main cycle of activity, which is training, unloading, competition, and regeneration (figure 10.8).

Often coaches become captivated by participating in many exhibition competitions and overlook proper training. They stress intensity at the expense of volume, and as a result the athletes peak much earlier than originally planned. A natural consequence is a poor show toward the end of the competitive phase when the main competitions are planned. Remember that training accumulation during the preparatory phase is not a bottomless bag. On the contrary, the bag must be continually replenished so that adequate physical and psychological support will last until the end of the competitive phase.

An important outcome of participation in competitions, especially for prospective athletes, is gaining competitive experience. All competitions included in an annual plan are subordinate to and must enhance achieving the main performance objective of the year, which is usually accomplished during the main competition. Selecting and planning competitions are therefore arts of their own.

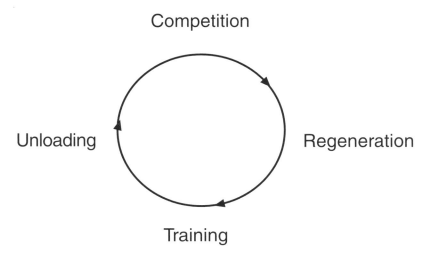

Figure 10.8 Cycle of activities in training

A competition is the real testing ground for athletes' preparation. During a contest, athletes can test their improvement levels on a given date, consolidate technique, and test tactics against direct opponents. At the same time, they can learn how to spend energy effectively and improve psychological traits such as willpower and perseverance. It is important, however, that the coach plans the specific objectives athletes are to achieve before participating in any competition. Orient and determine the objectives according to the type and characteristics of the competition in which athletes take part.

Classification and Characteristics of Competitions

We can classify most competitions into two groups: official or main and preparatory or exhibition.

Consider the official or main competitions as determining qualification or defining the final standing in a championship. They are of paramount importance, and customarily athletes strive to achieve a high or the highest possible performance. In heats or qualifying rounds, highest performance is not always necessary for further levels of competition. Main competitions may serve as a guideline to segregate the annual plan into macrocycles, especially for individual sports.

The preparatory or exhibition competitions are customarily planned to test and attain feedback from athletes or teams regarding certain aspects of training. Such competitions are an integral part of a microcycle and, therefore, the coach should not alter or unload his or her normal training plan. Although victory should not be the only objective, such competitions can help athletes arrive at an adequate state of readiness before the official competitions. This is possible because during such competitions they may endure maximal intensity, deplete energy reserves, surpass physical and psychological capacities, overcome emotion, and acquire experience against known and unknown opponents.

Consequently, all competitions in athletics have the following characteristics and orientations.

Victory in a competition captivates each athlete from early involvement in training. To be a victor in a competition requires long hours of hard work. Talent in athletics is an important asset, but hard work is a requirement. There are no shortcuts for hard work in the pursuit of becoming a winner.

Records, which you can closely link to victory, are the dream of many athletes. When athletes surpass their own and others' previously scored records, it means that under specific, ideal conditions they have defeated their weaknesses both physiologically and psychologically. Although records are not always beaten as a coach plans in a particular phase, such competitions are usually organized during the middle of the competitive phase. Organize no such meets within 2 or 3 weeks of the main competition of the year, because they exhaust athletes' physical and psychological capabilities.

Test competitions are organized with the scope of verifying athletes' potential and qualities on a given date. The objectives of such competitions are to test the athletes physically and psychologically and to validate their technique or tactical maneuvers. In team sports, because such competitions are informal, the coach may decide to stop the game from time to time and suggest tactics to test against opponents.

Adjustment to specific conditions of future competitions plays an important role in athletes' abilities to perform adequately. The coach may, therefore, choose to compete in a place that would familiarize the athletes with facilities and the quality of the equipment they will experience in a future major competition. Such a competition may be an exhibition; therefore, the coach should stress adaptation and adjustment to the specifics of the facilities rather than victory.

Planning the Competition

The competition schedule is usually set by the sport governing bodies, and in their decision they are concerned with the championship or league competitions only. The coach may, however, decide to select preparatory or exhibition contests also, according to the time available and specific objectives. Selecting and planning competitions are paramount processes in training that can enhance or adversely affect peaking for the major contests.

Misinterpretations often exist about selection procedures and the coach's role in the decision-making process. Some coaches follow the belief that athletes have to participate in every available competition with all possible effort. Obviously, in such a case athletes constantly experience stressful activities that might not lead to an optimal season climax. Similarly, such a heavy game or contest schedule requires many regeneration dates, which disturbs the normal course of training. The intense psychological stress athletes require to reach an adequate state of arousal for each competition is also a concern. Neglecting these two aspects may facilitate undesirable consequences, reflected through poor peaking for the main competition of the year.

Another unusual procedure for selecting competitions is coaches telling the athletes to make the decision. In most cases, the athletes obviously do not have the knowledge to use the proper methodological guideline for selecting and planning a competition. Consequently, the leadership should come from the coach who may decide to employ one of the two methods of planning the competition calendar for the annual plan: the grouping or the cyclic approach.

The grouping approach refers to the method of planning 2 or 3 weeks in a row, during which the athletes take part in tournaments or competitions, participating in several events or races per weekend. As illustrated by figure 10.9, such a phase is usually followed by a macrocycle of training only, allowing the athletes to train for another 2 or 3 weeks of group competitions.

The hypothetical example illustrated by figure 10.9 suggests that at the end of May the athlete or team takes part in a group of competitions spread

Training phase	Competitive phase																					
Dates	May					June				July					August				September			
	1	8	15	22	29	5	12	19	26	3	10	17	24	31	7	14	21	28	4	11	18	25
Macrocycles		6		7			8				9					10				11		
Calendar of competitions				X	X					X	X	X					◣					■

Figure 10.9 Planning the competitions based on the grouping approach

over 2 weeks. In each case, it may be that the coach organizes races or games over 2 or 3 days during each weekend. The first microcycle following these competitions is a lower intensity cycle with one peak at the end. The first part of the cycle (2-3 days) is dedicated to regeneration, with low-intensity nonstressful training lessons. The next two and a half microcycles are planned for hard training, followed by a short unloading phase of 2 or 3 days, and again three weeks of competitions. August 21 is the qualifying (regional) competition for the main championships of the year held during the weekend of September 25. For training, the macrocycles preceding the qualifying and final championships follow the same pattern as the previous ones.

The grouping approach is most suited to individual sports, in which the only two official competitions are planned in a manner similar to the previous example. For team sports, use such an approach only for national championships and international competitions, in which the grouping concept is a typical model training for an official international tournament. Use the cyclic approach for both individual and team sports. The term refers to competitions that are planned in a repetitive, cyclic manner (figure 10.10).

The competition during macrocycles 8 and 9 are league games planned for each weekend. Then at the end of macrocycles 10 and 11, the regional and final championships are planned. Because each microcycle ends with a game, you may structure each with one peak only, which usually should be on Tuesday or Wednesday. One or two days before the game, there is a progressive unloading phase to enhance supercompensation for the day of the game. For individual sports in which there are no league competitions, consider the cyclic approach for only the qualifying and finals (main competition of the year), as in figure 10.11. In such a case, the coach may decide to take part in other competitions organized by various clubs. Assuming that there are several competitions to choose from, the coach would plan to take part only in those that facilitate a

Training phase	Competitive phase																					
Dates	May					June				July					August				September			
	1	8	15	22	29	5	12	19	26	3	10	17	24	31	7	14	21	28	4	11	18	25
Macrocycles		7					8				9					10				11		
Calendar of competitions		X		X		X	X	X	X	X	X	X	X	X	X	X				◣		■

Figure 10.10 Cyclic approach for a team sport

Training phase	Competitive phase																		
Dates	November					December				January					February				March		
	1	8	15	22	29	5	12	19	26	3	10	17	24	31	7	14	21	28	4	11	18
Macrocycles	7					8									9				10		
Calendar of competitions	X			X		X		X		X		X									

Figure 10.11 Cyclic approach for a cross-country skier

cyclic approach. Consequently, athletes would compete every second weekend, devoting the time between competitions to training. This approach is advantageous because the coach can modify training programs according to the feedback received during competitions. Naturally, this will enhance an ideal preparation for the main competition.

Concerning the structure of microcycles for the cyclic approach, the microcycle following a competition must be low intensity during the first half to enhance recovery, and higher intensity during the second half. Structure the microcycle before the competition the opposite way, with the athletes training harder during the first half (highest peak on Tuesday or Wednesday) and unloading during the second half of the week (figure 10.12).

You may correctly assume that a pragmatic coach can employ a combination of both methods of selecting and planning for competitions. It may happen that in a certain part of the competitive phase a particular method prevails, and the other will remain for the balance of the year.

Planning the main competition, which is normally done by the national association or federation, should be on the date of future Olympic Games so coaches experience several annual cycles before the games. Such experimentation will optimally lead to an ideal annual plan that you must then duplicate for the Olympic year. This is an important concept that the national federation should consider and follow.

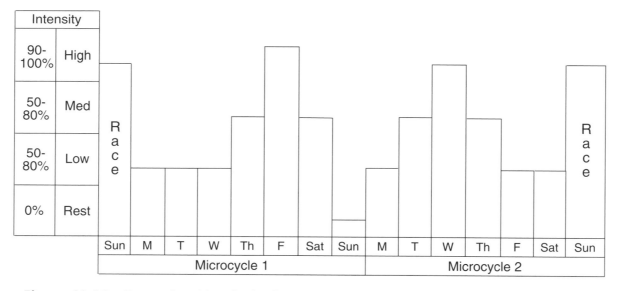

Figure 10.12 Curve of peaking the load in training during the interval between competitions

When there is a long period between the last competition and a major competition, such as the national championships, Olympic Games, world championships, and so on, you can organize a special macrocycle (table 10.2). The goals you assign for each microcycle are important because good planning facilitates decent training and a good peaking strategy to achieve the best performance.

Table 10.2 illustrates a normal macrocycle, consisting of 5 microcycles in this example, and a condensed one, in which the time between the two competitions is just 3 weeks. In the condensed cycle, assign each training objective a number of days rather than weeks.

TABLE 10.2 Objectives for a Macrocycle Before the Major Competition of the Year

Macrocycle's objectives	Normal (5 weeks)	Condensed (3 weeks)
Active recovery	1	3
Loading	2	7
Unloading	1	7
Competition	1	4

Event Frequency

Individual characteristics, experience, age, and sport characteristics are among the determining factors when deciding on the frequency and number of competitions to include in the annual plan. Another important factor to consider is the duration of the competitive phase: the longer the phase, the greater the number of competitions. Consider the characteristics of the sport as the paramount guideline when deciding the number and frequency of competitions. Athletes participating in sports of short duration (i.e., sprinting, jumping, diving) in which the physical demand is lower, experience a higher recovery rate. Consequently, the frequency and implicitly the number of starts (races, events) could be high. Ozolin (1971) suggests that in such sports, elite athletes may take part in 40 to 50 starts per year. On the other hand, sports demanding high energy and nervous expenditure, in which endurance, strength, and muscular endurance are either dominant or an important component of training (i.e., swimming, mid- and long-distance running, cross-country skiing, rowing, cycling, boxing, wrestling, etc.), the number of competitions should be much lower, 15 to 25 (table 10.3). Athletes participating in team sports often take part in more than 30 games per year. Concerning frequency, consider the time the athlete requires for recovery, which in the case of the latest group is long.

During the competitive phase, enter the athletes in two to four main competitions, which in most cases are qualifying meets for the main contest of the year and the main competition. In addition, include competitions of lesser importance in the calendar of competitions. As suggested by table 10.4, however, plan a short period of training between the preparatory (exhibition) competitions for the precompetitive subphase and the main competitions.

It is not necessary to organize a competition only in a specialized sport or event. Often, especially during the preparatory phase, you could organize special

TABLE 10.3 Suggested Number of Competitions Per Year in Athletics

Event	Beginners and prospective athletes		Elite athletes	
	Winter	Summer	Winter	Summer
Sprinters, hurdlers, jumpers, and throwers				
Specialized event	3-4	12-16	3-5	16-20
Other events/sports	2-3	4-6	1-3	3-5
Mid-distance				
800-1,500m	—	4-8	2-3	10-16
Shorter distances	2-3	8-10	2-4	8-10
Distance running and walking				
Marathon	—	1	—	2-3
50K walk	—	6-8	—	8-10
Combined events				
Decathlon	—	1-2	—	2-3
Heptathlon	—	2	—	2-4
Individual events	2-4	10-12	3-5	12-16

competitions to enhance general physical development. Plan such competitions mostly for beginners and prospective athletes who have not properly acquired technique. Often, coaches organize such competitions for elite athletes as well. In Eastern Europe it is common to see gymnasts and weightlifters competing in a 30-meter dash and standing high jump and rowers, cyclists, and canoeists competing in cross-country skiing, and so on. There is a psychological as well as a physical advantage to such competitions. When athletes are competing in activities that are part of their training or have similarities to their event, they are more motivated to work hard for improvement in their general or specific physical preparation.

Concerning participation in the interval between competitions, Bompa (1970) and Harre (1982) recommend that a coach consider the following aspects:

- An athlete should take part in a competition only when he or she is capable of achieving set objectives for each training factor: physical, technical, tactical, and psychological.
- The coach should select each competition carefully, in an order that increases the difficulty progressively.
- Unchallenging competitions do not motivate an athlete.
- Do not avoid opponents with superior capabilities.
- Too many competitions, especially road trips, diminish the coach's possibility to properly dose competitions and training. The result will be a decrease in the athlete's physical and especially psychological potential.
- Correct planning of the competition schedule should ensure the best peaking for the main competition.
- The main competition of the year is the only one that establishes an athlete's hierarchy in a sport. The others (except for league games) are just progressive steps that bring the athlete to that level.

TABLE 10.4 Guiding Objectives for the Competitive Subphase

Training phase	Competitive phase			
Subphases	**Precompetition**	**Spec. prep. for league comp.**	**League/official competition**	**Special preparation**
Objectives	Improve performance Gain competitive experience Determine main strengths and weaknesses Test technique and tactics under competitive circumstances	Correct deficiencies shown during the precompetition subphase Alter techniques and methods to improve athletes' competitive effectiveness	Reach high athletic potentials Prepare for qualifying competitions	Take part successfully in the main competition
Means of implementation	Competitions of progressively increasing difficulty Increase density of competitions Decrease slightly the volume of training	Extensive training Increase volume Some competitions without affecting training	Reduce volume and increase intensity according to the needs of the sport Take part in more demanding competitions	Special preparation for the main competition

Summary of Major Concepts

Many coaches and athletes consider peaking and the ability to reach a peak performance for a competition a heavenly favor. The ability to peak for a competition represents nothing more than a strategy you design, manipulating training to reach physical and psychological supercompensation before an important meet. When these two elements of supercompensation occur, then peak performance is a normal outcome.

The ups and downs of athletic performance often depend on the training an athlete performs during the preparatory phase, the ratio between volume and intensity of training, and the number of competitions in which an athlete takes part. Do not exaggerate the number of competitions, especially with the young athletes. Do not wear them down too early!

The following sequencing is essential for an athlete's ability to peak for competitions:

- You train to compete.
- You regenerate and recover before starting to train again.
- You train for the next competition.
- You manipulate training to supercompensate and reach a peak performance during the next competition.

Pay maximum attention to these training activities throughout the competitive phase.

PART III

Training Methods

Strength and Power Development

Of all the biomotor abilities discussed in chapters 11-13, strength and power are the most critical for many sports. All team sports and speed-power dominant sports rely on solid strength and power development. Understanding the mechanics and physics of strength training and incorporating those principles into your training program will give your athletes a competitive edge.

Biomotor Abilities

Most physical movements incorporate the elements of force, quickness, duration, complexity, and a range of motion to a certain extent. Further, you can distinguish individual motor aspects and physiological components, such as strength, speed, endurance, and coordination. For training, there will likely be more interest in perfecting the athlete through the physiological components, commonly known as biomotor abilities, than in perfecting the skill.

The ability of an individual to perform an exercise is the cause, and the movement itself is just the effect. What the athlete requires, therefore, is the ability to control the cause to perform a successful effect. The biomotor abilities, which are the foundations of a cause, are largely genetic or inherited abilities. In this chapter, I will refer to the ability to perform an exercise as a basic, natural ability and the outcome of combining certain biomotor abilities. Although flexibility is not a natural ability but an anatomical quality of the locomotor organ, I will also consider it because it is important in training.

A biomotor ability links with and depends on its quantitative sphere, in which the magnitude of the strength, speed, and endurance levels limit physical work, given the qualitative demands. Each exercise has a dominant ability, and when the athlete maximizes the load, it is a strength exercise. When the athlete maximizes quickness and frequency in an exercise, it is a speed exercise. When maximizing distance, duration, or the number of repetitions, the athlete experiences an endurance exercise. Finally, when an exercise requires a high degree of complexity, it is a coordination exercise. In training, however, one ability rarely dominates an exercise, and a movement is often the product or combination of two abilities. Figure 11.1 illustrates power, when strength and speed equally dominate, as in jumping and throwing events in athletics, or spiking in volleyball. Furthermore, combining endurance with strength, as in swimming, canoeing, wrestling, and so on, produces muscular endurance. The product of endurance and speed (events around 60 seconds) is speed-endurance or endurance of speed. The highly acclaimed agility in some sports is a combination of speed, power, and coordination. Finally, when agility and flexibility join, the result is mobility, or the quality of performing a movement quickly, with good timing and coordination, throughout a wide range of movement, as in diving, floor exercises in gymnastics, karate, wrestling, and team sports.

A relationship of methodical importance exists among strength, speed, and endurance. During the initial years of training, all abilities have to develop to build a solid foundation for specialized training. This phase is specific to national level and elite athletes whose programs aim for a precise, specialized, training effect. Thus, as a result of employing specific exercises, the adaptation process occurs in accordance with the athlete's specialization. For elite-class athletes, the relationship among the magnitude of strength, speed, and endurance, as the more determinant and difficult to develop biomotor abilities, depends on the particularities of the sport and the athlete's needs. Figure 11.2 illustrates such a relationship, in which each example shows strength or force (F), speed (S), or endurance (E) dominating. In each case, when one biomotor ability is strongly dominant, the other two do not share or participate to a similar extent. This example is, however, just theory, which you may directly apply to only a few sports. In most sports, the combination among the three biomotor abilities leads to a different outcome, in which each ability has a greater input. Figure 11.3 exemplifies a few sports, with the circle representing the dominant composition among strength, speed, and endurance.

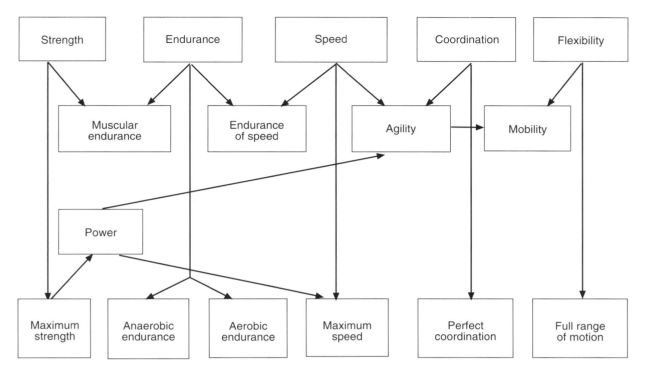

Figure 11.1   Interdependence among the biomotor abilities

Two factors determine the contribution of the biomotor abilities to attaining of high performance: the ratio among them reflecting the specifics of the sport and the development of each ability according to its degree of participation in performing the sport or event.

It is, therefore, crucial to appropriately select the means of training to meet the needs of the sport. This includes selecting in relation to the dominant composition of biomotor abilities and the training phase. Exclusively using technical elements or specific skills leads to a correct competition of abilities. The ratio of such a development is, however, much higher when you develop the biomotor abilities using specific exercises (refer to Physical Training in chapter 3).

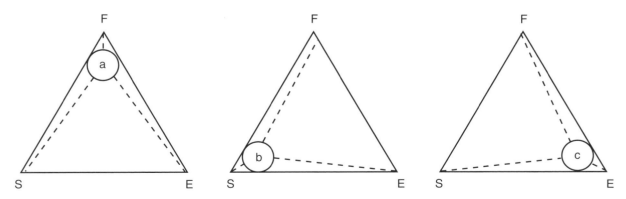

Figure 11.2   Relationship among the main biomotor abilities, in which strength (a), speed (b), and endurance (c) dominate (from Florescu, Dumitrescu, and Predescu 1969)

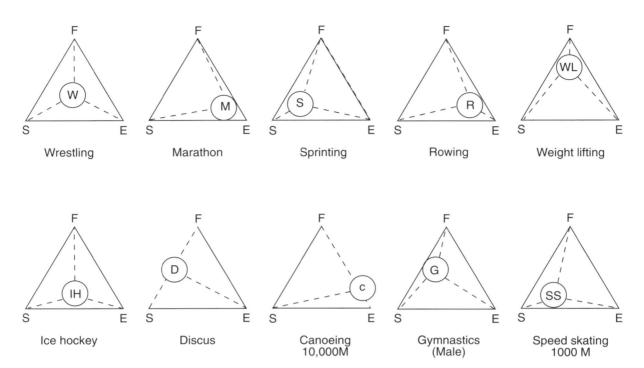

Figure 11.3 The dominant composition among the biomotor abilities for various sports

Developing a biomotor ability is specific and relates to the method you employ. When an athlete develops a dominant ability, for example strength, it indirectly affects the abilities of speed and endurance. Such an effort depends strictly on the degree of resemblance between the methods you employ and the specifics of the sport. Developing a dominant biomotor ability may, therefore, have a positive or negative transfer. When you attempt to develop strength, there may be a positive transfer to speed and even a certain degree to endurance. On the other hand, a weight-training program to develop maximum strength may have a negative transfer to aerobic endurance, such as that required in marathon running. Similarly, a training program aimed exclusively at developing aerobic endurance may, under certain circumstances such as training for marathon, have a negative transfer to strength and speed. Specific training for speed, on the other hand, always has a neutral effect.

There is a vast amount of information referring to both the scientific foundation and the methodology of developing biomotor abilities. The methodology of developing the biomotor abilities concerned training specialists for centuries. Researchers such as Lagrange in 1892, Schmidt in 1925, and Uhov in 1875 wrote the first information regarding these abilities in the methodical literature (Zatzyorski 1968; see also Novikov 1941), and it was only later that physiologists investigated it. Because such an enormous amount of information exists, and considering the objective and size of this book, I will keep this chapter to a minimum. The area that I will stress, however, is the practical or methodical area, which may be the most beneficial.

Strength Training

In simple terms, strength is the ability to apply force. Its development should be the prime concern of anyone who attempts to improve an athlete's performance. Although athletes preparing to compete in the ancient Olympic Games used primitive forms of strength development, there are still many coaches who do not take advantage of its benefits. Using several strength-development methods leads to faster growth, by 8 to 12 times that of using only skills available for a certain sport. For instance, a volleyball player may develop a faster jumping ability for spiking by using weight training than by simply performing several spikes during a volleyball practice. It seems that strength training is, therefore, one of the most important ingredients in the process of making athletes.

Theoretically, we can refer to force as a mechanical characteristic and a human ability. In the former case, force is the object of studies in mechanics, and in the latter, it is the scope of physiological and methodical investigation in training.

Force as a Mechanical Characteristic

You could determine force by direction, magnitude, or the point of application. According to Newton's Second Law of Motion, force is equal to mass (m) times acceleration (a), or the following:

$$F = m \cdot a$$

Consequently, an athlete can increase strength by changing one or both factors (m or a). Such changes result in quantitative alterations to consider when developing strength. The following two equations used in mechanics may illustrate this point:

$$F_{mx} = m_{mx} \cdot a \qquad (1)$$

$$F_{mx} = m \cdot a_{mx} \qquad (2)$$

F_{mx} is maximum force; m_{mx} is maximum mass; and a_{mx} means maximum acceleration.

In the first equation, maximum force develops by using the maximum mass (or load) possible; whereas the same result occurs in the second equation by using the maximum speed of movement. The force that an athlete can apply and the velocity at which he or she can apply it maintain an inverse relationship (which was demonstrated previously). This is also true for the relationship between an athlete's applied force and the time over which he or she can apply it. The gains in one ability are at the expense of the other. Consequently, although force may be the dominant characteristic of an ability, you cannot consider it in isolation because the speed and time component will directly affect its application.

The force-velocity inverse relationship was demonstrated by Hill (1922) and Ralston, Polissan, Inman, Close, and Feinstein (1949). An adaptation of Ralston's force-velocity curve is illustrated by figure 11.4, which demonstrates that when the mass is low, the acceleration is high, given maximum effort by the participant. As the mass increases the acceleration decreases, up to no movement at all, for instance, from a baseball throw, to shot put, to weightlifting, and up to a static muscular contraction for mass heavier than an athlete's maximum force.

The magnitude of the force directly relates to the magnitude of the mass. This relationship is linear only at the beginning, when the force increases as the mass of the moving object increases. A continuous elevation of a mass will not necessarily result in an equally large increase in applied force. The

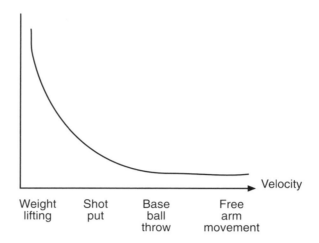

Figure 11.4 Force-velocity curve (adapted from Ralston et al. 1949)

per gram force that an athlete applies against a shot (shot putting in athletics) will, therefore, be greater than that for lifting a barbell. As suggested by Florescu et al. (1969), to put a shot of 7.250 kilograms a distance of 18.19 meters, an athlete displays a power of 6.9 horsepower (h.p.) or 5,147 watts, but to snatch (weightlifting) 150 kilograms requires only 4.3 horsepower or 3,207 watts.

Physiology of Strength Training

We can define strength as the neuromuscular capability to overcome an external and internal resistance. The maximum strength that an athlete can produce depends on the biomechanical characteristics of a movement (i.e., leverage, the degree to which larger muscle groups participate), and the magnitude of contraction of the muscles involved. In addition, maximum strength is also a function of the intensity of an impulse, which dictates the number of motor units involved, and its frequency. According to Zatzyorski (1968), the number of impulses per second may elevate from 5 or 6 at rest, up to 50 lifting a maximum load.

Following a strength-training program, a muscle enlarges itself (Morpurgo 1976) or hypertrophies as a result of the following factors:

- The number of myofibrils (the slender threads of a muscle fiber) per muscle fiber increases (hypertrophy).
- Capillary density per muscle fiber increases.
- Amount of protein increases.
- Total number of muscle fibers increases.

All these occurrences lead to the general increase in a muscle's cross-sectional area (Costill et al. 1979; Fox et al. 1989; Goldberg et al. 1975; Gregory 1981; MacDougall et al. 1976; MacDougall et al. 1977; MacDougall et al. 1979).

Zatzyorski (1968) considers that strength magnitude is a function of three factors: intermuscular coordination, intramuscular coordination, and the force with which the muscle reacts to a nervous impulse.

Intermuscular coordination is the interaction of various muscular groups during performance. In a physical activity requiring strength, there must be adequate coordination between the muscle groups that take part in the action. Often the muscles participate in a certain sequence. For instance, in clean and jerk (weightlifting), at the start and during the early part of the lift the trapezius muscle has to be relaxed. This muscle should, however, take part in the jerking phase. Often though, some elite athletes contract the trapezius from the beginning of the lift. This lack of coordination alters the technical pattern of the lift, and consequently produces in an ineffective performance. Similarly, in sprinting events the contraction of shoulder muscles often has a negative effect on the sprinter's performance. It seems, therefore, that the consequence of inadequate intermuscular coordination is a performance lower than an athlete's potential, and both the coach and athlete should pay attention to it. Relaxation techniques improve the coordination of muscular contractions.

Intramuscular coordination, which is an athlete's force output, depends also on the neuromuscular units that simultaneously take part in the task. According to Baroga (1978), if during an arm curl the muscle biceps brachii has a maximum force output of 25 kilograms, then electrical stimulation of the same muscle may result in elevating the muscle's force capacity by 10 kilograms. It is apparent that often the athlete is not capable of involving all the muscle fibers in any particular activity. Kuznetsov (1975) calls this phenomenon the force deficit. The athlete may improve it by using the maximum load or other training methods forthcoming in this chapter, which result in recruiting more neuromuscular units.

The force generated when the muscle reacts to a nervous impulse. A muscle reacts to a training stimulus with only about 30% of its potential (Kuznetsov 1975). Using the same methods or loads in training leads only to a proportional training adaptation. To elevate or bring about a superior threshold of adaptation, the athlete must use higher intensity stimuli, because maximum stimuli results in maximum effect. The consequences of a systematic training are, therefore, the progressive improvement of the nervous impulses' synchronization and the intensive activity of the antagonistic muscle (a muscle that acts in opposition to the action of another muscle) with the agonistic muscle (prime mover). A training program will enable muscle fiber groups to alternate. This means that when one group of muscle fibers exhausts, another group will start to contract, resulting in strength improvement.

The ability of an athlete to exert force also depends on the angle of the joint. Research performed in this area has yielded conflicting results. Although some findings suggest that an athlete achieves maximum strength when the joints are in full extension or close to it (Elkins, Leden, and Wakim 1957; Hunsicker 1955; Zatzyorski 1968), others reported higher muscular efficiency when flexing the joint 90 to 100 degrees. As Logan and McKinney (1973) put it, a muscle must be at its longest to exert its greatest force. The muscle is, however, contracting in the direct line of pull when flexing the joint at 90 degrees and is thus working at a greater mechanical efficiency. In figure 11.5a, contractions start from an open angle (arrow 2). In figure 11.5b, muscle contractions start from an acute angle (arrow 3). It seems safe to say that an athlete can produce more force from an open angle joint than if the same joint was acute. The force of pull is much higher when the myosin and actin start overlapping than at 90 degrees, when a good portion of overlapping has already occurred.

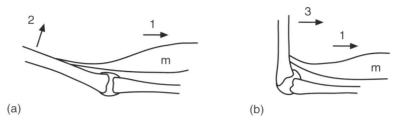

Figure 11.5 Joint angle and muscle efficiency

Types of Muscle Contraction

You can generate muscle contraction or tension by force of gravity, isokinetic apparatus, fixed resistance, and electrical stimulation.

Force of Gravity

When athletes use free weights they usually exert force against the force of gravity, which increases proportionally to the mass (load) of an object. You can attain tension in the muscle either by overcoming gravity or by opposing or resisting it. In either case, there occurs a dynamic contraction, which often is incorrectly called isotonic, from the Greek words *isos* meaning equal and *tonikos* meaning tension. Defining isotonic as equal tension is inaccurate, however, because the muscle tension is a function of the angle of flexion.

Defeating the force of gravity results in a type of contraction that is commonly called concentric (Latin *com-centrum* means having a common center) and denotes the case in which the muscle shortens. Concentric contraction or defeating the force of gravity is the common training technique of most athletes using free weights.

Resisting the force of gravity is a means of developing strength that athletes use less frequently, although it is extremely effective. This simply means that instead of lifting a weight (defeating the force of gravity), you lower it, slowly yielding to the force of gravity. During such an eccentric contraction, the muscles actually lengthen during the phase of stimulation. Such is the case when the shock of impact is absorbed after jumping down from a high object.

Isokinetic Apparatus

Several types of machines (Nautilus, Mini-Gym, Cybex, etc.) are used for strength training. In all cases, an isokinetic (equal or constant movement) contraction occurs, during which the resistance of the apparatus remains constant throughout a full range of motion. During the movement, which combines concentric and eccentric contractions, the machine provides a resistance that is equal to the force the athlete performs.

Fixed Resistance

A muscle can develop tension often higher than that developed during a dynamic contraction via a static or isometric condition. Athletes can apply force against specially built immobile frames or objects that will not yield to the force they generate. This makes the muscle develop high tension without altering its length.

Electrical Stimulation

Although not yet adequately investigated, it seems that electrical stimulation could lead to gains in a muscle's strength. Sources suggesting such improvements are mostly from Russia (Kots 1977; Webster 1975) and Japan (Ikai and Yabe 1969). According to Webster, Russian weightlifters improved their maximum strength as a result of employing electrical stimulation. Kots (1977) claimed that using electrical stimulation increases the muscle's hypertrophy and found gains not only in strength but also in endurance. Ikai and Yabe used a frequency of stimulation three times higher (up to 150 impulses per second) than the physiological frequency (1-50 impulses per second). They found strength increases to be 31% higher than those realized through voluntary maximum contractions.

Factors Affecting Strength Performance

The display of maximum strength depends on three main factors: muscle potential, the use of muscle potential, and technique.

Muscle potential is the sum of forces all the muscles perform in a movement. According to Kuznetsov (1975) and Baroga (1978), the potential to perform force is 2.5 to 3 times higher than the contemporary performances in weightlifting. Thus, on the basis of these claims, an athlete should be able to lift up to 800 kilograms, which obviously is much greater than current performances.

Using muscle potential refers to the ability to use many muscle fibers simultaneously, both central and peripheral. The ability to increase muscle potential is substantially facilitated by using specific exercises of both natures, defeating and opposing gravity. In addition, exercises athletes perform in a rhythm superior to that of a competition, with a high volume of work, and wise use of isometric with dynamic contractions are effective.

A muscle that has in vitro potential to lift 100 kilograms is physiologically limited to 30% of its potential (Baroga 1978) or 30 kilograms. As previously suggested, from a theoretical potential of 800 kilograms a weightlifter may lift a load of about 240 kilograms. Specific training aimed at improving the use of muscle potential, using technique as an intermediary, may improve athletes' ability to lift up to 80% of their maximum potential. As a result, weightlifters should be able to lift 640 kilograms and high jumpers to perform 2.60 to 2.70 meters. It seems that the possibility of achieving such performances lies in the ability to involve central and peripheral muscle fibers simultaneously in activity (Kuznetsov 1975).

Matching Strength Training to Performance

There are various types of strength that the coach has to be aware of to conduct more effective training. For instance, the ratio between body weight and strength has an important consequence, to the extent that it allows comparison between individual athletes and indicates whether an athlete has the ability to perform certain skills. The following types of strength should have importance to a coach.

General strength refers to the strength of the whole muscular system. As this aspect is the foundation of the whole strength program, the athlete must develop it highly, with a concentrated effort during the preparatory phase or during the first few years of training beginner athletes. A low level of general strength may be a limiting factor for an athlete's overall progress.

Specific strength is the strength of only those muscles that are particular to the movement of the sport (the prime movers). As the term suggests, this type of strength is characteristic for each sport. Any comparison between the strength level of athletes involved in different sports is invalid. Progressively incorporate specific strength, which athletes must develop to the maximum possible level, toward the end of the preparatory phase for all elite-class athletes.

Maximum strength refers to the highest force the neuromuscular system can perform during a maximum voluntary contraction. This is demonstrated by the highest load that an athlete can lift in one attempt.

Muscular endurance is the muscle's ability to sustain work for a prolonged time. It represents the product of stressing both strength and endurance in training.

Power is the product of two abilities, strength and speed, and is the ability to perform maximum force in the shortest time.

Absolute strength (AS) refers to the ability of an athlete to exert maximum force regardless of body weight (BW). Absolute strength must reach high levels to be successful in some sports (shot put, heaviest weight categories in weightlifting and wrestling). You measure absolute strength using dynamometers. In training, however, it is significant to know the maximum amount of weight that an athlete can lift in one attempt, as the basis for calculating the training load. Considering that an athlete follows a systematic training, absolute strength increases parallel with gains in body weight.

Relative strength (RS) represents the ratio between an athlete's absolute strength and his or her body weight, as in the following:

$$RS = \frac{AS}{BW}$$

Relative strength is important in sports in which athletes travel during performance or are divided into weight categories (i.e., wrestling, boxing). For instance, a gymnast may not be able to perform the iron cross on the rings unless the relative strength of the muscles involved is at least 1.0, which means that the absolute strength must be at least sufficient to offset the athlete's body weight. Table 11.1 illustrates a comparison of the relative strength of two record holders in weightlifting.

From table 11.2, it is evident that as the body weight increases, relative strength decreases. This is significant for sports in which power is the dominant ability. According to the data provided by Zatzyorski (1968), the former world record holder in high jump, Valerie Brumel had the highest relative strength among Soviet jumpers (table 11.2).

TABLE 11.1 Relative Strength of the Weightlifting Record Holders (Clean and Jerk) From the Lightest and Heaviest Weight Categories

No.	Weight category/kg	World record/kg	Relative strength (kg force per kg body weight)
1	52	140	2.7
2	>110	255	2.3

TABLE 11.2   Comparison of Relative Strength of Soviet High Jumpers

Name	Standing vertical jump/cm	Absolute strength/kg (full squats)	Relative strength/kg
Brumel	104	174	2.21
Dyk	81	135	1.73
Glaskov	78	130	1.83

Adapted from Zatzyorski 1968.

From the data provided, we can conclude that the increment of relative strength is a function of weight loss. If, however, weight loss is a requirement for performance improvement, the athlete must do it under the supervision of a physician and the guidance of a nutritionist. Above all, the coach should not forget that systematic training is the ideal means of increasing relative strength.

Although at this time it is inadequately investigated, *strength reserve* is the difference between absolute strength of an athlete and the amount of strength required to perform a skill under competitive conditions (Bompa, Hebbelinck, and Van Gheluwe 1978). For instance, strength gauge techniques used to measure rowers' maximum strength per stroke unit revealed values up to 106 kilograms, and the mean strength per race was 56 kilograms. The same subjects had an absolute strength in power clean lifts of 90 kilograms. Subtracting the mean strength per race (X = 56 kilograms) from absolute strength (90 kilograms), you will find the strength reserve, which in our example is 34 kilograms. The ratio of mean to absolute strength is 1:1.6. Similarly, other subjects had a higher strength reserve, with a ratio of 1:1.85. The latter subjects were obviously capable of achieving higher performances in rowing races. This allows us to conclude that an athlete with a higher strength reserve is capable of reaching a higher performance. Although the concept of strength reserve may not be meaningful to all sports, it is hypothesized to be significant in sports such as swimming, canoeing, rowing, jumping, and throwing events in athletics.

Methodology of Strength Training

An athlete can improve strength by overcoming internal (attempting to flex an arm while opposing it with the other one) or external resistance. You can consider the following training means, listed in a progressive sequence, among the main sources of external resistance:

- Individual body weight (e.g., push-ups) exercises with a partner (e.g., grip the hands and perform arm pulls against partner's resistance)
- Medicine balls (lifts, throws, etc.)
- Elastic bands and cords (either fastened to solid object or held by partner; as cord stretches resistance increases)
- Dumbbells
- Barbells
- Fixed resistance (isometric contraction)

Because athletes perform most strength-training programs with free weights (barbells), the coach should consider the following rules.

A strength-training program should use free weights with other means of training, such as medicine balls, apparatus, and bounding. The training effect is more complex because they complement each other and are therefore more beneficial to the athlete.

Weight-training exercises may use both analytic and synthetic exercises, because their training effects are different. An analytic exercise involves a small group of muscles or a body limb, and as a consequence, the effect is strictly local. The main advantage of such an approach is that the athlete can alternate muscle groups continually, and as a result, the summation of training loads could reach high levels. Although an athlete can improve local strength dramatically, it has a low transfer effect to general endurance. Sports requiring endurance should therefore consider synthetic exercises, multijoint exercises involving several muscle groups. Such exercises may not permit equally high amounts of work, but do provide a superior general and specific functional component.

Before working the active limb, the athlete should exercise the passive segment. In other words, before strengthening the arms, exercise the muscles and ligaments of the supporting segments (the vertebral column and the scapulo-humeral girdle). This concept is also valid for the warm-up before a weight-training lesson.

Before developing muscular strength, develop good flexibility to avoid eventual joint rigidity. Incorporate flexibility exercises in the second part of the warm-up (please refer to planning a training lesson in chapter 6) and during the rest periods between weight-training exercises. This will facilitate a faster recovery in the muscle because it will reach its normal resting length more quickly using flexibility exercises (Pendergast 1974). In addition, the efficiency of a movement depends not only on the force of the active muscles, but also on the relaxation of the antagonistic muscles.

Methodical Parameters Relevant to Strength Training

Strength is one of the most important biomotor abilities, and its role in an athlete's training is often paramount. Understanding the methodology of its development is primary because it affects both speed and endurance. When constructing a strength-training program, you must consider several parameters, included in the following explanations, that are paramount to any successful program.

The key to an effective program is adequate selection of exercises. In their desire to develop most muscle groups, some coaches overlook establishing an optimum number of exercises. and select too many. Obviously, the outcome is an ineffective and fatiguing training program.

You must select exercises in light of the following aspects.

• Age and performance level. One main objective of a training program designed for juniors or beginners is developing a solid anatomical and physiological foundation. Without such an approach, consistent improvement will be unlikely. For strength training, the coach should select many exercises

(9-12) that address the main muscle groups of the body. The duration of such a program may be up to 2 or 3 years, depending on the age of the athlete and the expected age of high performance (table 2.3). Considering these circumstances, one of the coach's high attributes must be patience. Training programs designed for advanced or elite-class athletes should follow a completely different approach. For these athletes, a main objective of training is elevating performance to the highest possible levels. Strength training has its own role in accomplishing such an objective. A strength program for elite-class athletes, especially during the competitive phase, has to be specific, directed precisely to the prime movers and containing only a few exercises (three to six).

• Needs of the sport. Select exercises for strength training, especially for elite-class athletes, to meet the specific needs of the sport. An elite-class high jumper may perform only three or four exercises; whereas a wrestler must elevate the number to five to eight to adequately strengthen all prime movers.

• Training phase. An athlete needs a general strength-training program during the commencement of the preparatory phase. Following the transition phase, the coach starts a new annual plan and designs the beginning to build the foundation of training to come. Because such a program has to involve most muscle groups, the number of exercises for strength training during the early preparatory phase must be high (9-12), regardless of the specifics of the sport. As the program progresses, reduce this number, concluding with the competitive phase when the athlete performs only the specific, essential exercises.

Succession of Strength-Training Exercises in a Training Lesson

Strength-training exercises are more effective when they follow exercises for developing speed (Baroga 1978). Apparently, powerful stimuli like those applied during speed training arouse the athlete's body and CNS for strength development. Often weightlifters from Eastern Europe apply this concept, although in most cases strength-training programs begin with exercises for developing strength.

Training Load

Load refers to the mass or amount of weight used in developing strength. As figure 11.6, you may use the following loads in training:

Supermaximum is a load that exceeds an athlete's maximum strength. In most cases, you should use loads between 100 and 175% by applying the eccentric or opposing (known also as negative) gravity method. Elite-class weightlifters often employ 105 to 110% of maximum strength two or three times per week with the concentric (or positive) method. When you use supermaximum loads, I advise that you have two spotters, one at each end of the barbell, assisting or guarding the performer to avoid accidents. For instance, in the bench press, employing the negative method a barbell may fall on the performer's chest.

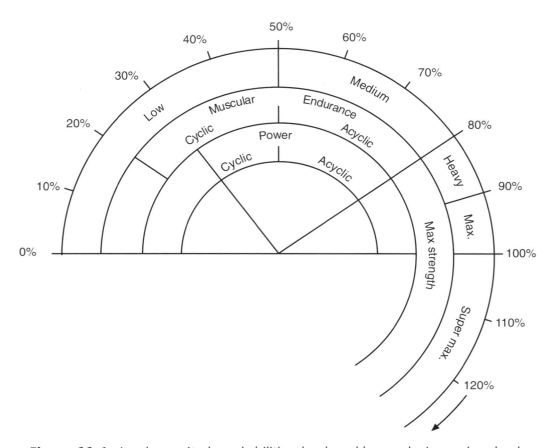

Figure 11.6 Load magnitude and abilities developed by employing various loads

Use supermaximum loads during maximum strength development only for those athletes with a strong background in strength training. Restrict most other athletes to a load of up to 100%. Maximum load, as indicated by the outer circle (figure 11.6), refers to a load of 90 to 100% of maximum. Heavy load is when you employ a load between 80 and 90% of maximum. Medium load refers to a percentage between 50 and 80% of maximum. Low is any load less than 50% of capacity. Athletes develop muscular endurance, both cyclic and acyclic, when the load is between 20 and 80%, but for power, you must employ a load between 30 and 80%.

Number of Repetitions and Rhythm of Execution

Both the number of repetitions and rhythm or speed of execution are functions of load; the higher the load, the lower the number of repetitions and rhythm of execution. As illustrated by figure 11.7, for developing maximum strength (90-175%), the number of repetitions is low (1-3) and performed slowly. For exercises developing power (30-80% of maximum), the number of repetitions is moderate (5-10) and performed dynamically. As for muscular endurance, the number of repetitions is high, sometimes up to the athlete's limit (250 or more), performed in a slow to medium rhythm. For acyclic muscular endurance, the number of repetition is between 10 and 30, and for cyclic, it approaches the athlete's limit.

The rhythm of breathing ought to be in harmony with the rhythm of performing a movement. An athlete usually inhales before the lift, holds his or her breath during the movement (apnea), and exhales toward the completion of the lift.

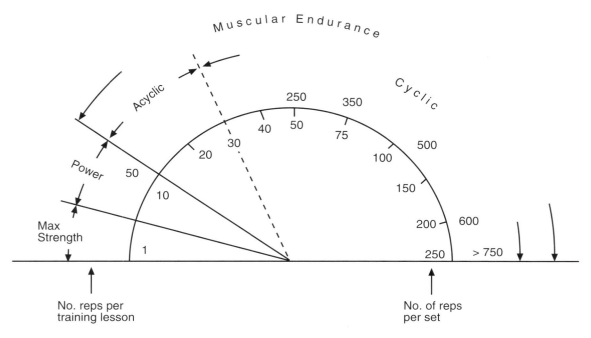

Figure 11.7 Number of repetitions required for developing various types of strength

Number of Sets

A set consists of a number of repetitions of an exercise followed by a rest interval. There is an inverse relationship between the training demand (load and number of repetitions in our case) and number of sets, which means that as training demand increases, the number of sets must decrease. The number of sets is also a function of the following factors: the athlete's abilities and training potential; the number of muscle groups to train (a higher number of sets is necessary when few muscle groups are involved); the number of exercises in a training lesson; and the phase of training. For instance, a high jumper in a specialized training program may use only 3 to 5 exercises and perform 6 to 10 sets per lesson. On the other hand, a wrestler who is interested in developing most muscle groups and uses more exercises may plan only 3 to 6 sets. Similarly, an athlete who wants to maintain only a certain level of strength during the competitive phase due to special circumstances, will use fewer sets than during the preparatory phase when developing strength was the main objective. The conclusion is that the number of sets may vary between 3 and 8, depending on specific training circumstances.

The notation of load, number of repetitions, and number of sets are expressed as follows:

$$\frac{\text{Load}}{\#\,\text{reps}}(\#\,\text{sets})$$

For example,

$$\frac{100}{8}\,4$$

The numerator (100) refers to the load to employ, the denominator (8) represents the number of repetitions, and the multiplier (4) illustrates the number of sets.

Rest Interval and Activity During Rest

As a general guideline, progressively reduce the rest interval as the athlete adjusts to training stimuli; however, prolong the rest interval as the load increases. The rest interval depends on the type of strength sought, the athlete's training status, the rhythm and duration of performance, and the number of muscles involved. Ozolin (1971) suggests that for exercises developing maximum strength, make the rest interval between 2 to 5 minutes. For all-out exercises, however, a longer rest interval of between 5 and 10 minutes may be recommended. For exercises to develop muscular endurance, the rest interval is shorter, often being 1 or 2 minutes. Scholich (1974) considers that the rest interval, especially for circuit training, has to be associated with the physiological response to a stimuli as indicated by the heart rate. When the heart rate decreases to 120 beats per minute, the athlete may perform another set. Finally, it is important that the coach consider the individual recovery rate, because each individual reacts differently to similar training stimuli. First, study and get to know the athlete; then prescribe precise training programs.

To facilitate a quicker recovery between sets, the coach should advise the athlete of the type of activity to perform during the rest interval. Relaxation exercises (i.e., shaking the legs, arms, and shoulders) and light massage are effective in facilitating a faster recovery between sets. Baroga (1978) claims that relaxation exercises are indicated especially because heavy load exercises increase the quantity of myostromin (a protein occurring within the framework of a muscle tissue) in muscles, which causes muscle rigidity.

Selecting the means and methods of training, the load, number of repetitions, and number of sets is essential to the success of a strength-training program. A summary of these training parameters is presented in table 11.3.

Using table 11.3 as a reference, you can see that the load of exercises to develop maximum strength is high, for power it is medium to low, and for muscular endurance it is medium to low. On the other hand, the table suggests that the rest interval to enhance maximum strength has to be high, for power it is high to medium, and for muscular endurance low to medium, because such exercises place a lower demand on the body.

Total Volume of Training for Strength Development

The total volume of strength training depends on the needs and specifics of the sport. It is common for weightlifters to lift 30 tonnes (33 short tons) per lesson. Because most international-class weightlifters train a minimum of 1,200 hours per year, lifting 40,000 tonnes (44,000 short tons) per year is a medium volume of work. The Bulgarian athletes train 1,600 hours per year, which is one reason they are among the best in the world.

A strength-training lesson may last 1 to 2 hours depending on the strength requirements of the sport, and other factors such as age, sex, sport classification, and training phase. Consider table 11.4 as a guideline for the volume of strength training for various sports and events.

These figures, specific for sports and events requiring strength or speed, refer to elite athletes. The total volume of strength training drastically alters for sports in which muscular endurance is an important component. Thus, for sports like wrestling, swimming, canoeing, and rowing, the yearly tonnage may be three to six times higher. For instance, canoers and rowers may lift as much as 20,000 tonnes (22,000 short tons) per year. One of the highest volumes of strength training per lesson ever recorded was that of an athlete involved in rowing: 118 tonnes, or 129 short tons (Bompa 1979).

TABLE 11.3 Dominant Parameters in Strength Training
and the Emphasis to Place on Each According to Ability

| | EXERCISES FOR | | |
	Maximum strength	Power	Muscular endurance
Load	H	M → L	M → L
# Repetitions	L	M	H
# Sets	H	M	L
Rhythm of performance	L	H	L → M
Rest interval	H	H → M	L → M

H = high; M = medium; L = low.

TABLE 11.4 Volume (Tonnes) of Strength Training for Various Sports (Men)

| | Volume per microcycle in training phases | | | Volume/year | |
Sport/event	Preparatory	Competitive	Transition	Minimum	Maximum
Shot put	24-40	8-12	4-6	900	1,450
Downhill skiing	18-36	6-10	2-4	700	1,250
High jump	16-28	8-10	2-4	620	1,000
Ice hockey	15-25	6-8	2-4	600	950
Speed skating	14-26	4-6	2-4	500	930
Basketball	12-24	4-6	2	450	850
Javelin	12-24	4	2	450	800
Volleyball	12-20	4	2	450	700
Sprinting	10-18	4	2	400	600
Gymnastics	10-16	4	4	380	600
Boxing	8-14	3	1	330	500

Modified from Bompa 1960 and Baroga 1978.

Methodical Sequence of Developing a Strength-Training Program

Develop a strength-training program considering the following systematic sequence. The coach should select the exercises to employ in the program.

Test the maximum strength in one attempt, or one repetition maximum (1RM) to determine the 100% strength of the athlete's prime movers. The coach should know each athlete's maximum strength in at least the dominant exercises of a training program. Often, the coach chooses the load and number of repetitions randomly or by following the programs of other athletes, instead of using objective data about the individual. This data is valid for only a certain cycle of training, usually a macrocycle, because the athlete's degree of training and potential alter continuously.

When the coach knows the individual's maximum strength, then he or she must decide the range of percentage of loads to use in training according to the characteristics of the sport, the athlete's needs, and the type of strength sought. For example, a basketball coach may decide to develop leg power by employing 75% of each player's maximum strength. Thus, if player AB has a maximum strength for leg press of 220 kilograms, then the load in training would be 165 kilograms (or 75% of maximum strength). Obviously, the percentage of load to use in training depends on the type of strength you will develop (see figure 11.6).

The next step is to test the athlete's maximum number of repetitions with the selected load. Let 12 be the maximum number of repetitions that player AB performed with 165 kilograms. Now you can calculate the number of repetitions (NR) to perform in a given training lesson by using the following equation:

$$\frac{RM(\%)}{100} = NR$$

RM represents repetitions maximum performed with the selected load, and % refers to the percentage of load (the selected load) of 1RM. By employing the figures from this example, you will find the following NR to use in training:

$$\frac{12(75\%)}{100} = 9$$

Thus the NR for the basketball player in a given phase of training is 9.

Develop the training program and apply it in a given phase of training. By now the coach knows the exercises to be performed, the athlete's maximum strength, the percentage of load to use in training, and the number of repetitions for each exercise. The coach must use all this data to make the training program for a macrocycle. This program cannot, however, be the same for each macrocycle. The coach must progressively increase the training demand so the athlete will adjust to an elevated workload, which will translate into an increase in strength. Increase the training demand by any of the following means: increase the load, decrease the rest interval, or increase the number of repetitions. In the last case, you can use the following equation:

$$\frac{RM}{DC} + PC = NR$$

The numerator represents the repetition maximum (in our example 12) and the denominator is a dividing constant (DC). The progression constant (PC) will be added to the product in each microcycle so the training demand will increase continually.

Both DC and PC are a function of the athlete's classification and potential (table 11.5).

Let RM be 12, DC 1.5, and PC 2. By substituting these figures into the equation, you will find the following number of repetitions in a given training phase:

$$\frac{12}{1.5} + 2 = 10$$

Add the PC increment cumulatively from the second microcycle only; therefore, considering these figures, the numbers of repetitions will be as follows: 12, 14, and 16. You do not have to follow this progression rigidly, but adjust it to suit the athlete's improvement rate.

TABLE 11.5 DC and PC Altered According to Athlete's Classification

Athlete's classification	DC	PC	Athlete's classification	DC	PC
Elite class	1.2	2	Prospective athletes	1.8	1
National level	1.5	2	Juniors and beginners	2	1

Test to recalculate the maximum strength and the number of repetition per selected percentage of maximum strength. This new test is necessary before a new macrocycle to ensure that progress prevails and training demand is adequate.

Write any strength-training program on a free sheet of paper, or even better in the training journal. Examples of formats to express a strength-training program are illustrated in tables 11.6 and 11.7.

TABLE 11.6 Headings of a Chart Presenting a Strength-Training Program

Exercise	Load/kg	Number of reps	Number of sets	Rhythm	Rest interval	Activity during rest
Leg press, etc.	120	20	6	Moderate	90 s	Relaxation and breathing exercises

TABLE 11.7 Condensed Chart Presenting a Strength-Training Program

Exercise	Load, # reps, # sets	Rhythm	Rest interval	Activity during rest
Leg press, etc.	$\frac{120}{20}_6$	Moderate	90 s	Relaxation

Methods of Strength Training

Developing strength takes several forms, depending on the characteristics of a sport. Some sports require more power, others more muscle endurance because the duration of activity is long. So, there is no one method that will address the needs of all sports.

Characteristics of Developing Maximum Strength

The main characteristic of a maximum strength-training program is involving exercise of all or at least most of the neuromuscular units. Everyone aiming to develop maximum strength must, therefore, frequently employ maximum and supermaximum stimuli.

Among the sports requiring maximum strength development are weightlifting, shot put, discus, and hammer throw. Other sports requiring power or muscular endurance may benefit from maximum strength development, at least during certain parts of the preparatory phase.

The strain on an athlete's body is especially high when employing maximum or supermaximum (negative method) loads. It seems, therefore, that alternating muscle groups for each training lesson facilitates a higher volume of work and a better recovery rate between lessons. For example, work the legs in one lesson and the arms and shoulders in the next.

Characteristics of Developing Power

The principal stimulus in power training is performing a movement dynamically linked with the force magnitude taking place in the same exertion. For

Alternating muscle groups helps lessen strain

instance, during sprinting an athlete's force of leg propulsion is three and one-half times that of his or her body weight, but the force used to throw a javelin is much smaller. Thus the force of acceleration is the main stimulus for power training. In acyclic sports (i.e., jumping events), power is the determinant ability for achieving a good result. On the other hand, in cyclic sports (i.e., sprinting), power is brought into action repetitively and rapidly. Consider these general characteristics of sports requiring power and reflect them in a strength-training program.

Acyclic Power

The main beneficiaries of developing acyclic power are athletes involved in throwing and jumping events in athletics, gymnastics (for most elements), fencing, diving, and every sport requiring a takeoff, for example volleyball. For these sports or athletic elements, power performed acyclically is the dominant factor in the performance. Although maximum strength is an important element of progression, exercises using lower loads and performed extremely quickly (i.e., exercises with medicine balls) ought to be part of the program as well.

Most strength-training exercises, such as power clean, snatch, and clean and jerk, are from the weightlifters' repertoire. This does not, however, exclude other exercises such as weight belts and vests, various jumps, for example deep jumps, over benches, and bounding exercises. The load for acyclic power is between 50 and 80% (figure 11.6) with the movement performed quickly. I recommend four to six sets with a rest interval of 3 to 5 minutes for an almost full recovery. Adequate recovery is paramount because only an almost completely recovered body can perform acyclic power exercises efficiently.

Cyclic Power

A characteristic of sports requiring cyclic power is that their relationship with speed is pronounced. These sports include sprinting in athletics, swimming, speed skating, and cycling, and all sports requiring speed. The strength component of a strength-training program employs slightly reduced stimuli (load 30-50%). You must link the improvement of cyclic power with sprinting endurance, which assists the athlete in avoiding a decrease in stride frequency toward the end of a race.

I recommend the load for cyclic exercises to be 30 to 50% of maximum (figure 11.6), performed in a dynamic rhythm, with up to 10 repetitions, and a long recovery interval (5 minutes). Relaxation exercises throughout a training program and alternating contraction with relaxation are mandatory requirements, because rigidity may affect a muscle's contraction rate.

Characteristics of Developing Muscular Endurance

We can divide muscular endurance according to the specifics of sports: acyclic, or shorter duration, and cyclic, or muscular endurance, for sports of longer duration. Often the difference between these two types of muscular endurance is visible; therefore I will examine them separately.

Acyclic Muscular Endurance

You can improve acyclic muscular endurance either by repeating parts of elements (routines of the sport) with an intensity slightly higher than in competition, or by using weight training. In the latter case, use a load between 50 and 80% of maximum with the number of repetitions between 10 and 30 (figure 11.7). Those involved in gymnastics, wrestling, and martial arts are

Cyclic power and speed go hand and hand

among the athletes who may benefit the most from this method. Considering that the needs of the athletes are often complex, they must combine developing acyclic muscular endurance with developing other strength components, which calls for using other methods.

Cyclic Muscular Endurance

For all cyclic sports having a performance time in excess of 2 minutes, regard the development of cyclic muscular endurance as one of the main factors leading to performance improvement. Sports such as swimming (400-1,500 meters), canoeing (1,000-10,000 meters), rowing, speed skating, and cross-country skiing can evidently benefit from perfecting this strength component. To model a strength-training program to the specifics of the sport, select and perform the exercise so phases of muscular contraction alternate with phases of relaxation. The load for this type of duration is 20 to 50% of the maximum.

In most of the sports and events listed previously, aerobic endurance is an important if not dominant component. Strength, especially muscular endurance, is also a key element, because in most of these sports, the athletes perform against water resistance. A strength-training program must relate to the distance and therefore to the objective requirements of the event. Consequently, for events of shorter duration, such as 400-meter swimming and 1,000-meter canoeing, the load may be between 40 and 50% or higher. The number of repetitions should be between 30 and 100. For events of longer duration, the load is slightly lower and the number of repetitions increases, up to maximum. The frequency or rhythm of repetition again must relate to the dynamics of the event, but generally between 30 and 50 repetitions per minute are adequate. The heart rate, as a guideline to the physiological reaction to training demand has to be, as suggested by Schroeder (1969), between 150 and 160 beats per minute.

As a summary of the means and methods employed in strength training, I invite you to study table 11.8, which was proposed by Harre (1982). Although Harre holds slightly different opinions from those explained in the present section, you still may gain a better comprehension of the subject from the table.

Maximum Strength Methods

Selecting a strength-training method has to relate to the type of strength sought. Consequently, there are training methods to develop maximum strength, power, or muscular endurance, which I briefly present here.

Although athletes can develop maximum strength through static, isokinetic, or electrical stimulation methods, the maximum strength method using free weights or other instruments is still the most common. The main element of progression is the intensity of stimulation realized through the load increment. As suggested by Baroga (1978), you can consider four variants to develop maximum strength. The progression each variant suggests refers to a training lesson. Selecting a variant depends on its effectiveness according to individual particularities.

Speed skaters benefit from perfecting cyclic muscular endurance

TABLE 11.8 Dosage and Methods Employed in Strength Training

Percentage of maximum strength	No. of repetitions per set	Rhythm of performance	Rest interval	No. of sets	Method	Applicability
100-85%	1-5	Moderate	2-5 min	Beginners 3-5 Advanced athletes 5-8	$\frac{85\%}{5} + \frac{95\%}{2\text{-}3} +$ $\frac{100\%}{1} + \frac{95\%}{2\text{-}3}$	To improve maximum strength for acyclic sports.
85-70%	5-10	Moderate to slow	2-4 min	3-5	$\frac{70\%}{10} + \frac{80\%}{7} +$ $\frac{85\%}{5} + \frac{85\%}{5}$	To improve maximum strength. Basic method for cyclic sports requiring maximum strength.
50-30%	6-10 at a maximum speed	Explosive	2-5 min	4-6	$\frac{30\%}{10} + \frac{40\%}{10} +$ $\frac{50\%}{10} + \frac{40\%}{10}$	To improve power.
75%	6-10	Very fast	2-5 min	4-6	$\frac{75\%}{10} + \frac{40\%}{10} +$ $\frac{75\%}{10} + \frac{75\%}{10}$	To improve power and maximum strength.
60-40%	20-30 (50-70% of maximum number of repetitions)	Fast to moderate	30-45 s	3-5	Circuit training	To improve muscular endurance.
40-25%	25-50% of maximum number of repetitions	Moderate to fast	Optimal	4-6	Circuit training	As above but for sports that do not require overwhelmingly this quality.

Adapted from Harre 1982.

- Variant A—the load increases continuously: 80%, 90%, 100%, 110%.
- Variant B—the load increases in steps: 80%, 80%; 90%, 90%; 100%, 100%; 110%, 110%.
- Variant C—the load increases and decreases continually (pyramid): 80%, 90%, 100%, 100%, 90%, 80%.
- Variant D—the load increases like a wave: 80%, 90%, 85%, 90%, 100%, 95%, 100%, 90%.

The number of exercises in a training lesson is between four and eight, and the number of repetitions is between one and five. Because the number of sets must relate to the athlete's abilities and to the total number of exercises, he or she may repeat an exercise in 4 to 10 sets. The rhythm of performing an exercise depends on the load. High loads do not allow a rapid rhythm. The athlete should, however, strive for a dynamic rhythm regardless of load.

The maximum strength method is beneficial to all athletes requiring maximum strength, and especially to weightlifters and throwers in athletics.

Static or Isometric Contractions

Hettinger and Müler (1953) and again Hettinger (1966) scientifically justified the merits of static contractions in developing maximum strength, although the concept was improperly used for some time. This method reached its climax in the 1960s and has since faded in popularity. Static contraction does not have a marked functional effect for muscular endurance, although it can still assist in developing maximum strength. Therefore, weightlifters and throwers may use it in their strength-training efforts. You can accomplish static conditions through three techniques: by attempting to lift a weight heavier than your potential; by applying force, either push or pull, against an immobile object; and by applying force with one limb and opposing it with another.

You can perform static contractions in various limb positions and angles, from a muscle that is completely elongated to one that is fully shortened. When using this method, regard the following methodological aspects:

- Static contractions are efficient when using 70 to 100% of maximum strength.
- Employ the method primarily in the training of mature athletes with a good background in strength training. If training juniors, use low intensity.
- Training dosage intensifies by increasing the number of exercises and not the effort per contraction.
- The duration of a contraction is between 6 and 12 seconds, with a total of 60 to 90 seconds of contraction per muscle group per training lesson.
- During the rest interval of 60 to 90 seconds, I recommend relaxation and breathing exercises. The latter is a compensatory necessity because athletes perform static contraction in apnea (breath holding). In addition, the intrathoracic pressure is elevated, which restricts circulation and thus the oxygen supply.
- For a more effective program, alternate static with isotonic contractions, especially for sports requiring speed and power. A variant of the static contraction, the intermediary contraction, during which the athlete may stop the lifted object several times for 4-8 seconds throughout the performance, seems to be more acceptable than the strictly static method.

Power

Developed by Belgian R. Molette (1963), this method aimed at developing power by employing three groups of exercise: free-weight exercises; exercises with medicine balls; and tumbling and flexibility exercises. The main elements of progression increase the number of repetitions and increase the speed of performance.

Determine the load by the amount of weight the athlete can lift correctly six times. Then, improve the speed of execution. When the execution speed is satisfactory, increase the number of repetitions from 6 to 12. When the speed for 12 repetitions is satisfactory, increase the load until the athlete can again complete only 6 repetitions. When the athlete cannot perform exercises correctly, training has to stop.

The rest interval is 2 or 3 minutes when exercising with a load below 85% maximum, and 3 to 5 minutes when the load exceeds this amount. The program consists of 12 exercises divided into four groups of three: one with barbells, one with medicine balls, another with barbells, and finally one with simple tumbling and flexibility exercises. Following each group of exercises, take a rest interval.

Athletes performing exercises with medicine balls must do it with a high speed. The main elements of progression are the increase in distance between two performers, and the increase and decrease of weights of balls. You can use power training for sports requiring power or complex biomotor abilities, such as jumping, throwing events in athletics, alpine skiing, most team sports, boxing, and wrestling.

Developing Muscular Endurance

At Leeds University, Morgan and Adamson (1959) developed a fitness and training method that proved successful for many decades. This method was called circuit training because all stations of the program were arranged in a circle. A similar concept was used in training before World War II, in which the main merit was alternating muscle groups. This concept was also employed in circuit training. Several other publications on this topic were printed during the following years. The books written by Jonath (1961) and especially by Scholich (1974) managed to further the scientific knowledge of this method.

Although circuit training was initially used to develop general fitness progressively, it was improved and became a complex method. As a result, by considering various strength-training methodical parameters, you may design circuit training programs to develop strength, speed, and coordination, as well as combinations of abilities such as power and muscular endurance. In developing a circuit training program, consider the following characteristics:

- A circuit may be short (6 exercises), normal (9 exercises), or long (12 exercises); therefore, its total duration may vary from 10 to 30 minutes. Usually, an athlete may repeat a circuit three times; however, its duration, the number of repetitions, and the rest interval depend on the athlete's background and the ability sought.

- Elevate the physical demand progressively and individually.

- Many athletes may participate simultaneously because there are set stations arranged before training, giving this method an organizational advantage.

- Arrange the circuit to alternate muscle groups; therefore, an athlete may exercise body segments as follows: leg, arms, abdomen, and back.

- You can precisely manage the training demand by indicating the exact time or number of repetitions for the athlete to perform. Variations of circuit training exist, however, in which you can perform a circuit without rest intervals or time limits or perform all exercises without rest intervals but with a time standard for one or three circuits.

- As an element of progression, you may reduce the time to perform a circuit without altering the number of repetitions or the load, or you may increase the load or number of repetitions.

- The rest interval between circuits is about 2 minutes, but may change according to the demand on the athletes. You could use the heart rate method to calculate the rest interval. When the rate falls to about 120 beats per minute, start another circuit (Scholich 1974).

According to the needs of the sport, Scholich (1974) suggests two variants of strict circuit training: intensive and extensive. You can use circuit training intensive with interval to develop acyclic muscular endurance. As the term suggests, the rhythm of repeating an exercise is dynamic, with a load between 50 and 80% of maximum and between 10 and 30 repetitions. The rest interval is two or three times higher than the execution time. You can use this variant for sprinting events (athletics, swimming, and speed skating), wrestling, boxing, football, and other team sports.

In contrast, circuit training extensive with interval, employs a lower load (20-50%) and an extensive number of repetitions (up to limits). The rhythm of performance is medium to slow, with a rest interval shorter than the intensive variant. Such a program is indicated for sports requiring cyclic muscular endurance, distance running, swimming, cross-country skiing, rowing, and so on.

Specificity Versus a Methodical Approach

By attempting to develop an optimal strength-training program, some coaches, based on their experience, suggested that the program has to be specific. This concept was then developed by some physiologists (i.e., Mathews and Fox 1976) into a principle of training. By strictly following this principle, you simulate the movement pattern while performing a skill, and perfect only the type of strength dominant in the sport, throughout an athletic career.

This concept is correct if you apply it only to elite athletes during the competitive phase. If children and beginners follow the same rule from their first day of training throughout their entire athletic career, and throughout all training phases, then the principles of training are misunderstood and violated.

Develop an optimal strength program with the determinant and prevalent biomotor abilities of the sport. Furthermore, the selected exercises ought to simulate the plane, direction, and specific angle in which the athlete performs the skill. Strength-development exercises have to involve the prime movers. However, consider these realities for elite athletes, and during the conversion and maintenance phases of an annual plan regarding strength training. Consequently, periodization is the leading concept in planning a strength-training program. On the other hand, a children's strength-training program has two phases: general or multilateral strength training and the specific phase.

The general and multilateral strength training, during which the coach develops all the muscle groups, ligaments, and tendons, thus strengthening and developing the base for future heavy loads and specific training, is desirable for the methodology of training, and it would be likely to lead to an injury-free athletic career. The duration of this phase may be between 2 and 4 years, depending on the athlete's age and abilities. Throughout this phase, a coach needs considerable patience. To look for a quick return in training is an unhealthy approach.

After developing the foundations of strength training, the coach may start the specific phase, which will be considered for the rest of the athlete's career.

This does not mean, however, that the coach will follow a strength-training program specific to the needs of the sport throughout all phases of an annual training plan. Rather, it must consider the concept of periodization of strength training, which always starts with a buildup or general strength development phase.

Summary of Major Concepts

We can trace many of the drastic improvements of athletic performance since the 1960s to the impact strength training has had on several sports. There is still a great deal of improvement athlete's can make by incorporating more strength training into their athletic programs.

Those who have used anabolic steroids in their quest to improve performance have done so as a result of ignorance regarding strength training. They try to increase the power of contraction artificially and dangerously for their health, without natural means such as strength training.

I would like to invite anyone in search of better athletic performance to learn more about strength training.

We can trace ignorance regarding strength training to using bodybuilding and weightlifting methods. None of these methods are applicable to the needs of sports' strength, especially for sports in which endurance is an important factor.

One of the most important factors to examine for developing strength to improve athletic performance in sports is applying the periodization concept to strength training. I encourage interested individual to thoroughly examine my book *Periodization Training for Sports* (Human Kinetics, 1999). In it I examine in detail which training methods to use and how to organize them for the specific need of a sport. You will experience improvements in performance beyond your greatest expectations.

Chapter 12

Endurance Training

For any nonstop sporting activity of 60 seconds or longer, endurance is an important, dominant contribution to the final performance. Factors affecting endurance, including willpower, speed reserve, and aerobic and anaerobic capacity, must be studied so training will thoroughly prepare athletes for the stresses of competition.

Classification of Endurance

Endurance refers to the length of time that an individual can perform work of a given intensity. The main factor that limits and at the same time affects performance is fatigue. A person has endurance when he or she does not easily fatigue or can continue work in a state of fatigue. An athlete is capable of doing this if he or she is adapted to the specifics of the work performed. Endurance depends on many factors, such as speed, muscle force, technical abilities of performing movements efficiently, the ability to use physiological potentials economically, and psychological status when performing work.

Considering the needs of training, there are two kinds of endurance: general and specific endurance. Ozolin (1971) considers general endurance to be the capacity of performing a type of activity that involves many muscle groups and systems (CNS, neuromuscular, and cardiorespiratory system) for a prolonged time. A good level of general endurance, regardless of the sport's specialization, facilitates success in various types of training activities. Athletes involved in sports in which endurance, and especially aerobic endurance, dominates do have a high level of general endurance. This suggests that there is a strong relationship between general and specific endurance. On the other hand, athletes taking part in sports of short duration or of high technical sophistication do not have a good level of general endurance. Every athlete needs general endurance. It assists in performing a high volume of work, overcoming fatigue in competitions of long duration, and recovering faster after training or competitions.

Specific endurance, which often is referred to as endurance of playing, sprinting, and the like, depends on the particularities of each sport or the many repetitions of the motor acts of each sport. Although specific endurance is imprinted in the characteristics of certain sports, it may be affected by the excitement of competitions, the performance of difficult athletic tasks, or the type of training performed. Also, a demanding tactical game often affects an athlete's specific endurance; thus, the athlete may be subject to technical and tactical faults during the second part of the contest. Consequently, the stronger the specific endurance the athlete develops from a solid base of general endurance, the easier he or she can overcome training and competition stressors.

The types of endurance presented are paramount to a successful performance in each sport. For cyclic sports, however, the following classification is often suggested (Pfeifer 1982).

- Endurance of long duration is required for sports that last for more than 8 minutes. Energy is supplied almost exclusively by the aerobic system, which greatly involves the cardiovascular and respiratory systems. During an endurance race in this category, the heart rate is high (over 180 beats per minute), the heart's minute volume (the volume of blood pumped by the heart in one minute) is between 30 and 40 liters, and the lungs ventilate 120 to 140 liters of air per minute (Pfeifer 1982). Obviously, for long duration races (i.e., marathon) these values are lower. The O_2 supply is a determining factor for a good performance. The vital capacity and the minute volume of the heart are, therefore, limiting factors for high athletic results. They also reflect the athlete's adaptation to the stress of such activities. Work of medium intensity favors the body's adaptation and capillary vascularization so vital for the supply of O_2 to the muscle cells (Mader and Hollmann 1977).

- Endurance of medium duration is specific for sports and events in which work is performed during 2 to 6 minutes. The intensity is higher than in sports requiring endurance of long duration. The O_2 supply cannot totally meet the body's needs; therefore, the athlete develops an O_2 debt. The energy produced by the anaerobic system is proportional to the speed magnitude. Pfeifer (1982) claims that for a 3,000-meter run, the anaerobic system supplies approximately 20% of the total energy the athlete needs and, for 1,500 meters, up to 50%. As in the previous case, the O_2 absorption has a determinant role in performance.

• Endurance of short duration refers to sports in which the duration of the distance traveled is between 45 seconds and 2 minutes. For sports in this category, the anaerobic processes participate intensely in supplying the energy required to perform the athletic task. Strength and speed play an important role in producing high results. The O_2 debt is high, and according to Pfeifer (1982), the anaerobic system provides 80% of the required energy for a 400-meter run and 60 to 70% for the 800-meter run. The basis for developing the anaerobic capacity is the aerobic capacity. Consequently, an athlete must develop a high aerobic capacity even for sports and events in this category. Muscle endurance, which I referred to in strength training, is facilitated by high strength development blended with adequate endurance. Sports such as rowing, swimming, and canoeing are the main beneficiaries of this combined ability.

• Endurance of speed represents athletes' resistance to fatigue under maximum intensity. Most of the work is done in apnea, which requires athletes to have both maximum speed and strength (also refer to speed training).

Factors Affecting Endurance

Endurance, so important for good performance, is of different types, and its effective development depends on several training methods. In your quest to improve athletic performance, it is important to be aware of several factors, which may negatively affect the development of endurance.

Central Nervous System (CNS)

During endurance training, the CNS adapts to the specifics of the training demand. As a result of training, the CNS increases its working capacity, which improves the nervous connections needed for well-coordinated functioning of the organs and systems. Fatigue, which often impairs training, occurs at the CNS level; therefore, decrease in the CNS working capacity is a major cause of fatigue. The struggle against fatigue is a battle of the nervous centers to maintain their working capacity.

Increasing CNS endurance and its optimal status ought to be one of the main concerns in training. The coach can facilitate this by selecting adequate and optimal means of training. Uniform work with moderate intensity improves and strengthens the entire activity of the CNS, namely the neuromuscular coordination specific for endurance activities. Similarly, long-duration endurance activity performed under increasing levels of fatigue increases nervous cell resistance to stressful work (Ozolin 1971).

Athletic Willpower

Willpower is a paramount ingredient in endurance training. The athlete requires it mostly when he or she has to perform work in a state of fatigue, or when the level of fatigue increases as a result of prolonged activity. This is even more obvious when intensity is an important component of training. The athlete cannot maintain the required level of intensity unless his or her desire and will order the nervous centers to continue the work or even increase it, particularly at the finish. Human beings do hold a great deal of endurance reserves, and we can maximize them only by appealing to the will to defeat the weaknesses, which may often result from fatigue. An important training objective, therefore, is to increase pain tolerance so athletes can psychologically tolerate the hurt, pain, and agony of training and competitions.

Aerobic Capacity

The aerobic potential, or the body's capacity to produce energy in the presence of O_2, determines the athlete's endurance capacity. Aerobic power is limited by the ability to transport O_2 within the body. Developing the O_2 transportation system should, therefore, be part of any program to improve endurance capacity. High aerobic capacity, which is vital to training, also facilitates faster recovery between and after training. A rapid recovery allows the athlete to reduce the rest interval and perform the work with higher intensity. As a result of shorter rest intervals, he or she can increase the number of repetitions, which increases the volume of training. A fast recovery rate, enhanced by high aerobic capacity, is also important in sports that require many repetitions of a skill (jumping events) or an increased number of bouts in team sports (hockey, football).

The organs and especially the respiratory system that supplies the oxygen become well developed during endurance training. In fact, certain organs are developed according to the training method employed. Thus, interval training strengthens the heart, and high altitude or long-duration training increases the O_2 using capabilities (Ozolin 1971). The aerobic capacity, however, relies on developing the respiratory system and correct breathing.

Breathing plays an important role in endurance training. The athlete must perform it deeply and rhythmically, because active exhalation is critical for an adequate performance. Most athletes have to learn how to exhale to evacuate as much air as possible from the lungs, because the O_2 has already been extracted. Without proper exhalation, the concentration of O_2 in the freshly inhaled air will be diluted, which will adversely affect performance. A forceful exhalation is even more important during the critical phase of a race or game, when an adequate supply of O_2 can enable athletes to overcome the difficulty.

A high aerobic capacity positively transfers to the anaerobic capacity. If an athlete improves his or her aerobic capacity, the anaerobic capacity also improves, because he or she will be able to function longer before reaching an O_2 debt and will recover more quickly after building an O_2 debt (Howald 1977). This finding is significant for most sports in which the anaerobic capacity is an important component. Most team sport athletes would maximize their technical and tactical knowledge by improving aerobic capacity. Improving aerobic endurance must be a permanent goal for most athletes.

A strong aerobic capacity also stabilizes speed. The competitive phase of many sports emphasizes anaerobic capacity, but often the consistency of anaerobic performance is affected by exaggerated, stressful, intense work. When anaerobic capacity is an important component of training, you must also introduce aerobic activities to prolong a successful performance. In such cases, training lessons stressing aerobic long-duration endurance alternate activities of various intensities. Under these new conditions, the body can regenerate and thus increase the durability of anaerobic power. The same concept is valid for the unloading (tapering) phase. When athletes reduce their training demands before important competitions, introduce training lessons of aerobic activity to

Endurance training enhances respiratory capabilities

replace stressful intensive activities. As a result, the body will regenerate, because the load is lighter, and the degree of training is not affected. Howald (1977) implies that there is a trend showing that athletes using long-duration submaximum training do have higher anaerobic thresholds than those using more high-intensity endurance and interval training. Consequently, based on these realities, coaches should revise their training concept and introduce a much higher percentage of aerobic activities into their training programs.

Anaerobic Capacity

In the absence of O_2, energy is produced by the anaerobic system for sports that demand maximum exertion and those requiring submaximum exertion during the initial stages. Energy contributed by the anaerobic system directly relates to the performance intensity. For example, if an athlete runs a 400-meter race with a velocity of 7.41 meters per second, the ergogenesis (the production of energy) is 14% aerobic and 86% anaerobic. Running the same distance with a velocity of 8.89 meters per second, the ratio is 7.7% aerobic and 92.3% anaerobic (Razumovski 1971). It appears, therefore, that the use of the two energy systems depends on the distance of the race and the classification or performance level of an athlete. It is obvious from this example that the two systems can provide energy in various proportions. The proportion of the aerobic component increases as the distance increases and the intensity decreases.

Ozolin (1971) claims that the body's anaerobic capacity is affected by the CNS processes, which facilitate continuing intensive work or work under exhausting conditions. Research also suggests that the anaerobic capacity is affected by hyperventilation, or inhaling additional O_2 through increasing the respiration rate before the start.

Specific training in the respective sport is the best method of improving the anaerobic capacity. As explained, however, anaerobic training often has to alternate with aerobic training. Aerobic training should predominate for sports that last longer than 60 seconds. Anaerobic training, such as the overemphasized interval training used in North America, will not necessarily make athletes faster who compete in sports lasting longer than 2 minutes. It is helpful only for the first part of the race.

Speed Reserve

One factor that affects endurance, especially specific endurance, is the speed reserve. Its importance in cyclic sports may often be determinant, although many coaches are still unaware of this or disregard it. Speed reserve is the difference between the fastest time achieved on a distance much shorter than the racing distance (i.e., 100 meters) and the same short distance during a longer race (i.e., 800 meters). To have validity, perform the test during the same time. An athlete who can cover a short distance fast will be able to travel longer distances at a lower speed more easily. Under such circumstances, an athlete with a higher speed reserve would spend less energy to maintain a given speed compared with others with a lower reserve.

You can perform a speed reserve test as follows. The coach should first determine the distance to test. A standard speed distance for mid-distance running is 100-meter dash; for swimming either 25 or 50 meters or one length of the pool; for rowing 500 meters, and canoeing 250 meters. Then test the athletes to determine the maximum speed with which they can cover the standard distance. The next step would be to test the athletes' speed over the standard distance, for example 100 meters, while they compete over the distances in which they specialize.

Let 11 seconds be the maximum speed over 100 meters and 12.4 seconds the time achieved over 100 meters while running 400 meters. The difference of 1.4 seconds is the speed reserve index; the larger the difference the greater the speed reserve. A good speed reserve and systematic specific endurance training will lead to high performance in the chosen event. Similarly, provided that athletes have a good speed, the smaller the index the better the specific endurance. Although this aspect of training is inadequately researched, it is obvious that there is a strong interdependence between speed reserve and athletes' ability to reach a high performance. An athlete running 100 meters in 10.6 seconds, even without much specific training, would cover 400 meters in 50 seconds. This means a speed reserve of probably 1.8 seconds and a mean speed of 12.5 seconds. An athlete with a speed of 12 seconds per 100 meters would, however, have a hard time or may even be unable to perform a similar time over 400 meters. Speed in general and a speed reserve in particular may, therefore, be a limiting factor in athletic progress.

Methodology of Developing Endurance

To improve endurance, athletes must learn to overcome fatigue, and they do this by adapting to the training demand. Any degree of adaptation is reflected in improved endurance.

Athletes must develop the two types of endurance, aerobic or anaerobic, primarily according to the specifics of the sport or event. Developing these two types of endurance depends on the type of intensity and the methods used in training. Although other classifications of intensities are used in training, the absolute intensity in endurance training is linked with the energy supply systems. Thus, Zatzyorski (1980) considers the following three intensities: subcritical, critical, and supracritical.

The subcritical intensity has reduced speed, a low energy expenditure, and an O_2 demand below the athlete's aerobic power. The O_2 supply meets the physiological demand; therefore, the athlete performs the work under the steady state condition.

The athlete achieves the critical intensity when the speed increases and the O_2 demand reaches the supply capacity. The athlete performs the critical intensity in the anaerobic threshold zone; thus, the speed is directly proportional to his or her respiratory potential.

Supracritical speed refers to activities that are faster than the critical speed. The athlete performs the work under O_2 demand, which usually increases faster than the performance speed.

Training Parameters for Aerobic Endurance

The physiological threshold of various organs and systems involved in aerobic activity increases and develops more efficiently when training consists of low-intensity, long-duration work. If the activity is continuous, it is a difficult task for an athlete's body to maintain the O_2 consumption so specific for aerobic endurance. Usually, the duration of work under maximum O_2 consumption cannot exceed 10 to 12 minutes, except highly trained athletes (Zatzyorski 1980). Elite-class athletes from sports such as running, cross-country skiing, rowing, swimming, and so on may maintain a velocity close to the critical level for between 1 and 2 hours (heart rate 150-166 beats per minute).

As a general outline, the following training parameters are significant for developing aerobic endurance.

• The intensity of training must be lower than 70% of the maximum velocity (Herberger 1977). As a criterion to follow, you can measure the intensity by the time of performance per a given distance, the velocity in meters per second, or the heart rate (140-164 beats per meter). Training stimuli that do not elevate the heart rate above 130 beats per minute do not significantly increase the aerobic capacity (Zatzyorski 1980).

• The duration of an isolated stimulus (i.e., one repetition) has to be of several varying magnitudes. Sometimes it must be 60 to 90 seconds to improve anaerobic endurance, which is an important component during the beginning of a race. Often, however, athletes use and need long repetitions of 3 to 10 minutes to perfect aerobic endurance. The general composition of a training program depends, however, on the phase of training, the characteristics of the sport, and the needs of the athlete.

• Calculate resting intervals so the following stimulus occurs during the period of favorable changes previous work provoked. According to Reindel, Roskamm, and Gerschler (1962), it has to be between 45 and 90 seconds. For aerobic endurance, however, the rest interval definitely should not exceed 3 or 4 minutes, because during a longer rest the capillaries (the blood vessels that connect the arteries with veins) shrink, and for the first minutes of work, blood flow is restricted (Hollmann 1959). The same author suggests that you can also consider the heart rate method for calculating the rest interval. Usually when the heart rate drops to 120 beats per minute, work can commence.

- Activity during the rest interval is normally a low intensity to stimulate biological recuperation. In athletics, walking or jogging are familiar activities for well-trained athletes.

- Determine the number of repetitions by the athlete's physiological capacity to stabilize O_2 consumption at a high level. If this stabilization does not occur at a sufficiently high level, the aerobic system will be unable to meet the energy demands. Consequently, the anaerobic system takes up the slack, which puts a severe strain on the body and results in fatigue. As suggested by Zatzyorski (1980), the heart rate may be a good indication of the level of fatigue. The heart rate increases as fatigue develops and the athlete performs equally strenuous repetitions. Once more than 180 beats per minute or so, which reflects a high level of fatigue, the heart has less contracting power, resulting in less O_2 to the working muscles. At this point, or shortly before, the athlete should cease training.

Training Parameters for Anaerobic Endurance

Anaerobic endurance represents an important physiological asset for many sports, including team sports. Most of the means for developing anaerobic endurance are cyclic and performed with high intensity. The coach may use the following brief presentation as a general guideline in training.

- The intensity may range from submaximum up to maximum limits. Although you use a variation of intensities in training, for improving anaerobic endurance, intensities around 90 to 95% of maximum ought to prevail.

- The duration of work may be between 5 and 120 seconds, depending on the type of intensity the athlete uses.

- The rest interval following an activity of high intensity must be long enough to replenish the O_2 debt. This may be within 2 to 10 minutes, because the interval of recuperation is a function of the intensity and duration of work. For more efficient recuperation and replenishment of fuel to provide required energy, I advise you to divide the total number of repetitions into a few series of four to six repetitions each. Plan the longest rest interval of 6 to 10 minutes between sets so the accumulated lactic acid will have sufficient time to oxidize. The athlete can then start the new set almost recovered.

- Activity during rest has to be light and relaxing. Total rest (i.e., lying down) is inadvisable, because the excitability of the nervous system may decrease to unacceptable levels (Zatzyorski 1980).

- The number of repetitions must be low to medium, because work for developing anaerobic capacity is intense and cannot have too many repetitions without accumulating lactic acid (LA). If work continues, the glycolytic resources become exhausted, which means that the aerobic system must assume responsibility for providing the required energy. Under this circumstance, the velocity decreases and, consequently, the work will not benefit the anaerobic capacity. It seems that the best method is to divide the planned number of repetitions into several sets, say four sets of four repetitions. The rest interval between repetitions may remain as planned (i.e., 120 seconds), but between sets it has to be long enough (i.e., up to 10 minutes) to replenish the O_2 debt and consequently oxidate LA.

Endurance-Training Programs Based on the Lactic Acid Method

Contemporary training is complex. To direct adequate programs, the coach often needs to discover precisely the internal dosage and how the body responds to training stimuli. The LA (lactic acid) method refers to detecting the quantity of LA present in the blood as a result of training. Although the method is not complicated, it does require the scientific assistance of a physiologist. To put it simply, a blood sample is taken from the ear lobe and analyzed to determine the LA concentration. According to the LA concentration, divide the effort in training into four zones (Marasescu 1980), illustrated in table 12.1.

TABLE 12.1 Four Zones of Effort
Based on the LA Method

Zone no.	Zone	LA composition
1	Compensation	0-23 mg
2	Aerobic	24-36 mg
3	Combined	37-70 mg
4	Anaerobic	71-300 mg

The first zone refers to activities such as jogging for warm-up, compensation activity between repetitions, and light activities at the end of a training lesson. The second zone is the more difficult work of aerobic endurance exercises. The third zone is a typical program combining aerobic and anaerobic programs. The last zone refers strictly to intense, anaerobic activities.

Data interpretation is simple. By comparing the LA concentration to the data in table 12.1, you can make alterations in the program, depending on the type of training required. Often a coach's intention is an aerobic workout, but based on the LA method, the reality may be that the athlete worked harder, performing an activity of the third or fourth zone. As a result, the coach must change the program. The LA method may also illustrate other features of the athlete's training. For instance, the lower the LA concentration is following hard work, the better the athlete's training capacity. On the other hand, the higher the LA concentration following an anaerobic training, the better the athlete mobilized the anaerobic mechanism.

The correct combination of work from the four zones (table 12.1) in training may lead to an objective method of directing a program. Table 12.2 illustrates two combinations that you could use as guidelines for a correct program in a given training phase.

The combination of activities for endurance training, and especially the percentage per combination, represents additional proof of the importance of the aerobic component in any endurance-training program.

TABLE 12.2   Combinations of Activities According to the Objective of Endurance Training

Combination number	Training objective	Type of activity	Percentage
1	Improve endurance	Aerobic combined Anaerobic Compensatory	$\geq 50\%$ $\leq 25\%$ Remaining percent
2	Improve speed	Aerobic combined Anaerobic Compensatory	$\leq 50\%$ $\geq 25\%$ Remaining percent

Methods to Develop Endurance

Throughout all development phases, especially the phase of perfecting endurance, adjustment to the physiological limitation of endurance training is crucial. Physiological limitation (tissue adaptation to work under the conditions of insufficient O_2 or hypoxia, an excess of carbon dioxide) is always accentuated when athletes reach a high state of fatigue. In addition to classical methods of furthering the body's adaptation to a higher endurance demand, which are briefly described here, you may consider other techniques. Breathing at a lower rate than the body and rhythm of performance demand may artificially create a state of hypoxia (i.e., to breathe once at every 3-4 swimming strokes). Training at a medium or high altitude where the partial pressure of O_2 is lower leads to the same result, which is training under the conditions of hypoxia. Many East European athletes do this twice a year for 2 to 4 weeks. Another positive result of using these two techniques is the increase of hemoglobin content in the blood. Hemoglobin is an iron-containing protein pigment present in the red blood cells and functions primarily in transporting O_2 from the lungs to the muscle tissue.

Long-Distance Training Methods

One characteristic of all training methods in this category is that work is not interrupted by rest intervals. The most commonly used methods are as follows: uniform or steady state, the alternative, and the fartlek method.

Uniform Method

The uniform method is characterized by a high volume of work without any interruptions. Although it is used throughout all annual training phases, this method dominates during the preparatory phase. I highly recommend it for sports requiring aerobic endurance, but mostly for cyclic sports with a duration of 60 seconds or more. The duration of one training lesson may be between 1 and 2.5 hours. You can properly calculate the intensity by using the heart rate method, and the rate should be between 150 and 170 beats per minute.

The main training effect is improving and perfecting aerobic capacity. Similarly, the steadiness of performance leads to consolidating technique (i.e., speed skating, swimming, canoeing, rowing), while improving the working efficiencies of the body's functions.

A variant of this method is to progressively increase the speed from moderate to medium intensity throughout a training lesson. For instance, the athlete

Training accentuates the body's adaptation to a higher endurance demand

may perform the first one-third of the training distance at a moderate speed, increasing it to intermediate, and finally to a medium intensity for the last one-third. This is an effective method of developing aerobic endurance because the progressive elevation challenges the athlete both physically and psychologically.

Alternative Method

The alternative method is one of the most effective methods of developing endurance. Throughout the lesson, the athlete changes the performance intensity over a predetermined distance. The intensity of work varies frequently from moderate to submaximum without any interruptions. You can determine the variation of intensities by external factors (terrain profile for running, cross-country skiing, and cycling); internal factors (athlete's will); and planned factors (coach's decision regarding the portion of distance to alter the intensity). Alternate the peak velocity of 1 to 10 minutes with moderate intensity, which will allow the body to recuperate slightly before another increase. For high velocity stimuli, the heart rate may reach values around 180 beats per minute, and the restoration phase may have the rate around 140 beats per minute (Pfeifer 1982), but not much lower than that. The rhythmical, wavelike approach in altering the intensity facilitates a high volume of work, improving the cardiorespiratory and CNS capacity significantly. In addition, this method promotes a flexible adaptation of the body's processes, resulting in a strong development of general endurance. You may apply this method with those

Sprint training adds variety in uniform running training

involved in cyclic sports during the precompetitive and competitive phases, as well as others (team sports, wrestling, boxing) during the preparatory and precompetitive phases.

An excellent variant of this method is to organize the entire training program into sets. Instead of performing uninterrupted work of say 90 minutes, divide it into three sets, with an active rest (i.e., walk) between each set.

Fartlek Method

The fartlek or speed-play method was developed by the Scandinavian and German runners from 1920 to 1930. While performing, the athlete inputs his or her own contribution by alternating uniform training at will with short portions of higher intensity performance. Such sprints are not planned and rely mostly on the athlete's subjective feeling and judgment. The use of the fartlek method is specific mostly, but not entirely, to the preparatory phase, to interject variety into the monotony of uniform training.

Interval Training

Interval training is a highly taxing type of training that we could compare with the extremely strenuous work performed by Sisyphus. According to Greek mythology, Sisyphus was the king of Corinth and well known for his craftiness, when Hades, the god of death, came to get him. Sisyphus tricked Hades and put him in chains. Hades eventually escaped and punished Sisyphus for his trickery. The sentence was that Sisyphus would eternally push a huge stone to the top of a hill. Every time Sisyphus reached the summit the stone would roll back down, forcing him to start his work again and again and again.

Those who want to experience interval training had better remember the work of Sisyphus!

The term interval training does not necessarily refer to a well-known method, but to all methods performed with a rest interval (figure 12.1).

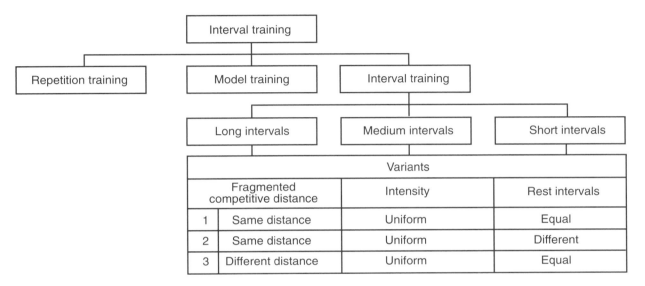

Figure 12.1 Variations of training with a rest interval

Repetition Method

The repetition method of distances longer or shorter than the racing distance, develops specific or racing endurance. Longer repetitions place a strong demand on the aerobic component of racing endurance, because the performance speed is close to the racing speed. On the other hand, shorter repetitions solicit the anaerobic component, because the performer often develops an O_2 debt. Obviously, in the latter case, the intensity is slightly higher than that of a race. An important asset of the repetition method is developing willpower through the demand to perform many repetitions. The total volume of work may be four to eight times that of the racing distance, with a rest interval between 5 and 10 minutes, depending on the repetition distance and intensity.

Model Training

Consider model training a variation of repetition training, because an athlete experiences repeating several training distances. The originality of this method lies in that it resembles the specifics of the race, hence the name model training. The first part of training consists of several repetitions that are much shorter than the racing distance, performed with an intensity close to (slightly higher or lower) racing velocity. Under such conditions, the anaerobic metabolic system provides the energy, as in a race. The midpart of training uses distances and intensities that improve and perfect the aerobic endurance. The last part of training again employs short-distance repetitions to exactly model the race, which resemble and develop the final kick capacity. The athlete performs these repetitions under a certain level of fatigue as in the race and heavily tax the anaerobic endurance, which considering its specifics we may call speed of endurance.

Calculate factors such as total volume of work, velocity, rest intervals, and the number of repetitions according to the individual's potential and the characteristics of the sport. You can use the heart rate method for calculating the rest interval. Considering its specificity, employ this method during the precompetitive and competitive phases.

Interval training, a method that was in fashion in Europe in the 1960s and overrated in North America even in the 1980s and 1990s, is rightly reconsidered for its merits in developing endurance. Most exaggeration about interval training came from the fact that repetitions of short duration were expected to improve everything, including aerobic endurance. Obviously, this was never the case. There is no one method that can do everything for everybody. Only a wise combination of all methods knitted together according to the needs of the athlete and the specifics of the sport may be successful. Interval training as it is best known, with duration of stimuli between 30 and 90 seconds, inadequately develops the aerobic energy production system and the capacity to maintain what development there is throughout the competitive phase.

Interval training refers to the method of repeating stimuli of various intensities with a previously planned rest interval, during which the athlete does not fully regenerate. The coach calculates the duration of the rest interval by the heart rate method. The athlete could repeat the portions of distance either by time (i.e., 12 × 3 minutes) or precise distance (12 × 800 meters). For a more efficient training effect, combine all three interval training methods.

- Short-distance interval training, between 15 seconds and 2 minutes, which mostly develops anaerobic endurance
- Medium-distance interval training, 2 to 8 minutes, which may develop both energy production systems
- Long-distance interval training, 8 to 15 minutes, with a main training effect of aerobic endurance improvement

The main elements of progression are intensity and duration of stimuli, the number of repetitions, rest interval, and activity during rest.

Specific Racing Endurance

You can develop specific endurance by what Pfeifer (1982) calls control or racing method. As the term suggests, using such a method exclusively develops the endurance specific for each event or sport. Calculate the training dosage so it corresponds specifically to physical, psychological, and tactical characteristics of the selected sport (figure 12.2).

Developing endurance is a complex task, because in most sports there are combinations of aerobic and anaerobic components. Consequently, to achieve a complex body adaptation, you must use several of these methods and variants. The physiological effect of a method does not, however, have to be the only criteria for selecting a training method, as there is also the psychological benefit of a method. Apparently from a psychological point of view, training methods developing aerobic endurance (uniform and alternative) are superior to interval training (Pfeifer 1982).

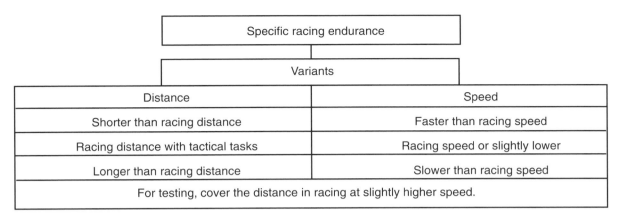

Figure 12.2 Variants of specific racing endurance (modified from Pfeifer 1981)

Training the Energy Systems— Five Intensity Values

In all athletic programs, you must alter the intensity of training throughout a microcycle to enhance the athletes' physiological adaptation to training and regeneration after a demanding training session. Such alternation of intensities depends, however, on the ergogenesis of the event and the characteristics of the training phase.

Concerning the physiological profile of an endurance event, energy demands are supplied by the phosphate system (ATP-CP) in the first 15 to 20 seconds, followed by the lactic acid (LA) system up to 1:30 to 2 minutes. If the event continues for a longer period, then energy demands are supplied by glycogen, which in the presence of O_2 is completely burned without producing lactic acid (figure 12.3).

As most sports use fuel produced by all the energy systems, training has to be more complex, exposing athletes to all energy systems, especially during the last part of the preparatory and the competitive phases.

I propose five intensity values in figure 12.3, to assist coaches in achieving scientific and well-planned training that considers the physiological profile and the energy requirements of a sport. These intensities are listed in order of magnitude of training demand, with number 1 being the most taxing and 5 being the least. For instance, the lactic acid tolerance training (LATT) is the most demanding physiologically and is, therefore, intensity number one (1). At the opposite end of the scale is the phosphate system training (number 4) and aerobic threshold training (number 5), because the body can tolerate them much easier.

The headings of figure 12.3 explain the physiological characteristics of each value, which you should regard as a training method. For instance, to use lactic acid tolerance training, the coach will employ one of the durations, with a set number of repetitions, and a rest interval (RI) sufficient to remove the lactic acid from the system. The coach will also consider the corresponding ratio of work to rest interval, lactic acid concentration in millimoles (mmol), and the heart rate (HR). To reach such physiological characteristics, I suggest that you use the percentages of maximum intensity for the early and late preparatory phases. The latter intensity also refers to the competitive phase. For a better understanding of the five intensities, I explain each method briefly.

Intensity symbol	Training for	Duration of reps	Number of reps	Rest interval	Ratio work/RI	LA conc. (mmol)	Heart rate	% of maximum intensity	
								Early	Late
1	Lactic acid tolerance training (LATT)	30"-60" / 2'-2.5'	2 x 2-4 / 4-6 (8)	10-15' / >5'	1:10-1:15	12-18 Max=20	Near max or max	>85	>95
2	Maximum oxygen consumption training (max VO2)	3'-5'	4-8 (12)	2'-3'	2:1	6-12	180	80-85	85-95
3	Anaerobic threshold training (AnTT)	1:30-7' / 8'-2ʰ	3-5 / 6-2	5' / 5'-45'	1:1 / 1:06-1:15	4-6	150-170	75-85	85-90
4	Phosphate system training (PST)	4-15"	10-30	1-3"	1:4-1:25				95
5	Aerobic threshold training (ATT)	10'-2ʰ	6-1	1-2'	1:1-1:25	2-3	130-150	>60	>60

Figure 12.3 Guidelines for training the five intensities of the energy system (" represents seconds, ' minutes, and ʰ hours)

Lactic Acid Tolerance Training (LATT)

Athletes who can tolerate the pain of acidosis can perform better longer. The scope of LATT therefore is to adapt to the acidic effect of LA; buffer the LA effect; increase lactate removal from the working muscle; and increase tolerance physiologically and psychologically to the hurt, pain, and agony of training and competition. Athletes who adapt and learn to tolerate increases in LA can work more intensely and produce more LA, because it should not be inhibiting. Thus, toward the end of an event, the athlete can produce more energy anaerobically. Athletes can reach maximum limits of LA tolerance in 40 to 50 seconds.

Recovery periods must be long enough to remove LA from the working muscle (15-30 minutes). If this is prevented, acidosis will be so severe that the reduction in energy metabolism will cause speed to drop below the level necessary to increase LA production. Consequently, the athlete will not realize the intended training effect. Work periods of less than one minute require several repetitions, that is four to eight. Longer work periods of 2 to 3 minutes are desirable, but only if the athlete sustains speed at a level high enough to cause excessive LA accumulation (12-16 millimole), thus producing high levels of aerobic power under conditions of extreme acidosis.

Psychologically, the purpose of LATT is to push athletes beyond the pain threshold. There should be caution, however, because overdoing the LATT can lead to undesirable training states, critical levels of fatigue, and ultimately overtraining. For these reasons, LATT should not exceed one or two workouts per week.

Maximum Oxygen Consumption Training (MaxVO₂T)

During training and competition, both parts of the oxygen transport system, central (heart) and peripheral (capillaries at the level of the working muscle), are heavily taxed to supply the required oxygen. Because the supply of O_2 at the working muscle level represents a limiting factor in performance and athletes with large $MaxVO_2$ capacity have demonstrated better performances in endurance events, $MaxVO_2T$ must be an important concern for both coach and athletes.

Increased $MaxVO_2$ results from improved transportation of O_2 by the circulatory system, and increased extraction and use of O_2 by the muscular system. Consequently, you must dedicate a large portion of the training program to developing $MaxVO_2$. This is best served by work periods of 3 to 5 minutes or longer, at 80 to 90% intensity (higher intensity for shorter duration and lower for more repetitions). The HR can be maximum or within 10 beats per minute of maximum.

Athletes can improve $MaxVO_2$ through shorter work periods (30 seconds-2 minutes), provided the rest interval is short as well (10 seconds-1 minute). Under such conditions, training effect will result through the accumulative effect of several repetitions (4-12) that will reach $MaxVO_2$ and not from one or two repetitions, which may primarily solicit the anaerobic system.

The athlete could perform repeated work periods for $MaxVO_2$ and the other methods in straight sets (i.e., 12 × 3 minutes with RI = 1:30 minutes) as well as in sets (i.e., 3 × 4 minutes with RI = 1:30 minutes, with RI between sets = 3 minutes). Because RI between sets is longer, the more extensive restoration allows the athlete to perform more work. Similarly, because intensive (but wise) work is often equated with improvement, coaches should test which method is more productive for their athletes.

Anaerobic Threshold Training (AnTT)

The AnTT refers to the intensity of an exercise at which level the rate of LA diffusion in the blood stream exceeds the rate of its removal (AnTT = 4-6 millimole).

Short, repeated work periods stimulate the anaerobic metabolism, but the level of LA produced in the muscles does not rise significantly above normal levels. The LA diffuses into adjacent resting muscles, thus lowering its concentration level; is metabolized in the working muscle; and is removed from the blood by the heart, liver, and muscles at the rate it is accumulated.

A training program designed to reach the AnTT must produce LA at a rate beyond the ability of these mechanisms to dispose of it. Such a program has to be 60 to 90% of the maximum speed with a HR of 150 to 170 beats per minute. The duration of a work period can vary, but the work to RI ratio should be 1:1.

The AnTT is a trainable factor that you can express as a percentage of $MaxVO_2$. Well-trained athletes can reach the AnTT at 85 to 90% of $MaxVO_2$. (The intent of AnTT training is to elevate the threshold beyond 4 millimole, so the athlete can maintain intensive work without accumulating excessive LA.) During such training programs, the subjective feeling of the athlete should be mild distress, with the speed slightly faster than what is comfortable.

Phosphate System Training (PST)

The intent of PST is to increase an athlete's ability to be fast with less effort. PST should improve the propulsion off the starting blocks and in the early part of the event without using maximum speed. This is possible by applying short work periods of 4 to 15 seconds, with a speed in excess of 95% of maximum.

Such a training program employs the phosphate energy system, and the outcome is an increase in the quantity of ATP-CP stored in the muscle and increased activity of the enzymes that release energy through the ATP-CP reaction.

Long recovery intervals between work periods (work to RI ratio = 1:4-1:25) are necessary to completely replace the muscles' CP supply. If the rest interval is short, the restoration of CP will be incomplete, and as a result anaerobic glycolysis will become the major source of energy rather than the phosphate reaction. This in turn will produce LA that will reduce speed, and the athlete will not realize the desired training effect. PST or sprint training should not, therefore, cause muscle pain, because this is a sign of anaerobic glycolysis.

Aerobic Threshold Training (ATT)

High aerobic capacity is a decisive factor for all events of medium and long duration. Similarly, it is determinant for all sports in which the O_2 supply represents a limiting factor. Using ATT is beneficial for most sports, for a number of reasons. It enhances quick recovery following training and competition; it develops the functional efficiency of the cardiorespiratory and nervous systems; and it enhances the economical functioning of the metabolic system. Finally, it increases the capacity to tolerate stress for long periods.

ATT is performed mostly through a high volume of work without interruption (uniform pace), interval training using repetitions longer than 5 minutes, and the progressive elevation of intensity from moderate to medium-fast speed within one training session.

The duration of an ATT session could be between 1 and 2.5 hours. The athlete achieves the intended training effect only when the LA concentration is between 2 and 3 millimoles, with a HR of 130 to 150 beats per minute (sometimes even higher). Less than these figures and the training effect is questionable. During ATT, the minute volume of blood is 30 to 40 liters, and the O_2 intake approximates 4 to 5.5 liters per minute.

ATT is often the primary training method for the preparatory phase. During the competition phase, you can plan ATT 1 or 2 times per week as a method of maintaining aerobic capacity and as a recovery session to reduce intensity but maintain the general fitness level.

Building the Program

Now that I have illustrated the five intensities of training, the critical question is how to incorporate them within a training program. Traditionally, a coach designs a training program by assigning certain physical, technical, or tactical objectives to certain days of a microcycle. Yet the critical element is training the energy systems, which represent the foundation of good performance. You must do this in cooperation with the technical and tactical elements, based on knowledge of the physiological profile prevailing in an event. When planning a microcycle, the coach should not write down the training content, but the mathematical values of the intensities needed in the cycle. This will suggest the components of the energy systems to emphasize in that training session (figures 12.5-12.9). The distribution per microcycle of the five intensities depends on the phase of training, the athlete's needs, and whether a competition is planned at the end of the cycle. As suggested in figures 12.5 through 12.9, when planning a microcycle the coach should first determine the five values in terms of percentages; then distribute the values per day to meet the decided proportion. Figure 12.4 is a comprehensive, graphic illustration of training the energy systems.

LA conc. (mmol)	Training for	HR	% of max intensity	Training effect	Training benefits
20.00	Maximum aerobic power	200			- High improvement in anaerobic endurance
		200			- Overemphasis may result in overtraining
12.0	Lactic acid tolerance	200	85-90%		
8.0	Max VO$_2$	190-200	80-90%		- Considerable improvement in aerobic endurance
		180			
4.0	Anerobic threshold	170	(60)-70-85%		- Observe intensity for optimal benefit
		160			
		150			
		140			- Improvement in aerobic endurance
2.0	Aerobic threshold	130	60%		
		120	50%		
		110			
		100			- Little improvement in aerobic endurance
1.1	Resting state	>80			

Figure 12.4 Effects of the five intensities on training the energy systems (made by Roaf 1988)

A major training concern for distributing intensity values in a microcycle is the athlete's physiological reaction to training and the level of fatigue a given intensity generates, as the dynamics of supercompensation illustrate (estimated at the bottom of figures 12.5-12.9). An intensity from the top of the intensity scale (figure 12.3), or intensity number 1, will constantly generate higher levels of fatigue, which are illustrated by the magnitude of the depth of supercompensation curve. Such a training session (figure 12.6 on Monday P.M.) is followed, therefore, by two sessions of intensity 5, which facilitate supercompensation by being less demanding. On the other hand, you can plan several training sessions for improving adaptation to LATT in two consecutive days (figure 12.8 Thursday and Friday). Such an approach, which is often necessary in training, results in high levels of fatigue, and supercompensation occurs only following the light training session planned on Saturday A.M. (intensity number 5) and the free weekend.

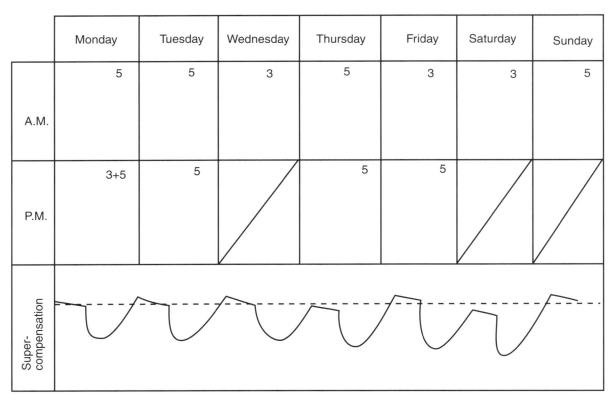

	Monday	Tuesday	Wednesday	Thursday	Friday	Saturday	Sunday
A.M.	5	5	3	5	3	3	5
P.M.	3+5	5		5	5		
Super-compensation							

Figure 12.5 Early preparatory microcycle in which the ratio of the five intensities is
ATT = 75% and AnTT = 25%

	Monday	Tuesday	Wednesday	Thursday	Friday	Saturday	Sunday
A.M.	5	5	3	5	5	1+3+5	3
P.M.	3+5	5		5	5		
Super-compensation							

Figure 12.6 Late preparatory microcycle with ratio of intensities ATT = 50%, AnTT =
25%, MaxVO$_2$T = 20%, LATT = 5%

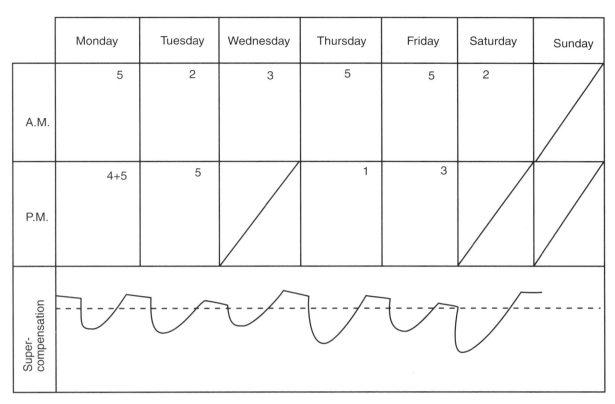

	Monday	Tuesday	Wednesday	Thursday	Friday	Saturday	Sunday
A.M.	5	2	3	5	5	2	
P.M.	4+5	5			1	3	

Figure 12.7 Precompetitive microcycle with ratio of intensities ATT = 40%, AnTT = 20%, MaxVO₂T = 20%, PSP = 10%, LATT = 10%

	Monday	Tuesday	Wednesday	Thursday	Friday	Saturday	Sunday
A.M.	5	3	5	4+5	3	1+5	
P.M.	4+5	4+5+1			2	1	

Figure 12.8 Competitive phase microcycle without competition on weekend with ratio of intensities ATT = 20%, LATT = 20%, MaxVO₂T = 20%, PST = 20%, AnTT = 20%

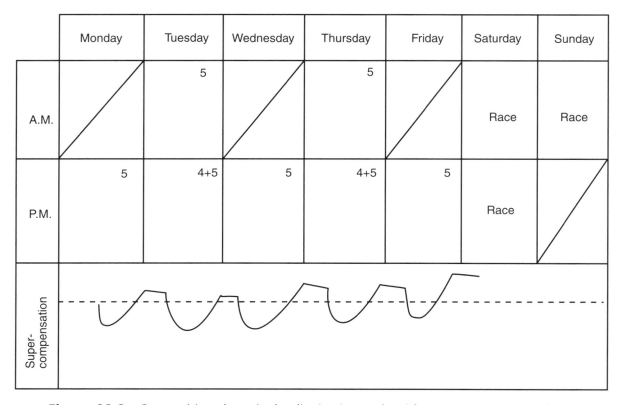

Figure 12.9 Competitive phase (unloading) microcycle with competition on weekend and ratio of intensities ATT = 80%, PST = 20%

Combinations of various intensities in a training session are often a necessity. For instance, a combination between intensities 1 and 5 or 4 and 5 suggests that after working an anaerobic component (i.e., number 1 and 4), which are the most taxing and fatiguing, you can plan a less demanding intensity (i.e., number 5). Such a combination will enhance the development or maintenance of aerobic endurance and will especially facilitate the recovery rate between training sessions.

Physiological adaptation to the profile of an event may result in other possible combinations as well. One such possibility could be 4 + 3 + 1. Such a combination models a race in which the beginning (an aggressive start) relies on the energy produced by the phosphate system (4); the body of the race uses the energy produced by the lactic and oxygen systems (3); and the finish, in which the athlete can tolerate the increased levels of lactic acid (1), makes the difference between winning and losing.

It is necessary to incorporate a scientific basis in the methodology of planning if a coach expects high efficiency from the time invested in planning the training. Applying the five intensities to the training plan incorporates the entire spectrum of energy systems necessary in all endurance-dominant or endurance-related sports, from the phosphate, to the lactic acid, then the aerobic system.

In this method, the coach plans mathematical values, which he or she rations and distributes in a microcycle depending on the ergogenesis of the sport, the phase of training, and the athlete's needs.

To avoid the undesirable effects of overtraining, consider the sequence and frequency of the intensity symbols while strictly adhering to the concept of supercompensation. Under such circumstances, planning becomes more scientific, has a logical sequence, and observes the important training requirement of alternating high- with low-intensity stimuli so fatigue is constantly succeeded by regeneration.

Training the Energy Systems for Aerobic-Dominant Sports

For the aerobic-dominant sports, in which the ergogenesis is more than 50% aerobic, the intensity values and their proportions are different from those in figure 12.3. The phosphate system training, or intensity 4, is therefore irrelevant. The aerobic compensation training is more important for the aerobic-dominant sports, because the scope is to compensate and regenerate between days of demanding training, supporting supercompensation. Figure 12.10 illustrates the five intensity values for aerobic-dominant sports, and figure 12.11 shows how you could plan these intensities during a microcycle.

Intensity number	Characteristics of training	Rhythm of activity	HR/min	% of total volume of training
1	LA tolerance training	Maximun	>180	85-95
2	Max$\dot{V}O_2$ consumption	Very high	170-180	80-90
3	Anaerobic threshold	High	160-170	80
4	O_2 threshold	Medium	150-160	70
5	O_2 compensation	Low	130-150	40-60

Figure 12.10 The five intensity values for endurance-dominant sports

Monday	Tuesday	Wednesday	Thursday	Friday	Saturday	Sunday
$^3/_5$	$^1/_2$ $^4/_5$	5	$^1/_3/_4$	4	$^2/_3/_5$	

Figure 12.11 Microcycle planning for the five intensity values for aerobic-dominant sports

Training the Energy Systems for Junior Athletes

For juniors, or any individuals in their early years of training, reduce the intensity values to three and dominate training by the aerobic threshold training (figure 12.12). Below the chart you will find a guideline for how to use the proportions of the three intensity values per microcycle.

You can examine training the energy systems for team sports in chapter 7, the microcycle.

Intensity number	Training for	Duration	Number of repetitions	Rest interval	LA conc. mmol	Heart rate
1	LA tolerance training	30"-2'	6-8	5-10'	>12	Near or max
2	Anaerobic threshold training	2'-7' >8'-30'	6-4 6-4	5-7' 5-15'	4	160-170
3	Aerobic threshold training	30'-2ʰ	3-1	2'	2-3	~150

Figure 12.12 Training the energy systems for junior athletes. Proportions per week of the three intensities for the preparatory phase (late prep.): intensity #1 = 5%; intensity #2 = 10-15%; and intensity #3 = 80-85%. For the racing season (competitive phase) consider: intensity #1 = 5-10%; intensity #2 = 20%; and intensity #3 = 70-75%.

Summary of Major Concepts

Most sports require a certain degree of endurance, which is proportional to the duration of a competition. In many sports, especially team sports, the importance of endurance and the way it is developed are grossly neglected. Furthermore, athletes perform endurance training by jogging, which is far removed from the specific requirement of the sport.

The best method to improve specific endurance for any sport is to consider the ergogenesis of the sport or the proportions between the anaerobic and aerobic components. Before ergogenesis training, which is most specific for the pre- and competitive phases, a coach should emphasize a phase of aerobic endurance.

Please examine in detail the suggestions regarding training the energy systems. This information and the suggested approach will help you a great deal in organizing your training in general and your specific endurance training in particular.

Often, especially for sports in which endurance is the dominant ability, aerobic training has a compensation role, facilitating recovery while performing a low-intensity activity. Do not miscalculate aerobic compensation training (figure 12.10).

Chapter 13

Speed, Flexibility, and Coordination Training

In addition to the important biomotor abilities of strength and endurance, many athletic skills and performances rely on qualities such as speed, flexibility, and coordination. Understanding the factors that influence speed, flexibility, and coordination helps the coach choose the proper technique for developing these abilities to their fullest potential.

Speed Training

One important biomotor ability required in sports is speed, or the capacity to travel or move quickly. Mechanically, speed is expressed through a ratio between space and time. The term speed incorporates three elements: reaction time, frequency of movement per time unit, and speed of travel over a given distance.

The correlation among these three factors assesses the performance of an exercise requiring speed. Thus, in sprinting, the outcome depends on the athlete's reaction at the start, the speed of travel throughout the body of the race (i.e., force of propulsion), and his or her stride frequency.

Speed is a determinant ability in many sports such as sprinting events, boxing, fencing, team sports, and others. For sports in which it is not a determinant factor, including speed activities in training enhances high-intensity training. Consequently, speed training represents an important concern for almost every sport.

Ozolin (1971) implies that there are two types of speed: general speed and specific speed. General speed is the capacity to perform any kind of movement (motor reaction) in a rapid manner. Both general and specific physical preparation enhance general speed. Specific speed on the other hand, refers to the capacity to perform an exercise or skill at a given speed, which is usually high. Athletes develop special speed, specific for each sport, through specific methods explained briefly in this section. Whatever type of speed you seek, you cannot expect a positive transfer unless the structure of movement, both kinematic and dynamic, is similar to the skill pattern.

A runner does not achieve maximum speed instantly but after accelerating at least 30 meters. The speedogram (graphical representation of speed over a given distance) shows that athletes reach maximum speed after the 40-meter mark, or 5 seconds after the start (Zatzyorski 1980), and can maintain it steadily for up to 80 meters. From that point on it fluctuates due to CNS fatigue and the showing of inhibition (Harre 1982). Athletes improve further only by improving power, speed-endurance, and power-endurance.

Factors Affecting Speed

Many elements influence speed development. Special factors include heredity, reaction time, the athlete's ability to overcome external resistance, technique, concentration and willpower, and muscle elasticity.

Heredity

Compared with strength and endurance, in which athletes may achieve spectacular improvements after adequate training without having extraordinary talents, speed is determined by heredity and requires more natural talent. Hence, the mobility of the nervous processes, the quick alternation between excitation and inhibition, and the capacity to regulate the neuromuscular coordination pattern (de Vries 1980) may lead to a high motor frequency. In addition, the intensity and frequency of the nervous impulses represent determinant factors in achieving high speed.

The property of skeletal muscle represents a limiting factor in speed potential (Dintiman 1971). This reflects the difference in makeup and proportion of slow-twitch fibers (red muscle) and fast-twitch fibers (white muscle), which contain a lower quantity of reddish pigments and look rather pale. The white muscle fibers contract faster than their red counterparts, which is a great asset for a sprinter. According to de Vries (1980), the ultimate maximum speed capacity is limited by the intrinsic speed of the muscle tissue, suggesting that heredity represents an important factor in performing quick movements.

Reaction Time

Reaction time is also inherited. Reaction time represents the time between exposure to a stimulus and the first muscular reaction, or the first movement performed. From a physiological standpoint, reaction time has five components (Zatzyorski 1980):

- The appearance of a stimulus at the receptor level
- The propagation of the stimulus to the CNS
- The transmission of the stimulus through the nervous path and the production of the effector signal
- The transmission of the signal from the CNS to the muscle
- The stimulation of the muscle to perform the mechanical work
  The most time elapses during the third component

Reaction time to both simple and complex or choice situations must be made in sports (Dintiman 1971). Simple reaction is the predetermined conscious response to a previously known signal performed unexpectedly (i.e., the gun in sprinting). Choice or complex reaction time, on the other hand, refers to when an individual receives several stimuli and has to choose between them. Obviously, the latter is the slower, and the time delay increases as the number of choices increases. Reaction time has to be distinguished from reflex time, which is an unconscious response to a stimulus (i.e., the tendon's reflex to an external contact). Similarly, movement time, or the time that elapses between the start and finish of a movement, is important in speed training. Reaction time is a determinant factor in most sports and athletes can improve it with proper training. Zatzyorski (1980) suggests that the reaction time to a visual stimulus is shorter for trained (0.15-0.20 seconds) as opposed to untrained individuals (0.25-0.35 seconds). The reaction time to sonar stimuli is slightly shorter: 0.17 to 0.27 seconds for untrained and 0.05 to 0.07 for international-class athletes.

Ability to Overcome External Resistance

In most sports, power, the force of a muscle contraction or the capacity of an athlete to display force, is one determinant factor in performing fast movements. During training and athletic competitions, external resistance to athletes' quick movements comes from gravity, the apparatus, environment (water, snow, wind), and the opponents. To defeat these opposing forces, athletes have to improve their power, so the increased force of muscular contraction makes them capable of increasing the acceleration of skills.

Often an athlete must perform a skill quickly and repeat it in the same manner for a long time. Consequently, in speed training, athletes must complement the development of power with the development of muscular endurance, which facilitates the display of quick but prolonged work.

Technique

Speed, frequency of a movement, and reaction time are often a function of technique. Acquiring a rational, effective form facilitates the performance of a skill quickly by shortening levers, correctly positioning the center of gravity, and using energy efficiently. In addition, the ability to perform a skill with ease and a high degree of coordination as a result of conscious and reflex relaxation of the antagonistic muscles is also important.

Concentration and Willpower

It seems that a high degree of power facilitates rapid movements. Consequently, the speed of a movement is determined by the mobility and harmonious character of the nervous processes, the frequency of the nervous impulses and their precise manner, and strong concentration. Willpower and strong concentration are important factors in achieving high speed; therefore, incorporating special sessions to solicit the athlete's psychological qualities are imperative in speed training.

Muscle Elasticity

Muscle elasticity and the ability to relax the agonistic and antagonistic muscles alternately are important in achieving a high frequency of movement and correct technique. In addition, joint flexibility is an important ingredient for performing movement with high amplitude (i.e., long strides), which is paramount in any sport requiring fast running. Consequently, including daily flexibility training is imperative, especially for ankles and hips.

Methods to Develop Maximum Speed

There are many methods to develop maximum speed, some more specific than others. However, in any of the following methods, there is a common element: the intensity of stimuli or the elements that excite the mind and the body to further develop maximum speed.

The following five methodological elements are significant to speed training and will aid in understanding the subsequent material.

Intensity of Stimuli

The intensity of stimuli employed in training should lie in the range between submaximum and supermaximum if you expect any improvement. A precondition to such intensity of training, however, is a good technique. The athlete must acquire good skill by employing stimuli of intermediate, medium, and sometimes submaximum intensities. The best training effect results when training stimuli are optimal, which usually occurs when speed training is preceded by only the customary warm-up. Furthermore, speed training is more effective when it follows days of rest or low-intensity training. Similarly, to develop these abilities in the same training lesson, you have to plan them for the end of the lesson.

Duration of Stimuli

The duration of stimuli, like any other component of training, has to be optimized. A minimum duration is the time required to accelerate to maximum speed. If the duration of stimuli is too short and the athlete does not reach maximum speed the only outcome is the improvement of the acceleration phase, but not optimal speed. Both the minimum and maximum duration of stimuli cannot be categorically specified, although for sprinters a suggested range is 5 to 20 seconds. A much longer duration would enhance anaerobic endurance. As in any other training component, the duration of speed-training stimuli is individual and necessitates a knowledge of the athlete's abilities, especially his or her potential to maintain maximum speed. When the athlete cannot maintain maximum speed as a result of fatigue, the exercise should stop.

Volume of Stimuli

Stimuli employed for speed training are among the most intensive that the CNS and neuromuscular system experience; therefore, the optimal volume, though individual differences exist, should be low. The volume of stimuli is a function of intensity and the training phase. Stimuli employed to develop aerobic endurance, present mostly during the preparatory phase, may prevail for up to 90% of the total volume of training, ranging between 10 and 20 times the competition distance per training lesson. Stimuli with maximum and supermaximum intensity may endure for two-thirds up to double the competition distance (Harre 1982), with a total volume of work between 5 and 15 times that of the competition distance.

Frequency of Stimuli

The total amount of energy expended during speed training is low compared with endurance training. The energy expenditure per time unit, however, is much higher than in many other events or sports. This explains why fatigue shows quickly in a speed-training lesson, which suggests that athletes may repeat maximum intensities five or six times per lesson, two to four times per week during the competitive phase (Harre 1982).

Rest Intervals

Between any repetition of training stimuli, the athlete requires a rest interval that ensures almost complete restoration of working capacity; otherwise, high-intensity work may be impossible to repeat. The rest intervals should, therefore, facilitate an optimal recovery, during which LA is reduced and O_2 debt is restored almost entirely. Lactic acid, which plays a restrictive role in speed training, reaches a maximum level between 2 and 3 minutes following the stimulus. On the other hand, the interval should not be so long that the CNS's excitability level fades away (Harre 1982). Consequently, considering individual characteristics, the rest interval between intensive stimuli may be around 4 to 6 minutes. If you use longer intervals, say 12 minutes, I recommend a short warm-up to elevate the CNS excitability level. Should the coach employ sets of short-distance repetitions, then following each set, a longer rest interval of 6 to 10 minutes is desirable.

   During normal intervals of 2 to 6 minutes, I advise an active rest such as light jogging or walking, and for intervals that exceed 6 minutes, I suggest a combination of passive and active rest.

Methods to Develop Reaction Time

The athlete may develop of simple reaction time by employing the following methods (Zatzyorski 1980).

Repeated Reaction

Repeated reaction is based on the arousal of an individual following a stimulus, either at the instant of a signal (visual or sonar) or altering the conditions of performing a skill. Some examples include repeated starts at varied time lapses between the get set and starting signal; changing the direction of travel at the coach's signal; anticipating and reacting differently to known skills or movements of opponents.

Analytic Method

The analytic method refers to performing parts of a skill or technical element under easier conditions, which facilitates the reaction to a signal or the movement speed. For instance, an athlete reacts faster to a starting signal if he or she elevates the hands slightly more than the feet. In this way, the athlete's body weight is not equally distributed; therefore, he or she may react faster with the arms than under standard conditions.

Sensomotor Method

The sensomotor method (Gellerstein 1980) refers to the liaison between reaction time and the ability to distinguish small time lapses, or microintervals of 10th of a second. It is assumed that those who can perceive the time difference between various repetitions have a good reaction time. Athletes ought to perform such exercises in three phases:

- Phase 1. At the coach's signal, the athlete performs starts with maximum speed over a short distance, say 5 meters. After each repetition, the coach tells the athlete the performance time.
- Phase 2. As above, but now the athlete has to estimate the performance time before the coach tells the exact time. In this way, the athlete learns the perception of his or her reaction time and speed.
- Phase 3. At this time, the athlete performs starts in times previously decided. As a result, the athlete learns to direct his or her reaction time.

Improving reaction time depends on the athlete's concentration and where he or she focuses attention. If the concentration is directed toward the movement to perform rather than on the starting signal, then the athlete's reaction time is shorter. The reaction time is also shorter if for a few 10ths of a second before the start the muscles are isometrically tense (i.e., press the feet against the starting blocks). Finally, reaction time depends on the time lapse before the starting signal. Zatzyorski (1980) suggests that optimal time between the get set and the start itself is 1.5 seconds.

The athlete develops complex (choice) reaction by fostering two abilities: reaction to a moving object and selective reaction.

Reaction to a Moving Object

Reaction to a moving object is typical for team sports and those involving two opponents. For instance, when a teammate passes the ball, the receiver has to see the ball, perceive its direction and speed, select his or her plan of action, and perform it. These four elements comprise the hidden reaction, which takes between 0.25 and 1.0 second (Zatzyorski 1980). The first element requires the longest time, especially if the player receives the object unexpectedly. The sensory time, the time necessary to perform the other three elements, is much shorter, 0.05 seconds. Consequently, during training the coach should stress mostly the first element, the ability to visualize the moving object. Various exercises that include sending the ball or action in boxing, fencing, and so on toward a player from unexpected positions and directions, or at unexpected speeds, enhance the reaction to moving objects. Also, using various games or playing in areas smaller than standard improves the reaction to a moving object.

Selective Reaction

Selective reaction is selecting an appropriate motor response from a set of possible responses to the actions of partners or opponents, or even to a quick alteration of the performing environment. For instance, a boxer takes a defense stance and chooses the best reaction to respond to his or her opponent's actions. Similarly, a downhill skier selects the optimal posture according to the slope and snow.

The athlete ought to develop selective reaction progressively. For instance, in boxing or wrestling the athlete first learns a standard reaction to a given technical element. As this skill is automized, the athlete then learns a second variation of this standard reaction. Now the athlete has to select which of the two variations is more efficient at a given time. At a later phase, the coach adds new elements until the athlete knows all the defense and counteroffense skills appropriate for a given action, and must select the most appropriate and effective one under various conditions. Zatzyorski (1980) implies that top-class athletes react with the same speed for simple and complex reactions. He suggests that each movement has two phases. First, isometric, or the phase when the muscle tone is high, equally distributed in the muscle, and ready to act; and second, the isotonic phase, when actual movement or reaction occurs. Often, top-class athletes have such a good reaction that they react even before opponents execute the second phase.

Methods to Develop Speed

Many methods are available to develop speed. The following methods are the most effective.

Repetition

Repetition is the basic method used in speed training. It refers to repeating a set distance several times at a given speed. Although the result sought is improving speed, this method may also lead to improving a skill or technical element, because a movement can become a dynamic stereotype only through repetition. The repetition method compensates for the fact that an athlete cannot maintain maximum speed for a long time. It serves a paramount role because performance improvement does not result from a single performance of the competitive distance. Several repetitions are necessary to achieve speed improvement, consistency of speed over a given distance, and superior training effects.

During repetition training the athlete's psyche, will, and maximum concentration are of paramount importance. What should dominate the athlete is a will to surpass his or her maximum speed by overcoming the limiting factors. The need to relax is of secondary importance, because relaxation is a normal training outcome. Ozolin (1971) claims that the athlete should direct thoughts, will, and concentration toward performing a repetition at maximum speed, because such psychological and mental preoccupation assists the athlete in reaching superior speed and neuromuscular coordination. Also, the athlete ought to direct concentration at performing a dominant movement rapidly, which will also result in accelerating the performance of associated movements. For instance, while sprinting an athlete should concentrate on accelerating the arm movement, which, based on coordination between them and the legs, will result in faster leg movement. Finally, an athlete must direct concentration toward accomplishing a specific task, such as covering a distance in a given time. This method is applicable for speed as well as for power training (i.e., reach an object placed at an optimal height with legs or arms).

The athlete can perform repetition training with maximum speed under standard conditions (i.e., flat ground) in two ways. The progressive method, in which the speed increases progressively until reaching maximum. This is advisable for beginning athletes or for sports that develop speed through technical and tactical skills. The athlete performs repetitions with maximum speed throughout the training lesson. This method is usually restricted to advanced athletes and those whose techniques are very good. Two variants of repetition training exist.

The first is repetitions performed with maximum speed under decreased resistance. This method applies to various sports, and the athletes perform it by reducing the external resistance. They can do this by using lighter implements in athletics, shortening the oar's leverage in rowing, reducing the surface of the blade in rowing and the paddle in canoeing, and so on. Similarly, athletes use external forces to achieve a superior speed, for instance run, cycle, row, or paddle with the wind blowing from behind, or cycle behind a motorcycle.

The second is repetitions with maximum speed under conditions of increased resistance. By employing this method, athletes achieve speed development indirectly. Thus, the speed of performing an exercise is superior if before it, for a short time, the athlete does weight training (Florescu et al. 1969) or performs against a resistance. To create resistance, athletes can swim, skate, or run while being held back by an anchored rubber cord; row or swim with a collar around the boat or swimmer's waist; ski or skate wearing a heavy vest.

Alternative Method

The alternative method refers to a rhythmically alternating movements (repetitions) with high and low intensities. The athlete adds and reduces speed progressively, while maintaining the phase of maximum speed. Such a method leads to increasing the speed and to performing with ease and relaxation.

Handicap Method

The handicap method allows athletes with different abilities to work together, provided that all have equal motivation. When a repetition is performed, each individual is placed (either ahead or back depending on his or her speed potential), so that all should reach the finish line, or the end of the acceleration phase, at the same time.

Relays and Games

Considering their emotional feature, you can use relays and games extensively to improve speed, especially for beginners or top athletes during the preparatory phase. One advantage is that this method will likely eliminate excessive strain and provide enjoyment and fun.

Speed Barrier

After applying standard methods, speed development reaches a certain ceiling, which Ozolin (1971) calls the speed barrier. By employing the same training methods with few variations and little excitement, the athlete reaches a level at which everything is monotonous, and as a consequence, he or she no longer improves speed. To break the speed barrier, the athlete requires new stimuli. New excitement has to break the monotony of training and the use of standard methods. Novelty in training represents stronger and more exciting stimuli, which will result in corresponding physical and psychological alterations.

Among the most efficient methods to surpass the speed barrier are those athletes perform under decreased resistance, in which the external resistance is reduced. Thus, inclined running, or running with the wind blowing from behind gives the athlete a new sense of speed that will lead to further improvements. Under these new conditions, the CNS, the neuromuscular coordination, will readapt to the new requirements of performing an exercise. The multiple

Novel training methods present more exciting stimuli

repetitions of new stimuli will create new and more rapid adaptations, resulting in an elevation of the speed ceiling. Decreased resistance methods have been used extensively by Soviet sprinters. The inclined track (2-3 degrees) seems to increase the athlete's speed by 17% over the descending portion and by 13% when the athlete entered the horizontal section (Obbarius 1971).

Using decreased resistance methods should, however, facilitate accelerations that the athlete could reproduce under normal competitive conditions. Further, you must restrict these methods to advanced athletes whose skills are firmly automized and who, as a consequence, can handle suprarapid accelerations.

Flexibility Training

The capacity to perform movement over a broad range is known as flexibility, or often mobility, and is significant in training. It is a prerequisite to performing skills with high amplitude and increases the ease with which the athlete can perform fast movements. The success of performing such movements depends on the joint amplitude, or range of motion, which has to be higher than that required by the movement. Thus, there is a need for a flexibility reserve, which the athlete must develop to be on the safe side.

An inadequate development of flexibility, or no flexibility reserve, may lead to various deficiencies, suggested by Pechtl (1982) as being the following:

- Learning or perfecting various movements is impaired.
- The athlete is injury prone.

- The development of strength, speed, and coordination are adversely affected.
- The qualitative performance of a movement is limited. (When an individual has a flexibility reserve, he or she can perform skills more rapidly, energetically, easily, and expressively.)

Factors Affecting Flexibility

Flexibility is affected by the form, type, and structure of a joint. Ligaments and tendons also affect flexibility; the more elastic they are, the higher the amplitude of a movement.

The muscles that pass or are adjacent to a joint influence flexibility. In any movement, the contraction of a muscle that acts actively (agonists) is paralleled by the relaxation or stretching of the antagonist muscles. The easier the antagonistic muscles yield, the less energy you spend to defeat their resistance. The capacity of a muscle fiber to stretch increases as a result of flexibility training. Flexibility is often limited regardless of the amount of training invested if the antagonistic muscles are not relaxed, or if there is a lack of coordination between contraction (agonists) and relaxation (antagonists). It is not surprising, therefore, that individuals with poor coordination, or an inability to relax the antagonistic muscles, may have a low rate of flexibility development.

Age and sex affect flexibility to the extent that younger individuals, and girls as opposed to boys, seem to be more flexible. Individuals reach maximum flexibility at 15 or 16 years of age (Mitra and Mogos 1980).

Both general body temperature and specific muscle temperature influence the amplitude of a movement. Wear (1963) found that flexibility increases by 20% following a local warm-up to 115° Fahrenheit (40° Celsius) and decreases by 10 to 20% by cooling the muscle to 65° Fahrenheit (18° Celsius). Similarly, a movement's amplitude increases following a normal warm-up because progressive physical activity intensifies blood irrigation of a muscle, making its fibers more elastic. Consequently, performing stretching exercises before warming up, which seems to be an accepted theory by many North American athletes, is undesirable to say the least. As indicated by the sequence of exercises to follow during warm-up (refer to chapter 6 on training lesson), flexibility exercises come after various types of easy jogging and calisthenics. By the time the athlete performs flexibility movements, the muscle temperature has increased, thus facilitating the muscle fibers to stretch without causing harm. Zatzyorski (1980) investigated the effects on flexibility of no warm-up, warm-up via physical exertion for 20 minutes, and warm-up via hot bath at 40° Celsius for 10 minutes. The results were as expected. The highest degree of flexibility was achieved following normal warm-up and was 21% greater than that resulting from the hot bath and 89% higher than that resulting from no warm-up.

Flexibility varies accordance to the time of day. The highest amplitude of movement seems to be between 10:00 A.M. and 11:00 A.M., and 4:00 P.M. and 5:00 P.M., and the lowest likely occurs earlier in the morning (figure 13.1). The explanation lies with the continuous biological changes (CNS and muscle tone) that occur during the day (Ozolin 1971).

A lack of adequate muscle strength inhibits the amplitude of various exercises (Pechtl 1982). Strength, therefore, is an important component of flexibility, and the coach should regard it properly. There are coaches and athletes, however, who think that strength gains limit flexibility or that substantial flexibility gains have a negative influence upon strength. Such theories are based

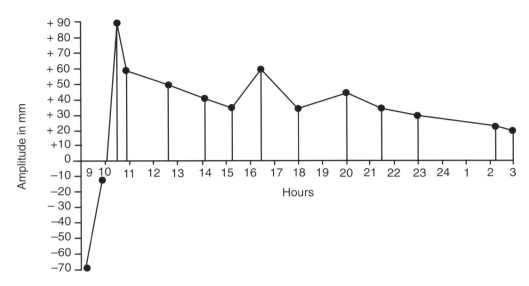

Figure 13.1 Range of movement varies with the time of day (from Ozolin 1971)

on the fact that the increase in muscle size decreases the joints' flexibility. The capacity of a muscle to stretch cannot, however, affect its ability to perform strength movements.

Strength and flexibility are compatible because the first depends on the cross section of the muscle, and the latter depends on how far a muscle can stretch. These are two different mechanisms and, therefore, do not eliminate each other. Gymnasts who are both strong and flexible are proof of this concept. Remember, however, that an incorrect methodology of developing strength or flexibility may lead to questionable results. Consequently, to avoid any surprise, strength training has to be concurrent with flexibility training.

Fatigue and the emotional state affect flexibility performance significantly. A positive emotional state has positive influence on flexibility compared with depressive feelings. Similarly, flexibility is affected by fatigue (Mitra and Mogos 1980), be it a general state of exhaustion or fatigue accumulated toward the end of a training lesson.

Methods to Develop Flexibility

Use one of the following three groups of methods to develop flexibility.

- The active method, comprised of a static method and a ballistic method
- The passive method
- The combined method, or proprioceptive neuromuscular facilitation (PNF) developed by Kabat in 1958

Before briefly exploring each method, it is important to mention that some contradiction exists regarding which method is most efficient. Many coaches and athletes prefer the static method, fearing that the ballistic method may lead to muscle pull. Although PNF has some limitations in its application, that is, it is applicable only to the hip and shoulder joints, coaches often prefer this method. Several authors (Zatzyorski 1980; Mitra and Mogos 1980; Pechtl 1982) however, viewed both the active and the passive methods as equally effective. Similarly, comparative studies (Norman

Age and gender affect flexibility. Young girls seem to be the most flexible.

1973) among the three groups of methods concluded that there is no difference between their effectiveness.

Active Method

The active method is a technique whereby an individual achieves maximum flexibility of a joint exclusively through muscular activation. This method refers to the extent to which the agonistic muscles flex, as well as the relaxation and yielding to such a force by the antagonistic muscles. When using the static method, the athlete flexes two segments of a limb to the utmost point of flexibility and holds the position for 6 to 12 seconds. The athlete performs the ballistic method through active swings of one segment of a limb that is mobile, against another limb that is still.

Passive Method

The passive method achieves maximum flexibility through the assistance of a partner or by employing a weight. In the first case, a partner holds or presses a limb toward its maximum point of flexibility without the subject's active involvement. This method is applicable for the following joints: ankle, hip, vertebral column, shoulder, and wrist. I recommend using weights (barbells, dumbbells) for improving ankle, knee, and shoulder flexibility. I do not suggest this for the hips or vertebral column, because the weight may exceed the athlete's pain tolerance or may press two segments of a joint to bend beyond their limits, resulting in eventual muscle pulls. In any case, the weight has to be low, carefully applied, and progressively increased. Always do such training under close supervision.

Combined Method

The combined method (PNF) requires the athlete to actively flex the limb to the joint's limit, then execute a maximum isometric contraction against the resistance of a partner. The athlete then lifts the limb voluntarily to a more acute angle beyond previous limits. Once again, the athlete performs the same routine, a strong isometric contraction against the resistance provided by a partner. The athlete may perform the isometric contraction for 4 to 6 seconds, with as many repetitions as he or she can physically tolerate and that are methodologically necessary.

Methodology of Developing Flexibility

The area of training methodology refers to two types of flexibility, general and specific. General flexibility refers to the idea that each athlete has to have a good mobility of all bodily joints, irrespective of specific requirements of a sport or event. Such flexibility is a requirement in training, and it assists the athlete in training tasks and performing substantial unspecific exercises or elements from related sports. On the other hand, specific flexibility implies the quality that is sport or joint specific (i.e., specific flexibility of a hurdler differs drastically from that of a butterfly swimmer).

Because developing flexibility is easier at a young age, it has to be part of the training program of each young athlete irrespective of sport specialization. If the athlete achieves a desired degree of flexibility, it does not mean that you should neglect flexibility training. On the contrary, from this point on, flexibility programs must maintain the achieved level.

Incorporate flexibility exercises in the warm-up part of a training lesson. As already indicated, precede flexibility exercises by a general warm-up (jogging and calisthenics) of at least 10 minutes. Relate the selection of exercises and their complexity and difficulty to the athlete's preparation level and the specifics of the sport. The athlete must perform each selected exercise in 3 to 6 sets of 1 to 15 repetitions (or up to a maximum of 60-90 repetitions per lesson). During the rest interval, consider relaxation exercises (shake the group of muscles that have performed or execute a light and short massage). Increase the amplitude of an exercise progressively and carefully throughout the performance. At first, the athlete performs exercises with an amplitude that is not challenging, then progressively increases up to the limits. From this point on, each repetition should aim to reach this superior limit and further it.

For the ballistic method, there is a high variety of exercises, flexions, extensions, and swinging. As suggested by Bompa, Bompa, and Zivic (1981), an athlete can achieve flexibility by employing free exercises, medicine balls, stall bars, and benches. Using medicine balls (i.e., flex the hips while holding the ball with arms extended) increases the leverage of a limb. It also accentuates the momentum, which results in more effective development of flexibility.

For both the static and PNF methods, the athlete tries to position the joints to enhance the sought flexibility. Then the performer statically maintains the position for 6 to 12 seconds (6-10 sets), for a maximum total of 100 to 120 seconds per training lesson for the chosen joints. The athlete can build up such time requirement progressively over 10 to 18 months. Throughout the performance of static flexibility, the performer should relax the antagonistic muscles so they will yield to the pull of the agonists, thus reaching a more acute angle between two limbs.

For the periodization of flexibility, you must achieve most of it during the preparatory phase. Regard the competitive phase as a maintenance period, when the athlete directs the energy and strain on muscle groups toward specific training. In either case, however, flexibility has to be part of an everyday training program and the athlete should perform it toward the end of the warm-up. Athletes attained best results when they trained flexibility twice a day (Ozolin 1971). Even athletes performing four to six training lessons per week still may develop flexibility during early morning training, thus ensuring an adequate flexibility.

Coordination Training

Coordination is a complex biomotor ability, closely interrelated with speed, strength, endurance, and flexibility. It is of determinant importance for acquiring and perfecting technique and tactics, as well as for applying them in unfamiliar circumstances. Such circumstances can include the alteration of terrain, equipment and apparatus, light, climate and meteorological conditions, and opponents. Coordination is also solicited in space orientation, either when the body is in unfamiliar conditions (vaulting, various jumps, trampolining) or when there is a loss of balance (slippery conditions, landing, quick stops, contact sports).

The level of coordination reflects an ability to perform movements of various degrees of difficulty quickly, with great precision and efficiency, and according to specific training objectives. It is considered that an athlete with good coordination is capable of performing a skill perfectly, as well as rapidly solving a training task to which he or she is unexpectedly exposed.

The physiological basis of coordination lies in the coordination of the nervous processes of the CNS. A human body is a unitary whole composed of various organs, systems, and functions. The complexity of the functions of the organs and systems is constantly regulated and coordinated by the CNS. One main CNS function is selecting and executing a fast and accurate response to a stimulus through the efferent (away from nervous center) nervous path to certain effectors (Mitra and Mogos 1980).

Athletes' movements, whether voluntary or reflex, simple or complex, are the result of muscular contractions, which may act to facilitate the movement (the agonists) or inhibit it (the antagonistic muscles). More complex movements that the athlete has not yet automized are limited by certain factors, especially an uncoordinated excitation, which might affect the ratio of agonist and antagonist involvement, resulting in uncontrolled and poorly coordinated movements. Regulating the motor activity implies differentiating and reacting to a stimulus with high precision and quickness. As a result of many repetitions of a skill or technical element, the fundamental nervous processes of excitation and inhibition become properly coordinated, which results in stable, well-coordinated, efficient, and fine motor skills.

Classifying Coordination and Its Complexity

Coordination, a very complex human quality, is influenced by several factors. In your quest for maximum skill improvements, consider the following guidelines.

General Coordination

General coordination governs the capacity to rationally perform various motor skills, irrespective of sport specialization. Every athlete following a multilateral development should acquire an adequate general coordination. Multilateral development must commence with the initiation into a sport, because by the time of specialization, general coordination has to be well assimilated. Under such circumstances, general coordination represents the basis from which an athlete can develop specific coordination.

Specific Coordination

Specific coordination reflects the ability to perform various movements in the selected sport quickly, but also flawlessly, with ease and precision. Thus, specific coordination is closely linked to the specificity of motor skills and equips the athlete with additional abilities to use in performing efficiently in training and competition. Specific coordination is achieved as a result of performing many repetitions of specialized skills and technical elements throughout an athletic career. Consequently, a gymnast may be extremely coordinated in his or her sport but uncoordinated in basketball.

Specific coordination incorporates developing coordination with other biomotor abilities, according to the characteristics of the selected sport. An athlete has coordination of speed, as in slalom skiing, freestyle swimming, or hurdling, when he or she can perform a skill fast, subject to a specific rhythm and tempo. Coordination of speed depends on three main factors (Mitra and Mogos 1980).

- The time necessary to acquire a complex skill with the specific and required precision and tempo (rate of speed or rhythm).
- The time necessary to react to a signal or an opponent's actions. (Because such coordination is closely linked to reaction and movement time, its development or a high innate ability is essential to performance.)
- The time required to adapt or adjust individual skills or movements to newly created situations or impeding actions. The degree of precision attained during quick changes occurring throughout a competition (i.e., team sports, alpine skiing) and the elapsed time between the signal or an opponent's action and an athlete's reaction are often determinant to the outcome. An athlete requires a high degree of coordination of speed to respond rapidly and correctly to a challenge.

Sports requiring strength necessarily require developing coordination of strength, as exhibited by the performance of wrestlers, weightlifters, hammer throwers, and gymnasts. In such sports, the precision, ease, and rapidity of a movement or skill requires high coordination, strength, and power. A less coordinated athlete usually performs with exaggerated strain, rigidity, and wasted energy. Finally, coordination of endurance implies the ability to perform highly coordinated skills over extended periods, as in team sports, boxing, and judo. Endurance is an essential component for this type of coordination, because a lack of it elevates fatigue, which in turn affects some of the CNS functions, including coordination.

A skill has various degrees of complexity according to its pattern, performance over time, and orientation in space. Zatzyorski (1980) proposed the following criteria to qualify coordination.

- Degree of difficulty. A skill or movement may be easy or difficult. Basically, cyclic skills are less complex and thus easier to acquire than acyclic skills. Those learning an acyclic skill may, therefore, claim to participate in more difficult tasks.
- Precision of performance. An athlete can perform a movement with a high degree of precision when it matches the challenge of a motor task in time, angles, and dynamics. Usually, a skill performed with high precision is

biomechanically sound and physiologically efficient. In other words, it is economical.

- Duration of acquisition. The complexity of a skill relates to the time required to acquire it. A well-coordinated individual acquires a skill much faster than someone with inferior ability. Similarly, in sports characterized by rapid alternation of rhythm, situations, or performance requirements and a high variety of skills (i.e., team sports, boxing, wrestling), the time the athlete needs to solve a technical or tactical problem (opponent action to individual reaction) determines the technical result. Under such circumstances, the athlete must have a high degree of specific coordination and adaptability.

Factors Affecting Coordination

Before discussing methods that would lead to developing coordination, it is important to outline factors that limit it, because their improvement will also improve coordination. One or more of the following factors may limit coordination.

Athletic Intelligence

An outstanding athlete impresses not only with amazing and superior skills or tremendous biomotor abilities, but also with his or her thoughts and ways of solving complex and unforeseen motor or tactical problems. This is not possible without specialized thinking based on years of training and experience. In many sports, skillfulness and cleverness are the results of precise and quick thinking. A determining factor is the ability to analyze, to select multiple information collected by motor, visual, and sensory analyzers. Following a quick analysis (separation of the information received by the CNS into elements), the athlete retains significant information and synthesizes it to produce the optimal reply. Through excellent coordination of contraction and relaxation, the muscle chains are selected and ordered to perform according to the specific time and situation of performance. The quickness of implementing the selected action often may ensure the superiority of an athlete or team over others. On the other hand, the suppleness of thinking is the result of the balance between the fundamental nervous processes (excitation and inhibition) and the rapidity originating from the power of those processes.

Finesse and Precision of the Senses

Finesse and precision of the sensory organs, especially the motor analyzers and kinesthetic sensors (the sensors of movements), as well as balance and the rhythm of muscular contraction represent important factors (Mitra and Mogos 1980). Kinesthesia improves through systematic training, resulting in an ability to perform more coordinated, precise, efficient, and quick skills.

Motor Experience

Motor experience, as reflected by a high variety of skills, constitutes a determining factor in coordination ability or the ability to learn quickly. The athlete develops and perfects coordination through a long process of learning varied skills and technical elements. Such a process, during which the athlete is continually exposed to new situations and environments, enriches motor experience and facilitates a fine coordination.

Developing Other Biomotor Abilities

The development level of other biomotor abilities, such as speed, strength, endurance, and flexibility, impact coordination because there is such a close relationship among them. A poor ability in one area represents a limiting factor on perfecting coordination.

Methods to Develop Coordination

There are not too many specific methods for developing coordination compared with other biomotor abilities, as coordination is a natural, inherited ability. For individuals not gifted with good coordination and who acquire complex skills slowly, it is erroneous to expect tremendous improvements as a result of applying the techniques in table 13.1.

A successful program for developing coordination should rely heavily on acquiring of a high variety of skills. Consequently, all the young athletes

TABLE 13.1   Methods for Developing Coordination

Method	Example of exercises
Unusual starting position of an exercise.	Various jumping exercises (long or deep jumps) sideways or backward.
Perform skills with the opposite limb or in an unusual position.	Throw the discus or put the shot with the opposite arm. Kick or dribble the ball with the opposite arm or leg. Box in a reverse guard.
Alter the speed or tempo/rhythm of performing a movement.	Increase the tempo progressively. Variations of tempo.
Restrict or limit the space for performing skills.	Decrease playing space in team sports.
Change technical elements or skills.	Employ unfamiliar long-jumping techniques (i.e., hitch kick). Perform the most comfortable jumping technique over apparatus or obstacles using the normal takeoff leg and the other leg.
Increase the difficulty of exercises through supplementary movements.	Various shuttle runs and relays using diversified apparatus, objects, and tasks to achieve.
Combine known with newly formed skills.	Parts or routines in gymnastics and figure skating. Play the game having the task of using a newly learned skill.
Increase the opposition or resistance of a partner.	Use varied tactical schemes against a team employing an additional player. Play or fight (wrestle) against various teams (partner) during the same match.
Create unusual performance conditions.	Variations of terrain (hilly) for running or cross-country skiing. Row or swim in wavy water. Perform skills with heavy vests. Play on various fields (asphalt, grass, synthetic, wood).
Perform related or unrelated sports.	Various games or plays. Technical elements or skills of various sports.

involved in a sport specialization should experience skills of other sports, which would ultimately improve coordination. Pechtl (1982) implies that all athletes should continually learn new skills from their specific or other sports; otherwise, coordination and consequently learning capacity decreases. Throughout phases of improvement in coordination, the coach should try to employ exercises with progressively increased complexity. You may increase the complexity and difficulty of a skill by employing various conditions, apparatus, and sport equipment (table 13.1). Include exercises for coordination in the first part of the training lesson when an athlete is rested and has a high concentration capacity. Finally, athletes acquire coordination most successfully at an early age, when the plasticity (ability to alter and adapt in conformity to the environment) of the nervous system is much higher than in adulthood (Pechtl 1982).

Summary of Major Concepts

It is known that fast athletes are the envy of those who are not blessed with a similar gift. You should not view speed only as linear, straightforward velocity, but also as the ability to quickly change directions and perform fast turns. For team sports, quick changes of direction are as important as linear velocity.

To be able to perform all these elements of speed one has to have strong legs, so I would like to point out an important and practical fact. Nobody will be fast before they are strong! Strength training must therefore be an important part of any training program for sports that require speed to be developed.

Flexibility is superficially developed in most sports, especially in team sports. Ankle and hip flexibility should be the focus of all athletes, and the majority of sports.

Many people believe that coordination is a hereditary gift. To a very high degree this is true, however coordination, or the lack of it, can be greatly improved, especially if one starts its development from childhood. Again, specificity of training is far from being enough to refine coordination. From childhood on, athletes must be exposed to all kinds of activities and skills, especially by using balls of any type.

Persistent work always pays off; even in the area of coordination training.

Appendix

**Blank Charts for Annual
and Four-Year Plans**

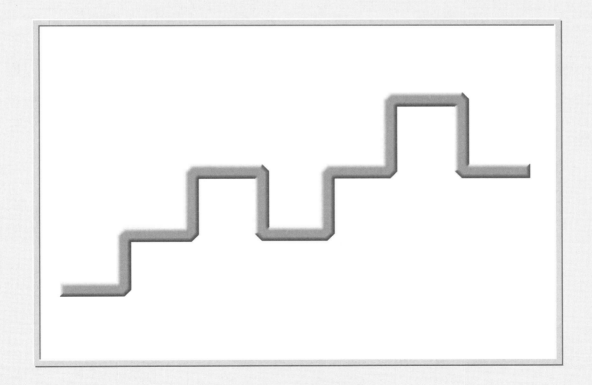

Chart of the Annual Plan

Type: Year: Coach:

Athlete's name(s)

Training objectives

Performance	Tests/standards	Physical prep.	Technical prep.	Tactical prep.	Psychological prep.

Dates
- Months
- Weekends

Calendar of competitions
- Domestic
- International
- Location

Periodization
- Training phase
- Strength
- Speed
- Endurance
- Psychological
- Nutrition
- Macrocycles
- Microcycles

1 2 3 4 5 6 7 8 9 10 11 12 13 14 15 16 17 18 19 20 21 22 23 24 25 26 27 28 29 30 31 32 33 34 35 36 37 38 39 40 41 42 43 44 45 46 47 48 49 50 51 52

Peaking index
Testing dates
Medical control dates
Camp/semicamp

%100
90
80
70
60
50
40
30
20
10

1
2
3
4
5
Peaking

Training factors
- —— Volume
- – – Intensity
- ···· Peaking
- ▮ Phys. prep.
- ▢ Tech. prep.
- ▢ Tact. prep
- ▨ Psych. prep.

Chart of the Annual Plan

Type: _____   Year: _____   Coach: _____

Dates	Months	
	Weekends	
Calendar of competitions	Domestic	
	International	
	Location	
Periodization	Training phase	
	Strength	
	Endurance	
	Speed	
	Psychological	
	Nutrition	
	Macrocycles	
	Microcycles	1 2 3 4 5 6 7 8 9 10 11 12 13 14 15 16 17 18 19 20 21 22 23 24 25 26 27 28 29 30 31 32 33 34 35 36 37 38 39 40 41 42 43 44 45 46 47 48 49 50 51 52
Peaking index		
Testing dates		
Medical control dates		
Camp/semicamp		

Peaking index scale:

%100	1
90	2
80	3
70	4
60	5
50	
40	
30	
20	
10	
	Peaking

Training factors legend:
— Volume
- - Intensity
· · · Peaking
▬ Phys. prep.
▢ Tech. prep.
▢ Tact. prep.
▨ Psych. prep.

Chart of the Annual Plan

Type: Year: Coach:

Athlete's name(s)

Training objectives

Performance	Tests/standards	Physical prep.	Technical prep.	Tactical prep.	Psych. prep.

Dates
- Months
- Weekends

Calendar of competitions
- Domestic
- International
- Location

Periodi-zation
- Training phase
- Strength
- Endurance
- Speed
- Psychological
- Nutrition
- Macrocycles
- Microcycles

Microcycles: 1 2 3 4 5 6 7 8 9 10 11 12 13 14 15 16 17 18 19 20 21 22 23 24 25 26 27 28 29 30 31 32 33 34 35 36 37 38 39 40 41 42 43 44 45 46 47 48 49 50 51 52

Training factors
- Optional exercises
- Skill acquisition
- Routines
- Peaking index
- Testing dates
- Medical control dates
- Camp/semicamp

Peaking index: %100 | 90 | 80 | 70 | 60 | 50 | 40 | 30 | 20 | 10

1 | 2 | 3 | 4 | 5   Peaking

Legend:
- —— Volume
- – – Intensity
- ···· Peaking
- ▮ Phys. prep.
- ▯ Tech. prep.
- ▯ Tact. prep.
- ▨ Psych. prep.

Chart of the Annual Plan

Year: Coach:

Dates	Months
	Weekends
	Domestic
	International
Calendar of competitions	Location
Periodization	Training phase
	Strength
	Endurance
	Speed
	Psychological
	Nutrition
	Macrocycles
	Microcycles

Microcycles numbered: 1 2 3 4 5 6 7 8 9 10 11 12 13 14 15 16 17 18 19 20 21 22 23 24 25 26 27 28 29 30 31 32 33 34 35 36 37 38 39 40 41 42 43 44 45 46 47 48 49 50 51 52

Peaking index
Testing dates
Medical control dates
Camp/semicamp

Training factors

Peaking index scale: 1 2 3 4 5 — Peaking

· · · · Peaking
—— Volume km/wk
– – – Speed % of mx.

389

Chart of the Annual Plan

Year: Coach:

Dates	Months																																																		
	Weekends																																																					
Calendar of competitions	Domestic																																																					
	International																																																					
	Location																																																					
Periodi-zation	Training phase																																																					
	Strength																																																					
	Endurance																																																					
	Speed																																																					
	Psychological																																																					
	Nutrition																																																					
	Macrocycles																																																					
	Microcycles	1	2	3	4	5	6	7	8	9	10	11	12	13	14	15	16	17	18	19	20	21	22	23	24	25	26	27	28	29	30	31	32	33	34	35	36	37	38	39	40	41	42	43	44	45	46	47	48	49	50	51	52
Peaking index																																																						
Testing dates																																																						
Medical control dates																																																						
Camp/semicamp																																																						

Training factors

Peaking
1
2
3
4
5

· · · · · Peaking
———— Volume
– – – Intensity

Training factors

Peaking
1
2
3
4
5

· · · · · Peaking
———— Volume
– – – Intensity

Training factors

Peaking
1
2
3
4
5

· · · · · Peaking
———— Volume
– – – Intensity

Year	Objectives			
	20	20	20	20
Performance				
Physical preparation				
Technical preparation				
Tactical preparation				
Psychological preparation				

Tests & standards

Training factors

	%100
Volume	90
Intensity	80
Peaking	70
Phys. prep.	60
Tech. prep.	50
Tact. prep.	40
Psych. prep.	30
	20
	10

Glossary

actin——A protein involved in muscular contraction.

action potential——The electrical activity a muscle or nerve cell develops during activity or depolarization.

active transport——The movement of substances or materials against their concentration gradients by expending metabolic energy.

acyclic——A skill consisting of constantly changing actions, which are not similar to other actions.

adaptation——Persistent changes in structure of function, particularly in response to increments in training load.

adenosine diphosphate (ADP)——A complex chemical compound, which when combined with inorganic phosphate (Pi) forms ATP.

adenosine triphosphate (ATP)——A complex chemical compound formed with the energy released from food and stored in all cells, particularly muscles.

adipose tissue——Fat tissue.

afferent nerve——A neuron that conveys sensory impulses from a receptor to the central nervous system.

agonistic muscles——Muscles directly engaged in a muscular contraction and working in opposition to the action of other muscles.

all-or-none law——A stimulated muscle or nerve fiber contracts or propagates a nerve impulse either completely or not at all.

alpha motor neuron—A type of efferent nerve that innervates extrafusal muscle fibers.

alveoli (plural), alveolus (singular)—Tiny terminal air sacs in the lungs where gaseous exchange with the blood in the pulmonary capillaries occurs.

amortization phase—The eccentric or yielding phase of an activity. Amortization occurs just before the active or push-off phase of an activity and includes the time from ground to the reverse movement.

anabolic—Protein building.

anaerobic—In the absence of oxygen.

anaerobic glycolysis—The incomplete chemical breakdown of carbohydrate. The anaerobic reactions in this breakdown release energy to manufacture ATP as they produce lactic acid (anaerobic glycolysis is the lactic acid system).

anaerobic threshold—That intensity of workload or oxygen consumption in which anaerobic metabolism accelerates.

androgen—Any substance that possesses masculinizing properties.

antagonistic muscles—Muscles that have an opposite effect on movers, or agonist muscles, by opposing their contraction.

ATP-PC system—An anaerobic energy system in which ATP is manufactured when phosphocreatine (PC) is broken down.

axon—A nerve fiber.

back extensor—Muscles involved in straightening the back.

ballistic—Dynamic muscular movements.

barbell—A bar to which you attach varying weights and usually hold with both hands.

biceps brachii—Elbow flexor of the upper arm.

bilateral exercise—Using both arms or legs at the same time to perform an exercise.

biomotor abilities—The capacity to perform a range of activities, such as strength, speed, and endurance. They are influenced by training and may be genetically determined.

bodybuilding—A sport in which muscle size, definition, and symmetry determine the winner.

bapillary—A fine network of small vessels located between arteries and veins where exchanges between tissue and blood occur.

carbohydrate—Any group of chemical compounds, including sugars, starches, and cellulose, containing only carbon, hydrogen, and oxygen; one of the basic foodstuffs.

cardiac output—The amount of blood the heart pumps in one minute.

cardiorespiratory endurance—The ability of the lungs and the heart to take in and transport adequate amounts of oxygen to the working muscles, allowing athletes to perform activities that involve large muscle masses (e.g., running, swimming, bicycling) over long periods.

central nervous system—The spinal cord and brain.

concentric contraction—The shortening of a muscle during contraction.

conditioning—Augmentation of the energy capacity of muscle through an exercise program. Conditioning is not primarily concerned with performance skill as would be the case in training.

cross bridges—Extension of myosin.

cyclic—A skill comprised of motions that are repeated continuously.

density—The mass per unit volume of an object.

detraining—Reversing adaptation to exercise. Effects of detraining occur more rapidly than training gains when there is significant reduction of work.

dumbbell—Small weight of fixed resistance, usually held with one hand.

eccentric contraction—The muscle lengthens while contracting (developing tension).

efferent nerve—A neuron that conveys motor impulses away from the central nervous system to an organ of response, such as skeletal muscle.

electrical potential—The capacity for producing electrical effects, such as an electric current, between two bodies (e.g., between the inside and outside of a cell).

endomysium—A connective tissue surrounding a muscle fiber or cell.

endurance—The capacity to perform work for an extended time.

energy—The capacity or ability to perform work.

energy system—One of three metabolic systems involving a series of chemical reactions, which form waste products and manufacture ATP.

enzyme—A protein compound that speeds a chemical reaction.

epimysium—A connective tissue surrounding an entire muscle.

estrogen—The female androgen.

excitation—A response to a stimulus.

exercise-recovery—Performing light exercise during recovery from exercise.

extracellular—Outside the cell.

extrafusal fiber—A typical or normal muscle cell or fiber.

fasciculus (singular), fasciculi (plural)—A group or bundle of skeletal muscle fibers held together by a connective tissue called the perimysium.

fast-twitch fiber (FT)—A muscle fiber characterized by fast contraction time, high anaerobic capacity, and low aerobic capacity, all making the fiber suited for high power output activities.

fat—A compound containing glycerol and fatty acids. One of the basic foodstuffs.

fatigue—A state of discomfort and decreased efficiency resulting from prolonged or excessive exertion.

fatty acid (free fatty acid)—The usable form of triglycerides.

flexibility—The range of motion about a joint (static flexibility), opposition or resistance of a joint to motion (dynamic flexibility).

force deficit—The inability to involve all the muscle fibers to perform an athletic action.

free weights—Weights not part of an exercise machine (i.e., barbells and dumbbells).

gamma motor neuron—A type of efferent nerve cell that innervates the ends of an intrafusal muscle fiber.

glucose—Simple sugar.

glycogen—The form in which glucose (sugar) is stored in the muscle and the liver.

glycogenesis—The manufacture of glycogen from glucose.

glycolysis—The incomplete chemical breakdown of glycogen. In aerobic glycolysis, the product is pyruvic acid; in anaerobic glycolysis (lactic acid system) the product is lactic acid.

golgi tendon organ—A proprioceptor located within a muscular tendon.

growth hormone—A hormone secreted by the anterior lobe of the pituitary gland that stimulates growth and development.

hamstring—The muscle on the back of the thigh that flexes the knee and extends the hip.

hemoglobin (Hb)—A complex molecule found in red blood cells that contains iron (heme) and protein (globin) and is capable of combining with oxygen.

homeostasis—Maintaining stable internal physiological conditions.

hormone—A discrete chemical substance secreted into the body fluids by an endocrine gland that has a specific effect on the activities of the other cells, tissues, and organs.

hyperplasia—An increase in the number of cells in a tissue or organ.

hypertrophy—An increase in the size of a cell or organ.

innervate—To stimulate, to transmit nervous energy to a muscle.

intensity—The qualitative element of training such as speed, maximum strength, and power. In strength training, intensity is expressed in load of 1RM.

intermittent work—Exercises performed with alternate periods of relief rather than continuous work.

interneuron (internuncial neuron)—A nerve cell located between afferent (sensory) and efferent (motor) nerve cells. It acts as a middleman between incoming and outgoing impulses.

interstitial—Pertaining to the area or space between cells.

interval training—A system of physical conditioning in which the body experiences short but regularly repeated periods of work stress interspersed with adequate periods of relief.

isokinetic contraction—Contraction in which the tension the muscle develops while shortening at constant speed is maximal over the full range of motion.

isometric (static) contraction—Contraction in which tension develops with no change in the muscle length.

isotonic—Pertaining to a solution having the same tension or osmotic pressure.

isotonic contraction—Contraction in which the muscle shortens with varying tension while lifting a constant load, also referred to as a dynamic or concentric contraction.

kilogram-meters (kgm)—A unit of work.

lactic acid (lactate)—A fatiguing metabolite of the lactic acid system resulting from the incomplete breakdown of glucose (sugar).

lactic acid system (LA system)—An anaerobic energy system in which ATP is manufactured when glucose (sugar) is broken down into lactic acid. High-intensity efforts lasting from 1 to 3 minutes draw energy (ATP) primarily from this system.

machine—Resistance training equipment that dictates the direction of the exercise movement and the body position.

macrocycle—A training phase of 2 to 6 weeks duration.

maturation—Progress toward adulthood.

metabolism—The sum of the chemical changes or reactions occurring in the body.

metabolite—Any substance produced by a metabolic reaction.

microcycle—A training phase of approximately one week.

millimole—One thousandth of a mole.

mitochondrion (singular), mitochondria (plural)—A subcellular structure in all aerobic cells in which the electron transport system take place.

mole—The gram-molecular weight or gram-formula weight of a substance.

motoneuron (motor neuron)—A nerve cell, which when stimulated effects muscular contractions. Most motoneurons innervate skeletal muscle.

motor end plate—The neuromuscular or myoneural junction.

motor unit—An individual motor nerve and all the muscle fibers it innervates.

multiple motor unit summation—The varying of the number of motor units contracting within a muscle at any time.

muscle bundle—A fasciculus.

muscle spindle—A proprioceptor surrounded by intrafusal muscle fibers.

muscular endurance—The ability of a muscle or a muscle group to perform repeated contraction for a long time.

muscle receptors—Proprioceptors that monitor systems related specifically to skeletal muscles. These receptors include the Golgi tendon organ and muscle spindle, which send information to higher brain centers about muscle tension, static length, velocity of stretch, and pressure.

myofibril—The part of a muscle fiber that contains two protein filaments, myosin and actin.

myoglobin—An oxygen-binding pigment similar to hemoglobin that gives the red muscle fiber its color. It acts as an oxygen store and aids in the diffusion of oxygen.

myosin—A protein involved in muscular contraction.

nerve cell—See neuron.

nerve impulse—An electrical disturbance at the point of stimulation of a nerve that is self-propagated along the entire length of the axon.

neuromuscular—The nerve and muscular systems.

neuron—A nerve cell consisting of a cell body (soma), with its nucleus and cytoplasm, dendrites and axons.

oblique—Muscle on the side of the abdominal area.

oxygen debt—The amount of oxygen consumed during recovery from exercise, above that ordinarily consumed.

oxygen system—An aerobic energy system in which ATP is manufactured when food (principally sugar and fat) is broken down. This system produces ATP most abundantly and is the prime energy source during long-lasting (endurance) activities.

perimysium—A connective tissue surrounding a fasciculus or muscle bundle.

periodization—A process of structuring training into phases.

periodization of strength—The structuring of training programs into phases to maximize the capacity to meet the specifics of strength, according to the needs of a sport event.

phosphagen—A group of compounds, collectively refers to ATP and PC.

phosphagen system—See ATP-PC system.

phosphocreatine (PC)—A chemical compound stored in muscle, which when broken down aids in manufacturing ATP.

plasma—The liquid portion of the blood.

plateau—Period during training when athlete makes no observable progress.

plyometrics—Drills or exercises linking sheer strength and scope of movement to produce an explosive-reactive type of movement. The term often refers to jumping drills and depth jumping, but plyometrics can include any drills or exercises using the stretch reflex to produce an explosive reaction.

power—Performance of work expressed per unit of time.

proprioceptor—Sensory organs found in muscles, joints, and tendons, which give information concerning movement and body position (kinesthesis).

protein—A compound containing amino acids. One of the basic foodstuffs.

psychotonic—A psychological technique of relaxation.

pange of motion—Movement allowed by the body's joints and position in a particular exercise.

peceptor—A sense organ that receives stimuli.

peflex—An automatic response induced by stimulating a receptor.

repetition—The number of work intervals within one set.

repetition maximum (RM)—The maximal load that a muscle group can lift in one attempt. Also called one repetition maximum (1RM).

resistance training—Using various methods or equipment that provide an external force against which to exercise.

rest—Resting during recovery from exercise.

sarcolemma—The muscle cell membrane.

sarcomere—The distance between two Z lines; the smallest contractile unit of skeletal muscle.

sarcoplasm—Muscle protoplasm.

sarcoplasmic reticulum—A network of tubules and vesicles surrounding the myofibril.

sensory fiber—See afferent nerve.

sensory neuron—A nerve cell that conveys impulses from a receptor to the central nervous system. Examples of sensory neurons are those excited by sound, pain, light, and taste.

set—The total number of repetitions an athlete performs before taking a rest interval.

slow-twitch fiber (ST)—A muscle fiber characterized by slow contraction time, low anaerobic capacity, and high aerobic capacity, all making the fiber suited for low power output activities.

somatotype—The body type or physical classification of the human body.

spatial summation—An increase in responsiveness of a nerve from the additive effect of numerous stimuli.

specific gravity—The ratio of the density of an object to the density of water.

specific heat—The heat required to change the temperature of a unit mass of a substance by one degree.

specificity of training—Principle underlying constructing a training program for a specific activity or skill.

stabilizers—Muscles that are stimulated to anchor or stabilize the position of a bone.

static contraction—See isometric contraction.

spotter—Individual responsible for the safety of a trainee who is performing a lift.

stimulus (singular), stimuli (plural)—Any agent, act, or influence that modifies the activity of a receptor or irritable tissue.

strength—The force that a muscle or muscle group can exert against a resistance.

stretch or myotatic reflex—A reflex that responds to the rate of muscle stretch. This reflex has the fastest-known response to a stimulus (in this case the rate of muscle stretch). The myotatic or stretch reflex elicits contraction of homonymous muscle and synergist muscles (those surrounding the stretched muscle that produce the same movement) and inhibition of the antagonist muscles.

synapse—The connection or junction of one neuron to another.

synergist muscle—Muscle that actively contributes to the agonist muscle during a muscle contraction.

temporal summation—An increase in responsiveness of a nerve resulting from the additive effect of frequently occurring stimuli.

testosterone—The male sex hormone secreted by the testicles, possessing masculinizing properties.

tetanus—Maintaining tension of a motor unit at a high level as long as the stimuli continue or until fatigue sets in.

tonus—Resiliency and resistance to stretch in a relaxed, resting muscle.

training—An exercise program to develop an athlete for an event. Increasing skill of performance and energy capacities are of equal consideration.

training frequency—The number of times per week the training workout occurs.

triglycerides—The storage form of free fatty acids.

troponin—A protein involved in muscular contraction.

twitch—A brief period of contraction followed by relaxation in a motor unit's response to a stimulus (nerve impulse).

valsalva maneuver—Making an expiratory effort with the glottis closed.

variation—Process of changing exercise variables to provide a different training stimulus.

vein—A vessel carrying blood toward the heart.

vitamin—An organic material in the presence of which important chemical (metabolic) reactions occur.

volume—A quantitative element of training.

watt—A unit of power.

wave summation—The varying frequency of contraction of individual motor units.

weightlifting—An Olympic competitive sport in which the highest total poundage in two lifts—snatch and clean and jerk determine the winner.

weight training—A strength-training program employing the resistance of weights, such as barbells and dumbbells.

work—Applying a force through a distance. For example, applying one pound through one foot equals one foot-pound of work.

Z line—A protein band that defines the distance of one sarcoma in the myofibril.

References

Alexeev, M. 1950. About the physiological mechanisms of developing motor skills based on I.P. Pavlov's findings. *Teoria i Praktika Fizicheskoi Kulturi* (Moscow) 12: 9-15.

Allen, D., H. Westerbald, J. Lee, and J. Lannergren. 1992. The role of excitation-contraction coupling in muscle fatigue. *Sports Medicine* 13(2): 116-126.

Alpine Canada. 1990. Physiological profile of skiing events. Newsletter 32.

Altenberger, H. 1993. Ubertraining—Eine ständig laudernde gefahr (Overtraining—An always lurking danger). *Laufsport-Magasine* (St. Pölten) 1/2(S): 42-43.

Andrews, E. 1991. *Muscle management.* London: Thorsons.

Appell, H. 1990. Muscular atrophy following immobilization: A review. *Sports Medicine* 10(1): 38-42.

Appell, H., J. Soares, and J. Duarte. 1992. Exercise, muscle damage and fatigue. *Sports Medicine* 13(2): 108-115.

Armstrong, R. 1986. Muscle damage and endurance events. *Sports Medicine* 12(3): 184-207.

Armstrong, R. 1991. Mechanisms of exercise-induced muscle fiber injury. *Sports Medicine* 12(3): 184-207.

Arnheim, D. 1985. *Modern principles of athletic training* (6th ed.). St. Louis: Times Mirror/Mosby College.

Asmussen, E. 1936. Deflective exercises. *Legemsovlser* 2: 25-35.

Asmussen, E., and O. Boje. 1945. Body temperature and capacity of work. *Acta Physiologica Scandinavica* 10: 1-23.

Astrand, P., and K. Rodahl. 1970. *Textbook of work physiology.* New York: McGraw-Hill.

Astrand, P., and K. Rodahl. 1977. *Textbook of work physiology: Physiological basis of exercise.* New York: McGraw-Hill.

Astrand, P., and K. Rodahl. 1985. *Textbook of work physiology.* New York: McGraw-Hill.

Astrand, P., and B. Saltin. 1961. Maximal oxygen uptake and heart rate in various types of muscular activity. *Journal of Applied Physiology* 16: 2115-2119.

Babij, P., and W. Booth. 1988. Biochemistry of exercise: Advances in molecular biology relevant to adaptation of muscle to exercise. *Sports Medicine* 5: 137-143.

Bacon, T. 1989. The planning and integration of mental training programs. *Science Periodical on Research and Technology in Sport* (SPORT) 10(1): 1-8.

Baechle, T. (Ed.) 1994. *Essentials of strength training and conditioning.* Champaign, IL: Human Kinetics.

Balaban, E. 1992. Sports anaemia. *Clinical Sports Medicine* 11: 313-325.

Balch, J., and P. Balch, 1997. *Prescription for nutritional healing* (2nd ed.). New York: Avery.

Balyi, I. 1996. Long-term planning of athlete development phase. *British Columbia Coach* 1: 9-14.

Banister, W. 1985. Ammonia as an indicator of exercise stress: Implications of recent findings to sports medicine. *Sports Medicine* 2: 34-46.

Baracos, V. 1984. Effects of temperature on protein turnover in isolated rat skeletal muscle. *American Journal of Physiology* 246: C125.

Barnard, R., G. Gardner, N. Diaco, R. MacAlpern, and R. Hedman. 1973. Cardiovascular responses to sudden strenuous exercise, heart rate, blood pressure and ECG. *Journal of Applied Physiology* 34(6): 833-837.

Baroga, L. 1978. Tendinte contemporane in metodologia dezvoltarii fortei (Contemporary trends in the methodology of strength development). *Educatia Fizica si Sport* 6: 22-36.

Barolin, G. 1978. Retrospective on eight years of psychohygienic training with sports champions. *Medizinische Psychologie* 28(6): 119-125.

Belinovich, V. 1958. *Obuchenie v fisycheskom vospitanii* (The teaching process in physical education). Moscow: Fizkultura i Sport.

Benson, H. 1975. *The relaxation response.* New York: Morrow.

Berg, A. 1994. The cytokine response to strenuous exercise. *International Journal of Sports Medicine* 15: 516-518.

Berger, R. 1962. Effects of varied weight training programs on strength. *Research Quarterly* 33: 168.

Bergeron, G. 1982. Therapeutic massage. *Canadian Athletic Therapy Association Journal* Summer: 15-17.

Berglund, B. 1992. High altitude training: Aspects of haematological adaptation. *Sports Medicine* 14(5): 289-303.

Bergstrom, J., L. Hermansen, E. Hultman, and B. Saltin. 1967. Diet, muscle glycogen and physical performance. *Acta Physiologica Scandinavica* 71: 140-150.

Bernstein, D., and T. Borkovec. 1973. *Progressive relaxation training.* Champaign, IL: Research Press.

Bielz, M. 1976. *Rating the effort in high performance rowing.* Doctoral thesis, Institute of Physical Culture, Leipzig.

Bigland-Ritchie, B. 1981. EMG/force relations and fatigue of human voluntary contractions. In Doris Miller (Ed.), *Exercise and sport sciences reviews: Vol. 9.* Salt Lake City: Franklin Institute Press. 75-117.

Bigland-Ritchie, B., N. Dawson, R. Johansson, and O. Lippold. 1986. Reflex origin for the slowing of motorneuron firing rates in fatigue of human voluntary contractions. *Journal of Physiology* 379: 451-459.

Bigland-Ritchie, B., R. Johansson, O. Lippold, and J. Woods. 1983. Contractile speed and EMG changes during fatigue of sustained maximal voluntary contractions. *Journal of Neurophysiology* 50(1): 313-324.

Binkhorst, R., L. Hoofd, and C. Vissers. 1977. Temperature and free-velocity relationship of human muscle. *Journal of Applied Physiology* 41: 471-475.

Blohin, I. 1970. In A. Gandelsman and K. Smirnov (Eds.), *Fisyologischeskie osnovi metodiki sportivnoi trenirovki* (The physiological foundations of training). Moscow: Fizkultura i Sport.

Bloomfield, H. 1996. *Hypercium (St. John's wort) and depression.* Los Angeles: Prelude Press.

Bohus, B., R. Bemus, D. Fokkema, J. Koolhaas, and C. Nyakas. 1987. Neuroendocrine states and behavioral and physiological stress responses. *Progress in Brain Research* 72: 57-70.

Bompa, T. 1956. Antrenamentul in periooda pregatitoare (Training methods during the preparatory phase). *Caiet Pentre Sporturi Nautice* (Bucharest) 3: 22-24.

Bompa, T. 1960. *Antrenamentul in diferite perioade de pregatire* (Training content in different stages of preparation). Timisoara, Romania: Cjefs.

Bompa, T. 1964. *Analiza fiziologica a pistelor din campionatul mondial de canotaj, 1964* (A physiological analysis of the rowing races during the 1964 world rowing championships). XI Research Conference in Physical Education and Sport, Timisoara, Romania.

Bompa, T. 1968a. Criteria pregatirii a unui plan depatra ani (Criteria of setting up a four year plan). *Cultura Fizica si Sport* (Bucharest) 2: 11-19.

Bompa, T. 1968b. *Individualizarea: Un factor psihologic de antrenam.* (Individualization: A psychological factor of training). International Symposium on Sports Psychology, Moscow.

Bompa, T. 1969. *Unele aspecte ale refacerii psihologice dupa efortful de competitie* (Some aspects of the athletes psychological recovery following the strain of performance). Conference for Research in Sports Psychology, Bucharest, Romania.

Bompa, T. 1970. *Planul psihologic al atletilor in competitie* (Athlete's psychological plan for competition). Symposium of Psychology of Coaching, Brasov, Romania.

Bompa, T. 1975. *The national rowing squad plan for the 1976 Olympic Games.* Montreal: Canadian Rowing Association.

Bompa, T. 1976. *Theory and methodology of training.* Toronto: York University.

Bompa, T. 1979. *The model of the national rowing team plan for the 1980 Olympic Games.* St. Catharines: Canadian Rowing Association.

Bompa, T., T. Bompa, and T. Zivic. 1981. *Fitness and body development exercises.* Dubuque, IA: Kendall/Hunt.

Bompa, T., M. Hebbelinck, and B. Van Gheluwe. 1978. *Biomechanical analysis of the rowing stroke employing two different oar grips.* The XXI World Congress in Sports Medicine, Brasilia, Brazil.

Bondarchuk, A. 1986. *Track and field training.* Translated by James Riordan. Kiev: Zdotovye.

Booth, R. 1993. Exercise, overtraining and the immune response: A biological perspective. *New Zealand Journal of Sports Medicine* (Auckland) 21: 42-45.

Brooks, G., and T. Fahey, 1985a. *Exercise physiology.* New York: Macmillan.

Brooks, G., and T. Fahey, 1985b. *Exercise physiology: Human bioenergetics and its applications.* New York: Macmillan.

Brotherhood, J. 1984. Nutrition and sports performance. *Sports Medicine* 1: 350-389.

Brouha, L. 1945. Training specificity of muscular work. *Review of Canadian Biology* 4: 144.

Brown, A., and R. Herb. 1990. Dietary intake and body composition of Mike Pigg—1988 triathlete of the year. *Clinical Sports Medicine* 2: 129-137.

Bucher, C. 1972. *Foundation of physical education.* St. Louis: Mosby.

Bucur, I. 1979. *Metode si mijloace utilizate pentru revenirea atletilor* (Techniques and methods employed for athlete's recovery). Timisoara, Romania: National Sports Council.

Bucur, I., and M. Birjega. 1973. *Sinteza cursului de educatie fizica* (Synopsis of the theory of physical education). Timisoara, Romania: Institut Politecnic.

Calder, A. 1996. Recovery. In R. de Castella and W. Clews (Comps.), *Smart sport, The ultimate reference manual for sports people—athletes and players, coaches, parents and teachers.* Australia: RWM Publishing Quality Ltd. 7-1 to 7-17.

Carlile, I. 1956. Effect of preliminary passive warming-up on swimming performance. *Research Quarterly* 27: 143-151.

Carlson, R. 1988. The socialization of elite tennis players in Sweden: An analysis of the players' backgrounds and development. *Sociology of Sport Journal* 5: 241-256.

Catina, V., and Bompa, T. 1968. *Antrenamentul stiintific al atletilor* (A scientific approach to athlete's training). International Symposium on Sport Medicine, Cluj, Romania.

Cercel, D. 1974. Posibilitatile de aplicare a antrenamentului modelat in handbal (Means of applying modeling in training handball). *Educatia Fizica si Sport* 53: 13-18.

Chariev, R. 1974. A comparison of two variants of training structures under the conditions of weekly competitions. *Scientific Research Collection* (Moscow): 63-80.

Chudinov, V. 1960. Specific exercises for the development of the motor abilities. *Teoria i Praktika Fizicheskoi Kulturi* (Moscow) 11: 16-21.

Cinque, C. 1989. Massage for cyclists: The winning touch? *The Physician and Sports Medicine* 17(10): 167-170.

Clarkson, P., K. Nosaka, and B. Braun. 1992. Muscle function after exercise-induced muscle damage and rapid adaptation. *Medicine and Science in Sports and Exercise* 24(5): 512-520.

Claustrat, B., J. Brun, M. David, G. Sassolas, and G. Chozot. 1992. Melatonin and jet lag: Confirmatory result using a simplified protocol. *Biological Psychiatry* 32: 705-711.

Colgan, M. 1993. *Optimum sports nutrition: Your competitive edge.* New York: Advanced Research Press.

Colliader, E., and P. Tesch. 1990. Effects of eccentric and concentric muscle actions in resistance training. *Acta Physiologica Scandinavia* 140: 31-39.

Conlee, R. 1987. Muscle glycogen and exercise endurance: A twenty year perspective. *Exercise and Sport Sciences Reviews* 15: 1-28.

Cooper, D., J. Gallman, and J. McDonald. 1986. Role of aerobic exercise in reduction of stress. *Dental Clinics of North America* 30 (Suppl.4): S133-S142.

Costill, D., E. Coyle, W. Fink, G. Lesmes, and F. Witzmann. 1979. Adaptations in skeletal muscle following strength training. *Journal of Applied Physiololgy* 46(1): 96-99.

Counsilman, J. 1971. *Handling the stress and staleness problems of the hard training athletes.* International Symposium on the Art and Science of Coaching, Vol. I. Toronto, Canada. 15-22.

Couzy, F., P. Lafargue, and C. Guezennec. 1990. Nutrition and other factors. *International Journal of Sports Medicine* 11: 263-266.

Coyle, E., D. Feiring, T. Rotkis, R. Cote, F. Roby, W. Lee, and J. Wilmore. 1981. Specificity of power improvements through slow and fast isokinetic training. *Journal of Applied Physiology: Respiratory Environment and Exercise Physiology* 51: 1437-1442.

Cratty, B. 1967. *Movement behaviour and motor learning.* Philadelphia: Lea and Febiger.

Cratty, B. 1970. Coaching decisions and research in sport psychology. *Research Quarterly* 13: 28-34.

Cratty, B. 1973. *Psychology in contemporary sport.* New Jersey: Prentice Hall.

Cratty, L. 1962. A comparison of learning of a fine motor skill to learning a similar gross motor task, based upon kinesthetic cues. *Research Quarterly* 33: 212-221.

Dal Monte, A. 1983. *The functional values of sport.* Firente: Sansoni.

Dal Monte, A., F. Sardella, P. Faccini, and S. Lupo. 1985. *Metabolic requirements in boxing.* I.S.A.S. Roma.

Deabler, H., E. Fidel, R. Dillenkoffer, and S. Elder. 1973. The use of relaxation and hypnosis in lowering high blood pressure. *American Journal of Clinical Hypnosis* 17(2): 75-83.

Deacon, S., and J. Arendt. 1994. Phase-shifts in melatonin, 6-sulpha-toxymelatonin and alertness rhythms after treatment with moderately bright light at night. *Clinical Endocrinology* 40: 413-420.

Deci, E. 1971. Effects of externally mediated rewards on intrinsic motivation. *Journal of Personality and Social Psychology* 18: 105.

De Lorme, T., and A. Watkins. 1951. *Progressive resistance exercises.* New York: Appleton-Century-Crofts.

DeLuca, C., R. LeFever, M. McCue, and A. Xenakis. 1982. Behavior and human motor units in different muscles during linearly varying contractions. *Journal of Physiology* 329: 113-128.

Demeter, A. 1972. Refacerca organismului in football (Organism recovery following soccer training). *Football* 312: 8-14.

Dempster, W. 1958. Analysis of two-hand pulls using free body diagrams. *Journal of Applied Physiology* 13(3): 469-480.

de Vries, H. 1963. The looseness factor in speed and O_2 consumption of an anaerobic 100 yard dash. *Research Quarterly* 34: 305-313.

de Vries, H. 1980. *Physiology of exercise for physical education and athletes* (3rd ed.). Dubuque, IA: Brown.

Dintiman, G. 1971. *Sprinting speed.* Springfield, IL: Charles C. Thomas.

Dishman, R. 1992. Physiological and psychological effects of overtraining. In K.D. Browell (ed.), *Eating, bodyweight, and performance in athletics: Disorders of modern society.* Malboro, PA: Leigh & Fabinger. 48-72.

Dons, B., K. Bollerup, F. Bonde-Petersen, and S. Hancke. 1979. The effects of weight-lifting exercise related to muscle fiber composition and muscle cross-sectional area in humans. *European Journal of Applied Physiology* 40: 95-106.

Donskoy, D. 1971. Cited by L. Trodoresau and C. Florescu in E. Ghibu (Ed.), *Some directions regarding the perfection and masterness of technique and strategy.* Bucharest: Stadion. 49-62.

Dorland's illustrated medical dictionary (25th ed.). 1974. Philadelphia: Saunders.

Doubt, J. 1991. Physiology of exercise in the cold. *Sports Medicine* 11(6): 367-381.

Dragan, I. 1978. *Refacenea organismuliu dupa antrenament* (Organism recovery following training). Bucharest: Sport-Turism.

Dragan, I., V. Constantinescu, A. Popovici, and D. Carmen. 1978. *Aspecte biologice a formei sportive* (Biological aspects of peaking). Bucharest: National Sports Council.

Dragan, I., and I. Stanescu. 1971. *Refacerea organismului dupa antrenament: O necesitate* (Organism recovery following training: A requirement of contemporary athletics). Bucharest: Stadion.

Dudley, F., P. Tesch, B. Miller, and P. Buchanan. 1991. Importance of eccentric actions in performance adaptations to resistance training. *Aviation and Space Environment Medicine* 62: 543-550.

Dyachikov, V. 1960. How the Russian high jumpers succeeded at Rome. *Legkaia Atlatika* 12: 30-36.

Dyachikov, V. 1964. The perfection of athlete's physical preparation. In N. Ozolin (Ed.), *Sovremenaia sistema sportivnoi trenirovki* (Athlete's training system for competition). Moscow: Fizkultura i Sport.

Ebbing, C., and P. Clarkson. 1989. Exercise-induced muscle damage and adaptation. *Sports Medicine* 7: 207-234.

Edgerton, R. 1976. Neuromuscular adaptation to power and endurance work. *Canadian Journal of Applied Sports Sciences* 1: 49-58.

Edgerton, V. 1970. Morphology and histochemistry of the soleus muscle from normal and exercise rats. *American Journal of Anatomy* 127: 81-88.

Edington, D., and V. Edgerton. 1976. *The biology of physical activity.* Boston: Houghton Mifflin.

Eiselen, G. 1854. *Gymnastic übungen* (Gymnastics exercises). Berlin: Verlag.

Ekman, A., J. Leppaluo, P. Huttunen, K. Aranko, and O. Vakkuri. 1993. Ethanol inhibits melatonin secretion in healthy volunteers in a dose-dependent randomized double blind cross-over study. *Journal of Clinical Endocrinology and Metabolism* 77: 780-783.

Ekstrand, J., and J. Gillquist. 1982. The frequency of muscle tightness and injuries in soccer players. *American Journal of Sports Medicine* 10(2): 75-78.

Ekstrand, J., and J. Gillquist. 1983. Soccer injuries and their mechanisms: A prospective study. *Medicine and Science in Sports and Exercise* 15(3): 267-270.

Elkins, U., U. Leden, and K. Wakim. 1957. Objective recording of the strength of normal muscles. *Archives of Physical Medicine* 33: 639-647.

Enoka, R. 1996. Eccentric contractions require unique activation strategies by the nervous system. *Journal of Applied Physiology* 81(6): 2339-2346.

Epuran, M. 1974. *Psihologia sportului contemporan.* (Psychology and the contemporary athletics). Bucharest: Stadion.

Erdelyi, G. 1962. Gynecological survey of female athletes. *Journal of Sports Medicine* 2: 174-179.

Espenshade, A. 1960. Motor development. In W.R. Johnson (Ed.), *Sciences and medicine of exercise and sports.* New York: Harper & Row. 66-91.

Fabiato, A., and F. Fabiato. 1978. The effect of pH on myofilaments and the sacroplasmic reticulum of skinned cells from cardiac and skeletal muscle. London: *Journal of Physiology* 276: 233-255.

Fahey, D. 1991. How to cope with muscle soreness. *Power-Research*

Fahey, T. D. 1994. *Basic weight training for men and women.* Mountain View. CA: Mayfield Publishing. 23.

Faraday, G. 1971. In N.G. Ozolin, *Sovremennaia systema spartivnoi trenirovky* (Athlete's training system for competition). Moscow: Fizkultura i Sport.

Farfel, V. 1960. *Physiologi v sportom* (Sport's physiology). Moscow: Fizkultura i Sport.

Fenz, W. 1976. Coping mechanisms and performance under stress. *Medicine Sport* 29: 96.

Fieldman, H. 1966. Effects of selected extensibility exercise on the flexibility of the hip joint. *Research Quarterly* 37(3): 326-329.

Finnbogi, J., K. Borg, L. Edstrom, and L. Grimby. 1988. Use of motor units in relation to muscle fiber type and size in man. *Muscle & Nerve* 11: 1211-1218.

Fleck, J., and W. Kraemer. 1982. The overtraining syndrome. *National Strength and Conditioning Association Journal* August/September: 50-51.

Florescu, C., V. Dumitrescu, and A. Predescu. 1969. *Metodologia desvoltari calitatilor fizice* (The methodology of developing physical qualities). Bucharest: National Sports Council.

Fox, E. 1979. *Sports physiology.* Philadelphia: Saunders.

Fox, E. 1984. *Sports physiology* (2nd ed.). New York: Saunders College.

Fox, E., R. Bowes, and M. Foss. 1989. *The physiological basis of physical education and athletics.* Dubuque, IA: Brown.

Fox, E., and D. Mathews. 1974. *Interval Training.* Philadelphia: Saunders.

Francis, C., and P. Patterson. 1992. *The Charlie Francis training system.* Ottawa: TBLI.

Friden, J., and R. Lieber. 1992. Structural and mechanical basis of exercise-induced muscle injury. *Medicine Science and Sports Exercise* 24: 521-530.

Friman, G. 1979. Effects of clinical bed rest for seven days of physical performance. *Acta Medica Scandinavica* 205(5): 389-393.

Frost, R. 1971. *Psychological concepts applied to physical education and coaching.* Reading, MA: Addison-Wesley.

Fry, R., A. Morton, and D. Keast. 1991. Overtraining in athletics: An update. *Sports Medicine* 12(1): 32-65.

Gallway, W. 1976. *Inner tennis*. New York: Random House.

Gandelsman, A., and K. Smirnov. 1970. *Physiologicheskie osnovi metodiki sportivnoi trenirovki* (The physiological foundations of training). Moscow: Fizkultura i Sport.

Gazzah, N., A. Gharib, I. Delton, P. Moliere, G. Durand, R. Christon, M. Largarde, and N. Sarda. 1993. Effect of an N-3 fatty acid-deficient diet on the adenosine-dependent melatonin release in cultured rat pineal. *Journal of Neurochemistry* 61: 1057-1063.

Gellerstein, C. 1979. Quoted by Zatzyorski in L. Matveyev and A. Novikov (Eds.), *Teoria i metodika physicheskogo vospitania* (The theory and methodology of physical education). Moscow: Fizkultura i Sport.

Ghibu, E. 1978. *Mijloace si proceduri pentru pregatirea jocurilor olimpice din 1980* (Means and procedures regarding the preparation for the 1980 Olympic Games). Bucharest: National Sports Council.

Ghibu, E., C. Simonescu, C. Radut, A. Hurmuzescu, N. Navasart, and C. Florescu. 1978. *Aspecte psihologice ale formei sportive* (Psychological aspects of peaking). Bucharest: National Sports Council.

Ghircoiasu, M. 1979. Energia metabolismului (The energetic metabolism). Bucharest: Sport-Turism.

Gibson, H., and R. Edwards. 1985. Muscular exercise and fatigue. *Sports Medicine* 2: 120-132.

Gionet, N. 1986. Is volleyball an aerobic or an anaerobic sport? *Volleyball Technical Journal* 5: 31-35.

Gippernreiter, S. 1949. *Weather, temperature, and organisms' reactions*. Moscow: Fizkultura i Sport.

Glick, J. 1980. Muscle strains: Prevention and treatment. *Physician and Sports Medicine* 8(11): 73-77.

Goldberg, A., J. Etlinger, D. Goldspink, and C. Jablecki. 1975. Mechanism of work-induced hypertrophy of skeletal muscle. *Medicine and Science in Sports* 7(3): 185-198.

Goldspink, G. 1964. The combined effects of exercise and reduced food intake on skeletal muscle fibers. *Journal of Cellular Composition Physiology* 63: 209-216.

Gollnick, P., R. Armstrong, C. Sanbert, W. Sembrowich, R. Sepherd, and B. Saltin. 1973. Glycogen depletion patterns in human skeletal muscle fibers during prolonged work. *Pfügers Archives* 334: 1-12.

Gollnick, P., R. Armstrong, W. Sembrowich, R. Sepherd, and B. Saltin. 1973. Glycogen depletion pattern in human skeletal muscle fiber after heavy exercise. *Journal of Applied Physiology* 34(5): 615-618.

Gollnick, P., K. Piehl, C. Scubert, R. Armstrong, and B. Saltin. 1972. Diet, exercise, and glycogen changes in human muscle fibers. *Journal of Applied Physiology* 33: 421-425.

Goncharov, N. 1968. Cited in V. Zatsyorski, *Athlete's physical abilities*. Moscow: Fizkultura i Sport.

Gordon, E. 1967. Anatomical and biochemical adaptation of muscle to different exercises. *Journal of the American Medical Association* 201: 755-758.

Grantin, K. 1940. Contributions regarding the systematization of physical exercises. *Theory and Practice of Physical Culture* 9: 27-37.

Gregory, L. 1981. Some observations on strength training and assessment. *Journal of Sports Medicine* 21: 130-137.

Grimby, G. 1992. Strength and power in sports. In P. Komi (Ed.), *Strength and Power in Sports*. Oxford: Blackwell Scientific Publications.

Guilford, J. 1958. A system of psychomotor abilities. *American Journal of Psychiatry* 71: 164-174.

Gündhill, M. 1997. *Ironman*. Oxnard, CA: Ironman Publishing. 134-139.

Guyllemin, R., P. Brazeau, P. Bohlen, S. Esch, N. Ling, W. Wehrenberg, B. Bloch, C. Mougin, S. Zeytin, and A.

Baird. 1983. Somatocrinin, the growth hormone releasing factor. In N. Greep (Ed.), *Recent progress in hormone research: Proceedings of the 1983 Laurentian Hormone Conference*. New York: Academic Press. 40: 233-299.

Hackney, A., S. Pearman, and J. Nowacki. 1990. Physiological profiles of overtrained and stale athletes: A review. *Journal of Applied Sport Psychology* 1: 21-33.

Hahn, E. 1977. The transition phase and the psychological preparation. *Leichtathletik* 28: 377-380.

Hainaut, K., and J. Duchateau. 1989. Muscle fatigue: Effects of training and disuse. *Muscle and Nerve* 12: 660-669.

Hakkinen, K. 1989. Neuromuscular and hormonal adaptations during strength and power training. *The Journal of Sports Medicine and Physical Fitness* 29(1): 9-26.

Halliwell, W. 1979. Strategies for enhancing motivation in sport. In P. Klavora, *Coach, athlete and the sport psychologist*. Toronto: Twin Offset. 211-232.

Harma, M., J. Laitinen, M. Partinen, and S. Suvanto. 1993. The effect of four-day round trip flights over 10 time zones on the circadian variation of salivary melatonin and cortisol in airline flight attendants. *Ergonomics* 37: 1479-1489.

Harre, D. (Ed.) 1982. *Trainingslehre*. Berlin: Sportverlag.

Hellebrandt, F., and S. Houtz. 1956. Mechanisms of muscle training in man: Experimental demonstration of the overload principle. *Physical Therapy Review* 36: 371-383.

Hennig, R., and T. Lomo. 1987. Gradation of force output in normal fast and slow muscles of the rat. *Acta Physiologica Scandinavica* 130: 133-142.

Herberger, E. 1977. *Rudern*. Berlin: Sportverlag.

Hettinger, T. 1966. *Isometric muscle training*. Stuttgard: Georg Thieme.

Hettinger, T., and E. Müler. 1953. Muskelleistung and muskeltraining. *Arbeitsphysiologie* 15: 111-126.

Hill, A. 1922. The maximum work and mechanical efficiency of human muscles and their most economical speed. *Journal of Physiology* 56: 19-41.

Hirtz, P. 1976. The perfection of coordination: An essential factor in physical education. *Körpererziehung* 26: 381-387.

Höger, H. 1971. The structure of long-term training programs. In D. Harre (Ed.), *Trainingslehre*. Berlin: Sportverlag.

Hollmann, W. 1959. *Der arbeits and trainingseinflus auf kresilauf und atmung*. Darmstag: Sportwisenshaft.

Hollmann, W. 1993. Serotonin Im Gehirn—Verantwortlich Für Die Syndrome Sportentziehungs-Erscheinungen Und Übertraining? *Sportmedicine* 44: 509-511.

Horrobin, D. 1994. Modulation of cytokine production in vivo by dietary essential fatty acids in patients with colorectal cancer. *Clinical Science Colon* 87: 711.

Houmard, A. 1991. Impact of reduced training on performance in endurance athletes. *Sports Medicine* 12(6): 380-393.

Howald, H. 1977. Objectives measurements in rowing. Minden: *Rudersport* 4: 31-35.

Hultman, E. 1967a. Physiological role of muscle glycogen in man, with special reference to exercise. *Circulation Research* 20-21 (Suppl. 1): I99-I114.

Hultman, E. 1967b. Studies on muscle metabolism of glycogen and active phosphate in man with special reference to exercise and diet. *Scandinavian Journal of Clinical Laboratory Investigation* 19 (Suppl.): 1-63.

Hultman, E., and K. Sahlin. 1980. Acid-base balance during exercise. *American College of Sport Medicine* 8: 41-128.

Hunsicker, P. 1955. *Arm strength at selected degrees of elbow flexion*. Wright-Patterson Air Force Base, OH: Wright Air Development Center.

Ikai, M., and K. Yabe. 1969. Comparison of maximum muscle strength produced by voluntary and electric stimulation. Cited in W. Schroeder, The correlation of force with the other motor abilities. *Theorie und Praxis der Körperkultur* 12: 98-121.

Iliuta, G., and C. Dumitrescu. 1978. Criterii medicale si psihice ale evaluarii si conducerii antrenamentului atletilor (Medical and psychological criteria of assessing and directing athlete's training). *Sportul de Performanta* (Bucharest) 53: 49-64.

Illin, S. 1959. In V. Zatzyorski, *Athlete's physical abilities.* 1968. Moscow: Fizkultura i Sport.

Israel, S. 1963. Das akute entlastungssyndrom. *Theorie und Praxis der Körperkultur* 12: 3-12.

Israel, S. 1972. The acute syndrome of detraining. *GDR National Olympic Committee* (Berlin) 2: 30-35.

Israel, S. 1976. Zur problematic des ubertrainings aus internistischer und leistungphysiologischer sich. *Medicine und Sport* 16: 1-12.

Ivanova, T., and A. Weiss. 1969. In W. Schroeder, The correlation between force and the other motor abilities. *Theorie und Praxis der Körperkultur* 12: 98-110.

Jacobsen, E. 1938. *Progressive relaxation.* Chicago: University of Chicago Press.

James, M. 1996. The effects of human TNF alpha and IL-1 beta production of diets enriched in N-3 fatty acids from vegetable and fish oil. *American Journal of Clinical Nutrition* 63: 116.

Jonath, W. 1961. *Circuit-training.* Berlin: Limpert.

Kabat, H. 1958. Proprioceptive facilitation in therapeutic exercises. In M. Licht (Ed.), *Therapeutic exercises.* Baltimore: Waverley Press.

Kaijser, L. 1975. Oxygen supply as a limiting factor in physical performance. In J. Keul (Ed.), *Limiting factors in human performance.* Stuttgart: Theime. 39-47.

Kalinin, V., and N. Ozolin. 1973. The dynamics of athletic shape. *Legkaia Atlatika* (Moscow) 10: 20-22.

Kanehisa, H., and M. Miyashita. 1983. Specificity of velocity in strength training. *European Journal of Applied Physiology* 52: 104-106.

Karlsson, J. 1971. Muscle ATP, CP, and lactate in submaximal and maximal exercise. *Department of Physiologica and Gymnastics.* 382-391.

Karlsson, J., and B. Saltin. 1971. Oxygen deficit and muscle metabolites in intermittent exercise. *Acta Physiologica Scandinavica* 82: 115-122.

Karpovich, P., and W. Sinning. 1971. *Physiology of muscular activity.* Philadelphia: Saunders.

Karvonen, J. 1992. Overtraining. *Medicine and sport science.* Zurich: Karger. 174-188.

Karvonen, M., E. Kentala, and O. Mustala. 1957. The effects of training on heart rate. A longitudinal study. *American Medical and Experimental Biology* 35: 307-315.

Keast, D., K. Cameron, and A. Morton. 1988. Exercise and the immune response. *Sports Medicine* 5: 248-267.

Kessler, R., and D. Hertling. 1983. *Management of common musculoskeletal disorders.* Philadelphia: Harper & Row. Chapter 10.

Keul, J., E. Doll, and D. Keppler. 1969. *Muskelstoffwechsel.* Munich: Barth.

Klissouras, V., F. Pirnay, and J. Petit. 1973. Adaptation to maximal effort: Genetics and age. *Journal of Applied Physiology* 35(2): 288-293.

Knox, S., T. Theorell, B. Malmberg, and A. Lindquist. 1986. Stress management in the treatment of essential hypertension in primary health care. *Scandinavian Journal of Primary Health Care* 4: 175-181.

Korcek, I. 1974. The assessment of quantitative and qualitative indices in team sport's training. *Trener* (Bratislava) 2: 6-9.

Korman, A. 1974. *The psychology of motivation.* Englewood Cliffs, NJ: Prentice Hall.

Korobov, A. 1971. In N. Ozolin, *Sovremenaia systema sportivnoi trenirovky* (Athlete's training system for competition). Moscow: Fizkultura i Sport.

Kots, I.M. 1977. *Lecture series.* December. Montreal: Concordia University.

Kraus, H. 1975. The need for relaxation in athletics. *Journal of Sports Medicine* 3(1): 41-43.

Krestovnikov, A. 1938. *Sports physiology.* Moscow: Fizkultura i Sport.

Krestovnikov, A. 1951. *The physiological basis of physical education.* Moscow: Fizkultura i Sport.

Krüger, A. 1973. Periodization, or to peak at the right time. *Track Techniques* 54: 1720-1724.

Kruglanski, A. 1971. The effects of extrinsic incentive on some qualitative aspects of task performance. *Journal of Personality* 39: 606-617.

Kuipers, H. 1991. Overtraining. *En Sport* 24: 90-94.

Kuipers, H. 1994. Exercise induced muscle damage. *International Journal of Sports Medicine* 15: 132.

Kuipers, H., and H. Keizer. 1988. Overtraining in elite athletes: Review and directions for the future. *Sports Medicine* 6: 79-92.

Kunst, G., and C. Florescu. 1971. *The main factors for performance in wrestling.* Bucharest: National Sports Council.

Kuperian, T. (Ed.) 1982. *Physical therapy for sports.* Philadelphia: Saunders.

Kuznetsov, V. 1975. *Kraftvorbereitung. Theoretische Grundlagen Der Muskelkraftwiklung.* Berlin: Sportverlag.

Lachman, S. 1965. A theory relating learning to electrophysiology of the brain. *Journal of Physiology* 59: 275-281.

Lagrange, S. 1968. In V. Zatzyoski, *Athlete's physical abilities.* Moscow: Fiskultura i Sport.

Laizan, L., and E. Zub. 1976. The index of the athletic shape. *Legkaia Atletika* (Moscow) 6: 30-31.

Landers, D. 1980. The arousal-performance relationship revisited. *Research Quarterly for Exercise and Sport* 5(1): 77-90.

Lange, L. 1919. *Uber funktionelle anpassung.* Berlin: Springer Verlag.

Lauru, L. 1957. Physiological study of motion. *Advanced Management* no: 22-27.

Lawther, J. 1972. *Sport psychology.* Englewood Cliffs, NJ: Prentice Hall.

Lazarus, R. 1976. *Patterns of adjustment.* New York: McGraw-Hill.

Legros, P. 1992. Le Surentrainement. *Science Et Sports* (Paris) 7: 51-57.

Lehman, B. 1955. In N. Ozolin, *Sovremennaia systema sportivnoi trenirovky* (Athlete's training system for competition). 1971. Moscow: Fizkultura i Sport.

Lehmann, M., C. Foster, and J. Keul. 1993. Overtraining in endurance athletes: A brief review. *Medicine & Science in Sport and Exercise* 25(7): 854-862.

Lemmer, B., T. Bruhl, K. Witte, B. Pflug, W. Kohler, and Y. Tourtou. 1994. Effects of bright light on circandian patterns of cyclic adenosine monophosphate, melatonin and cortisol in healthy subjects. *European Journal of Endocrinology* 130: 472-477.

Leshaft, P. 1910. *Children's education.* Moscow: Sport Performance Books.

Letunov, S. 1950. In N. Ozolin, *Sovremenaia systema sportivnoi trenirovky* (Athlete's training system for competition). 1971. Moscow: Fizkultura i Sport.

Levine, M., A. Milliron, and L. Duffy. 1994. Diurnal and seasonal rhythms of melatonin, cortisol and testosterone in interior Alaska. *Arctic Medical Research* 53: 25-34.

Levy, S., R. Hebereman, M. Lippiman, and T. d'Angelo. 1987. Correlation of stress factors with sustained depression of natural killer cell activity and predicted prognosis in patients with breast cancer. *Journal of Clinical Oncology* 5: 348-353.

Lievens, P. 1986. The use of cryotherapy in sport injuries. *Sports Medicine* 3: 398.

Lippin, R. 1985. Stress release, emerging tool in total stress management program. *Occupational Health and Safety* 54(6): 80-82.

Loat, C., and E. Rhodes. 1989. Jet-lag and human performance. *Sports Medicine* 8(4): 226-238.

Logan, G., and W. McKinney. 1973. *Kinesiology*. Dubuque, IA: Brown.

Lowe, R., and J. McGrath. 1971. Stress, arousal and performance. *Project Report: AF11*. Air Force Office of Strategic Research. 61-67.

Ludu, V. 1969. *Coordonarea si metodica desvoltarii ei* (Coordination, and its methodology of development). Bucharest: National Sports Council.

Lukes, H. 1954. *The effect of warm-up exercises on the amplitude of voluntary movement*. Master's thesis, University of Wisconsin, Madison.

Luthe, W. 1963. Method, research and application in medicine. *American Journal of Psychotherapy* 17: 174-195.

Luthe, W., and J. Shulz. 1969. *Autogenic therapy* (Vol. 1). New York: Grune & Stratton.

Lysens, R., Y. Vanden Auweele, and M. Ostyn. 1986. The relationship between psychosocial factors and sports injuries. *Journal of Sports Medicine and Physical Fitness* 26(1): 77-84.

MacDougall, J. 1974. Limitations to anaerobic performance. *Proceedings: Science and the Athlete*. Hamilton: Coaching Association of Canada and McMaster University.

MacDougall, J., D. Sale, G. Elder, and J. Sutton. 1976. Ultrastructural properties of human skeletal muscle following heavy resistance training and immobilization. *Medicine and Science in Sports* 8(1): 72.

MacDougall, J., D. Sale, J. Moroz, G. Elder, J. Sutton, and H. Howald. 1979. Mitochondrial volume density in human skeletal muscle following heavy resistance training. *Medicine and Science in Sports* 11(2): 164-166.

MacDougall, J., G. Ward, D. Sale, and J. Sutton. 1977. Biochemical adaptation of human skeletal muscle to heavy resistance training and immobilization. *Journal of Applied Physiology* 43(4): 700-703.

Mace, R., and C. Carroll. 1986. Stress inoculation training to control anxiety in sport: Two case studies in squash. *British Journal of Sports Medicine* 20(3): 115-117.

Mace, R., C. Eastman, and D. Carroll. 1986. Stress inoculation training: A case study in gymnastics. *British Journal of Sports Medicine* 20(3): 139-141.

Mader, A. 1985. Personal communication with author. Vancouver, British Columbia.

Mader, A., and W. Hollmann. 1977. The importance of the elite rowers metabolic capacity in training and competition. *Beiheft zu Leistungssport* 9: 9-59.

Mainwood, G., and J. Renaud. 1984. The effect of acid-base balance on fatigue of skeletal muscle. *Canadian Journal of Physiology and Pharmacology* 63: 403-416.

Marasescu, N. 1980. Metode noi pentru antrenamentul de mare performanta (New methods in high performance training). *Education Fizica si Sport* 5: 34-39.

Margaria, R., P. Ceretelli, P. Aghemo, and G. Sassi. 1963. Energy cost of running. *Journal of Applied Physiology* 18: 122-128.

Marsden, C., J. Meadows, and P. Merton. 1971. Isolated single motor units in human muscle and their rate of discharge during maximal voluntary effort. *Journal of Physiology* (London) 217: 12P-13P.

Martens, R. 1970. Influence of participation motivation on success and satisfaction in team performance. *Research Quarterly* 41: 31-35.

Martin, B., S. Robinson, D. Wiegman, and L. Anlick. 1975. Effects of warm-up on metabolic responses to strenuous exercise. *Medicine and Science in Sports* 7(2): 146-149.

Mathews, D., and E. Fox. 1971. *The physiological basis of physical education and athletics*. Philadelphia: Saunders.

Mathews, D., and E. Fox. 1976. *The physiological basis of physical education and athletics*. Philadelphia: Saunders.

Matsuda, J., R. Zernicke, A. Vailns, V. Pedrinin, A. Pedrini-Mille, and J. Maynard. 1986. Structural and mechanical adaptation of immature bone to strenous exercise. *Journal of Applied Physiology* 60(6): 2028-2034.

Matveyev, L. 1965. *Periodization of sports training*. Moscow: Fizkultura i Sport.

Matveyev, L., V. Kalinin, and N. Ozolin. 1974. Characteristics of athletic shape and methods of rationalizing the structure of the competitive phase. *Scientific Research Collection* (Moscow): 4-23.

Matveyev, L., and A. Novikov. 1980. *Teoria i medodika physicheskogo vospitania*. (The theory and methodology of physical education). Moscow: Fizkultura i Sport.

McClements, J., and C. Botterill. 1979. Goal-setting in shaping of future performance in athletics. In P. Klavora and J. Daniel (Eds.), *Coach, Athlete and the Sport Psychologist*. Toronto: Twin Offset. 81-96.

Meichenbaum, D. 1977. *Cognitive behavior modification*. New York: Plenum Press.

Meyers, C. 1974. *Measurement in physical education*. New York: Ronald Press.

Mitra, G., and A. Mogos. 1980. *Metodologia educatiei fizice scolare* (Methodology of high school physical education). Bucharest: Sport-Turism.

Molette, R. 1963. *Power training*. Brussels: Cross Promenade.

Monteleone, P., M. Maj, M. Fusco, C. Orazzo, and D. Kemali. 1993. Physical exercise at night blunts the nocturnal increase of plasma melatonin levels in healthy humans. *Life Sciences* 47: 1989-1995.

Morehouse, L., and L. Gross. 1977. *Maximum performance*. New York: Simon & Schuster.

Morehouse, L., and A. Miller. 1971. *Physiology of exercise*. St. Louis: Mosby.

Morgan, R., and G. Adamson. 1959. *Circuit training*. London: G. Bell and Sons.

Morpurgo, B. 1976. In D. Mathews and E.L. Fox, *The physiological basis of physical education and athletics*. Philadelphia: Saunders.

Muido, L. 1948. The influence of body temperature on performance in swimming. *Acta Physiologica Scandinavica* 12: 102-109.

Muresan, I. 1973. *Ciclul saptaminal de antrenament* (The weekly training cycle). Bucharest, Romania: National Council of Sports.

Myers, B., and P. Badia. 1993. Immediate effects of different light intensities on body temperature and alertness. *Physiology and Behaviour* 54: 199-202.

Nadori, L. 1989. *Theoretical and methodological basis of training planning with specific considerations within a microcycle*. Lincoln, NE: National Strength and Conditioning Association.

Nagorni, M. 1978. *Facts and fiction regarding junior's training*. Moscow: Fizkultura i Sport. 6.

Neilson, N., and C. Jensen. 1972. *Measurement and statistics in physical education*. Belmount: Wadsworth.

Neugebauer, H. 1971. Planning and organization processes of training. In D. Harre (Ed.), *Trainingslehre*. Berlin: Sportverlag. 64-81.

Newsholme, E., E. Blomstrand, N. McAndrew, and M. Parry-Billings. 1992. *Biochemical causes of fatigue and overtraining*. Oxford: Blackwell Scientific. 351-364.

Nideffer, R. 1976. *The inner athlete: Mind plus muscle for winning.* New York: Crowell.

Nieman, D., and S. Nehlsen-Cannarella. 1991. The effects of acute and chronic exercise on immunoglobins. *Sports Medicine* 11(3): 183-201.

Nikiforov, I. 1974. About the structure of training in boxing. *Scientific Work* (Moscow) 6: 81-91.

Noakes, T. 1991. *Lore of running.* Champaign, IL: Leisure Press.

Nordfors H., and D. Hatvig. 1997. Hypericum perforatum in the treatment of mild depression. *Läkartidningen* 94: 2365-2367.

Norman, S. 1973. *The influence of flexibility on velocity of leg extension of the knee.* Master's thesis, University of Illinois, Chicago.

Novikov, A. 1941. Physical abilities. *Treoria i Prakika Physicheskoi Kulturi* 1: 2-12.

Nudel, D. (Ed.) 1989. *Pediatric sports medicine.* New York: PMA.

Obbarius, D. 1971. In N. Ozolin, *Sovremenaia systema sportivnoi trenirovky* (Athlete's training system for competition). Moscow: Fizkultura i Sport.

O'Connor, J., and P. Morgan. 1990. Athletic performance following rapid traversal of multiple time zones: A review. *Sports Medicine* 10(1): 20-30.

Ohashi, W., and T. Monte. 1992. *Reading the body, Ohashi's book of Oriental diagnosis.* New York: Penguin.

Orlick, T., and R. Mosher. 1978. Extrinsic awards and participant motivation is a sport related task. *International Journal of Sport Psychology* 8: 49-56.

Oxendine, J. 1968. *Psychology of motor learning.* New York: Appleton-Century-Crofts.

Ozolin, N. 1971. *Sovremennaia systema sportivnoi trenirovky* (Athlete's training system for competition). Moscow: Fizkultura i Sport.

Paha, M. 1994. Temperature modulates calcium homeostasis and ventricular arrhythmias in myocardial preparations. *Cardiovascular Research* 28: 391.

Parry-Billings, M., V. Matthews, E. Newsholme, R. Budgett, and J. Koutedakis. 1993. *The overtraining syndrome: Some biochemical aspects.* London: E & FN Spon. 215-225.

Patel, C., and M. Marmot. 1987. Stress management, blood pressure, and quality of life. *Journal of Hypertension* 5 (Suppl.): S21-S28.

Paul, G. 1969. Physiological effects of relaxation training and hypnotic suggestion. *Journal of Abnormal Psychology* 74: 425-437.

Pavlov, I. 1927. *Conditioned reflexes.* London: Oxford University Press.

Pavlov, I. 1951. *Twenty years of experience in studying the nervous system activity.* Moscow: U.S.S.R. Academy of Science.

Pechtl, V. 1982. The basis and methods of flexibility training. In D. Harre (Ed.), *Trainingslehre.* Berlin: Sportverlag. 120-139.

Pelletier, K. 1977. *Mind as a healer, mind as a slayer.* New York: Delta.

Pendergast, D. 1971. *Physiological aspects of physical activity.* Buffalo: Graduate Court, State University of New York at Buffalo.

Penman, K. 1969. Ultrastructural changes in human striated muscle using three methods of training. *Research Quarterly* 40: 764-772.

Perkins, K., P. Dubbert, J. Martin, M. Faulstich, and J. Harris. 1986. Cardiovascular reactivity to psychological stress in aerobically trained vs. untrained mild hypertensives and normotensives. *Health Psychology* 5(4): 407-421.

Petrie, K., A. Dawson, L. Thompson, and R. Brook. 1993. A double-blind trial of melatonin as a treatment for jet lag in international cabin crew. *Biological Psychiatry* 33: 526-530.

Pfeifer, H. 1982. *Methodological basis of endurance training.* In D. Harre (Ed.), *Trainingslehre.* Berlin: Sportverlag. 210-229.

Phillips, W. 1963. Influence of fatiguing warm-up exercises on speed of movement and reaction latency. *Research Quarterly* 34: 370-378.

Philostratus. 1964. *Gymnasticus.* Referred to in C. Kiritescu, *Palestrica.* Bucharest: Editura Uniunii de Cultura si Sport.

Pierrefiche, G., G. Topall, G. Courbin, I. Henriet, and H. Laborit. 1993. Antioxidant activity of melatonin in mice. *Research Communication in Chemical Pathology and Pharmacology* 80: 211-223.

Popescu, O. 1957. *Coeficientul de oboseala in cursele de canotaj* (The fatigue coefficient of rowing races). Bucharest: National Council of Sports.

Popescu, O. 1958. Principii privind antrenamentul cu greutati. (Some principles regarding weight training programs). *Studii si Cercetari* 4: 20-16.

Popescu, O. 1975. Metode de recuperare in sporturile de apa (Techniques of recovery employed in aquatic sports). *Educatia Fizica si Sport* 10: 48-52.

Popovici, F. 1979. Personal communication with the author. Bucharest.

Prentice, J. 1990. Therapeutic modalities. In *Sports Medicine* (2nd ed.). St. Louis: Times Mirror/Mosby College. 1-7, 73-74, 89-122, 129-142, 257-283.

Puni, A. 1974. Some theoretical aspects of athlete's volitional preparation. In M. Epuran (Ed.), *Psihologia sportului contemporan* (The psychology of contemporary sports). Bucharest: Stadion.

Radut, C. 1973. Biometric measurements for rowing talents. Bucharest: National Sports Council.

Ralston, H., M. Polissan, V. Inman, J. Close, and B. Feinstein. 1949. Dynamic feature of human isolated voluntary muscle in isometric and free contractions. *Journal of Applied Physiology* 1: 526-533.

Razumovski, E. 1971. In N. Ozolin, *Sovremenaia systema sportivnoi trenirovky* (Athlete's training system for competition). Moscow: Fizkultura i Sport.

Reindel, H., H. Roskamm, and W. Gerschler. 1962. *Interval training.* Munich: Johan Ambrosius Barth.

Reiter, R. 1991. Norepinepherine and its effect on melatonin release. *New Physiological Science* 6: 223-227.

Renström, P., and J. Johnson. 1985. Overuse injuries in sports. A review. *Sports Medicine* 2: 316-333.

Reynolds, S. 1984. Biofeedback, relaxation training, and music: Homestatis for coping with stress. *Biofeedback and Self-Regulation* 9(2): 169-179.

Riddle, K. 1956. *A comparison of three methods for increasing flexibility of the trunk and hip joints.* Doctoral dissertation, University of Oregon, Portland.

Ritter, I. 1982. Principles of training. In D. Harre (Ed.), *Trainingslehre.* Berlin: Sportverlag. 33-47.

Roaf, A. 1988. Personal communication with the author. Banf, Alberta.

Rose, J., and M. Rothstein. 1982. General concepts and adaptations to altered patterns of use. *Muscle Mutability Part 1* 62(12): 1773-1785.

Rosen, G. 1977. *The relaxation book.* Englewood Cliffs, NJ: Prentice Hall.

Roskamm, H. 1967. Optimum patterns of exercise for healthy adults. *Journal of Canadian Medical Association* 22: 19-31.

Rowland, T. 1990. Developmental aspects of physiological function relating to aerobic exercise in children. *Sports Medicine* 10(4): 253-266.

Rudik, P. 1967. The idiomotor representation and its importance in training. *Sport Wyczynowy* (Warsaw) 8: 11-18.

Ruff, L. 1989. Calcium sensitivity of fast- and slow-twitch muscle fibers. *Muscle & Nerve* 12: 32-37.

Ryan, D. 1962. Relationship between motor performance and arousal. *Research Quarterly* 33: 279-287.

Sahlin, K. 1986. Metabolic changes limiting muscular performance. *Biochemistry of Exercise* 16: 77-87.

Sahlin, K. 1992. Metabolic factors in fatigue. *Sports Medicine* 13(2): 99-107.

Sale, D. 1989. Neural adaptation in strength and power training. In L. Jones, N. McCartney, and A. McComas (Eds.), *Human Muscle Power*. Champaign, IL: Human Kinetics. 289-307.

Saltin, B., and P. Astrand. 1967. Maximum oxygen uptake in athletes. *Journal of Applied Physiology* 23: 202-226.

Sandman, K., and C. Backstrom. 1984. Psychophysiological factors in myofascial pain. *Journal of Manipulative and Psychological Therapeutics* 7(4): 237-242.

Sauberlich, H., R. Dowdy, and J. Skala. 1974. *Laboratory tests for assessment of nutritional status*. Cleveland: CRC Press.

Schmidt. 1968. In V. Zatsyorski, *Athlete's physical abilities*. Moscow: Fiskultura i Sport.

Scholich, M. 1974. *Kreistraining*. Berlin: Bartels & Weritz.

Schöner-Kolb, I. 1990. *Das verhalten ausgewählter physiologischer, biochemischer und physchologischer parameter während und nach einem übertrainingsversuch an normalpersonen im alter von 23-30 jahren*. Doctoral thesis, German Sport University, Cologne.

Schroeder, W. 1969. The correlation between force and the other motor abilities. *Theorie und Praxis der Körperkultur* 12: 98-49.

Schutt, N., and D. Bernstein. 1986. Relaxation skills for the patient, dentist, and auxiliaries. *Dental Clinics of North America* 30 (Suppl. 4): S93-S105.

Serban, M. 1979. Aspecte psihologice ale formei sportive (Psychological aspects of peaking). *Educatia Fizica si Sport* 6: 38-46.

Setchenov, I. 1935. *On the question of the increase of the human muscle working capacity. Selected works*. Moscow: National Academy of Science.

Siclovan, I. 1972. *Teoria antrenamentului sportiv* (Theory of training). Bucharest: Stadion.

Siclovan, I. 1977. *Teoria antrenamentului sportiv* (Theory of training). Bucharest: Sport-Turism.

Siebert, W. 1929. The formation of skeletal muscle hypertrophy. *Journal of Clinical Medicine* 109-350.

Simoneau, J., G. Lortie, M. Bouley, M. Marcotte, M. Thibault, and C. Bouchard. 1985. Human skeletal muscle fiber type alteration with high-intensity intermittent training. *European Journal of Applied Physiology* 54: 250-253.

Singer, R. 1977. Motivation in sport. *International Journal of Sport Psychology* 8: 3-21.

Singer, R., D. Lamb, J. Loy, R. Malina, and S. Kleinman. 1972. *Physical education: An introductory approach*. New York: Macmillan.

Smith, R., T. Sarason, and V. Sarason. 1978. *Psychology: The frontiers of behavior*. New York: Harper & Row.

Sopov, K. 1975. Guidance of training the training process. *Sport Za Rubezhon* (Moscow) 9: 6-7.

Spielberger, C., P. Gorserch, and R. Lustene. 1970. *STAF Manual*. Palo Alto, CA: Consulting Psychologists Press.

Stokkan, D., and R. Reiter. 1994. Melatonin rhythms in arctic urban residents. *Journal of Pineal Research* 16: 33-36.

Strassman, R., C. Quahs, J. Lisansky, and G. Peake. 1991. Elevated rectal temperature produced by all-night bright light is reversed by melatonin infusion in men. *Journal of Applied Physiology* 71: 2178-2182.

Szogy, A. 1976. *An optimal model for talent identification in rowing*. Bucharest: National Council of Sports.

Talyshev, F. 1977. Recovery. *Legkaya Atletika* 6: 25-29.

Teodorescu, L. 1975. *Aspecte teoretice si metodice ale jocurilor sportive* (Theoretical and methodological aspects of team sports). Bucharest: Sport-Turism.

Teodorescu, L., and C. Florescu. 1971. Some directions regarding the perfection and masterness of technique and strategy. In E. Ghibu (Ed.), *The content and methodology of training*. Bucharest: Stadion. 66-81.

Terjung, R., and D. Hood. 1986. Biochemical adaptations in skeletal muscle induced by exercise training. In D. Layman (Ed.), *Nutrition and aerobic exercise.*. Washington, DC: American Chemical Society. 8-27.

Tesch, P. 1980. Muscle fatigue in man. *Acta Physiologica Scandinavica Supplementum* 480: 3-40.

Tesch, P., G. Dudley, M. Duviosin, B. Hather, and R. Harris. 1990. Force and EMG signal patterns during repeated bouts of concentric or eccentric muscle actions. *Acta Physiologica Scandinavia* 138: 263-271.

Thibodeau, G. 1987. *Anatomy and physiology*. St. Louis: Times Mirror/Mosby College.

Thorndike, E. 1935. *Fundamentals of learning*. New York: New York Teachers College.

Timofeev, V. 1954. *The mechanism of formation the motor skills*. Lecture at the University of Moscow.

Topalian, G. 1955. In N. Ozolin, *Sovremnaia systema sportivnoi trenirovky* (Athlete's training system for competitions). 1971. Moscow: Fizkultura i Sport.

Torngren, L. 1924. *The Swedish gymnastics book*. Stockholm: Esslingen.

Totterdell, P., S. Reynolds, B. Parkinson, and R. Briner. 1994. Associations of sleep with everyday mood, minor symptoms and social interaction experience. *Sleep* 17: 466-475.

Trager, M. 1982. Psychophysical integration and mentastics: The Trager approach to movement education. *Journal of Holistic Health* 7: 15-25.

Trager, M., and C. Guadagno. 1987. *Trager mentastics: Movement as a way to agelessness*. New York: Station Hill Press.

Tschiene, P. 1989, June. *Finally a theory of training to overcome doping*. Presentation to the Second IAAF World Symposium on Doping in Sports. Monte Carlo.

Tucker, L., G. Cole, and G. Friedman. 1986. Physical fitness: A buffer against stress. *Perceptual and Motor Skills* 63 (2 pt): 955-961.

Tutko, T., and J. Richards. 1971. *Psychology of coaching*. Boston: Allyn & Bacon.

Uhov, V. 1968. In V. Zatzyorski, *Athlete's physical abilities*. Moscow: Fiskultura i Sport.

Uhtomski, A. 1950. *Learning about the dominant*. Leningrad: University of Leningrad.

Urmuzescu, A. 1977. Contributii pentru un model de forma sportiva pentru probele de rezistenta (Contribution for a model of athletic shape in endurance events). *Educatia Fizica si Sport* 9: 38-38.

Vander, J., J. Sherman, and D. Luomo. 1990. *Human physiology: The mechanisms of body function*. New York: McGraw-Hill.

Van der Beek, E. 1985. Vitamins and endurance training: Food for running or faddish claims? *Sports Medicine* 2: 175-197.

Vanek, M. 1972. *Sports psychology, its use and potential in coaching*. Toronto: Fitness International Productions.

Vanek, M., and J. Cratty. 1970. *Psychology of the superior athlete*. Toronto: Macmillan.

Van Erp-Baart, A., W. Saris, R. Binkhorst, J. Vos, and J. Elvers. 1989. Nationwide survey on nutritional habits in elite athletes. Part II Mineral and vitamin intake. *International Journal of Sports Medicine* 10: S11-S16.

Van Huss, W., L. Albrecht, R. Nelson, and R. Hagerman. 1962. Effect of overload warm-up on the velocity and accuracy of throwing. *Research Quarterly* 33: 472-475.

Van Reeth, O., and J. Sturis. 1994. Nocturnal exercise phase delays circadian rhythms of melatonin and thyrotropin secretion in normal men. *American Journal of Physiology* 266: E964-E974.

Voelz, C. 1976. *Motivation in coaching a team sport.* Washington, DC: American Association of Health, Physical Education, and Recreation.

Wallace, K. 1970. Physiological effects of transcendental meditation. *Science* 167: 1751-1754.

Wardlaw, M., P. Insel, and M. Seyler. 1992. *Contemporary nutrition: Issues & insights.* St. Louis: Mosby Year Book.

Wear, C. 1963. Relationships of flexibility measurements to length of body segments. *Research Quarterly* 34: 234-238.

Weber, E. 1914. Eine physiologische methode, die leistungsfähigkeit ermudeter menschlicher muskeln zu erhöhen. *Archives of Physiology* 385-420.

Webster, D. 1975. Soviet secret weapon. *International Olympic Lifters* 2: 24-26.

Weinberg, T. 1988. The relationship of massage and exercise to mood enhancement. *Sports Psychologist* 2: 202-211.

Wickstrom, R., and C. Polk. 1961. Effect of the whirlpool on the strength-endurance of the quadriceps muscle in training male adolescents. *American Journal of Physical Medicine* 40: 91-92.

Willmore, J., and D. Costill. 1980. *Training for sport and activity: The physiological basis for the conditioning process.* Dubuque, IA: Brown.

Wu, I. 1996. Effects of dietary N-3 fatty acids supplementation in men with weight loss associated with the acquired immune deficiency syndrome in relation to indices of cytokines. *Journal of Acquired Immune Deficiency Syndrome* 11: 258.

Yakovlev, N. 1967. *Sports biochemistry.* Leipzig: Deutche Hochschule für Körpekultur.

Zalessky, M. 1977. Coaching, medico-biological, and psychological means of recovery. *Legkaya Atletika* 7: 20-22.

Zatzyorski, V. 1968. *Athlete's physical abilities.* Moscow: Physkultura i Sport.

Zatzyorski, V. 1980. The development of endurance. In L. Matveyev and A. Novikov (Eds.), *Teoria i metodica physicheskoi vospitania* (The theory and methodology of physical education). Moscow: Fizkultura i Sport. 271-290.

Zauner, C., M. Maksud, and J. Melichna. 1989. Physiological considerations in training young athletes. *Sports Medicine* 8(1): 15-31.

Index

Page numbers in italics refer to the table or figure on that page.

About the Author

Tudor O. Bompa, PhD, is recognized worldwide as the foremost expert on periodization training. He first developed the concept of "periodization of strength" in Romania in 1963, as he helped the Eastern Bloc countries rise to dominance in the athletic world. Since then, Bompa has used his system to train 11 Olympic and world championship medalists and elite athletes.

A full professor at York University in Toronto, Bompa has authored several important books on physical conditioning, including *Serious Strength Training* (Human Kinetics, 1998), *Periodization Training for Sports* (Human Kinetics, 1999), and *Power Training for Sport: Plyometrics for Maximum Power Development*, as well as numerous articles on the subject. He has made presentations on periodization training in more than 30 countries. His publications, conferences, and ideas are highly regarded and enthusiastically sought out by many top professional athletes and training specialists. Bompa is married and lives in Sharon, Ontario.

Bompa currently offers certification programs in strength training, planning, and periodization. "The Tudor Bompa Training System" is designed for personal trainers, instructors, coaches, athletes, and educators. For more information, contact Dr. Tudor Bompa, P.O. Box 95, Sharon, ON, L0G 1V0, Canada.